THE IRISH ABOARD TITANIC

SENAN MOLONY

MERCIER PRESS

IRISH PUBLISHER – IRISH STORY

For Brigid & Philippa

MERCIER PRESS

Cork

www.mercierpress.ie

First published in 2000 by the Wolfhound Press.

This revised edition first published in 2012.

© Senan Molony, 2000, 2012
sennbrig@indigo.ie

Passages from *A Night to Remember* © 1955, 1976, by Walter Lord. Reprinted by permission of Henry Holt and Company LLC.

Extract from the *Daily Mail*, 3 April 1998 reprinted by permission of the *Daily Mail*.

The author has made every reasonable effort to contact the copyright holders of photographs and texts reproduced in this book. If any involuntary infringement of copyright has occurred, sincere apologies are offered and the owners of such copyright are requested to contact the author.

ISBN: 978 1 85635 883 5

10 9 8 7 6 5 4 3 2 1

Printed and bound in the EU.

CONTENTS

APPALLING DISASTER

TITANIC LOST

COLLIDES WITH ICEBERG

2,358 ON BOARD

ONLY 675 SAVED

187 IRISH PASSENGERS

MEAGRE DETAILS

CONFLICTING MESSAGES

Headline, The Cork Examiner, *Tuesday 16 April 1912, p. 5.*

ACKNOWLEDGEMENTS

I must pay tribute to my eyes and ears on the American side, Phillip Gowan of Myrtle Beach, North Carolina, to whom I am immensely indebted. I am also obliged to Bob Bracken of Midland Park, New Jersey.

The following have also generously provided information, pictures and assistance: Maureen Heslin Anderson, John Arkins, Fay Blettner, Róisín Brady, Sheila Brogan, Nora Buckley, Anne Burrows, Sue Babcock Byrd, Mary Noon Capuano, Helen Cassells, Chapin Memorial Library, Willie Charters, Ed Coghlan, Pat Colbert, Maura Conlon, Tony Cox, Ita Cusack, Julia Lynch Danning, Bernard Delaney, Con Dennehy, Chris Dohany, David Donohoe, Tony Donohoe, Moira Dooley, Frank and Essie Dwan, Mary Edward, Denzie and Johnny Egan, Con English, Al Ermer, Bernard Evers, Charlie Evers, Paddy and May Flanagan, Billy Flynn, Mary Flynn, Cathleen Foerster, Barbara Foland, Jerry Foley, Liz and Cathy Foyle, Paddy Gallagher, Erin Garry, Dr Denis Griffiths, Molly Harten, Margaret and Donal Hickey, Mary LaSha Higgins, Philip Hind, Michael Hopkins, Nancy Hopkins, Alan Hustak, Charles Jones, Edna Draper Jones, Karen Kamuda, Nellie Keane, William and Patsy Keane, Michael Kilgannon, Bob Knuckle, Jacqueline Komay, Beatrice Lacon, Mimi Lai, Helen Landsberg, Jack and Margaret Leniston, Jimmy Lennon, Don Lynch, Maureen Lynch, John and Margaret Lynn, Diana Ylstra Maher, Anthony and Clare Mangan, Anne Manning, Johnny Mannion, Susan Markowitz, John Martin, Ruth Jermyn McElhenny, Brian Meister, Arthur Merchant, Mick Molloy, Patrick and Nora Mullane, Tom and Kathleen Mullen, Tom Mullins, National Archives staff, National Library staff, Regina Nau, Esther Naughton, Derek Newcomb, Henry Noon, Margaret and Joseph Nuesse, Gearóid O'Brien, Mona O'Brien, Lorcan O'Connor, Mary Alice O'Connor, Kitty O'Donovan, Nellie O'Heney, Derry O'Riordan, Sister Angela Perry, Robert Prior, Noel Ray, Benny and Teresa Reilly, Mary Reilly, Sheila and Joe Riordan, Mary Rogers, Audrey R. Sampson, Patrick Shaughnessy, Tom Shiel, Daniel Sinnott, Mona Sinnott, Dympna Slater, Tommy Smith, Dick Stokes, Mary Foley Taylor, Johnny Thompson, Diana Thorpe, Brian Ticehurst, Jack Toohey, Rita Guilfoyle Townsend, Dermot Walsh, Mike Walter, Kathy Weir.

Senan Molony, 2012

Senan Molony is the Political Editor of the *Irish Daily Mail*, and is the author of several books, including *Titanic: Victims & Villains*, *Titanic and the Mystery Ship*, *Titanic Scandal: The Trial of the Mount Temple* and *Lusitania, an Irish Tragedy*, the latter also published by Mercier, along with *The Phoenix Park Murders*. Honoured at the inaugural National Newspapers of Ireland journalism awards in October 2011, he is a lecturer on the centenary re-creation of *Titanic*'s maiden voyage.

Lawrence O'Connor's shop in Church Street, Ennistymon, County Clare, taken in 1912, with a poster outside advertising the Olympic *and* Titanic. *The little girl pictured here subsequently emigrated to America.*

INTRODUCTION

The tumult began when the waters closed over the *Titanic*, and it has hardly ceased since. The awfulness of the cries of the dying faded within an hour and the sea was stilled, save for sobbing and the gentle slopping of oars. But the news soon reached New York and new cries were going up.

Newspapers led and fed the cacophony. A single ship, lost at sea like thousands since time immemorial, became a fever that touched every door. It was the only topic of conversation for weeks afterwards. It affected home and hearth, industry, empire, everything. Once so sure of itself, western society was forced to question and think anew.

In the decades since, the topic has remained submerged yet embedded in the public consciousness. *Titanic* is the Rolls Royce of shipwrecks. She glittered with the finery and wealth of millionaires and was the zenith of industrial accomplishment at the time, ushering in a host of refinements. And when all mankind's efforts in creating her were set at nought, she launched a thousand sermons on our follies and our foibles.

All this is true, but there is also something else, something differently spiritual. Why do we hanker after the lost ship? What is it about that 'tide in the affairs of men' in far-off 1912 that exercises such an unfathomable pull on imaginations still? Certainly, she stands as an object of desire, an emblem of opportunities forgone, and a glimpse of how the other half lived – with the added, secret comfort that rich and poor went down alike.

But we have heard too much about the rich. We are surfeited on Grand Staircases, on the ridiculous roe of sturgeon, on starched collars and feather boas. If we look closely at the *Titanic*, we can also see ourselves, not in how we enviously hope to be, but in how we are. Everyone can project themselves into the desperate dilemma of that night and how they might have acted, while perhaps forgetting that the vessel already carried a representative sample of us through all classes, creeds, ages and races. The *Titanic* certainly fulfils a need for those who yearn for the ways of yore. And, in actuality, she provides a detailed picture of the way things were. The way things were for officers, crew, society, Finns, Syrians, Americans, Irish …

Two of the oft-repeated catch cries of that night to remember are 'Women and children first!' and 'Be British!', the latter phrase attributed to Captain E. J. Smith in his efforts to stiffen the resolve of the crew close to the end. Hackneyed as they are, they offer a superficial impression of the values that informed the conventions of the Edwardian age. Men were expected to be gallant, to behave like gentlemen, to elevate the weak at the expense of the strong. In large part on that night of 14–15 April 1912, they lived up to the image they had created for themselves. It was part of belonging to the 'civilised' world, part of being British in the larger sense, even if one was Argentinian, German, Swiss or any one of the other nationalities in First Class. The underlying assumption was that civilisation set certain races apart. In the aftermath of the tragedy, commentators seized upon the fact of monied men standing back from the boats as triumphant proof of the superiority of the Anglo-Saxon mindset. If such complacency had helped to bring about the disaster, many continued to find it a refuge thereafter.

It is, after all, a stupid thing to crash full tilt into an iceberg. But the undoubted heroism shown by many that night was puffed up into mythic proportions. One paean of praise for the lost proudly trumpeted that the Englishman had shown the world how to die. Articles on both sides of the Atlantic pointed out with some distaste that the Chinese custom was not to prioritise the women and children, but to save the men. Men first, then the women, then children. Men work and produce, they can find new wives. If the women survive too, so much the better. The children can be replaced.

So much for the Chinese. Their near neighbours in Japan could also be disparaged. The *Titanic's* Fifth Officer, Harold Lowe, led lifeboat No. 14 back to the scene of the wreck a while after the hopeless cries had ended. His boat passed by a floating door to which a 'small Japanese' had lashed himself with a rope. Charlotte Collyer, a Second-Class passenger, wrote in a magazine in May 1912 that the officer had hesitated about trying to save him. 'What's the use?' said Mr Lowe. 'He's dead likely, and if he isn't, there's others better worth saving than a Jap!'

Lowe actually moved his lifeboat on, but then changed his mind and went back. The Japanese man was hauled aboard, and one of the women rubbed his chest while others chafed his hands and feet. He opened his eyes, and in five minutes had recovered his strength. He next took over at the oar from an exhausted crewman, prompting Lowe to remark: 'By Jove! I'm ashamed of what I said about the little blighter. I'd save the likes o' him six times over if I got the chance.'

But the reality was that the 'likes of him' did not make it into the lifeboats. The strong, who supposedly elevated the weak, somehow saw to it that the strong remained strong and the weak, weak – at least in racial and economic terms, if not quite so obviously in relation to women and children, although here too a steerage child was in a far weaker position than First-Class offspring. A woman in Third Class had just a 50–50 chance of being saved, while just one in eight of the Second-Class women were lost, and as few as three in a hundred of those at the top of the social tree. So the famous cry might as well have been 'First-Class women and First-Class children first!'

We shall look again at what it meant to be among the lower orders, like the Irish and other emigrants who were lower physically on the vessel's decks and much further away from the boat deck and the means of salvation. But let us also re-examine the attitudes exhibited to those not fortunate enough to be British, or at least conform to the Anglo-Saxon stereotype.

Alongside Officer Lowe in lifeboat No. 14 was steward Fred Crowe, who testified to the American inquiry that at the time of its launching 'there were various men passengers, probably Italians or some foreign nationality other than English or American, who attempted to rush the boats'. It would be difficult to think of a more neat summation of a generalised and unshakeable conviction in the order of things, and of peoples.

Wherever there was chaos or panic on the *Titanic* that night, the transcript points to 'Italians', 'foreigners' and 'Mediterranean-looking' men at the heart of it all. The Italians in particular were singled out for negative references. Despite the reality that there were very few Italians aboard the *Titanic* (far more serving as waiters in Signor Luigi Gatti's concession restaurant than were booked aboard as passengers), that nationality came in for unwarranted criticism, so much so that the Italian ambassador protested during the hearings of the US inquiry and Fifth Officer Lowe was obliged to apologise. Lowe later met the ambassador and a certified declaration was read into the record of the inquiry:

> I, Harold Godfrey Lowe … stated that I fired shots to prevent Italian immigrants from jumping into my lifeboat. I do hereby cancel the word 'Italian' and substitute the words 'immigrants belonging to Latin races' … I did not intend to cast any reflection on the Italian nation … I feel honoured to give out the present statement.

This rather odd affair points to something else that may be salient: the thinness of different skins in 1912. Clearly national pride was a matter of such supreme importance that the Royal Ambassador of Rome should feel it necessary to stand over Welshman Lowe as he composed his breast-beating public statement. No doubt Lowe himself was 'honoured' in return, while the parcel of blame was summarily passed on to other Latins.

Why should the Italians be the focus of barely disguised scorn from many crew-members? The answer must lie in conditioning. The previous October a British newspaper had described Italy as a 'pirate and brigand' nation, arising from Italian interference in Libya. King Victor Emmanuel had joined the scramble for Africa. In February 1912, the Italians, announcing themselves as a military power, bombed Beirut, opening an ambitious war against the Ottoman Empire. Britain, which had clothed much of the world in imperial pink, did not take kindly to such upstart behaviour, particularly since she controlled Egypt, Libya's eastern neighbour, and had designs on Palestine.

Put simply, Britain and Italy, like all other European powers, were heading inexorably for war. In this context, vaunted and sensitive feelings of national self-worth meant that even appalling disasters became fodder for the mythmakers. The worse they were, the greater that necessity. Britain had placed Lord Gordon of Khartoum on a pedestal because he was killed on the steps of his headquarters in the Sudan in 1885. Sieges of British forces at Mafeking and Ladysmith, once relieved, had been celebrated as great victories. Isandhlwana in 1879 saw hundreds of redcoats wiped out, and the last order given to 'fix bayonets and die like British soldiers do'. The same day saw the illustrious stand at Rorke's Drift when eighty-five South Wales Borderers won seventeen medals in an afternoon, eight of them Victoria Crosses. In 1852, some 200 British troops aboard the sinking *Birkenhead*, off Cape Town, had maintained perfect discipline when drawn up in companies on deck to drown as the vessel settled in shark-infested waters many miles from shore. Being British meant stiff upper lips and going down with the ship, literally and metaphorically.

The *Titanic* joined the ranks of legend and became even greater than all of them. Who today remembers the *Birkenhead*? Yet it is astonishing to note that Captain Edward Smith of the *Titanic* had been asked in a social setting with Harland & Wolff directors before the ship had even left Belfast whether courage and fearlessness in the face of death existed among seamen as of old. He replied that if any disaster like that of the *Birkenhead* should occur, they would go down as those men had done.

Indeed they did – at least by the time the mythmakers were finished. Waltz music drifted across the deck and 'Nearer My God to Thee' was played. The notion that a band member might have had tears streaming down his cheeks was judiciously omitted from the official version, while unsavoury happenings – once dragged into the light of the US inquiry – were ascribed to 'Italians', who in turn officially supervised the onward denigration of other peoples.

In this vainglorious context, the militarists were not alone in striving to avoid disgrace. Industrial might and popular pride was bound up in all of it, so that even such questionable achievements as being first to the South Pole or winning the blue ribbon for the fastest crossing of the Atlantic – the ribbon itself being an appropriately fabled, not actual laurel – were prizes sought after among the competing powers.

The South Pole actually gave Britain its first ice disaster of 1912, but this too was reinvented as a benchmark of nobility through the medium of courage and heroism. Roald Amundsen and Robert Falcon Scott had launched separate bids for the pole in October 1911, with the Norwegian winning the race on 14 December, but only managing to relay news of the victory in March 1912. He saw no sign of Scott, who had reached the pole in January, being crushed by the sight of the Norwegian flag. Ill-provisioned, Scott and his team turned back but were ambushed by bad weather. Trapped with little food, Captain Lawrence Oates sacrificed himself for the sake of his comrades, walking from shelter into a blizzard with the words: 'I am just going outside, I may be some time.' His conduct did not save the others, who all died, but his supreme act had been noted in Scott's later recovered diary of their last hours.

Such was the calibre of some men in 1912, which in part seemed to stem from old aristocratic principles such as *noblesse oblige*, that status conferred obligations. But a rich vein of shimmering, if catastrophic, failure – upon which the *Titanic* would place the tin hat, at least until the tin-hat days of Dunkirk – only serves to mask some deeper truths. It can certainly be argued that Britain and America's outlook imposed no obligations on persons of other nationalities to live up to standards of behaviour inculcated over decades, if not centuries, of conquest, civilisation and self-congratulation. Why should Third-Class passengers patiently 'wait their turn' in steerage? Who made the rules?

It will be seen in the accounts contained in this book that Third-Class passengers were undoubtedly discriminated against in leaving the *Titanic*. But if there was prejudice, it was institutionalised by reason of the class system. All subconsciously seemed to accept that a person who paid thousands for a First-Class ticket had a greater right to a place in a lifeboat than one who had paid less than £8 for their passage.

Daniel Buckley, a young man from Ballydesmond, County Cork – which in 1912 was known by the rather absurd yet telling name of Kingwilliamstown – certainly did not question the way things were. He told the US inquiry into the disaster that a sailor had hurried to lock an unlocked gate as he and fellow steerage passengers rushed up a staircase. Breathtakingly, Buckley, when asked by Chairman Senator William Alden Smith whether the steerage had any opportunity at all of getting out, responded: 'I think they had as much chance as the First- and Second-Class passengers.' Before the enormity of such a statement could sink in, Smith asked whether such equal chances had come about after the locked gate had been smashed in. Again Buckley's reply is instructive: 'Yes, because they were all mixed. All the steerage passengers went up on the First-Class deck at this time, when the gate was broken. They all got up there. They could not keep them down.'

Another steerage passenger, Olaus Abelseth, also displayed blithe acceptance of a hierarchy of human life. He spoke of steerage being allowed onto the forward well deck, where further advance was prevented to higher decks where the lifeboats were. But he also told his audience of incredulous senators that steerage passengers still had plenty of opportunity to get up. It turned out he was talking about the danger-fraught route of climbing up the deck cranes and inching along their freezing metal arms to jump over railings and onto the forbidden territory of B deck.

Equally, it was unquestioningly assumed that the lifeboats were for passengers, and that the crew had no entitlement to them other than to serve as basic lifeboat crews. Indeed, there was resentment of sailors saved in some lifeboats, particularly among First-Class ladies who had left husbands behind. Somehow the crew were not playing the game by swimming to lifeboats or shinning down ropes. This distaste manifested itself in criticism of crewmembers for smoking, alleged but unlikely drunkenness, coarse talk and incompetence.

If some members of the crew looked after themselves and their own in a few instances, few today would blame them. They did it when they could and when officer backs were turned. One account in this book mentions the strange expression on stewards' faces as passengers were helped into boats, an intimation of sickly envy knowing what was in store for they themselves, but still following orders.

At officer level there was no question of taking a place in the boats. Devotion to duty was paramount, and with it the maintenance of discipline – so much so that officers were prepared to fire their guns. Meanwhile senior surgeon William O'Loughlin swung his lifebelt in his hand and joked to colleagues that he wouldn't be needing it – even as the foaming water roared up the wall of the forward well deck mere yards away. Second Officer Charles Lightoller, a survivor, who had straddled some lifeboats the better to help load them, bristled when later asked how he had left the ship. He replied to the effect: 'I didn't leave the ship. The ship left me.'

The honourable way of leaving the ship was an important consideration for many. A judgemental society which could write off whole nations as cowards reserved the sanction of total ostracisation for those who failed, for whatever reason, to live up to such exacting standards. The managing director and chairman of the White Star Line, J. Bruce Ismay, who left in collapsible C, was vilified as J. 'Brute' Ismay and shunned by much of society for the rest of his days, many of them spent at a Connemara retreat.

Some saw it coming. Canadian yachtsman Arthur Peuchen, while still aboard the rescue ship *Carpathia*, asked Officer Lightoller for a testimonial that he had climbed down a rope to a boat when instructed to do so because of his experience in yachting. Yet numbers of men who came home alive suffered calumny and backbiting gossip that they had dressed like women to enter boats.

One Irishman, Edward Ryan, freely admitted posing as a woman for this purpose. Another, the aforementioned Daniel Buckley, had womanhood thrust upon him in the shape of a shawl placed over his head by a sympathetic lady as other men who had entered a boat were ordered out. Officer Lowe, our everyman for the attitudes of the day, told of discovering a man wearing a shawl when transferring passengers prior to going back for survivors. He 'pitched him in' to the stand-by boat because he was 'not worth being treated better'. And his nationality? 'Italian.' Meanwhile, one Irish survivor, Nellie O'Dwyer, recounted hearing of five or six Chinese who had escaped by fixing their hair down their backs and wrapping blankets about them in order to be taken for women. She parroted the line that 'the Italians were the worst'.

Even having been left behind, and in the hopeless effort of trying to swim to a lifeboat, one could be up against more than just the perishing cold, according to fireman Charles Judd, saved in collapsible A and quoted in the *Daily Herald* soon after arriving home in Plymouth. He was never called to an inquiry:

> I learned from other members of the crew why more Third-Class passengers were not saved. It is because somebody among the officers started the cry 'British first'. This, of course, did not discriminate against Americans, but it encouraged forcing back into the water Portuguese (even the women), Italians, and other foreigners to save people who cried for help in English.
>
> 'A British life above all others', was the word passed round, said a seaman to me. There was no command as far as I know to get the steerage people up onto the decks ready for the boats. There were many babies on the deck during the last moments. One Portuguese woman had three. God knows where they all went to, but we're all pledged to tell all we know, no matter who suffers.

This book must examine the role of race because it is perforce the story of one ethnic group, the Irish, who made up part of the *Titanic*'s multicultural mosaic. In many ways race was quite simply synonymous with status. 'Foreigners' of all nationalities were regarded as a threat to the existing way – therefore they were not just excluded from decision-making but relegated to a subordinate position when it came to the evacuation, lest they jeopardise operations. Deep-seated attitudes and assumptions were at work.

John Edward Hart, a steward, admitted that the steerage passengers were falsely reassured and kept below decks until 1.15 a.m., when most of the boats were already gone. Clearly large numbers of crew had been delegated to this task – that of restraint. It has to be assumed that a policy of containment was decided upon at the most senior level, that of the bridge, since it was a truism that did not need to be enunciated that foreigners were hot-tempered, impervious to discipline and could be relied upon for nothing except panic. They would rock the boat.

So it was that for reasons of order, discipline, efficiency etc., most of the boats were loaded with those who were on the scene and queuing patiently, meaning First and Second Class. And there is absolutely no question that determined efforts were made to keep the steerage below decks and that at least some gates were locked to this end and hatches fastened.

Seaman John Poingdestre took a crazy risk, three-quarters of an hour after the collision, in returning to his quarters for a pair of boots. A Third-Class bulkhead burst on E deck and he was buffeted by a torrent of freezing water up to his waist. He climbed to the forward well deck and saw a hundred Third-Class men who had already evacuated, waiting with their baggage beside the only means of escape – a single ladder to Second Class. The same rules were in force at that time as always, he testified. They were not allowed up, and 'no doubt' they would have been kept back if they attempted to rise. At this point Lord Mersey interrupted to ask: 'Don't you know that all barriers were down?' But Poingdestre refused to be intimidated. All barriers were not down, he held firm. He never saw *any* that were down.

Was this all premeditated murder, or a necessary measure to achieve the most good in a limited time? The question is an open one, since not all doors were locked and evidence suggests a kind of controlled release of manageable numbers of steerage passengers was put into effect. Hart, the steward, led two small groups from Third Class to the boat deck and saw them into lifeboats. They were all women and children. The steerage men, as if by unspoken edict, could stand by to drown like most of their male betters above.

For those crowded nervously below, knowing the ship was sinking beneath them, having no sense of what was happening above, but naturally suspecting betrayal, there were few alternatives. They could strike out on their own through the belly of the ship looking for an escape route to ascend, try to be patient, or force their way past crew and gates. It is no wonder that large numbers of them simply broke the rules – rules that favoured the elite and middle class – and in the desperation and rage of doing so, ironically confirmed the poor opinion of them that had led to their containment in the first place.

In his book, *Titanic at Two*, Paul Quinn recounts Colonel Archibald Gracie's description, first published in 1913, of large numbers of steerage passengers suddenly emerging from the First-Class entrance to the Grand Staircase. 'There arose before us from the decks below, a mass of humanity several lines deep, covering the boat deck facing us … there were women as well as men and they seemed to be steerage passengers who had just come up from the decks below.'

These people would have had no reason to fight their perilous way along different decks, some half-filled with water flowing from *above*, given the curious dynamics of the sinking, nor to surmount obstacles and meet the challenges of finding their way in a warren of avenues, if they had not been restrained from the normal means of progress. Quinn recreates their possible routes in a detailed and fascinating commentary, but it is enough to observe that the time at which they appeared on the boat deck was seconds before the ship lurched at the bows, flooding this mass of humanity in a giant wave and sweeping them all to their doom.

The Irish did enjoy one advantage: 'At least this lot speak English.' They could also read notices and understand precisely what was being said to them, a colossal boon. The phrase about speaking English had been uttered by a steward at Queenstown as the *Titanic* was taking on board her rag-tag cohort of Irish emigrants four days earlier – and one can only imagine what remark might have been passed as the rejoinder.

What is undeniable is that most of the Irish survivors who feature in this book were saved in some of the last boats to leave. They entered only a few boats in substantial numbers – Nos 13 and 15 on the starboard side, 14 and 16 on the port – and it is no coincidence that the earliest that any of these four boats departed the *Titanic* seems to have been 1.27 a.m., more than one and three-quarter hours after the ship first began taking on water. In that time, ten other boats had gone. Thus, despite an apparently orchestrated attempt by White Star Line employees at both inquiries to flatly deny any restriction of access to the boat deck, such a policy must have been forcibly maintained.

Not that the British inquiry wanted to examine that issue. The Americans may have called three steerage passengers to testify, but the subsequent British examination did not call any. Third Class did win the right to representation, but when their counsel attempted to raise a newspaper report of an Irish witness describing crewmembers beating back passengers aboard *Titanic* while also 'fastening doors and companionways' to prevent their progress, he was ruled out of order. The question was never considered, but swept under the carpet. On separate serious allegations against the crew by two Irish male survivors, Lord Mersey, the Wreck Commissioner, asked whether the penniless pair intended coming to England from America to state their claims! Asked if their evidence could be taken on commission, Lord Mersey replied: 'I think we are very unlikely to do that.'

The British inquiry followed immediately after the American one concluded. Not that the Americans hadn't done a good job, although the London press, an unassailable bastion of empire in 1912, lambasted their transatlantic cousins for their nautical ignorance, not to mention the 'disrespectful' treatment of important men. In consequence, J. Bruce Ismay, the White Star's managing director who left more than 1,000 paying customers behind on *Titanic*, was cheered to the echo by sympathisers at Liverpool when he walked down the *Adriatic*'s gangplank on returning.

Roger Casement, the Irish nationalist (who contributed £4 to *The Irish Times*' disaster appeal fund), had earlier taken his own delight in British discomfiture at what was happening in Washington. In a letter of 23 April 1912, he wrote with acid irony: 'I certainly think the USA Senate is a beauty! I wonder no one has yet drawn attention to these monstrous proceedings of a foreign parliament enquiring into the loss of a British ship on the high seas, issuing subpoenas and having "flashlight" court sittings. A fine body to elicit truth! No one to me seems to realise the enormous impertinence of these proceedings ...'

The British inquiry duly fulfilled its underlying function, that of producing a report which whitewashed the shortcomings of the Board of Trade, the body responsible for the legal insufficiency of lifeboats, while also absolving the owners and operators of the White Star liner. The Attorney General, Sir Rufus Isaacs, KC, MP, had opined during the sittings that passengers had no useful light to shed on the facts into which the court was inquiring, and Lord Mersey agreed, delivering the truly extraordinary remark: 'Survivors are not necessarily of the least value.' It was clear which survivors he was talking about – since the final report accepted the evidence of surviving officers who had a vested interest in minimising much of what had happened, or in resorting to outright mendacity.

An obvious example is the inquiry's finding that the *Titanic* did not break in two when she went down. She could not do so – after all, she was the very apex of British shipbuilding. Second Officer Lightoller said she slid gracefully beneath the waves 'absolutely intact'. Since discovery of the wreck in 1985, the world has known the opposite. The public could also have known it in 1912, had Third-Class passengers been called to give evidence. The Irish, who did not need interpreters, were among the last to the boats. Some of them were on the ship to the very end and survived on rafts or were plucked from the water. Their tales herein are emphatic and agreed: *Titanic* snapped in two.

What else were the Irish telling the truth about? One possible area is that of shootings as the ship went down. The inquiries, of course, heard only about warning shots to quell panic; but some of the Irish relate very different stories of actual killings. The reader will have to make up his or her own mind, with the added caveat that this area is a minefield of suggestibility and possible embroidery and is subject to all the usual cautions about eyewitness accounts.

Yet the Irish stories contained in these pages are not just important for the illumination they throw on the many mysteries still surrounding those last hours of the largest steamer in the world. They are also of importance in themselves, because the *Titanic* was an ocean-going time capsule. Here the Irish nation of the time presents itself – in all its outlooks, attitudes and values.

The survivors' letters, and newspaper reports about the lost fill these pages with the sights and sounds of early last century, while placing us on the deck of the *Titanic*. Such touchstones as religion, kindred, politics and emigration are all dwelt upon, and come into sharper focus from these contemporaneous outpourings. And 1912 was an important year for Ireland. Home Rule was a burning issue and the Bill to give it effect was introduced the same week *Titanic* sank. By the time of the British inquiry into the loss, the Bill had just been passed.

On 9 May 1912, trimmer George Cavell told how Third-Class men stood back as his packed No. 15 lifeboat began its descent with women and children. Counsel Sir John Simon asked whether the women in his boat were foreigners and was told they were Irish. He brought forth laughter in court when he observed: 'A nice question, whether they were foreigners or not.' The Irish boarding the *Titanic* were taking their opinions overseas, they were part of an emigration stream draining Ireland of much of her lifeblood while simultaneously transfusing America and permanently colouring much of political discourse there.

Nearly 30,000 Irish emigrated west in 1912, with more than two-thirds going to the United States and another 6,000 to Canada. It was an extraordinary human traffic that had been going on since the famine, sixty-five years before. The *Titanic* passenger list shows who those emigrants were in 1912: overwhelmingly young, single men and women, Roman Catholic, from labouring or farm backgrounds. They were aged in their early twenties or late teens, and they largely did not ever expect to return home. The merriment and music of 'American wakes' could not hide the heartache of impending separation. Older children were parting from their younger siblings (the census returns of 1901 and 1911 are startling in showing how populous Irish families could be) and the hurt remained behind. They left on sidecars, on horseback or on foot, heading to the local train station. They had saved for years to be able to afford to make the journey and they brought pitifully little with them in clothes, bags and wealth. Many had only been able to go because a family member already in the United States had sent back enough money, or a prepaid ticket, to 'bring the next one out'.

An enormous industry had grown up on the back of Irish emigration. Any town of any consequence had its own shipping agent or sub-agent. One such outlet, O'Connor's of Ennistymon (pictured on page 8), sold tickets, steamer trunks and religious statuary. The operators reported that almost every intending emigrant also bought some religious item to accompany them on their journey – and Irish bodies taken from the sea had Rosary beads or protective scapulars. Some brought relics. Mary McGovern had clay from a saint's grave, promising protection against death by fire or drowning. She was saved.

Meanwhile the little girl pictured in the front door of O'Connor's herself became an emigrant and moved to Britain, where she served as a nun.

Shipping lines made a fortune from the one-way tide. So too did others. One letter home, posted in Queenstown by a man who was lost, complained about the high cost of his party's overnight accommodation. In Queenstown alone no fewer than twenty establishments described themselves as emigrant lodging houses in 1912, with a further unspecified fourteen boarding homes and one or two hotels. All this in a town of a few thousand, making it a kind of Klondyke in reverse.

Just one week before the *Titanic* sailed, the local correspondent of *The Cork Examiner* wrote:

THE TITANIC'S FIRST AND ONLY CALL AT QUEENSTOWN LAST THURSDAY.

> Standing on the highway of Queenstown (in) those days, a stranger would think it a remarkable spectacle to see thousands of country people pouring into the town carrying their belongings. But to us the spectacle is no new one, as it has been repeated year after year for decades. Time was when 20,000 people poured through the gateway of Queenstown in the first three months of the year. Formerly, by Queenstown, 100,000 would leave in one year.
>
> Parents and every member of the family all went together. They carried their humble bedding and food vessels with them. Nowadays they come in broadcloth and minus bedding and utensils. No longer do we see parents joined up with their youngsters in the exodus. America is a closed door now, save to vigorous young people, without blemish and subject to triple medical examinations before getting passports. One of the saddest features contributing to the blood-letting of Ireland is the prepaid ticket, accounting for more than one-third of the annual drain.

The emigration rate was 6.7 per 1,000 of the population in 1912. Since the enumeration of Irish emigrants began on 1 May 1855, no less than 4,847,360 Irish people had left the country by the end of the *Titanic* year. Females were in a majority, with 2.6 million departures compared to 2.2 million males.

The poor cross-subsidised the rich. White Star, Cunard and others could not have afforded to extend the race for bigger, faster ships had not the emigrants provided the steady, year-long business that brought huge turnover and massive cash flow. After the disaster, one Irish newspaper observed plaintively that it did not much matter to the emigrant what day – let alone what time – he or she arrived in New York. But when striking seamen cancelled a sailing of the *Olympic* soon after the sinking, the British papers carried a businessman's pompous claims that every hour's delay was costing him hundreds of pounds.

The White Star's annual report, published in May 1912, recorded a profit of £1,074,752 and one shilling. Nearly half the money was paid out in dividends, but the under-insured *Titanic* had wiped out the year's work. The report declared: 'The loss of this fine vessel is a source of deep regret to your directors, but it is of minor importance compared with the terrible loss of so many valuable lives.' Curious syntax, some might think.

Newspapers had always fallen in line with the age's obsession with both success and excess. Pictures of castings for the White Star's *Gigantic*, noting that she would be a larger vessel than even the *Titanic*, appeared on the front page of *The Irish Post* on 4 May. And barely a week short of the tragedy's first anniversary in April 1913, *The Cork Examiner* carried a picture of the *Olympic*'s first voyage from Cork following her expensive safety refit. Without a trace of irony, the caption noted: 'In addition to the increased bulkheads, she has also been fitted with a strong inner shell of steel, rendering her practically unsinkable.'

Nor did the emigrants themselves have any questions. Those joining the big liners were walking into a standard of living, even in Third Class, that they could only dream about at home. They had electric light, warmth, planked floors, and three or more square meals a day – for most, vast improvements on what they had at home. And standards in steerage on the *Titanic* were incomparably ahead of anything else afloat. No wonder the Irish partied.

On Thursday 11 April 1912, two tenders bringing 113 Third-Class, seven Second-Class and three First-Class passengers left Deepwater Quay, Queenstown, for the anchorage of the *Titanic* off Roches Point. The *America* and the *Ireland* also ferried a small mountain of luggage and 1,385 mail sacks. They returned with the Irish mails and confident, optimistic messages to loved ones from many of those on board. They also brought back a single deserter. Why did stoker John Coffey, originally from Queenstown, desert? Had he been receiving abuse in the furnace-environment below decks or been offended by anti-Catholic slogans chalked on the flue boxes?

Those looking for insensitivity did not have to look far in the immediate aftermath of the sinking. Notes sent to bereaved families by the White Star's agents in Queenstown a month after the tragedy were composed on a letterhead still bearing the boast that the *Titanic* was one of the two largest steamers in the world. Worse, when White Star itself published its final list of survivors and casualties, the names of the Irish who boarded at Queenstown contained a series of grotesque errors – with two female passengers unforgivably transformed into men through the careless mistranscription of the simple names Julia and Bridget, into 'Julian' and 'Bert'. Other surnames were hopelessly transmogrified – such that it led to the grimmest of confusion about whether loved ones might have been on board or not.

Southern Irish attitudes seem initially to have soured against the *Titanic* in the early years after her sinking. The ship stood for 'Black' Belfast, for anti-Catholic sentiment, with reports of Home Rule protest slogans daubed on the hull receiving wide currency, to the exclusion of many other considerations. As usual, Ireland's political and religious squabble was narrowing horizons and limiting visions. It was only in 1998 that the first outdoor *Titanic* memorial was erected in southern Ireland, at the liner's last port of call.

The Royal Mail Steamer *Titanic* was built, crewed and passengered in large part by the people of Ireland. She belongs to all of Ireland as much as the whole world, and to those who recognise that dreams and death and hopes and life are common to all humans of every status and allegiance.

Piper Eugene Daly played a farewell dirge to his homeland as the *Titanic* weighed anchor at Queenstown and began her journey into destiny. The air he chose was *Erin's Lament*. Like hymns on the boat deck, the strains still carry … and come wafting like a memory, across the distant water.

NOTE TO THE READER:

The following includes verbatim reports from a variety of sources, which can give rise to inconsistencies when collated. The headline information for each person should then be considered correct. For example, ages are commonly wrong in census information, where shown, particularly for females. There are also variations in the spelling of names and places. Census material is omitted in some cases for space reasons. Ticket numbers could vary widely, but the first digit generally indicates the class of travel.

The original caption for this image, printed on page 10 of The Cork Examiner *of Thursday 18 April 1912, read:* This photo was taken on Thursday last at Queenstown. It shows the entrance to the *Titanic*, and here passed through from the tender to the liner all those who joined her at Queenstown. The picture was taken but a few seconds before the door was closed in for ever, and as the two officers shown at the entrance were calling a farewell to some of the officials they knew on the tender.

Opposite page: *The sister ship* Olympic *(1911) conveys the immensity of the* Titanic *and also her social striation, although Second Class occupied the aft end of the boat deck and could thus look down on the First–Class promenade deck immediately below. B Deck, above the stairway, was also a Second–Class area, with steerage confined to the well deck below (a notice on the gate at the top of the steps informed them they were not allowed to go further). Hundreds of steerage gathered in the well deck of the* Titanic *as the crisis unfolded. It can be seen how they were completely cut off from the lifeboats. The cargo cranes are important, as their arms were climbed in a bid to gain access to higher decks.*

Below: *Internally, the* Titanic *was also a series of social tiers, down to the stokers who worked far below the waterline in stifling heat at the very bottom of the vessel. Steerage males were accommodated forward and had to flee aft. The way the ship flooded resulted in occasional anomalies whereby water would pour down in a torrent from a higher deck.*

IRISH PASSENGERS RMS *TITANIC*

JULIA BARRY (26) LOST

Ticket number 330844. Paid £7 12s 7d, plus 5s extra for upgrade.
Boarded at Queenstown. Third Class.
From: Killeentierna, Currow, Farranfore, County Kerry.
Destination: 14 West 36th Street, New York city.

The Hennessy girl and her friend Julia Barry were having a wonderful day visiting the Lakes of Killarney. They had joined a pleasure boat and were now 200 yards from shore when Julia, perhaps spinning her parasol in evocation of the good life, suddenly lost control of it. The umbrella fell from her grasp and sank in the lake.

Julia exclaimed and the Hennessy girl was horrified. But worst affected was the boatman. Wildly superstitious, he turned his boat immediately and headed back for shore. He could not be persuaded otherwise by anyone on board.

On tying up, the skipper told his passengers that Julia Barry would die at sea. Kerry folklore says the prophecy came true a few weeks later when Julia lost her life in the wreck of the *Titanic* off the Grand Banks of Newfoundland.

Julia had already been living in America for many years when she returned to Ireland to nurse her ailing mother – who shared her Christian name – at the beginning of 1912. She had previously been living in Yonkers, New York, with brothers and sisters. Her stated destination on the return voyage was to be her sister Nellie's at West 36th Street.

Almost all the family had emigrated from a brood of fourteen children born to Julia Snr and her husband Michael, a stonemason. The family started off in a crowded cottage in the village of Currow, where her father was employed by local landlords on the construction of walls around their estate. Begun initially as famine relief, the employment lengthened and the Barrys moved to a house opposite a lake at Scartaglin where Julia was born in early 1882.

The *Irish Independent* pictured Julia in the wake of the disaster, noting: 'She was returning to New York after coming home to nurse her mother, who is now dead. She was about 26 and the mainstay of her aged father.' The omen on the Lakes of Killarney came about because she resolved to see again the splendour of the place that many Americans had asked her about when she was in the United States.

On 11 April 1913, the first anniversary of her boarding the *Titanic* at Queenstown, her father brought a high court writ against the Oceanic Steam Navigation Co., the incorporated operators of the White Star Line. He is thought to have received a small settlement for the loss of his daughter, without admission of liability.

1911 census – Killeentierna, County Kerry.
Michael Barry (80), mason, widower.
Julia, daughter (25), single.

JOHN BOURKE (41) LOST
CATHERINE BOURKE (32) LOST
MARY BOURKE (39) LOST

John and Catherine's joint ticket number 364849. Paid £15 10s.
Mary's ticket number 364548. Paid £7 15s.
Boarded at Queenstown. Third Class.
All from: Carrowskehine, Lahardane, County Mayo.
Destination: All bound to stay with Catherine's sister, Ellen McHugh, 66 Ruby Street, Chicago.

John and Catherine Bourke had been married for just over one year. She had been
Catherine McHugh, falling in love on a visit home to Ireland. Soon after the wedding the
couple resolved to sell up and go to the United States. John's younger sister Mary opted to
accompany them on the great adventure to Chicago where Catherine had previously lived.

Their story is told by the *Chicago Evening World* of May 1912:

FLOWER OF MAYO'S YOUTH SANK WITH HANDS JOINED ON THE TITANIC
Of fifteen merry lads and colleens seeking
fortune, only two arrive

The Chicago 'Evening World' says – Of
twelve young Irishmen and girls, two
young men and a boy, comprising a party
of fifteen from the County Mayo who
started for Chicago on the *Titanic,* only
two have arrived here – two colleens,
Annie Kelly and Annie McGowan.

The rest are at the bottom of the
ocean for they went down with the
Titanic and there is grief here in Chicago
where relatives mourn and grief back in
County Mayo over the sudden end to
the dreams and plans of thirteen of the
flower of Ireland's youth.

It was a family party, all the
members being bound by ties of kinship
or of lifelong companionship. In it were
John Bourke, a sturdy young farmer, and
his Kate, the bride of less than a year, and
John's sister Mary, all from the farming

country around Crossmolina; Kate McGowan, a former resident of Chicago, and her niece Annie McGowan, a girl of 16; Annie Kelly, aged 18, of Castlebar, the county town of Mayo, a few miles from Crossmolina; Patrick Canavan, 18, a cousin of Annie Kelly; Mary Manion [*sic*], bound to join her brother in Chicago; a boy Patrick, and Mary Flynn his sister; three blue-eyed rosy-cheeked girls named O'Donohue, Mahan and Driscoll, and Nora Fleming and Mary Glynn.

Romance of Ireland comes into Kate's life
The mysterious workings of destiny contributed to the formation of this ill-fated little squad of ocean-travellers. Some ten years ago, Kate McHugh and Kate McGowan, then little more than children, came to Chicago from their homes near Crossmolina.

They prospered, and about fifteen months ago Kate McHugh went back to Ireland for a visit. She met John Bourke, a playmate of her childhood days, and he married her out of hand, for an old affection both had forgotten leaped into love. It was the intention of Bourke and his wife to live out their lives in Ireland.

Kate McGowan went back to Ireland last October. She owned a rooming house in this city, and it was her intention to return in the spring. Right industriously did she sing the praises of Chicago in the homes of those she visited in County Mayo and the result of it was that when she came to start back there were fourteen ready to accompany her, among them the Bourkes, who had sold their farm and planned to invest their money in a teaming business in this city.

The night before the fifteen started for Queenstown to board the *Titanic*, there was what the Irish call a 'live wake' at Castlebar. Hundreds of friends of the young people gathered and made merry that they might start with light hearts and merriment. Never were fifteen voyagers to a strange land launched on their journey with such a plenitude of goodwill and good wishes.

The immense *Titanic* overshadowing everything in Queenstown harbour was a revelation to thirteen of the little party as they came alongside in the tender. Some of them had never seen an ocean liner before.

The Mayo delegation were given a section of the Third-Class quarters remote from the Lithuanians and Herzegovinians and Slavs, who had boarded the vessel the day before at Cherbourg and were already filling the steerage with strange odours.

Although travelling Third Class, the little party was prosperous. All had money and good clothing and many little trinkets they were carrying to loved ones who had gone before to the far-off and mysterious and magical Chicago. All fifteen kept to themselves, spending the days on deck in the fresh air and sunshine.

They were all asleep when the *Titanic*, rushing along at 23 knots an hour, tore a hole in her hull against an iceberg. The jar did not disturb the third cabin where the rush of water and the throb of engines were always heard.

It was half an hour or more after the *Titanic* struck when a steward roused the County Mayo travellers and told them the ship had struck something but there was no danger.

Although they believed the stewards, they did not go to sleep again. There was apprehension in the hearts of the lads and colleens from Mayo, and when Mrs Bourke suggested prayer, they all knelt. One of them recited the Rosary and the others, with their beads in hand, intoned the responses aloud. They were calm then, but they did not sleep.

Just twenty minutes before the boat went down, stewards ran through the steerage shouting orders for all passengers to go up on deck. There was no time for those who had neglected to clothe themselves to dress. They swarmed to the companionway leading to the upper decks, but were held back by officers who said things were not ready.

John Bourke and Patrick Canavan knew there was a ladder leading to the upper decks. Gathering the women and girls about them, they started for the ladder. Just then a steward who had talked on several occasions to Annie Kelly, a roguish Miss, happened along and saw her, frightened and confused, dropping behind her friends.

Grasping her hand, the steward dragged her up the stairway to the deck where the lifeboats were loading. She was clad only in a nightgown. A boat was just about to be launched. The steward pushed her in. It was only half full.

Then John Bourke and his wife and his sister Mary and the little Flynn boy appeared on deck. The stewards tried to push the two women into the boat after Annie Kelly.

'I'll not leave my husband', said Kate Bourke. 'I'll not leave my brother', said Mary Bourke.

The crew of the lifeboat would not let the little Flynn aboard, although he was a slight boy and not able to take care of himself. The last Annie Kelly saw of John Bourke and his wife and his sister and little Patrick Flynn, they were standing hands clasped in a row by the rail, waiting for the end.

The end came in a few minutes. The great *Titanic* went down and of all that left County Mayo on that ship, Annie Kelly thought she was the sole survivor.

But the next day, when she had recovered from the effects of the shock and exposure, she found Annie McGowan lying beside her. The two girls were cared for in an hospital in New York and sent to their relatives in this city scantily clothed, for they say the clothing given to them in New York was so ragged and dirty they could not wear them.

Annie McGowan does not know how she was saved; in fact she is unable to tell any connected story of the horror.

All gone but two of that merry group that boarded the *Titanic* in Queenstown, fresh from the County Mayo. And the two, young as they are, bear the marks of sorrow that will never leave them.

(Reprinted by *The Connaught Telegraph*, 25 May 1912)

The tragedy resulted in more wakes in County Mayo, days after the American wakes:

Titanic *Disaster Lahardane Victims*

One of the saddest sights ever witnessed in the west of Ireland was the waking of the five young girls and one young man from a village near Lahardane, who went down with the ill-fated *Titanic*.

They were all from the same village, and when the first news of the appalling catastrophe reached their friends the whole community was plunged into inutterable grief. They cherished for a time a remote hope that they were saved, but when the dread news of their terrible fate arrived, a feeling of excruciating anguish took the place.

For two days and two nights, wakes were held. The photograph of each victim was placed on the bed on which they had slept before leaving home and kindred. The beds were covered with snow-white quilts and numbers of candles were lighted around.

The wailing and moaning of the people was very distressing and would almost draw a tear from a stone. The name of the young man who drowned was Michael Bourke [*sic*], and in his case his loss is rendered all the sadder by the fact that his young wife went down with him to a watery grave.

A strange story is told by Bourke's brother in connection with the tragic affair. He states that at the time of the disaster he dreamt he saw his brother in the attitude of shaving himself in his own house.

(*Western People*, 4 May 1912)

John Bourke, baptised on 25 May 1869, was the son of William Bourke and Mary O'Boyle. His parents died and he married Catherine McHugh on 17 January 1911, in Lahardane.

Catherine, originally from Tawnagh in the locality, was related to another passenger, Catherine McGowan of Terry, Massbrook, County Mayo, while the Bourkes lived next door to fellow passenger Mary Mangan.

The 1911 census shows John and Kate to be aged 40 and 31, married for under one year, with the farmer's sister Mary in the same household, aged 38.

Local history states that John Bourke bought a new spade in early 1912 intending to put down a crop, but changed his mind and decided to emigrate instead. Local folklore also insists that Catherine and Mary were in a lifeboat (possibly No. 16 on the port side) and when they saw that John was to be left behind, returned to the ship and were lost.

BRIDGET DELIA BRADLEY (22) SAVED

Ticket number 334914. Paid £7 14s 6d.
Boarded at Queenstown. Third Class.
From: Ballinahulla, County Kerry; bordering Kingwilliamstown, County Cork.
Destination: 29 William Street, Glen Falls, New York.

She was saved – sitting securely in a lifeboat that was beginning its jolting descent to the water. But Bridget Delia Bradley felt she had to escape from the vessel of her salvation. Demented with fear, she tried to get back on the doomed ship:

There was a girl from my place, and just when she got down into the lifeboat, she thought that the boat was sinking into the water. Her name was Bridget Bradley. She climbed one of the ropes as far as she could and tried to get back into the *Titanic* again, as she thought she would be safer in it than in the lifeboat. She was just getting up when one of the sailors went out to her and pulled her down again.

(Daniel Buckley, testifying to the US inquiry, day 12, 3 May 1912)

Buckley also mentioned Bridget in a letter he wrote home from the safety of the rescue ship *Carpathia:*

Thank God some of us are amongst the saved. Hannah Riordan, Brigie Bradley, Nonie O'Leary and the Shine girl from Lismore are all right.

(Letter printed in The Cork Examiner, 13 May 1912)

Bridget's family believed she was rescued in lifeboat No. 4, launched from the starboard side of the sinking *Titanic* at 1.55 a.m., but this is inconsistent with her being seen by Daniel Buckley, whose own lifeboat departed a little earlier.

Bridget was interviewed by the *Daily Times* while still recovering from her ordeal at St Vincent's Hospital in New York:

I was in bed at the time the accident occurred and the shock, which was a comparatively slight one, did not disturb me greatly. A knock on the doors of our rooms caused us to get up and dress ourselves. I slipped on a lightweight black dress and wrapped a small shawl about me, the only clothes I saved, and went to the deck where I found the most of the passengers assembled.

There was no disorder on the deck that amounted to anything, and all the officers acted in a manner that convinced us the ship was not in grave danger. The story that the men on board acted like heroes is true in every detail, and it was 'women first' in nearly every case except for a few of the steerage passengers who tried to fight their way to the lifeboats and who I have been told were shot by officers of the boat.

All the lifeboats were lowered while I was on deck and it looked for a time as if I would be left. I saw men lead their wives to the lifeboats and leave them there, returning to the deck, and we on deck were not so horribly frightened as might be thought. Every one of us thought that it was impossible to sink the ship.

Just as the last lifeboat, the one with Mr Ismay in it, was launched over the side, one of the officers shouted 'There's more room in that boat' and I and eleven other women were crowded into it. This was after 1 o'clock. I don't know how much, but it was after one. The lifeboat was manned by enough men to care for it properly and immediately on touching the water, the men rowed with all their strength to get away from the ship, so that, if it did go down, we would not be caught in the suction.

The night was extremely cold, and we womenfolk had little wraps to keep us warm and we huddled there in clusters watching the great ship as it slowly sank. Not until we got off the boat did we fully realise the danger. Then we saw that the boat had tilted forward and that slowly, but surely, she was sinking.

We saw the bottom row of lights disappear under the water and watched as line after line disappeared, showing us the rapidity of the sinking of the ship. We were entirely surrounded by large cakes of ice and there was no food or water on the boat, and in the long wait for the *Carpathia* the majority of us prayed for the coming of the ship. When the welcome ship hove in sight many of us were too much exhausted to realise the greatness of the disaster …

We were picked up at 6 o'clock and I am informed that every one of the boats that were launched from the *Titanic* were picked up, with the exception of one which turned over and drowned every one on board. The relief that we experienced when on board the *Carpathia* is beyond description, but there was with many a fear that this ship might meet the same fate as the *Titanic* and it was not until the ship touched the port of New York that we all felt safe.

To realise what we passed through is impossible for anyone who was not on the ship. The hand of death was over us and as we floated out in the frail lifeboats, with no food or water, and as our thirst began to increase, the thought that we might not be picked up, and huddled up in this manner should die of starvation, made us beside ourselves, and as we prayed the smoke-stack of the *Carpathia* hove in sight …

Practically two out of every three who sailed on the *Titanic* are now at the bottom of the ocean, and when I realise that I was one of the last twelve to leave the ship, I cannot help thinking what might have been.

The brave men who went down have left a memory in the hearts of every one of us survivors that will linger as long as we live. The 'women first' rule was carried out to the letter and those who had womenfolk on board devoted their time to getting the women in the small boats while they themselves were content to remain on deck.

A few men, including six Chinese, had hidden under the seats of the lifeboats and were carried out, according to the stories on the *Carpathia* on Monday night, but it is said that two of them were crushed to death by the weight thrown upon them. There were none of them in our boat.

Bridget was the fifth eldest of nine children who lived in a cottage with no bath or electricity. She occasionally went to school barefoot. Older siblings Mary and Michael emigrated to the United States, both settling in Glen Falls, where Mary became a domestic and her brother a fireman.

On discharge from hospital, a penniless Bridget was assisted by the American Red Cross, receiving $125. She worked as a domestic in Glen Falls for two years before moving to New York and becoming engaged by the wealthy Nicholls family.

She lodged a court claim against the Ocean Steam Navigation Company, owners of the *Titanic*, in the US District Court, southern district of New York, in company with numerous other litigants. Her claim was for $153 worth of lost personal effects, made up as follows:

Three pairs high shoes, at $3.50 – $10.50; One lady's suit, woollen consisting of coat and skirt, $25; Two suits union underwear, flannel $1 – $2; Three pairs woollen stockings, $.50 – $1.50; Three pairs half hose $.50 – $1.50; One lady's hat with trimmings, $3; One toilet set consisting of brush, comb, soap, tooth brush, one bath towel, two plain towels, one silver soap case, one silver hair pin case and leather case for set – $5; One leather valise – $3.50; Two lady's dresses, cotton, $3.50 – $7; One black dress, mixed goods, $28; Six white shirt waists, $1 – $6; Cash $25; One large steamer trunk, $10; Paid for medical attendance as result of the collision, $25. Total: $153.

In 1925 Bridget met the supervisor of the Nicholls' summer estate on Howe Island in the St Lawrence river in Canada. She was 32, he was 40. They were married two days after the following Valentine's Day at St Patrick's Cathedral on Fifth Avenue, New York. She was now Mrs Bernard LaSha, and she adopted the first name Delia, a familiar name for Bridget.

They settled in Gananoque, Ontario, where their first child, Mary, was born in September 1927. John Joseph arrived fourteen months later, and Rose Henrietta two years after that. Joan Margaret was born in 1931.

By 1929, Delia LaSha, *Titanic* survivor, had become a boat owner herself. Her husband ploughed his savings into a tour boat, named the *Sun Dance*, to take passengers around the islands of the St Lawrence. In the autumn of 1932 he suffered a seizure and on 29 March 1933 died aged 47, at the height of the Great Depression. A few months later, heart worn and suffering from shingles, his widow gave birth to their fifth child, who lived only a few days and was buried with his father.

Bridget could not face the water commerce business herself. She hired a man to operate the *Sun Dance*, which cut down on her own income, and she took up babysitting to try to make ends meet. In 1951, she suffered a stroke which severely impaired her speech and paralysed her right arm and leg. The boat was sold.

When the film *Titanic* was shown in the local cinema that same decade, Delia LaSha was guest of honour. Her daughter Mary Higgins recounted: 'Mom became very emotional during the movie and at times kept shaking her head as if to say it didn't happen that way. If able to speak, I am sure she would have had many comments to make.'

Three years later she was dead, having outlived her husband by twenty-three years. According to her death certificate, she was born on 10 January 1893, and passed away on 24 January 1956, aged 63.

ARTHUR JACKSON BREWE (45) LOST

Ticket number 112379. Paid £39 12s.
Boarded at Cherbourg. First Class.
From: Drumgriffin, County Galway.
Destination: returning to Philadelphia.

First-Class passenger Dr Brewe was from Drumgriffin, County Galway. He was aged 45, and was returning to Philadelphia from a grand tour. He boarded the *Titanic* at Cherbourg in the company of friends – the same embarkation port as the 'Unsinkable' Molly Brown, his contemporary. She later wrote to passenger Colonel Archibald Gracie describing a conversation with Dr Brewe on Sunday night before the disaster:

> In telling of the people she conversed with that Sunday evening, she refers to an exceedingly intellectual and much-travelled acquaintance, Mrs Bucknell, whose husband had founded the Bucknell University of Philadelphia; also to another passenger from the same city, Dr Brewe, who had done much in scientific research.

During her conversation with Mrs Bucknell, the latter reiterated a statement previously made on the tender at Cherbourg while waiting for the *Titanic*. She said she feared boarding the ship because she had evil forebodings that something might happen.

(Mrs Emma Bucknell, 60, and her maid were rescued in boat No. 8)

The *Irish Weekly Independent* of 25 May 1912 reported:

Distinguished Galway man who went down on the Titanic
Amongst the victims of the *Titanic* disaster, of whose last moments on the ill-fated vessel nothing is known, was a distinguished Galway man, Dr Arthur Jackson Brewe of the Netherlands, Forty-fourth and Chestnut Streets, Philadelphia.

Dr Brewe was the eldest son of Mrs Butler, of Winterfield House, Drumgriffin, County Galway, and a brother of Mrs Glynn, the wife of Dr Glynn of Waterview House, Turloughmore, Athenry.

Born in Galway 45 years ago, he was educated in a preparatory school in Glencoe and subsequently at Clongowes, whence he matriculated to Trinity College, Dublin. Soon after taking his degree, he emigrated to the United States, first living in New York, and then moving to Philadelphia, where he made his home …

Dr Brewe, who had been on a tour of Africa, joined the *Titanic* from Cherbourg, having travelled through Rome, Naples, Florence, and Paris. His last letter was posted to his sister, Mrs Glynn, Waterview House, Turloughmore, immediately before he sailed, and she little thought as she read his graphic pen-pictures of his tour that he was fast approaching his doom.

CATHERINE BUCKLEY (22) LOST

Ticket number 329944. Paid £7 5s 8d.
Boarded at Queenstown. Third Class.
From: Springmount, Ovens, County Cork.
Destination: 71 Mount View Street, Roxbury, Massachusetts.

Catherine Buckley was travelling out to visit her sister Margaret in West Roxbury, near Boston, since her British army boyfriend had been posted to Hong Kong. She finally arrived in the local St Joseph's Cemetery after her body was recovered from the Atlantic, brought to Canada, and shipped south to Margaret – with reimbursement of her steerage fare by the White Star Line. Hers was the only Irish body returned to relatives.

Margaret had wanted her sister to come out and join her. Her parents, Julia and Jeremiah, both in their sixties when Catherine sailed, wanted their youngest to stay home in Ireland, fearing she would stay in the New World. They wanted her to care for them in their old age. Catherine finally defied their wishes, booked passage on the *Titanic* and was drowned. The parents never forgave their older daughter for urging Kate to her doom. When a bereft and distraught Margaret travelled home later that same year, the story is told that the homestead door was slammed in her face. 'Murderer!' was the bitter label hurled at Margaret by her own parents.

In fact Catherine had been one of a number of Irish passengers originally booked to cross the Atlantic on the White Star liner *Cymric*, which ought to have sailed on 7 April, but was trapped by the coal strike which had paralysed shipping. The passengers were transferred to the newest and grandest addition to the White Star fleet.

A full two weeks after the numbing disaster, on 28 April 1912, the search vessel *MacKay-Bennett* recovered Catherine's body. It was embalmed on board and returned to Halifax, Nova Scotia. There, in an ice rink converted into a morgue, the body was identified by means of Catherine's ticket:

> Body No. 299 Female. Estimated age 18. False teeth top. Dark.
> Clothing – Long blue overcoat; blue serge jacket and skirt; white blouse; blue corsets; grey knickers; 10s in silver; £1 in gold; $5 note in purse; satchel; Third Class ticket no. 329944. Third Class. Name – Catherine Buckley.

Catherine had been a maid to two old ladies, Annie and Emma Evans, at 3 Adelaide Terrace in Cork, where her name appears in the 1911 census. She wrote from this address to her sister on 19 March: 'just a hurried line, hoping you are well and to tell you I am to sail for the U. States on 11th April by the new steamer *Titanic*.' She added: 'Too bad I couldn't go direct to Boston on the account of the coal strike … there is a lot of liners put off on account of the strike, so I have to go the way I am told.'

Her army boyfriend, George, wrote to her sister in July 1912: 'Margaret, I am very sorry to hear that she has gone to her eternal home and left me in this dark world of ours alone.'

The Titanic International Society marked Catherine's grave with a new headstone in May 2010 in a ceremony attended by the Irish consul general.

DANIEL BUCKLEY (21) SAVED

Ticket number 330920. Paid £7 12s 7d, plus 3s 10d extra.
Boarded at Queenstown. Third Class.
From: Kingwilliamstown (now Ballydesmond), County Cork.
Destination: 855 Trement Avenue, Bronx, New York city.

Daniel Buckley lived because a woman in a lifeboat threw a shawl over him. Her action cloaked his presence as officers fired shots and ordered men who had rushed a boat to leave it – or die. A moment's humanity had turned Dannie Buckley female.

He was an ambitious and enterprising young man who wanted to go to America to make some money, as he told Senator William Alden Smith at the US inquiry. 'I came in the *Titanic* because she was a new steamer.'

But his good luck lasted for only another six years. Daniel Buckley was killed in 1918, a month before the end of the First World War, while helping to evacuate American Expeditionary Force wounded from the front line on the French/Belgian border.

Buckley was born on 28 September 1890 and baptised the same day in the Church of the Immaculate Conception in Boherbue, County Cork. His proud parents were Daniel Snr and Abigail Sullivan. The family moved to neighbouring Kingwilliamstown in 1905, where Daniel Snr became the town baker.

By 1912, Buckley and a number of young friends had decided on emigration to the United States, where opportunities would be better for a jobbing labourer like himself. The night before the party left for Queenstown to embark, there was an American wake in the town with strong drink, set-dancing and a singsong send-off. Buckley had penned a ballad to 'Sweet Kingwilliamstown', a tuneful tribute that endures in the area, but chose that night to sing an optimistic valediction: 'When the Fields are White with Daisies, I'll Return'.

Aboard the White Star vessel, Buckley and three friends found a Third-Class compartment near the bow. He shared the cramped room with his near neighbours Patrick O'Connell, Patrick O'Connor and Michael Linehan. Here is Buckley's account in a letter to his mother composed three days after rescue:

On board the *Carpathia*, 18 March [*sic*], 1912.

Dear Mother,
I am writing these lines on board the *Carpathia*, the ship that saved our lives. As I might not have much time when I get to New York, I mean to give you an account of the terrible shipwreck we had.

At 11 p.m. on the 14th, our ship *Titanic* struck an iceberg and sank to the deep at 2.20 a.m. on the 15th. The present estimation is 1,500 lost, 710 saved. Thank God some of us are amongst the saved.

Hannah Riordan, Brigie Bradley, Nonie O'Leary and the Shine girl from Lismore are all right.

There is no account of Patie Connell (25), Michael Linehan from Freeholds, or Jim Connor, Hugh's son, from Tureenavonacane. However I hope they were taken into some other ship.

There were four of us sleeping in the same apartment. We had a bed of our own and in every apartment there were four lifebelts, one for each person. At the time when the ship got struck I heard a terrible noise. I jumped out of bed and told my comrades there was something wrong, but they only laughed.

I turned on the light and to my surprise there was a small amount of water running along the floor, I had only just dressed myself when the sailors came along shouting 'All up on deck, unless you want to get drowned!'

We all ran up on deck. I thought to go down again to my room for a lifebelt and my little bag. When I was going down the last flight of stairs the water was up three steps so I did not go any further. I just thought of Dan Ring's saying 'stick to your lifebelts and face a tearing ocean'.

We were not long on deck when the lifeboats were prepared. There were only sixteen boats and that amount was only enough to carry a tenth of the passengers. The third boat that was let down, I went on it. There were about forty men in it.

We were only fifteen minutes in the boat when the big ship went down. It was a terrible sight. It would make the stones cry to hear those on board shrieking.

It made a terrible noise like thunder when it was sinking. There were a great many Irish boys and girls drowned. I got out without any wound. There were a lot of men and women got wounded getting off the steamer.

A good many died coming out on the lifeboats and after getting on the *Carpathia*. It was a great change to us to get on this strange steamer as we had a great time on the *Titanic*. We got a very good diet and we had a very jolly time dancing and singing.

We had every type of instrument on board to amuse us, but all the amusement sank in the deep. I will write a note when I get to New York. Good-bye at present.

Dannie

Dannie was paid $100 in relief assistance by the American Red Cross. On 4 May 1912, he sent home a postcard of the *Carpathia*, telling his brother John: 'I am sending you the picture of the ship that saved my life. Tell my mother to keep it and frame it. I hope she got better alright. I am getting on fine. Hoping ye are all well. Love to all. Dannie.'

Buckley testified before the Senate inquiry into the disaster, the only Irish passenger to do so. Senator Smith, chairman of the subcommittee, took his evidence separately and the questions posed emanate from this source:

This night of the wreck I was sleeping in my room on the *Titanic*, in the steerage. There were three other boys from the same place sleeping in the same room with me. I heard some terrible noise and I jumped out on the floor, and the first thing I knew my feet were getting wet; the water was just coming in slightly. I told the other fellows to get up, that there was something wrong and that the water was coming in. They only laughed at me. One of them says: 'Get back into bed. You are not in Ireland now.'

I got my clothes on as quick as I could, and the three other fellows got out. The room was very small, so I got out, to give them room to dress themselves. Two sailors came along, and they were shouting: 'All up on deck! Unless you want to get drowned.'

When I heard this, I went for the deck as quick as I could. When I got up on the deck I saw everyone having those lifebelts on only myself; so I got sorry, and said I would go back again where I was sleeping and get one of those life preservers; because there was one there for each person.

I went back again, and just as I was going down the last flight of stairs the water was up four steps, and dashing up. I did not go back into the room, because I could not. When I went back toward the room the water was coming up three steps up the stairs, or four steps; so I did not go any farther. I went back on the deck again, and just as I got there, I was looking around to see if I could get any of those lifebelts, and I met a First-Class passenger, and he had two. He gave me one, and fixed it on me.

Then the lifeboats were preparing. There were five lifeboats sent out. I was in the sixth. I was holding the ropes all the time, helping to let down the five lifeboats that went down first, as well as I could.

When the sixth lifeboat was prepared, there was a big crowd of men standing on the deck. And they all jumped in. So I said I would take my chance with them.

Who were they?

Passengers and sailors and firemen, mixed. There were no ladies there at the same time. When they jumped, I said I would go too. I went into the boat. Then two officers came along and said all of the men could come out. And they brought a lot of steerage passengers with them; and they were mixed, in every way, ladies and gentlemen. And they said all the men could get out and let the ladies in. But six men were left in the boat. I think they were firemen and sailors.

I was crying. There was a woman in the boat and she had thrown her shawl over me, and she told me to stay in there. I believe she was Mrs Astor. Then they did not see me, and the boat was lowered down into the water, and we rowed away from the steamer.

The men that were in the boat at first fought, and would not get out, but the officers drew their revolvers, and fired shots over our heads, and then the men got out. When the boat was ready, we were lowered down into the water and rowed away from the steamer. We were only about 15 minutes out when she sank.

What else happened?

One of the firemen that was working on the *Titanic* told me, when I got on board the *Carpathia* and he was speaking to me, that he did not think it was any iceberg; that it was only that they wanted to make a record, and they ran too much steam and the boilers bursted. That is what he said.

We sighted the lights of the big steamer, the *Carpathia*. All the women got into a terrible commotion and jumped around. They were hallooing and the sailors were trying to keep them sitting down, and they would not do it. They were standing up all the time.

When we got into the *Carpathia* we were treated very good. We got all kinds of refreshments.

Did you feel a shock from the collision when the ship struck?

Yes, I did.

And did that wake you up?

It did. I did not feel any shock in the steamer; only just heard a noise. I heard a kind of a grating noise.

Did you get right out of bed?

Yes, I did.

When you got out, you got into the water? There was water in your compartment in the steerage?

Yes; water was there slightly. There was not very much.

How much?

The floor was only just getting wet. It was only coming in under the door very slightly.

You had two or three boys with you?

Yes; three boys that came from the same place in Ireland.

What became of those other three boys?

I cannot say. I did not see them any more after leaving the room where I parted from them.

They were lost?

Yes, they were lost.

Was there any effort made on the part of the officers or crew to hold the steerage passengers in the steerage?

I do not think so.

Were you permitted to go up to the top deck without any interference?

Yes, sir. They tried to keep us down at first on our steerage deck. They did not want us to go up to the First-Class place at all.

Who tried to do that?

I cannot say who they were. I think they were sailors.

What happened then? Did the steerage passengers try to get out?

Yes, they did. There was one steerage passenger there, and he was getting up the steps, and just as he was going in a little gate a fellow came along and chucked him down; threw him down into the steerage place. This fellow got excited, and he ran after him, and he could not find him. He got up over the little gate. He could not find him.

What gate do you mean?

A little gate just at the top of the stairs going up into the First-Class deck.

There was a gate between the steerage and the First-Class deck?

Yes. The First-Class deck was higher up than the steerage deck, and there were some steps leading up to it, 9 or 10 steps, and a gate just at the top of the steps.

Was the gate locked?

It was not locked at the time we made the attempt to get up there, but the sailor, or whoever he was, locked it. So that this fellow who went up after him broke the lock on it, and he went after the fellow that threw him down. He said if he could get hold of him he would throw him into the ocean.

Did these passengers in the steerage have any opportunity at all of getting out?

Yes, they had.

What opportunity did they have?

I think they had as much chance as the First- and Second-Class passengers.

After this gate was broken?

Yes, because they were all mixed. All the steerage passengers went up on the First-Class deck at this time, when the gate was broken. They all got up there. They could not keep them down.

How much water was there in the steerage when you got out of the steerage?

There was only just a little bit. Just like you would throw a bucket of water on the floor; just very little, like that.

But it was coming in, was it?

Yes, it was only just commencing to come in. Then I went down the second time, to get one of the life preservers, there was a terrible lot of water there, in a very short time.

How much?

It was just about three steps up the stairs, on the last flight of stairs that I got down.

Did you find any people down in the steerage when you went back the second time?

There were a number, but I cannot say how many. All the boys and girls were coming up against me. They were all going for the deck.

Were they excited?

Yes, they were. The girls were very excited, and they were crying; and all the boys were trying to console them and saying that it was nothing serious.

Were you crying at the time?

Not at this time. There was a girl from my place, and just when she got down into the lifeboat she thought that the boat was sinking into the water. Her name was Bridget Bradley. She climbed one of the ropes as far as she could and tried to get back into the *Titanic* again, as she thought she would be safer in it than in the lifeboat. She was just getting up when one of the sailors went out to her and pulled her down again.

How many people were there in the steerage when you got out of bed?
I cannot say.
Could you see many people around?
Yes, sir; there was a great crowd of people. They were all terribly excited. They were all going for the decks as quick as they could. The people had no difficulty in stepping into the lifeboat. It was close to the ship.
I want to ask you whether, from what you saw that night, you feel that the steerage passengers had an equal opportunity with other passengers and the crew in getting into the lifeboats?
Yes, I think they had as good a chance as the First- and Second-Class passengers.
You think they did have?
Yes. But at the start they tried to keep them down on their own deck.
But they broke down this gate to which you have referred?
Yes, sir.
And then they went on up, as others did, mingling all together?
Yes, they were all mixed up together.
Have you told all you know, of your own knowledge, about that?
Yes.
Were you where you could see the ship when she went down?
Yes, I saw the lights just going out as she went down. It made a terrible noise, like thunder.
I wish you would tell the committee in what part of the ship this steerage was located.
Down, I think, in the lower part of the steamer, in the after part of the ship, at the back.
That is all. Thank you.

Buckley told the *Daily Times* on landfall: 'The lights were kept burning until the ship sank from sight. Men fought with women down in the steerage, and time and again officers would drag men from the boats in order to let women have their places.'

Daniel Buckley is buried in his native Ballydesmond, County Cork. The inscription on his grave reads: 'Of your charity, pray for the soul of Dannie Buckley, Ballydesmond, who was killed in action in France, on Oct 15th 1918, aged 28 years. Survivor of Titanic.'

Brave Irish American Soldier Second Lieutenant Daniel Buckley
A survivor of the ill-fated *Titanic*, he volunteered for active service under the stars and stripes in the 69th Irish (Rainbow Division) on American entrance to the war.

He came to France with his regiment in October 1917, saw fighting in several battles, had some miraculous escapes, the same Supernatural power which aided him in the *Titanic* still appearing to come to his assistance.

He was wounded, though not seriously, in April last, and fell, paying the supreme penalty, fighting under the flag of his adopted country, just previous to the cessation of hostilities. He was a native of Kingwilliamstown, County Cork, where he was extremely popular previous to his departure for the States.

(*The Cork Examiner*, 15 January 1919)

Buckley had joined the US army in June 1917, reasoning that it was better to choose his unit rather than wait to be conscripted. He wrote home having left his job in a Manhattan hotel: 'Well mother, I am after volunteering to go with the 69th regiment. The regiment is composed of all Irish fellows, about 2,000 strong ... I hope you won't be vexed, but proud that there is one of the family gone in at least to put some nails in the Kaiser's coffin.'

He trained at Camp Mills in Long Island and arrived in France that fall with Company K of the 165th US infantry. His early letters complained of overcharging by locals – 'they think we must be all millionaires when we come from the US' – while adding that he had little of his $15 a month pay left having contributed $6.70 to an insurance scheme. He also arranged for much of the pay to be channelled directly to his family.

He was soon in the trenches, and though censorship meant he could not describe military activity, wrote glowing generalised accounts: 'We had some great battles with the huns, but they run away when they see an American bayonet shining in the sunlight.'

Reality intruded, and he sustained some wounds which he passed off with brief references. A letter written on captured German paper related the death of a friend, Jack Reardon. 'He was a fine fellow and loved by all his pals as he was full of life. God have mercy on his soul. I hope he is better off, as this is a rough life over here. He was not killed instantly, but died in hospital. I have had some narrow escapes myself, but thanks to God I have been lucky so far ...'

His last letter was written on 9 October 1918, six days before his death:

My dear mother,

I am writing you a few lines hoping you are well, also Nonie, Julian, Jack and Neal, also all in Kingwilliamstown.

I wrote a couple of weeks ago and did not get a chance since, as we are very busy drawing the huns back on all fronts. I believe the war will soon be over, as the Germans are getting a great licking.

I received the medals you sent me, also the cigarettes, but only 15 packets were left. I was glad to get them as I was at the front then. At present I am behind the lines a little way and the music of our big guns is ringing all around. Last Sunday we attended Mass in the woods, + as Father Duffy says, with the music of the cannon to take the place of the organ.

I hope you receive the allotment as it will soon be five months due, as it started June 1st. Tell Nell Herlihy I received her letter + will write later as I get no paper at present. This is a wild place and all towns are in a level with the ground. I got a cold already and I hope we will be out of here before winter.

I will close now and say Good Bye, Good luck to all at home.

Your fond son,

Pvt Daniel Buckley.

Dannie Buckley was reported shot dead by a sniper while helping to retrieve wounded, somewhere on the Meuse-Argonne front.

He was initially interred in France, his remains only returning to Ireland in the spring of 1919 for burial in 'sweet' Kingwilliamstown. It was the first time he had been back since 1912 – and the locals standing in the graveyard noted that the surrounding fields were indeed 'white with daisies'.

JEREMIAH BURKE (19) LOST

Ticket number 365222. Paid £6 15s.
Boarded at Queenstown. Third Class.
From: Ballinoe, White's Cross, Upper Glanmire, County Cork.
Destination: Mrs Burns, 41 Washington Street, Charlestown, Massachusetts.

Jeremiah Burke is the passenger fabled to have thrown a despairing message in a bottle from the decks of the sinking *Titanic*. Miraculously, the bottle washed up on the shoreline just a short distance from his home in Ireland just over a year later.

The message contains an unclear date which could variously be 10, 12 or 13 April 1912. The *Titanic* struck the berg at 11.40 p.m. on 14 April. Interestingly, an article in the *Irish News*, published on 20 April 1912, observed that very few authentic messages from shipwrecks had ever come to safety and 'very many … are cruel hoaxes'.

Jeremiah's grieving family believed the message found by a coachman on the shore at Dunkettle, close to their home, was authentic. The message reads: 'From *Titanic*. Good Bye all. Burke of Glanmire, Cork'. Kate Burke, his mother, recognised her son's handwriting. She announced that the bottle was the same holy water bottle she had given to her boy on the day of his departure.

Jeremiah Burke was only 19, and stood six feet two inches in his stockinged feet. He was the youngest of seven children who had all worked on the 70-acre family farm, and stated on embarkation that he was an agricultural labourer.

Two of his sisters had previously emigrated to the US and he was resolved to join them when a letter arrived from Charlestown with money for his passage. His cousin Nora Hegarty, from neighbouring Killavarrig, decided to accompany him on the expedition to America.

Jeremiah's father William drove the cousins to Queenstown in his pony and trap. He reported seeing them making friends with another intending passenger, a piper identified as Eugene Daly. He survived, while both Jeremiah and Nora drowned.

More Cork Victims

The sympathy of the people of Cork will go out in full measure to the parents of Miss Nora Hegarty of Killavallig, Whitechurch, and Mr Jeremiah Burke, of Upper Glanmire, both of whom were only 19 years of age and who lost their lives in the *Titanic* disaster.

They left Queenstown full of hope for a bright and happy career in the United States. They were seen off by a number of relatives and friends and with them they cheerfully discussed their future prospects, but alas their young hopes and schemes were doomed by cruel disappointment.

They were both very popular in the Glanmire and Whitechurch districts and the shock which their death occasioned was general and acute. Their parents and relatives will have the sympathy of all in the great sorrow into which they have been plunged.

(*The Cork Examiner*, 27 April 1912)

Then in early summer 1913, the Royal Irish Constabulary contacted the family with the news that a man walking his dog had picked up the message in a bottle at Dunkettle, where the river in Glanmire meets the Lee and flows to the sea. The note is now on public display at the Queenstown Experience visitor attraction in Cobh.

His grandniece has said: 'The bottle and note were all his mother had, and in a way it was like a tombstone. He wouldn't have thrown away a bottle of holy water his mother gave him. There was an element of panic to it.'

Last Hour Messages

The possibility that messages from some of the people left on the doomed *Titanic* may have been committed to the deep is discussed ... Such notes, enclosed in bottles, may have been thrown overboard; and if so, their chances of being found are a hundred times better than those of any messages ever given to the sea. The US cruiser [*sic*] *MacKay-Bennett* is only one of the many ships that will be sent specially to search the scene of the shipwreck, and the possibility of salvaging something from the wreckage is certain to draw many Newfoundland fishing boats to the spot.

It is of course true that very few authentic messages from wrecks have ever come to safety. Very many that were first reported turned out to be cruel hoaxes. The bottle-messages that purported to come from the *Yongala*, which went down off Queensland, and from the Allan liner *Huronian*, which was lost in the North Atlantic, and from the *Waratah*, whose fate was never known, were all discovered to be false.

One of the few cases that were considered authentic was the bottle-message that was found some time after the *Bay of Bengal* sailed from England, saying that she had been wrecked almost immediately after putting to sea. Nothing more was ever heard of this ship.

(*Irish News*, 20 April 1912)

The theme of the ship that sailed and was never seen again has always had a horrible fascination. The White Star steamer *Naronic* was built in 1892 and was described as the finest and safest vessel ever launched.

She left Liverpool for New York on 11 February 1893, and then disappeared forever. But six weeks afterwards a champagne bottle was found on the beach at Ocean View,

Virginia, containing a letter alleged to have been written by John Olsen, a cattleman on board.

'The *Naronic* is fast sinking. It is such a storm that we cannot live in the small boats. One boat with its human cargo has already sunk. We have been struck by an iceberg in the blinding snow. The ship has floated for two hours. It is now 3.20 in the morning, and the deck is level with the sea.' That is all we have ever heard of the *Naronic*.

(*Galway Express*, 27 April 1912)

But here is a case of a Corkman's bottle, thrown overboard in mid-ocean, which indeed drifted for a year before making landfall, albeit on a different coast:

THE VOYAGE OF A BOTTLE FROM THE NORTH ATLANTIC TO THE FLORIDA COAST
Long Journey of a Corkman's Message

On the 23rd February 1931 when the *Dresden* was 2,125 miles from Cove, Mr Michael O'Sullivan, who originally hailed from the Mallow district, dropped a bottle overboard containing the following message –

February 21, 1931. Tourist cabin 336A. – On board the SS *Dresden* from Bremerhaven via Cherbourg and Queenstown to New York … This note in airtight bottle has been cast overboard 2,125 miles from Queenstown and at a latitude N. 41.32, and longitude W. 62.18. Finder please send to *Cork Weekly Examiner*, Patrick Street, Cork city, Ireland, giving your name and address and where found and when …

On Saturday last, 26 March, the Editor received a letter enclosing the message from Miss A. McBride, the Belleview Biltmore Hotel, Belleair, Florida. Miss McBride had picked up the bottle on the beach at Belleair while bathing on March 6, 1932. Here is her letter:

'While bathing at a local beach here in Florida I found the enclosed note which was dropped from the SS *Dresden* by a Mr O'Sullivan and I am carrying out his instructions by sending it to you – sincerely Miss A. McBride.
PS: March 6th, 1932, when I found this bottle washed onto the beach.'

We leave it to our nautical readers to calculate the exact mileage covered by that bottle. It must have drifted over one thousand miles almost exactly in twelve months. We hope that Mr O'Sullivan will communicate to us his present address when we will have much pleasure in returning to him his note, which is in marvellously good condition, after its adventurous voyage.

(*Cork Weekly Examiner*, 2 April 1932)

Jeremiah Burke left total assets of just £10, according to a subsequent application for administration of his estate by his father.

1911 census – William Burke (55) Farmer; wife Kate (54). Married 28 years, nine children, seven alive. Kitty (23), William (20), **Jeremiah (18)**, Laurence (16).

MARY BURNS (17) LOST

Ticket number 330963. Paid £7 12s 7d, plus extra 5s.
Boarded at Queenstown. Third Class.
From: Kilmacowen, Knocknarae, County Sligo.
Destination: 942 Kent Avenue, Brooklyn, New York city.

Mary Delia Burns could have been killed by her own kindness. It was reported from one source that the teenager chose to attend Kate Hargadon on board the *Titanic* as the latter was suffering from nausea and was unable to climb a ladder to the boats.

Mary, known as Delia by her family, had been rooming in the single women's quarters at the stern of the vessel with fellow Sligowoman Kate and her own near-neighbour Margaret Devaney. They were in compartment Q-138 on E deck.

The *Irish World* published Margaret Devaney's account of what happened to the trio in its edition of 4 May 1912:

> There were four of us from Knocknarae, County Sligo – Mary Burns and Kitty Hargadon and a boy we knew. We were all on deck, not thinking it was serious, when the boy comes along and said: 'You girls had better get into a boat.' Then he held out his hand, saying: 'I hope we'll meet again.'
>
> I got into the boat, but Mary Burns and Kitty Hargadon held back, thinking it was safer to remain on the ship. I never saw them again.

Seventeen-year-old Mary thought she was used to the sea. She lived in a tiny two-storey home less than 100 yards from the beach at the end of a narrow boreen that gives onto Ballysadare Bay. Mary had often helped carry seaweed up to the parcel of land they called a farm to act as fertiliser for the soil.

In the 1911 census, her age appears correctly as 16, with a brother Joseph, aged 12. Her parents, Thomas, a labourer, and Mary, née Monaghan, were aged 43 and 37 respectively. Mary's date of birth was 15 November 1894.

Like many another young girl, she hoped to become a housemaid for a wealthy family in New York and was travelling to the home of her aunt, Mary Sheridan, where she had been promised room and board.

As with the overwhelming number of Irish victims, her body was never recovered. 'Her death was never spoken about in the house afterwards because it was so sad,' said a younger sister, still alive at the century's end, who asked not to be identified.

The Cork Examiner of Saturday 20 April 1912, noted:

> There are two names of Mary Burns and Ellen Shine on the passenger list of the *Titanic*, while on the list of those saved, the names Burns without a Christian name and Axel Shine appear and probably mean the same. There is therefore some doubt about these passengers.

Ellen Shine was indeed rescued, but about the fate of Mary Burns there was no doubt at all – she drowned in the North Atlantic.

Mansion House Titanic Relief Fund, 1913 Report: Case No. 446. Burns, parents, £25.

MARY CANAVAN (23) LOST

Ticket number 364846. Paid £7 15s.
Boarded at Queenstown. Third Class.
From: Tonacrick, Addergoole, County Mayo.
Destination: 236 East 53rd Street, New York city.

PATRICK CANAVAN (21) LOST

Ticket number 364858. Paid £7 15s.
Boarded at Queenstown. Third Class.
From: Knockmaria, Nephin, County Mayo.
Destination: 1512 Diamond Street, Philadelphia.

Patrick (shown opposite) and Mary Canavan were first cousins. They were among a large group of fourteen young men and women from the parish of Addergoole, County Mayo, who embarked on the *Titanic*. Only two survived.

Patrick was a cousin of another *Titanic* passenger, Annie Kate Kelly, and was travelling to stay with his sister, Miss Kate Canavan, of Diamond Street, Philadelphia. Survivor Annie Kate makes fleeting reference to Patrick in her account of the tragedy, seeming to place him in the after well deck of the *Titanic*, behind the fourth funnel and close to the stern:

> John Bourke and Patrick Canavan knew there was a ladder leading to the upper decks. Gathering the women and girls about them, they started for the ladder.

Patrick, a general labourer, was the son of Anthony Canavan and Bridget Kelly (the latter was linked to Annie Kate Kelly) and was born and baptised on 14 September 1890. He had a brother Tom, three years older, who had also already emigrated west. By 1911, Pat was the eldest son at home, although nine years younger than his sister Annie. He was the sole remaining big brother to Bridgie (17) and Anthony (13).

Mary Canavan was a little older than her cousin Patrick. She was lost because agents canvassing for the shipping lines persuaded her to travel on 'a brand new ship' long before her intended crossing. Said a descendant: 'If the canvassers hadn't come around, Mary wouldn't have been on the *Titanic*. That was the big regret for years afterwards.'

Family members say one of the reasons so many were lost from Lahardane was because of the enthusiastic sales-pitches of agents seeking emigrants, who called to homes in early 1912. Mary fully intended to travel to the USA – she was just waiting for her American-based brother Paddy to come up with the fare. He had travelled over the previous year at the age of 24 and had promised to remit the passage money. He had not done so by the time the large group from Mayo prepared to leave, and Mary was reduced to begging her parents for an advance. Although wanting her to stay at home for another year, they finally capitulated.

Mary Canavan was the daughter of Thomas Canavan and Mary Earley. By the 1911 census returns, Mary Canavan was aged 22, and her parents Mary and farmer Anthony were 55 and 58 respectively. Annie Kate Kelly, the young survivor, spoke of 'Mary Flynn' being on board the *Titanic*, seemingly a reference to Mary Canavan because of the Flynn family connection. Mary intended to stay with her cousin Anthony Flynn when she reached New York. Anthony was the brother of another *Titanic* passenger, James Flynn.

Word of Mary's death came by messenger to her father when he was preparing to take animals to a fair to help recoup his outlay for her ticket. Her brother Paddy, who had not managed to earn the passage money, was killed a few years later when a tree fell on him while lumberjacking in California.

JANIE CARR (45) LOST

Ticket number 368364. Paid £7 15s.
Boarded at Queenstown. Third Class.
From: Castlerock, Aclare, County Sligo.
Destination: 7 Hamilton Street, Hartford, Connecticut.

Probably victim of liner's wreck
Now practically no hope that Miss Jennie Carr survived disaster

New York, April 19. There is practically no hope that Jennie Carr of Windsor Locks, Conn., who was a passenger aboard the *Titanic* returning to her home from Ireland, was saved from the steamer.

Inquiry at the White Star Line office this afternoon elicited the information that Ellen Carr and Jennie Carr sailed as Third-Class passengers and that Ellen Carr is the survivor. Jennie Carr is listed as 'missing'. The White Star Line does not know the point of destination of either women but is certain that the woman who was saved is Ellen Carr.

Miss Carr, formerly a resident of Springfield, had been living with her brothers and sisters in Ireland for the past three years but the failure of the Windsor Locks bank, where the savings of her lifetime were deposited, caused her to come back to this country to go to work again.

Her relatives in this city, two nieces, Katharine and Mary Carr of Pine Street and her nephew, Michael Carr of Lowell Street, were not aware that she had started to return until they heard from Mrs Michael O'Leary of Windsor Locks, a former employer of Miss Carr.

The message said that she had sailed from Queenstown for New York on the day that the *Titanic* put out. When the list of survivors first came out, Miss Jennie Carr was named among the Third Class passengers, but the name was later changed to Ellen Carr and Miss Carr's relatives thought that a mistake had been made in the name.

The *Carpathia* docked and the rescued passengers landed, but the relatives of Miss Carr got no word as to her whereabouts. They were confident that she had been saved and were fearing that her mind might have been unbalanced by the long exposure and the horror of the past few days.

As no message came during the day yesterday they became more anxious and tried to learn from the steamship company whether or not she was saved.

Miss Katherine Carr, who is employed as a domestic at 235 Pine Street, was notified last evening that her aunt had undoubtedly gone down with the *Titanic*. At first she could hardly believe that the words were true and when it finally dawned on her that the Carr woman registered as saved was not her aunt, she was greatly affected.

The other relatives are still hoping that their aunt will turn up in due time, although no hope is held out.

Miss Carr first came to this country about twenty years ago making her home in Springfield. She worked as a cook in several families, later working in a Chicopee Falls hotel. Besides her relatives in Ireland and this city she leaves three nephews and one niece in Hartford.

(*Springfield Union*, 20 April 1912, p. 7)

A single woman, Janie found herself torn between other people's offspring on both sides of the Atlantic. She had worked as housekeeper to a rich Connecticut banker and his family before going home in 1911. The return to Ireland was prompted by the sudden death of her widowed sister Catherine (56), which had left six children without parents. By the following spring, Janie had determined that she would make her future in Ireland. But then devastating news arrived from America: her former employer had killed himself. Selfless Janie immediately felt the need to return there to see what she could do. The visit back to Windsor Locks, Connecticut, also gave her the chance to settle her affairs before moving to Ireland permanently. It was another Good Samaritan journey, but it cost Janie her life.

A kind of surrogate mother to everyone in her family of seven surviving brothers and sisters, Janie had spent more than twenty years in the USA, having originally made the trip *c.* 1887. Her parents, Tom Carr, a settler from Fermanagh, and Bridget Goldrick, were both dead. Now she was leaving Ireland again after only her third trip home. Margaret Carr, Janie's teenage niece, planned to go with her but failed to get her papers in order in time, so Janie sailed alone.

She signed aboard the *Titanic* as a 37-year-old spinster, although it is known that she was in fact eight years older, with a date of birth of 11 February 1867. Janie was listed aboard as 'Jeannie' Carr, and a grant of administration of the substantial estate she left at home in Sligo named her as 'Jennie', although her birth and baptismal entries positively name her Jane. She left £113 – the total of an account in the Hibernian Bank.

DAVID CHARTERS (21) LOST

Ticket number 13032. Paid £7 14s 8d.
Boarded at Queenstown. Third Class.
From: Garvagh, Ballinalee, County Longford.
Destination: 310 West 108th Street, New York city.

David Charters demonstrated for his family how large the *Titanic* would be. He walked out of his front door and to the top of a ridge in front of the house, nearly one-fifth of a mile away. The walk is still remembered by his surviving family.

He had ten sovereigns in his pocket when he left his picturesque home place to travel to Edgeworthstown to catch a train to Queenstown. A man cannot live on scenery, even in lovely Garvagh, especially in a large household. It was a house that was repeatedly touched by tragedy. A brother, Jimmy, died aged seven on the kitchen table when undergoing a primitive operation to remove a growth on his jaw. Another brother, Robert, was killed in action in the Great War. A third brother died at the hands of the IRA. Willie Charters, nephew of David Charters, remembers that his Uncle Willie was taken out of the same homestead by an IRA flying column in 1921 and later executed for alleged informing. His body, 'riddled with bullets' in his nephew's phrase, was found in nearby Gorteen Lake. A fourth brother, Alec, died young of a brain haemorrhage, and a sister, Anne, died in childbirth.

The bad luck began with the *Titanic*. Described as a general labourer, David was going to join his uncle David Vance at an address in New York city.

Two of David's brothers, Alec and Dickie, later risked the long walk and emigrated to America. The latter lived to age 94, having begun by sweeping the streets that he had been led to believe were paved with gold, earning enough to progress to owning a small shop on Long Island.

1911 census – William (52) and Marianne (42). Married 20 years, with ten children, all still living. **David (19)**, general servant; Annie (14), John (12), Sarah E. (11), Richard (8), Mary Jane (6), Alexander (4), James W. (2).

PATRICK COLBERT (24) LOST

Ticket number 371109. Paid £7 5s.
Boarded at Queenstown. Third Class.
From: Kilconlea, Abbeyfeale, County Limerick.
Destination: Sherbrooke, Quebec, Canada.

Patrick was going to Canada to become a religious brother. But he was also concerned with the things of this world. He was off to serve God, but retained an affection for mammon. He took an extraordinary sum out of the bank before he left – some say it was as much as £600, but this seems truly fanciful – and carried it with him on the *Titanic*. His father had argued that he should take only a little, for his needs, and transfer the rest when he was safely settled. But Patrick took the money in cash – and after the shock and grief of bereavement, it somehow rankled in the family ever afterwards that such a fortune could have gone down in the Atlantic.

Patrick was one of the 'praying' Colberts, as distinct from the 'fighting' Colberts, a family of cousins with whom they shared land – one of whom, Edmond, was an All-Ireland tug-of-war champion in 1910. Patrick, one of whose brothers was already a Christian Brother in Cork, was due to stay with his brother Christopher – himself a man of the cloth and known to all as Brother Christopher – at a religious house in the Canadian industrial town of Sherbrooke on the Magog river.

Why he should have needed to take all his money with him was beyond anyone's understanding. In the wake of his death, there were stories in the locality of him being weighed down in the water by the sheer poundage of gold sovereigns. Others noted acerbically that it was not after all so hard for a rich man to enter the kingdom of Heaven.

Pious Patrick Colbert had amassed his money as a railway porter in bustling Abbeyfeale, a short distance from his home place. The youngest of seven children, he was born on 5 November 1887 to farmer John Colbert and his wife Kate of Kilconlea, County Limerick.

Patrick was one of those originally booked to travel on the strike-bound White Star liner *Cymric*.

County Limerick victims, Abbeyfeale, Sunday
The list of survivors published today contains no reference to the name of Mr Patrick Colbert, Kilconlea, Abbeyfeale, Mr James Scanlan, Rathkeale, nor of other young men said to have been on board from East and North Kerry.

Pat Colbert, for whose parents and family the greatest public sympathy is felt, was until his recent departure for the States, a porter at the railway station here, and a young man noted for his industry, intelligence and temperate habits.

There were some other intending emigrants about to sail in the *Titanic* from this district, but on the advice of an Irish American friend waited and sailed on another steamer.
(*The Cork Examiner*, 22 April 1912)

1911 census – Colbert; Kilkinlea, Abbeyfeale.
John (67), farmer, Kate (65); married 39 years, ten children, eight living. Michael (36), cattle buyer, Nora (34), Denis (29), and Tim (27), cattle buyers. **Pat (23)**, railway porter.

EDWARD POMEROY COLLEY (37) LOST

Ticket number 5727. Paid c. £28 10s, then £6 extra aboard.
Boarded at Southampton. First Class.
From: 17 Orwell Road, Upper Rathgar, Dublin.
Destination: Victoria, British Columbia, Canada.

Edward Pomeroy Colley died on his thirty-seventh birthday – 15 April 1912. In the weeks thereafter, several women wrote to his family in Ireland claiming to have been his girlfriend or even fiancée. He had indeed been an eligible bachelor. An engineer and land surveyor from Dublin and a relative of the Duke of Wellington, victor at Waterloo, Colley was returning alone to Canada and his mining interests. He occupied cabin E58, amidships on E deck.

Two days before he boarded at Southampton he had escorted a young lady to George Bernard Shaw's *Man and Superman* in the West End and wrote that it was 'rather improper in places'. Another flame was on his mind aboard the *Titanic*. Colley wrote a letter on ship stationery, dated 11 April 1912 (taken off at Queenstown), in which he belatedly congratulated his first cousin Norah Webber on her marriage to an officer of the 30th Lancers in the Punjab.

'My dear Norah', he began, before launching into the expansive style that won him so many female admirers:

I am a No. 1 sized elephantine pig and I shouldn't have let
the fact of your being faithless to me + marrying ANOTHER have the effect of coolness. As a matter of fact, it's not coolness at all, but I've been putting it off 'til I could send you a wedding present, which I have been unable to do. The Bank are not treating me well, + I'm afraid a cheque might be treated with dishonour. But I will some day, + meantime you have my broken heart at your shell-like feet …

I hear that all you married Webbers are absurdly happy. I don't think you + Adie [her sister Adelaide] ought to be really, when you consider you each of you broke my poor tender little heart. But then I was always too tender hearted where BEAUTY was concerned!!

Goodbye little Norah + write like a decent cousin to Eddie Colley. My love to you and my regards to my cousin-in-law, whom everyone tells me is too nice for words. Love from Eddie.

A day earlier, on 10 April, Colley wrote to his sister-in-law Edith. The missive reveals more of the man's intriguing struggles with affairs of the heart. It has been edited here:

This is a huge ship. Unless lots of people get on at Cherbourg and Queenstown, they'll never half fill it. The dining room is low-ceilinged, but full of little tables for 2, 3 and more in secluded corners. How I wish someone I liked was on board, but then nice people don't sit at tables for two unless they're engaged or married. I wonder my blue blood didn't tell me that?

They also have a restaurant where you can pay for meals if you get bored with the ordinary grub. Our most distinguished passengers seem to be W.T. Stead, Chas. M. Hays and E.P. Colley. Oh, and the Countess of something, but her blood is only black blue (give me good red corpuscles. I seem to know more about them. And they circulate faster.)

We nearly had a collision to start with. Coming out of Southampton we passed close to a ship that was tied up alongside the *Oceanic*, and the suction of our ship drew her out into the stream, and snapped the ropes that held her, and round she swung across our bows!

She had no steam up, so had to be pulled back by tugs, and we have to reverse. The name of her was the *New York* in case you see it in the papers. It proves conclusively the case of the *Hawke* and *Olympic* …

Don't you think that it is I who am common and second-rate and not my friends? I always prefer my funny friends to your pretty people. The blue people find me dull and the red ones don't.

I think my best plan is to make love unplatonically to A__ who owns the books. She has manners that would go down anywhere, dresses like an English girl, and knows all the better people in Victoria (did you know there were some?). She is not beautiful, but very nice, and in fact she would do charmingly but wouldn't please my relations. I am not a snob and you would be the first to call me one if I did more than draw attention to the fact.

On board R·M·S·"TITANIC."

April 11 1912

My dear Norah,

I am a *ho 1 sized elephantine pig* and I shouldn't have let the fact of your being faithless to me & marrying ANOTHER have the effect of coolness … as a matter of fact it not coolness at all, but I've been putting it off till I could send you a wedd— present, which I have been unable to do. The Bank are not treating me well, & I'm afraid a cheque might be treated with dishonour … but I will some day, & meantime you have my broken heart at your shell-like feet.

But Edie you have never met any of my supposedly dreadful friends, and I have lost all confidence in my power of choosing anyone for fear of family disapproval, that I can't face it. You can have this letter printed if you like, and circulated, and the proceeds of the sale given to the society for aged and infirm chaperones.

I hope to meet Mr and Mrs Kane, and her sister's child, in New York. She will be the ideal chaperone at any rate.

Goodbye Edie, you're a darling and wish you had a sister. I'd hypnotise her into thinking I wasn't common by inclination!

Love from Eddie [Letter auctioned for £15,000, September 2006]

On board the *Titanic*, Colley was reported by fellow passenger Colonel Archibald Gracie to be a smiling Irishman, one of a group of six rich gentlemen who offered their services as escorts to Mrs Helen Churchill Candee, a wealthy writer and socialite who survived the sinking in lifeboat No. 6. Colonel Gracie said the group comprised 'our coterie', which was determined to keep Mrs Candee amused and accompanied at all times. One writer later described Colley as a 'roly-poly Irishman who laughed a lot but said little', apparently quoting the lady herself.

On the night of the sinking, the coterie and Mrs Candee attended a concert in the First-Class reception area on D deck, forward, until just after 11 p.m. Colley retired for the night after a visit by some members of the party to the Café Parisien on B deck aft, starboard side, at 11.20 p.m. Twenty minutes later the *Titanic* struck the iceberg.

Edward Colley was born on an estate at Lucan, County Dublin, on 15 April 1875. The Colleys were a distinguished family. Henry was a magistrate and landlord, married to Elizabeth. They had four sons and six daughters. Edward's sister Constance, a pioneering doctor, contracted TB from a patient she was treating in Edinburgh, and died early in 1912 – the event that brought Edward home from Canada.

Major Colley's Journey
I have learned, on the most reliable authority, that our respected and popular Resident Magistrate is about to proceed to British Columbia to look after the estates of his brother, Major Edward Pomeroy Colley, who was one of the heroes who sacrificed his life for others in the terrible *Titanic* disaster.

His brother was an extensive mining engineer, having interests abroad as well as in Dublin and Limerick, and when the sad news that he had paid the penalty of his heroism with the foundering of the monster liner was made known, all creeds and classes in Tipperary and the surrounding district tendered their sympathetic condolences to a popular gentleman in a most trying time.

(*Tipperary Star*, 25 May 1912)

His uncle was Sir George Pomeroy Colley, a career soldier who rose to prominence in the British army and became governor of Natal. He fought in China, India, Afghanistan and South Africa – until shot through the forehead by Boers in an assault on Majuba Height in 1881.

When Edward Pomeroy Colley boarded the *Titanic* at Queenstown, he was following in the footsteps of his distinguished uncle who had boarded the troopship *Punjaub* for his first overseas posting from the same port fifty-eight years earlier. On that journey, which took fifty-nine days to reach Table Bay, Sir George had time to compose a prayer at sea – which his family respectfully memorialised after his death. It reads in part:

And when grim Death in smoke-wreaths robed / Comes thundering o'er the scene
What fear can reach the soldier's heart / Whose trust in Thee has been?
And if 'tis Thine immortal will / My spirit hence to call
'Thy Will be done', I'll whisper still / And ever trusting, fall.

THOMAS HENRY CONLIN (31) LOST

Ticket number 21332. Paid £7 14s 8d.
Boarded at Queenstown. Third Class.
From: Arvagh, County Cavan.
Destination: North Fairhill Street, Philadelphia.

Thomas Henry Conlin (31) was returning to America after a brief visit home. He had first emigrated from Ireland in the late 1880s. Described as a general labourer on embarkation records, he was travelling back to his sister Rosa in Philadelphia, where another sister, Annie, also lived.

The *Irish World*, published in New York on 11 May 1912, contained this assessment of him:

Thomas Conlin, Jr, thirty years old, of 2238 North Fairhill Street, this city, is counted among the victims of the *Titanic* disaster. He was seen on the ill-fated boat by survivors who knew him and was not among those rescued by the *Carpathia*.
He was born in Ireland, came to this country when very young and attended the St Edward's School. He was a member of the parish total abstinence society, the B.V.M. Sodality and the Holy Name Society. He was an agent for a machine company and had gone to Ireland to visit his old home.

Those aboard *Carpathia* who knew Tom Conlin were the Murphy sisters, Kate and Margaret, and it is recounted that Conlin took off his coat and threw it to these girls, who were dressed only in their nightclothes, as they were about to descend in a lifeboat. He knew he would not need it. It also appears that Tom and the Murphy girls were cousins.

One story around Cormore, County Cavan, claims that Thomas Conlin was engaged to an American woman named Lena Keyes, who later moved to Dobbs Ferry in New York, where she worked as a housekeeper. She never married and died in her nineties.

MICHAEL CONNAUGHTON (31) LOST

Ticket number 335097. Paid £7 15s.
Boarded at Queenstown. Third Class.
From: Tang, County Westmeath.
Destination: 965 DeKalb Avenue, Brooklyn, New York city.

Born at Lisaquill, Tang, adjoining Ballymahon in neighbouring County Longford, Michael was a trolley car operator (horse-drawn) in Brooklyn at the time of his death. He was returning from his third trip to visit his relatives, and was much mourned by married sisters Kate Horan and Mary Conlon, who revered their brother as the person responsible for bringing them to New York. Kate lived at his stated destination.

It is thought that Michael could have been rooming with his fellow Athlone man, Eugene Daly, in compartment C-23 on F deck, starboard bow, very close to where the iceberg impacted. In a letter home, Eugene's cousin Marcella, notes that 'that boy Connaughton … perished'.

KATE CONNOLLY (23) SAVED

Ticket number 370373. Paid £7 15s.
Boarded at Queenstown. Third Class.
From: Curtrasna, County Cavan.
Destination: 309 East 88th Street, New York city.

Kate Connolly saved a boy as the *Titanic* slipped to her grave. She carried the toddler, aged only two or three, into a lifeboat and kept him warm all night. After rescue by the *Carpathia*, the child was reunited with his mother who came down into the steerage area of the Cunard liner and took him back, rather ungratefully, according to the Irishwoman.

Kate was saved in lifeboat No. 13 on the starboard side. 'Kate jumped ought [*sic*] into the boat,' wrote her fellow survivor, Julia Smyth, who followed her. The escape came in the midst of chaos. Julia talked of a huge crowd, 'thousands', in front of the women, each one anxious to escape. One of their cabin mates, Mary McGovern, also saved, spoke of sailors desperately linking arms to create a human chain while armed officers held the crowd at bay. This happened around collapsible D, all the way forward on the port side, and possibly earlier, further aft, as steerage passengers surged up from the stern.

Even as 23-year-old Connolly was saving herself however, a 35-year-old namesake, also Kate Connolly, was being condemned to death by freezing immersion.

The surviving Kate Connolly was born in Curtrasna, Drumlymmon, County Cavan, on 14 June 1888, and baptised the same day. By 1901 the family consisted of father James (57), a farmer, mother Catherine (46), née Fagan, and children James (28), Catherine herself (13) and Mary (3). An older sister, Nellie, had emigrated to America, becoming Mrs John

McGuckian. In 1912, Kate Connolly was on her way to join her sister at East 88th Street, Manhattan.

Kate met her fellow passenger, Julia Smyth, at Ballywilliam train station in Cavan as both waited for a locomotive to bring them on the long journey south to Cork. The pair became firm friends and shared a cabin on *Titanic*. Kate, her new acquaintance Julia, and fellow Cavan girl Mary McGovern all roomed together on board, along with another Irish girl, Mary Agatha Glynn from Clare. All four were saved.

Afterwards, however, Kate was in need of the assistance of the American Red Cross, as instanced in its 1913 report: 'No. 85. (Irish.) Domestic servant, 21 years old, injured. $100'.

Kate Connolly became a live-in maid at a New York city brownstone. In 1914 a near neighbour followed her to the States. Two years her junior, William Arkins had lived only a mile from Kate's homestead in Cavan. They were married in St Patrick's Cathedral in 1916. William worked in a New Jersey shipyard during the First World War. In 1919 their first child, James, was born, followed by John the next year. Peter arrived in 1925, but a fourth son, Thomas, died after just a month of life in 1926. By this time the family had progressively amassed enough money to own several apartment buildings. Kate took care of the tenants and collected rents – and tried to forget about the *Titanic*. She died from a stroke at 9.45 p.m. on 3 July 1948 at her home in 147th Street, Whitestone, New York. She had just turned 60.

'She never liked to talk about the *Titanic*, but might comment on anniversaries,' said her son John. 'She said the sailors were mainly British and treated the Third Class like dirt. They prevented them from getting to the decks. During the sinking, she said, two or three of the young men found other ways to get up to the deck and came back and directed the young ladies.'

Local lore in Cavan suggests that Kate Connolly was the first to wake in her cabin and pulled the other girls out of bed 'by the hair of their heads' because they were unwilling to take the reported accident seriously.

KATE CONNOLLY (35) LOST

Ticket number 330972. Paid £7 12s 7d.
Boarded at Queenstown. Third Class.
From: Bank Place, Tipperary town, County Tipperary.
Destination: Bound to stay with J. Bunbury, Dobbs Ferry, New York.

The loss of the *Titanic* is still the topical subject of discussion here, and all news of the terrible disaster to the ill-fated monster is eagerly devoured.

Great regret is expressed locally that despite all the hopes cherished by reason of the unhappily uncorroborated messages, Miss Katie Connolly, of Bank Place, must have gone to a better land, either with the doomed vessel, or as a result of the terrible exposure to which delicately nurtured women were no proof against in most cases.

Stereotyped expressions of sympathy are but farcical in cases of such national and universal catastrophe.

(*Tipperary Star*, 27 April 1912)

Kate's widowed mother, a 67-year-old shopkeeper had been hoping against hope that her daughter had lived. A mistaken report that she had indeed been rescued must have brought elation and relief – the later confirmation of her death, over a week later, only crushing sorrow.

The newspaper reports indicate the roller-coaster of emotion experienced in late April 1912 by mother Kate Snr and her family of Margaret (37), a music teacher, Edward (33), who made piecemeal money as a blade sharpener, and Richard (29), who had been running a cycle business, but was now a porter.

First *The Cork Examiner* of 20 April 1912:

There were two Kate Connollys amongst the passengers. One has been saved, but it is impossible to say which.

Then this wrong report in the same newspaper three days later:

Tipperary lady saved
Major Pomeroy Colley, Resident Magistrate, Tipperary, proceeded to Dublin to make enquiries regarding the fate of his brother, Edward Pomeroy Colley, on board the ill-fated liner.

On Friday he found that the name of Kate Connolly, Bank Place, Tipperary, was on the list of the saved, and with great consideration and kindness he wired the fact to the relatives.

Miss Connolly was returning to America after a visit to her aged mother and her brothers here, and much satisfaction prevails at the news.

In fact, Kate Connolly had drowned – apparently because she trusted too much in the security of the big ship, even when alerted to the collision with the iceberg, as her fellow traveller Katie McCarthy told in a letter carried by *The Cork Examiner* of 11 May 1912:

> About 12 o'clock on Sunday night, Roger Tobin called us to get up, but told us not to be frightened as there was no danger. To make sure however of our safety, he told us to get lifebelts. There were three of us in the room: Katie Peters, Katie Connolly and myself.
>
> When Roger Tobin called me I wanted them to come up on deck, but they would not come. They appeared to think there was no danger. That was the last I saw of them.

The American Red Cross later aided the Connolly family:

> No. 86. (Irish.) A daughter was drowned while coming out to this country to get employment in order to help her family in Ireland. The family consisted of the mother, 70 years old, a sister 50, and two brothers, 44 and 38 years respectively.
>
> The sister has tuberculosis and earns only $2 a week giving music lessons. The elder brother is a knife sharpener and the other is a porter, both earning small wages. The daughter's passage, amounting to $39, was paid by her second cousin, who lives in this country.
>
> He at first requested that this amount be refunded to him, but later gladly accepted the suggestion that it be sent instead to the mother in Ireland to meet her immediate needs. The English Committee later gave the family £40.

PATRICK CONNORS (66) LOST

Ticket number 370369. Paid £7 15s.
Boarded at Queenstown. Third Class.
From: Charleville, County Cork.
Destination: 361 West 12th Street, New York city.

Although travelling in Third Class, Patrick Connors (birth name O'Connor) was as rich as Croesus compared with the rest of steerage. Indeed, he had more money on his body when found than the average Irish passenger was worth in total assets. He could certainly have afforded to travel Second Class – where access to the lifeboats was easier, although it is statistically true that a greater percentage of men were saved in Third Class than in Second. But Mr Connors prided himself on having pulled himself up by his bootstraps and on knowing the value of a dollar. He had been living in the United States for four decades, but was returning from a visit to his home place in Charleville (Rath Luirc), County Cork.

Charleville man one of the victims
News has been received in Charleville that Patrick O'Connor, a native of that town, is to be counted with those who went down with the SS *Titanic*. The deceased gentleman had been 38 years in America, where he had amassed a considerable fortune, and had last June decided upon paying a visit to the old land.

He stayed in Charleville at the house of his sister, Mrs M. Shanahan, for ten months and presented a splendid appearance of robust health.

Information was received a few days ago to the effect that his body had been picked up. The report has since been verified, and identification has been made an easy matter by reason of letters and other documents found in his clothes.

Mr O'Connor was only 24 years when he emigrated, being just 62 last month [*sic*], and his reminiscences of his early struggles in the States were extremely interesting. Needless to say, the greatest sympathy is felt for Mrs Shanahan over his sad and untimely end, and it is to be hoped that her claim to a share out of the funds collected for the relatives of those who went down with the ill-fated vessel will be recognised when the benevolent work of distribution is commenced.

(*Cork Free Press*, May 1912)

From the Public Archives of Nova Scotia:

Body No 171. Male. Estimated age 70. White Hair.
Clothes – Black overcoat; cardigan jacket; blue pants; blue shirt; black boots.
Effects – Letter of credit £80; £12 in Irish notes; £2 in purse; silver watch and chain; 7s 10 and a half d.
Third Class. Name – Patrick Connors.

ELLEN CORR (16) SAVED

Ticket number 367231. Paid £7 15s.
Boarded at Queenstown. Third Class.
From: Corglass, Moyne, Arva, County Longford.
Destination: 38 East 75th Street, New York city.

Ellen Corr, aged 16, was rescued in lifeboat No. 16. Launched from the port side, the British inquiry determined that it went away with a total of fifty-six persons aboard, all Second- and Third-Class women and children, with six crew. It probably went much earlier than its 'official' departure time of 1.35 a.m.

Barely more than a child herself, Ellen was emigrating to New York, where two elder sisters already lived. They were Mary (19), who was married to a Patrick Farley, of 1368 Third Avenue, and Honor (20), of 38 East 75th Street. A third elder sister, Bridget (18), may also have been in the US by 1912.

A domestic servant, Ellen's household in her native Corglass included seven of the ten children born to her loving – but crowded – parents. In 1911 the packed house looked like this: Farmer Charles Corr (64), and his wife Bridget, who was very much younger at 43; their children – Ellen (16), Anna Maria (14), Teresa (11), Maggie (9), George (7), Lizzie (5), and James P. (3). Ellen, baptised with the name Helen, was born on 28 July 1895.

Report of the American Red Cross (Titanic Disaster) 1913:
No. 90. (Irish.) Girl, 16 years old. ($100)

Ellen Corr later worked as a waitress at the Royal restaurant in John Street, New York, rising to become head waitress. She married an Irishman named Patrick Sweeney in a ceremony at St Patrick's Cathedral. They lived at 245 East 207th Street, the Bronx, but were never blessed with children. Ellen died on 9 March 1980, at the House of the Holy Comforter Hospital in the Bronx, and was buried in the Gate of Heaven Cemetery in Mount Pleasant, New York. Her family say that she refused absolutely to ever talk about her *Titanic* experiences.

1901 census:
Father Charles Corr (50), farmer. Wife Bridget (32) née Masterson.
Children: Honor (9), Mary K. (8), Bridget (7), **Ellen (5)**, Anne (3), Theresa, eight months.

MARY COUTTS (36) SAVED

Ticket number 3761. Paid £15 18s.
Boarded at Southampton. Third Class.
From: Monaghan and Belfast.
Destination: 148 Fourth Avenue, Brooklyn, New York city.

Known as 'Minnie', Mary Coutts was dramatically handed a lifejacket by a steward who told her: 'If you're saved, pray for me.'

Minnie was originally from Monaghan town. She had married a Belfast man named William Coutts, surrendering her maiden name of Treanor. The couple had two children. William then decided upon emigration to the United States, went on alone, and in April 1912 sent for his family to join him. Minnie therefore booked tickets on the *Titanic* for herself and her children William Leslie (9) and Neville (3). The family had lived in London and boarded at Southampton. All three were saved in lifeboat No. 2, the seventh and last-but-one lowered from the port side of the stricken ship.

The *Irish News* reported on 20 April 1912:

The formal list of survivors issued up to the present includes also Robert Hopkins, able seaman, of Belfast, and persons named Coutts, who are stated to belong to this neighbourhood, but who have not yet been definitely traced.

Report of the American Red Cross (Titanic Disaster) 1913:
No. 91. (Irish.) A mother, 37 years of age, with two children, nine and three years old, coming to join her husband in Brooklyn, lost five cases of household goods. She was not injured. The husband, employed as engraver, earns a fair salary but assists his aged mother in Ireland and was unable to furnish his home without assistance. ($750)

Happily reunited, the Coutts family went to live in Maplewood, New Jersey. Minnie died at her home at South Pierson Road on 29 February 1960. She was a widow, aged 84. Her remains were cremated and the ashes passed to her son, 51-year-old stocks and bonds salesman Neville, the boy of three she had scooped up from the deck of the *Titanic* as she entered a lifeboat with his older brother.

The older brother, William Leslie, a widower, had predeceased his mother, dying on Christmas Day 1957 in Steubenville, Ohio.

EUGENE DALY (29) SAVED

Ticket number 382650. Paid £6 19s.
Boarded at Queenstown. Third Class.
From: 2 Wolfe Tone Terrace, Athlone, County Westmeath.
Destination: E.G. Schuktze, 477 Avenue E, Brooklyn, New York city.

Eugene Daly was on board the *Titanic* until the very end. His sensational story tells of an officer shooting two men dead – before another shot rings out and the officer himself falls. Daly's account of the panic and of his own escape is probably the most graphic of any told by any survivor. He was in compartment C-23 on F deck, very far forward on the starboard side, so close to the impact that he was almost thrown out of bed:

> I was in compartment 23, Deck C, steerage [there was no steerage accommodation on C Deck]. Two other men were with me. I was in my bunk asleep on the Sunday night (the night of the disaster). A crash woke me up. It nearly threw me from my bed. I got up and went to the door. I put on my trousers and shoes.
>
> I met the steward in the gangway. He said there was nothing serious and that I might go back. I went back for a little while. Then I went up on deck as I heard a noise there. People were running around. Then I went down and went to the room where Maggie Daly and Bertha Mulvihill were.
>
> They came out with me, but a sailor told us there was no danger. He said the ship would float for hours. He also said to go back, and that if there was any danger he would call us.
>
> I went for a lifebuoy in the stern and Maggie and Bertha came with me. I had a scuffle with a man for a lifebuoy. He would not give it to me, but he gave it to Maggie Daly.
>
> There was a great deal of noise at this time and water was coming in. We knelt down and prayed in the gangway. Then the sailor said there was danger. We went to the deck

but there were no boats going off. Then we went to the second cabin deck. A boat was being lowered there. It was being filled with women. Maggie and Bertha got in, and I got in. The officer called me to go back, but I got in. Life was sweet to me and I wanted to save myself. They told me to get out, but I didn't stir. Then they got hold of me and pulled me out. Then the boat was lowered and went off.

There was another boat there, but I went up to the first cabin. The steerage people and second cabin people went to the first cabin part of the ship. They were getting women into the boats there. There was a terrible crowd standing about. The officer in charge pointed a revolver and waved his hand and said that if any man tried to get in he would shoot him on the spot.

Saw two men shot

Two men tried to break through and he shot them both. I saw him shoot them. I saw them lying there after they were shot. One seemed to be dead. The other was trying to pull himself up at the side of the deck, but he could not. I tried to get to the boat also, but was afraid I would be shot and stayed back. Afterwards there was another shot and I saw the officer himself lying on the deck. They told me he shot himself, but I did not see him.

Then I rushed across the deck, and there was a sort of canvas craft there. I tried with six or seven men to get it out, but we could not. It was stuck under a wire stay which ran up to the mast. The water was then washing right across the deck. The ship lurched and the water washed the canvas craft off the deck into the ocean. I was up to my knees in water at the time. Everyone was rushing around, but there were no boats. Then I dived overboard.

When I struck the water I swam for the boat that had been washed over. When I got to her she was upside down. I helped myself up on her. About fifteen people got upon her the same way. At the time I jumped there were a lot of people jumping overboard.

As I stood on the craft I saw the ship go down. Her stern went up and she gradually sunk down forward. Her stern stuck up high. I thought she would fall over on us, and she seemed to be swinging around, but she did not. There was no suction at all that we felt. Our craft was not drawn in at all.

(*Daily Sketch*, 4 May 1912, reprint of *New York Herald*)

Eugene Daly was finally rescued on collapsible B, a life-raft lashed to the roof of the officers' quarters on the port side until washed off by the onrushing sea. He had previously seen his cousin Maggie and his Athlone neighbour Bertha Mulvihill into lifeboat No. 15, all the way aft on the starboard side, which loaded from A Deck and from which he himself was bodily pulled having defied orders.

The boat where men were gunned down appears to have been collapsible A, all the way forward on the starboard side, since Daly says he then 'rushed across the deck' to collapsible B on the port side. In 1913 evidence he cited two shot dead, but no officer.

Dr Frank Blackmarr, a passenger on board the *Carpathia*, noted that Eugene Daly was unconscious when carried to his cabin, where he was revived with stimulants and hot drinks. Dr Blackmarr later took down Daly's dictation of his experiences as they approached New York on 18 April 1912. This was his first account of what transpired:

> I left Queenstown with two girls from my own home town who were placed in my charge to go to America. After the accident, we were all held down in steerage, which seemed to be a lifetime. All this time we knew that the water was coming up, and up rapidly.
>
> Finally some of the women and children were let up, but, as you know, we had quite a number of hot-headed Italians and other peoples who got crazy and made for the stairs. These men tried to rush the stairway, pushing and crowding and pulling the women down, some of them with weapons in their hands.
>
> I saw two dagos shot and some that took punishment from the officers. After a bit, I got up on one of the decks and threw a big door over the side. I caught hold of some ropes that had been used setting free a lifeboat. Up this I climbed to the next deck because the stairs were so crowded that I could not get through.
>
> I finally got up to the top deck and made for the front. The water was just covering the upper deck at the bridge and it was easy to slide because she had such a tip.
>
> ([Blackmarr's note:] Here this man fell back on his pillow crying and sobbing and moaning, saying: 'My God, if I could only forget!' After a bit he proceeded.)
>
> My God, if I could only forget those women's cries. I reached a collapsible boat that was fastened to the deck by two rings. It could not be moved. During that brief time that I worked on cutting one of those ropes, the collapsible was crowded with people hanging upon the edges. The *Titanic* gave a lurch downwards and we were in the water up to our hips.
>
> She rose again slightly, and I succeeded in cutting the second rope which held her stern. Another lurch threw this boat and myself off and away from the ship into the water. I fell upon one of the oars and fell into a mass of people. Everything I touched seemed to be women's hair. Children crying, women screaming, and their hair in their face. My God, if I could only forget those hands and faces that I touched!
>
> As I looked over my shoulder, as I was still hanging [on] to this oar, I could see the enormous funnels of the *Titanic* being submerged in the water. These poor people that covered the water were sucked down in those funnels, each of which was twenty-five feet in diameter, like flies.
>
> I managed to get away and succeeded in reaching the same boat I had tried to set free from the deck of the *Titanic*. I climbed upon this, and with the other men balanced ourselves in water to our hips until we were rescued. People came up beside us and begged to get on this upturned boat. As a matter of saving ourselves, we were obliged to push them off. One man was alongside and asked if he could get upon it. We told him that if he did, we would all go down. His reply was 'God bless you. Goodbye.'
>
> I have been in the hospital for three days, but I don't seem to be able to forget those men, women and children who gradually slid from our raft into the water.
>
> Signed, Eugene Daly. Collapsible B.

After safe arrival in New York, Daly wrote a letter to his mother in which he clearly and casually glossed over all that had happened:

> Dear Mother, got here safe. Had a narrow escape but please God, I am all right, also

Maggie. I think the disaster caused you to fret, but things could have been worse than what they were.

(The Cork Examiner, 7 May 1912)

But the *Irish World* of New York, in its 4 May 1912 issue, offered another picture:

> Eugene Daly of County Athlone [*sic*] bore the marks on his face of blows from sailors who fought with him against entering the last boat as it was lowered with many vacant seats. With five other men he launched a life raft and put off, picking up a score or more of passengers and crew who were struggling in the water.
>
> 'We were only a little distance from the *Titanic* when I saw her sinking and sinking, but I mistrusted my eyes until I looked and saw that the sea covered the place where she had been.'

It had all been so different when Daly first set out to join the *Titanic* at Queenstown. A 29-year-old weaver in Athlone Woollen Mills, he was also a mechanic and a prominent member of the Clan Uisneach War Pipers' Band, the Irish National Foresters Band and the local Gaelic League. He had been working for ten years at the woollen mills when he decided to leave that job and the terraced family home which faced directly onto a salmon weir that roared and foamed with the rushing waters of the broad and majestic Shannon river. He bought his passage in Butler's of the Square, Athlone.

Travelling with his 30-year-old cousin Maggie, Eugene played airs on his bagpipes on the tender *America* ferrying passengers from Queenstown to the *Titanic* anchorage at lunchtime on Thursday 11 April 1912. *The Cork Examiner* of 9 May reported that as the tender cast off from the quay, he played 'A Nation Once Again', his performance being received with delight and applause by his fellow travellers.

> He played many native airs on board the tender and as the latter moved away from the liner, the pipes were once more giving forth *A Nation Once Again*. Those who were on board the tender that day heard with extreme pleasure of his being amongst the survivors.

Daly's pipes are visible from his right ear downwards as he stands with them on the tender *America* in a little-known photograph taken on the day the *Titanic* sailed by *Cork Examiner* photographer Thomas Barker (see page 2).

The *Westmeath Independent* played up its local hero on 4 May 1912:

> *Eugene Daly's courage*
> The courage credited to Eugene Daly in the foregoing will not surprise his fellow townsmen, who knew him as a man of principle and pluck. In the present deplorable disaster, he appears to have upheld the traditions of the Gael, and one can well imagine that when the Captain seized the megaphone and roared: 'Be British!' Daly thought of the Pipers' Club in the old Border Town and determined to 'Be Irish', as he ever has been.

The Cork Examiner (7 May 1912) said he was an Athlone man who 'acted the part of a hero. He fought his way to the boats and was the means of saving two of his town's women.' Actually another passenger, Katie Gilnagh, also credited Daly with helping to save her life. The Longford woman told how she was woken by a man she had seen playing the bagpipes on deck earlier that day. He told her to get up, 'Something is wrong with the ship.'

The famous bagpipes were actually Irish uileann pipes, and Daly later claimed $50 compensation from the White Star Line for their loss. He was very pleased with the level of compensation and considered it more than the pipes were worth. A set of pipes has been recovered from the *Titanic*'s debris field which may have belonged to Daly. They are undergoing restoration. Not everyone who heard them was impressed with his playing, however. Lawrence Beesley, a teacher in Dulwich College, wrote in his survivor's account, *The Loss of the SS Titanic*:

> Looking down astern from the boat deck or from the B deck to the steerage quarter, I often noticed how the Third-Class passengers were enjoying every minute of the time; a most uproarious skipping game of the mixed-double type was the great favourite, while 'in and out and roundabout' went a Scotchman with his bagpipes playing something that [W. S.] Gilbert said 'faintly resembled an air'.

The *Westmeath Examiner* spoke of the same festive feeling:

> *Athlone piper's story of* Titanic *disaster: scene of jollity*
> In a letter to a former colleague in the Athlone Pipers Band, Mr Eugene Daly describes the scene of jollity on board immediately before the *Titanic* ran into the iceberg. They were, he said, having a great time of it that evening in steerage.
> 'I played the pipes and there was a great deal of dancing and singing. This was kept up even after we had struck, for the stewards came through and told us that we need not be afraid, that everything was all right. There was no danger, they said.
> 'Most of those assembled believed them until it was too late. That is why so many of the steerage were drowned. When they tried to get on deck the rush had begun and they could not get to the boats.
> 'I lost my pipes, which were a presentation, and which I prided myself so much on possessing. I lost my clothes and £98 which it had taken me many years to save in anticipation of this voyage to the United States ...'

Daly later attested to the fact that his thick overcoat had saved his life in the freezing water. He dubbed it his lucky coat, and wore it religiously thereafter.

> *Report of the American Red Cross (Titanic disaster) 1913:*
> No. 99. (Irish.) Mechanic, 29 years of age, lost $250. Had delicate sister, aged 17, dependent on him in Ireland. ($250)

Daly told US immigration in New York that he was from Lisclougher, County Meath, where his mother, Mrs Catherine Daly, was born. His younger sister named to the Red Cross was Maggie, the same name as his cousin who accompanied him on board the *Titanic*. The 1911 census report showed that his mother, Kate Daly, was a 60-year-old widowed housekeeper, while Maggie was a 21-year-old dressmaker, and Eugene's brother John a 19-year-old warper of wool.

Finally, the *Irish American* newspaper of 4 May 1912, reported that the irrepressible Daly was quickly back to his pipes:

> GAELIC FEIS IN CELTIC PARK
> *Athlone Piper Who Lost His Kilts and Pipes in* Titanic *Wreck to Play the Old Tunes*
> The Gaelic Feis to be held in Celtic Park on May 19 … One of the competitors in the War Pipes is a survivor of the *Titanic* disaster, and he has recovered sufficiently to be confident of marching off with the prize. His name is Eugene Daly, from Athlone, Ireland. Eugene was coming from Ireland to compete at the New York Feis and sailed on the ill starred liner. He lost his Irish kilts and bag-pipes when the *Titanic* went down and he himself was floating on a raft for over two hours before he was picked up.

Eugene did not win the competition, but he stayed in New York for much of his life, occasionally returning to Ireland to visit relatives. On at least one occasion when he did so, he related that 'six or seven' men had been shot on board the vessel and that there had been pandemonium in the final struggles for survival. It was not at all as noble or as civilised as had been suggested, he said. He told his nephew Paddy Daly that by the time his lifeboat reached the *Carpathia* there were many already dead, 'frozen solid'. Many years later, Daly was interviewed in Ireland in connection with script preparation for the 1958 film *A Night to Remember*.

He returned permanently to the United States in the early 1960s and died on 30 October 1965, at the age of 82, and was buried in St Raymond's Cemetery, the Bronx. He and wife Lillian had an only daughter, Marian Joyce, later Marian Van Poppe.

Athlone woman Bertha Mulvihill told the *Providence Evening Bulletin* of 19 April 1912, that a boy named Eugene 'Ryan' from her home town had told the group on leaving Queenstown that he had dreamt the *Titanic* was going to sink: 'Every night we were at sea he told us he had dreamt that the *Titanic* was going down before we reached New York. On Sunday night just before we went to bed, he told us the *Titanic* was going to sink that night. It was uncanny.'

Daly certainly knew Bertha and seems to have been keen

Athlone Man

GIVES THRILLING

DESCRIPTION

OF THE GREAT WRECK.

MR. EUGENE DALY.

A   Terrible   Experience.

SAW TWO MEN SHOT.

Jumped Overboard Himself.

How He Saved Miss Maggie Daly and Miss Mulvihill.

SENSATIONAL NARRATIVE

on her. On 20 August 1912, he sent a postcard to 'Miss Mulvihill' at the City Hospital in Providence, Rhode Island. The card was a *Titanic* memorial card. Daly placed an X on the front illustration to indicate where his sleeping quarters had been and wrote on the reverse that he had 'got home safe', apparently after a visit to Bertha. He added: 'Hope you keep well until we meet again and perm. me to be ever your friend, Eoghan O'Dalaigh, a survivor. xxx'

MAGGIE DALY (30) SAVED

Ticket number 382650. Paid £6 19s.
Boarded at Queenstown. Third Class.
From: Irishtown, Athlone, County Westmeath.
Destination: 356 East 157th Street, New York city.

Maggie was a cousin of Eugene Daly. She planned to join her older brother John Daly, who was a policeman in New York. She had previously lived in America and declared herself a citizen of the United States. After the disaster, Maggie wrote to her sister, Mary, a 41-year-old seamstress who lived with their widowed mother, Bridget Daly, at No. 98 Upper Irishtown. The parentheses are her own:

Dear Mary,
I am sure you think by this time I must have been at the bottom of the sea. Well I must say I am one of the lucky ones. I and Bertha Mulvihill are all that remains (11 left Athlone). That little girl from Summerhill (Delia Henry) and that boy Connaughton (Athlone), and I think Mrs Rice and her five boys perished.
It was a night I shall never forget. 20 people out of 200 Irish saved … all I have to regret is that I lost my clothes. I thought I would have a hard fight and I never would have been saved but for Eugene. He fought very hard for our lives.
(*The Cork Examiner*, 7 May 1912)

Anxious relatives receive good news
This afternoon a cable was received by Miss Mary Daly, Irishtown, in the following terms: 'Maggie and Eugene saved'.
The cable was despatched at New York by Miss Mary Daly's brother who met Miss Maggie Daly on the arrival of the *Carpathia*. The name Eugene refers to Mr Eugene Daly (a namesake) about whom his friends have been anxiously awaiting news for some days past.
Miss Margaret Daly has already spent many years in America, and came home about two years ago to her mother and sister, who reside in the old home in Irishtown. She was returning to join her brother and sister, who anxiously awaited her arrival in New York …
(*Westmeath Independent*, 27 April 1912)

Report of the American Red Cross (Titanic Disaster) 1913:
No. 100. (Irish.) Domestic servant, 30 years old. ($100)

MARGARET DEVANEY (23) SAVED

Ticket number 330958. Paid £7 12s 7d, plus 5s extra.
Boarded at Queenstown. Third Class.
From: Kilmacowen, County Sligo.
Destination: 861 Sixth Avenue, New York city.

A knife given to Margaret Devaney as a parting gift by her teenage brother John was the implement that helped to save her and a boatload of others. Margaret was originally reported rescued in lifeboat No. 12 on the port side, launched relatively early. Once it reached the sea there were difficulties unhooking the boat from its falls, and a woman lent a pocketknife to able seaman John Poingdestre to enable him cut through the ropes.

Her children, however, believe Margaret to have been saved in collapsible C, launched from all the way forward on the starboard side at around 1.40 a.m. They believe the knife was used to cut ropes binding the oars in the boat. Margaret also spoke of having to reach out and help push the lifeboat away from the side of the stricken ship as it was lowered, which was the experience of people in collapsible C because the vessel they were abandoning was by now listing heavily to port. Her daughter, Helen Landsberg, declares

firmly: 'I know my mother was in collapsible C.' Margaret told her that when she arrived the lifeboat was full, but two men climbed out, allowing her a seat, thereby sealing their own fates.

Margaret was horrified at the screams of the drowning as the *Titanic* went down, and said she spent the whole night adrift praying on her Rosary. She later recalled how she had earlier been so happy peeling apples with John's knife and chatting with friends in the *Titanic's* Third-Class common room after an evening meal of ragout beef and potatoes. She said it was a lucky thing she had the knife when the call came to prepare to abandon ship.

Her grandson, Peter Mastrolia, says Margaret had left the steerage, coat in hand, for some fresh air on deck before going to bed when she felt a 'tiny bump', that of the iceberg striking the ship, as she climbed the stairs. Later she tried to go back below to find her three travelling companions, but was 'literally thrown into a boat'. Once away, and after the screaming had stopped, the occupants rowed for flickering pinpoints at the edge of the horizon. 'You rowed toward a light and it would just be a star …'

Miss Mary Devaney, who is here with her sister, at No. 861 Sixth Avenue, told of burning her large straw hat in the night of terror they spent on the seas trying to attract help.
(*New York Herald*, 29 April 1912)

On arrival in New York, Margaret was equipped with a metal White Star flag emblem taken from her lifeboat and presented to her by a *Carpathia* crewman as a souvenir. Her family believes the gesture was a thank-you for providing the knife that helped her boat get away. Margaret also kept her steerage boarding card, stamped with the allocation of Q41, which placed her in a multi-berth cabin on E deck, all the way aft.

Margaret told US immigration on arrival that she was heading to join her sister Mary, and named her next of kin as her father John Devaney of Kilmacowen. She gave her occupation as a domestic. Also in America was her brother Michael (26), who was a stable groom to no less a personage than John D. Rockefeller, and who had sent her the fare to America. This expert horseman reportedly commandeered a police horse to force his way through the 10,000-strong quayside throng awaiting the rescue ship's arrival. When he did so, he discovered with relief that Margaret – who was not listed among the initial escapees – had been taken to St Vincent's Hospital.

Margaret Devaney, who found refuge in the home of her sister at No. 861 Sixth Avenue, in telling of her experiences, said:

> There were four of us from Knocknarae, County Sligo – Mary Burns and Kitty Hargadon and a boy we knew. We were all on deck, not thinking it was serious, when the boy comes along and said: 'You girls had better get into a boat.' Then he held out his hand, saying: 'I hope we'll meet again.' I got into the boat, but Mary Burns and Kitty Hargadon held back, thinking it was safer to remain on the ship. I never saw them again.
>
> We were in the third cabins when the alarms were sounded. The doors leading to the other decks were closed on us and we had to climb up ladders to the boat deck. The last thing I remember after being in the boat was the cries of the drowning. I said the Rosary for them, and thought it didn't matter much what became of me, only I knew my parents would grieve.
>
> (*Irish World*, New York, 4 May 1912)

In a later interview, Margaret indicated that the boy who had alerted the girls to the danger was Henry Hart, also from Sligo. Having gone up on the after well deck, the women returned to their cabin to put on life jackets. Margaret said Kitty Hargadon began suffering from seasickness or was nauseated with fear. She couldn't climb a vertical ladder – meant for crew use only – from the aft well deck to the Second-Class area. Mary Burns remained with Kitty while Margaret went on to attempt to locate a boat they could all use. Miss Devaney then said she was caught up in the crowd and forced into a boat alone.

On arrival in New York she stated her age to be 19, as she had on embarkation, trimming some years off. The 1901 census showed the family ages to be as follows: father John (40), mother Margaret (38), seven siblings – Michael (15), Mary (14), Maggie herself (12), Kate (10), John (8), Tim (5) and Dominic (3). Margaret appears to have been born on 15 May 1891, but she later adopted her husband's date of birth of 3 May 1892. She lived to be 83, a year older than her obituaries show.

Report of the American Red Cross (Titanic Disaster) 1913:
No. 118. (Irish.) Girl, 19 years of age, injured. ($100)

Margaret got work as a housemaid for a New York gynaecologist, helping to look after his young son. In 1914 she met her future husband on Long Island beach. John Joseph O'Neill was a plumber, and the couple were married in St Patrick's Cathedral in the heart of New York. They soon experienced heartbreak – their first child, Matthew, died after only one day of life in April 1921. Another baby, who went unnamed, lived for only twenty minutes after birth in October 1930.

The couple had four other children, two boys and two girls, who all lived long lives and brought joy to their parents. Margaret visited Ireland once, forty years after the *Titanic*, aboard the *Mauretania*. She found that little had changed with her home place. She visited the grave of W. B. Yeats in Drumcliffe, the poet to whom she had had a lifelong devotion.

Margaret Devaney O'Neill died on 12 June 1974, and lies buried in the Holy Name Cemetery in Jersey city. Her husband had predeceased her by fourteen years, dying in 1960, aged 65.

Margaret's knife, metal White Star burgee and ticket stubs were placed on display for many years in the immigration museum at the base of the Statue of Liberty.

BRIDGET DONOHUE (21) LOST

Ticket number 364856. Paid £7 15s.
Boarded at Queenstown. Third Class.
From: Cum, Addergoole, County Mayo.
Destination: 319 Central Avenue, Highland Park, Chicago.

The White Star Line turned Bridget Donohue into a man. The steamship company, in its final catalogue of the casualty toll from the world's worst shipping disaster, named her 'Bert O'Donoghue'. The error has continued for decades, with many lists of the lost containing the name Bert O'Donoghue, when in fact that final indignity stems from a careless misreading of her handwritten name in the embarkation records. Bridget had been abbreviated to 'Brt'.

Bridget was the daughter of David Donohue and Catherine Moyles, and was born on 11 January 1891. She was baptised three days later. Her mother died from complications of childbirth after the next baby, John, was delivered prematurely four years later, at just seven months. Their father struggled with his grief and two young children, but married again before the end of the century. His second wife was Ellen Cawley.

Bridget grew up as the mother hen to three stepsisters, Honoria, Ellen and Katie. They were aged just 13, 11 and 9 when she opted to leave home for a new start in the Windy City. She was on her way to her cousin Bridget Burke, who had offered accommodation and a leg up in life. She was 21 when she sailed on the *Titanic* with a large group of fourteen others from the general Lahardane area of County Mayo. Survivor Annie Kate Kelly described Bridget Donohue to the *Chicago Evening World* as one of 'three blue-eyed rosy-cheeked girls', the others being Delia Mahon and Bridget Driscoll, although this is likely to be journalistic licence.

As in the case of most of the Irish victims, Bridget's body was never recovered.

United Irish League, Lahardane Branch
The members of the above branch met on Sunday to transact business of great importance, but the Chairman, Mr James Early said that he knew that every member of the branch felt awfully sad at the great many fine boys and girls who from their parish were lost by the *Titanic* disaster.

He himself felt extremely sorry that they had even some of the committee, who were at all times supporters of the cause, and who on that day four weeks, came into the league room and wished them to be successful until their isle would be crowned a nation.

Others who were lost were the sons and daughters of the good fighting nationalists of this parish, and as a token of sympathy for their parents and relatives they would adjourn the business of the meeting to another date.

(*Western People*, 4 May 1912)

The Titanic *Disaster: An Appeal to the Public*
Sir – the whole parish of Lahardane, a poor district around Nephin, was plunged into grief when it became known that out of thirteen young girls and boys who embarked from there for America on the *Titanic*, only two were saved.

The young people left their native homes full of hope that they would soon be able to relieve the distress of their poor parents who have tried in vain to support themselves and their families on small uneconomic holdings of mostly reclaimed bog. The condition of the parents of those who went down with the *Titanic* may now be better imagined than described.

(*Western People*, 22 May 1912)

1911 census:
Parents: David (54) and Ellen (51).
Children: **Bridget (20)**, John (16), Honoria (12), Ellen (10), Kate (8).

PATRICK DOOLEY (38) LOST

Ticket number 370376. Paid £7 15s.
Boarded at Queenstown. Third Class.
From: Patrickswell, Knockainey, Lough Gur, County Limerick.
Destination: 142 East 31st Street, New York city, for onward to Chicago.

A postcard written by Patrick Dooley from Queenstown declared: 'I am sailing today, Thursday, on *Titanic* on her maiden trip to New York, her first trip on the Atlantic. Good bye. Love, Patrick Dooley'. The postcard showed a man standing in a roadway, cap in hand. Titled 'The Irish Emigrant', a poem beneath ran:

> I'm bidding you a long farewell, my Mary kind and true
> But I'll not forget you Darling, in the land I'm going to;
> They say there's bread and work for all, and the sun shines always there,
> But I'll never forget Ould Ireland were it fifty times as fair, were it fifty times as fair.

Patrick J. Dooley, by all accounts, was an extremely generous and considerate man:

> Much regret was felt by the people of Bruff and Loughguir districts when it was learned that Mr Patrick Dooley, son of Mr Edmond Dooley of Patrickswell, was amongst the number who went down with that ill-fated vessel.
>
> Mr Dooley was home on holidays from Chicago, chiefly for the purposes of seeing his aged father, and left in good spirits.
>
> He was a fine type of our exiled countrymen and on several occasions won distinction in American athletics. Mr Dooley was also one of the truest Irishmen that ever emigrated to the Great Republic of the West and never kept his purse closed when the cause of Ireland needed it.
>
> (*The Cork Examiner*, 16 May 1912)

Dooley had been living in Chicago for nine years, having emigrated in early 1903, and worked in a hotel. He was on the verge of coming home for good and was only travelling back to the United States for a short time. A letter found in his estate administration papers suggests this strongly, and was written by a solicitor acting for Dooley's elderly father, who is presumably the source of the lawyer's information:

> 1st July, 1913.
> Dear Mr Travers,
> I enclose papers for Grant of Administration intestate herein. The deceased was drowned on the *Titanic* and the only property he left was a deposit receipt in the Munster & Leinster Bank for £104 deposited a few days before he sailed out. He may have taken some little money with him, but he was not to remain long over. Have I the place of death described correctly? If not, please return to be amended.
>   Yours faithfully,
>   Roger Fox.

The described place of death was 'in mid-ocean, being a passenger on board the *Titanic*'. The single slip of paper lying behind in some safe place at home, signifying a hoard at the bank branch in Bruff, is a poignant image, somehow conveying again Patrick Dooley's detachment from money as an end in itself. His father, Edmond, who is illiterate, declared in the application to inherit the money left behind that his son was a 38-year-old bachelor, a labourer, who left only his father and one brother surviving in Ireland.

A number of the family had emigrated from the tiny hamlet of Patrickswell, not to be confused with a town of this name in the same county.

The American Red Cross nonetheless had to step in to assist other relatives left in the lurch by the loss of Mr Dooley. The details vary in this description, but there is little doubt that he is the person concerned since that organisation alphabetised its caseload:

Report of the American Red Cross (Titanic Disaster) 1913:
No. 87. (Irish.) A motorman, 34 years old, was drowned while returning from a visit to his parents in Ireland. A widowed sister and four children were dependent upon him for support, and his brother and wife and two children had also been helped by him.

The appropriation made will be administered by the local charity organisation Society for the benefit of the dependent sister and her family. ($468)

The occupation described here is likely to be most accurate, whereas 'labourer' was almost a generic term for 'Irishman' when it came to filling out legal papers. As regards age differentials, Patrick Dooley claimed to be 32 when signing aboard the *Titanic*, while posthumous legal papers put him six years older.

What is known is that Pat Dooley had planned to stay with his brother Richard (37) at East 31st Street, New York. They had only met once during Pat's near-decade in the USA. Their widowed father, Edmond, still farming, was into his seventies by 1912. It may have been intended that Pat would take over running the farm.

Patrick also had a sister Mary (41), and brothers Michael (39) and John (33). Many of these lives would not have been so damaged had the *Cymric* sailed as scheduled, four days before the *Titanic*, on Easter Sunday, 7 April.

ELIZABETH DOYLE (26) LOST

Ticket number 368702. Paid £7 15s.
Boarded at Queenstown. Third Class.
From: Bree, Enniscorthy, County Wexford.
Destination: 123 West 80th Street, New York city, for onward to Chicago.

There was strong optimism that 'bright, sunny' Lizzie Doyle had been saved because she had convinced her home people of her intent to buy a Second-Class ticket for the *Titanic*. It would have cost her around £10 10s. The news that large numbers of Second-Class women had been saved (84 per cent, against 55 per cent for Third-Class women by final White Star figures) led to neighbours competing to discover the good news of her survival in the latest newspapers.

But devoted daughter Lizzie – who had rushed home from America the previous year to nurse her widowed father in his final illness – may have felt uneasy about lavishing such a high standard of care on herself. She finally opted to save around £2 15s, and bought a Third-Class ticket, and she drowned with most of steerage.

Lizzie was travelling to Chicago from her home in Bree, Enniscorthy, County Wexford. She booked on the *Titanic* through a New Ross agent and was travelling in the company of her cousin Robert Mernagh, also lost. The pair may have finalised their travel intentions at the funeral of Robert's aunt Margaret Murphy, who died on the last day of February 1912, six weeks before the sailing.

Lizzie was listed as due to stay with Bridget Fox at West 80th Street, New York city. Bridget was a relative of Patrick Fox, another Irish *Titanic* passenger. Both Lizzie and Robert Mernagh intended onward travel to Chicago.

> Titanic *victims: Miss Lizzie Doyle, Bree, and Mr Robert Mernagh, Ballyleigh, Ballywilliam.* Sincere and widespread regret was felt in Bree and the surrounding district when on Saturday week last it became known that Miss Lizzie Doyle, who was one of the passengers on the ill-fated *Titanic*, was not amongst the survivors.
>
> Poor 'Lil', as she was familiarly called by her most intimate friends, was youngest daughter of the late Mr Martin Doyle, Bree, and was one of the most talented and popular young ladies in the district; her charming manners and bright, sunny disposition won for her the respect and admiration of all, and the untimely ending of her young life, so full of hope and promise, has cast a gloom over the whole district.
>
> She had been in Philadelphia two years previously, and only returned home last June in time to be present at the deathbed of her late lamented father. Having recovered somewhat from the shock occasioned by that sad event, she decided to return once more to America, and on the 10th April last she said good bye to her host of friends in Bree, and in company with her cousin, Mr Robert Mernagh, Ballyleigh, Ballywilliam, set out for Chicago.
>
> But alas for human hopes and aspirations, they were destined never to reach their journey's end. From the first, little hope was entertained of the safety of Mr Mernagh, but being Second Class passengers, a large percentage of the women of which were reported to be saved, the friends of Miss Doyle had great hopes for her safety, and from the moment the first news of the disaster reached Bree the newspapers were eagerly scanned day after day by anxious friends, all eager to be the first to find the good news, but without success, and on Saturday week their fond hope was dashed to the ground when the news came to her sorrowing relatives that neither she nor her cousin were amongst the survivors.
>
> On the following Sunday morning, when at 8 o'clock Mass Canon Sheil asked the prayers of the congregation for the repose of their souls, a pin might be heard falling in the church, so deep were the feelings of those present. The deepest sympathy is felt with their heartbroken relatives, and the church was thronged with sorrowing friends, all anxious to pay the last tribute to the memory of one who will not soon be forgotten.
>
> (*Enniscorthy Echo*, 18 May 1912)

Margaret Doyle had a vision of her sister Lizzie, according to a tale in the district, when she was putting out washing a few days after the departure. She saw the wraith and came into the house as white as any sheet she had just hung on the line.

A letter written by Elizabeth Doyle survives from 1909 and shows something of her character. It was written on 12 December that year from an address at 1244 Snyder Avenue, Philadelphia:

My dear Aunt,

No doubt you will think that when I left dear old Ireland I forgot all my relatives, but you will see that I still have a corner in my heart for you all still.

Of course you have heard long since of my safe arrival etc., so I won't waste time and paper telling you again. I am feeling splendid and as happy as a king here. Mr and Mrs O'Brien are awfully good and kind to me. How are you and uncle keeping since, or have you been over to Bree lately? Maggie is quite busy now with the tradesmen and all, so I know she won't have much time for going about …

This is a grand country, aunt, and the weather has been beautiful up to now, but it's getting much colder tho' still nice and fine. There is no twilight here. The night falls all of a sudden. But it's never dark as all electric lights are on all night …

Now dear aunt, as this is the last day for Christmas Irish mails and I have a few more to write, I hope you will forgive me for this hurried note and accept my best wishes for a Happy Christmas and a glad New Year.

With lots of love to uncle and your own dear self,

Your loving niece,

Lizzie Doyle.

Her estate came to just £10, granted to her brother Jeremiah on 12 March 1913. Legal papers noted that Lizzie 'died at sea in an accident to the steamship "Titanic".'

She is named on a family tombstone in Davidstown Cemetery, near Enniscorthy.

BRIDGET DRISCOLL (27) SAVED

Ticket number 14311. Paid £7 15s.
Boarded at Queenstown. Third Class.
From: Letter, Ballydehob, County Cork.
Destination: 522 Grove Street, Jersey city, New Jersey.

Bridget Driscoll was a dutiful child who had returned to Ireland to nurse her mother in her final illness. But Mrs Kate Driscoll had died and been buried by the time her daughter arrived – and Bridget soon faced the imminent prospect of joining her in the next world.

She was rescued in collapsible D, the last boat to be lowered from the davits. It went off around 2 a.m., when *Titanic* had short minutes to live. Her forecastle was under water, so too the forward well deck, and the water was climbing steadily to the boat deck. Women were put to the oars and collapsible D was about 100 yards off when the queen of the seas made her final plunge.

Bridget later told how she helped 'another lady from Ballydehob' – it could only have been Annie Jermyn – into collapsible D (pictured overleaf), which had been ready to lower earlier until more women were found at the last moment.

Bridget and Annie had travelled with Mary Kelly on successive tickets issued in Ballydehob. She initially indicated on official forms that she would be staying with cousins in New York, but later told US immigration that she was a 24-year-old domestic and would be staying with her cousin Mrs Minnie Fenn in Jersey city. In fact, Bridget had been born on 18 January 1885, but it was common for women of all ages to be grudging in their acknowledgement of the march of time.

Census records show that Bridget's parents had been married for thirty-six years. They had seven children, one of whom died in infancy. By 1911, Kate and John Driscoll were recorded as aged 59 and 63 respectively, with son Eugene (35) having taken over the farm,

yet the 1901 census had stated parents John and Kate to be 54 and 52 respectively, and children Eugene (24), Timothy (16), Bridget (16), Mary (14), and John (6).

Bridget and Timothy were twins, and he later became a policeman in Canada with the RCMP. Bridget herself married a man named Dominic Joseph Carney in the United States. They ran a grocery store at City Island, New York. She went on to have four children – Cathy, Joe, Patsy and Bill. Their first, Cathleen, was born six years after the disaster, on 19 September 1918. After her husband died in 1963, Bridget moved to Houston, Texas, to stay with her daughter Cathy at 5918 Yarwell.

Bridget Driscoll died in the Bellaire Hospital from acute renal failure on 28 December 1976, aged 91. She had survived more than sixty-four years since escaping the sinking of the *Titanic*.

FRANK DWAN (67) LOST

Ticket number 336439. Paid £7 15s.
Joined at Queenstown. Third Class.
From: Knockmahon, Bunmahon, County Waterford.
Destination: Morris Plains, New Jersey.

It is the last chance you will get in your life! That was the advice that sent the oldest Irish passenger aboard the *Titanic* to sea.

The last chance in question for 67-year-old Frank Dwan was the opportunity to visit his children, all of whom had emigrated to the United States. They had been begging him to come over, had sent him the passage money, and had finally persuaded his wife, Bridget, to scold him into going.

Heavily bearded Frank had enjoyed the prospect of a trip in the big ship. A fisherman for much of his life, he had an abiding love of the sea, and his enjoyment of the dawning adventure can be seen in a startling photograph taken on board the tender *Ireland*, on 11 April 1912 (see page 2). The little boat is about to cast out from the quay to ferry the passengers to the 882-foot leviathan now lying at anchor off Roche's Point. A photographer from *The Cork Examiner*, capturing the moment from the tender *America* alongside, finds Frank Dwan in his lens, smiling happily in conversation with Eugene Daly, who has his back to the rail.

Yet there is evidence that on the night before he sailed, Frank Dwan had a premonition of disaster and even spoke of the liner sinking to fellow passengers. Nonetheless he spurned an offer to take another ship and boarded the pride of the White Star fleet.

Frank had been married for forty-five years when he took his journey into fate. He and Bridget, his senior by four years, had had eight children, four of whom remained alive. One, Daniel, then aged 29, was one of the offspring who were all working as orderlies and porters in Morris Plains Insane Asylum in New Jersey. Two sons later became chauffeurs for the Rockefeller family and became rich themselves by the standards of the emigrant Irish.

Frank's name was misspelled 'Dewan' in the official White Star passenger list. He had been described on embarkation records as an agricultural labourer, and in the 1901 census had termed himself a general labourer. By 1911 he had reverted to the calling of fisherman. Frank wore his 'lucky' Norwegian fishing cap as he boarded the *Titanic*. His death effectively robbed his widow, who had urged him to travel, of all family companionship. His body, like so many others, was never found.

The Cork Examiner reported on Frank Dwan's short stay in Queenstown in its coverage of the disaster on 17 April 1912, in a piece filed by their local correspondent:

Frank with son Daniel, and grandson.

I heard many pathetic stories of those Irish travellers who were here for a day or so before they sailed on the ill-fated ship, but there was one old man amongst the many who came here on last Wednesday night. He was a hale old fellow, from Bunmahon, County Waterford. He asked the lodging house keeper on arrival if he knew him, and the reply was no. 'Well then,' he replied (his name was Duane [*sic*]), 'every child of mine that went to America stayed in this house, and I'm going out now to stay with them for a bit. My wife was out lately, and it's my turn to have a spell now, but I'm coming back again as soon as I stay a bit with my children.'

He thought £8 1s, the steerage passage money, high, and was told that if he waited for the *Celtic* till next morning he'd get his ticket for £7 16s, but he wouldn't have it, as every hour was too long until he'd meet the children, and they'd be waiting for him, and he wired his wife for some additional money, which she sent, and he booked his passage full of high hopes that ere a full week elapsed he'd meet his children on American soil.

Strangely enough, on that Wednesday night, the eve of his departure, he and many other travellers booked by the *Titanic*, commenced discussing the big crowd the *Titanic* would be taking, and Duane remarked what an awful thing it would be if she were sunk with all her passengers. It surely was a strange remark. The feelings of Duane's children, looking forward to a meeting they had longed for years can easily be imagined. They had been pressing him for years to go out, but he refused all along, until finally the inducements of wife and children made him go, and possibly he now lies numbered amongst the dead.

Frank Dwan is commemorated by a plaque and sculpture of his face at Saleen Church in his birthplace of Bunmahon, where he had married Bridget Walsh in 1867.

JAMES FARRELL (25) LOST

Ticket number 367232. Paid £7 15s.
Boarded at Queenstown. Third Class.
From: Clonee, Killoe, County Longford.
Destination: 420 East 80th Street, New York city.

He helped to save others, but for James Farrell there was no escape. His body was recovered from the sea, still clutching Rosary beads. It was sealed in canvas and weighted, given a brief religious service, and reconsigned to the deep.

Katie Gilnagh, an Irish *Titanic* survivor, recounted to author Walter Lord that a seaman at a barrier had blocked her, Kate Mullins and Kate Murphy:

> Suddenly steerage passenger Jim Farrell, a strapping Irishman from the girls' home county, barged up. 'Great God, man!' he roared. 'Open the gate and let the girls through!' It was a superb demonstration of sheer voice-power. To the girls' astonishment, the sailor meekly complied.
>
> Walter Lord, *A Night to Remember*

> In a letter to her father, Katie Gilnagh stated that James Farrell of Clonee was very kind to her and another girl. As they were leaving the ill-fated vessel, he gave her his cap to cover her head, and shouted 'Good-bye for ever.'
>
> (*Irish Independent*, 15 May 1912)

The story of the thrown cap is widespread in Longford, and Miss Gilnagh kept it for many years.

Farrell certainly appears to have been a very gregarious man. His body was later recovered, and from the list of effects it seems he may have swopped a coin for some souvenir kronor with one of the Scandinavian steerage passengers. Making conversation in the linguistic melting-pot below decks must have been interesting.

The following report comes from the Halifax coroner's office, which would have received details of the deceased as well as their effects from the search boat:

No. 68. Male. Estimated age 40. Hair dark. Moustache light.
Clothing – Dark suit; black boots; grey socks.
Effects – Silver watch; two purses (one empty), the other with $10.00,
3s. 2 and a half d., and 10 kronor; two studs; cameo; beads, left on body.
Name on Third Class ticket No. B67233 [*sic*] – James Farrell, Longford.

The corpse was recovered eight days after the sinking. The *MacKay-Bennett* recovery vessel had a policy of not returning heavily decomposed or crushed bodies to port, at least bodies identifiable as being from Third Class. Passenger bodies of other classes were packed in ice and placed in storage, while there were caskets aboard for First-Class corpses. James Farrell was buried at sea on 24 April 1912. He had been due to join a brother, Michael, in New York.

1901 census – Clonee, County Longford.
Parents John (40), farmer; Ellen (36). Children: Catherine (17), Michael (15), **James (14)**, John (12), Mary (11), Edward (9), Thomas (7).

HONORA FLEMING (22) LOST

Ticket number 364859. Paid £7 15s.
Boarded at Queenstown. Third Class.
From: Carrowskehine, Addergoole, County Mayo.
Destination: 542 West 112th Street, New York city.

It was Honora's twenty-second birthday the night the *Titanic* sank. She would likely not have remained long in her chair in steerage as a succession of young men used a heaven-sent excuse to request a dance with this beaming, if bashful, birthday girl. Many are the accounts of gaiety throughout Third Class on that fateful Sunday night, and it is likely that celebrations for the young Mayo girl occupied one small part of the general festivities.

Listed aboard as 'Nora', she was a housemaid, as was her sister Catherine (25), who had previously emigrated to New York city. Catherine Fleming Wynne sent money home to enable her younger sibling to come to America in 1911, but family legend says it was spent on a cow. Then she sent money again, and her sister was finally on her way.

Honora was among those wakened by stewards who said the Rosary in a gangway in the company of her Mayo friends. According to teenage Irish survivor Annie Kate Kelly, the group was then encouraged to go back to bed and did so. Honora was roused a second time as realisation of the danger spread, but there is no account of any later movements. She drowned and her name was later misspelled 'Hemming' in the official White Star casualty list.

Born and baptised on the same day, 14 April 1890, she appears in the parish baptismal record as Honora, a daughter of Thomas Fleming and Mary Callaghan. The 1901 census erroneously records her as 'Honor', and her age as 12 years. In the 1911 census she is listed under the pet name 'Onnie', short for Honora, aged 21. Her father, Thomas, is listed as a 60-year-old farmer, and her mother, Mary, as 58. The other children include Thomas (27), Josie (11), Bridget (15) and Ellie (13).

She appears to have been related to Margaret Devaney of Sligo, who told the *New York Herald* that 'Anna' Fleming (the name 'Onnie' or 'Honor' may have been misheard) was 'entertaining us with Irish songs when the first word of trouble came. She went down with the *Titanic*, poor girl, and I believe she was singing or joking at the time, she was that jolly.'

JAMES FLYNN (28) LOST

Ticket number 364851. Paid £7 15s.
Boarded at Queenstown. Third Class.
From: Cuilkillew, Addergoole, County Mayo.
Destination: 236 East 53rd Street, New York city.

James Flynn was travelling to join his younger brother Anthony, who lived in New York, at East 53rd Street. His age and occupation were given on embarkation as a 27-year-old labourer. The *Report of the American Red Cross* says: 'No. 141. (Irish.) A young man was lost.' His brother asked for assistance in recovering the body, and the necessary steps were taken for that purpose, but the body was not recovered.

James was from Cuilkillew, and was the son of James Flynn Snr, a 70-year-old farmer in 1912, and his wife, Anne, who was 64. He was baptised on 13 September 1883. He had turned 28 by the time he joined the great ship at Queenstown. He was related to both the Kelly and the Canavan families, which also provided *Titanic* passengers from Mayo.

Titanic survivor Annie Kate Kelly makes extensive references in her accounts of the tragedy to a passenger named 'Patrick Flynn', which could be construed as meaning James Flynn, the only male Flynn passenger among the large Mayo party on board the *Titanic*. Annie makes pathetic references to the 'little Flynn boy' being refused a place in the lifeboat and being pushed back, even though he was slight and not able to take care of himself. 'It was pitiful that they wouldn't allow the boy stay on the lifeboat, and he only a child and it not full.' While James may have been small in stature, he was certainly no boy, and definitely not a child, as one American newspaper had it.

Little 'Patrick' Flynn is last seen by Annie Kelly holding hands with John and Catherine Bourke as they stood by the deck rail of the *Titanic*, waiting for the end.

JOHN FLYNN (42) LOST

Ticket number 368323. Paid £6 19s.
Boarded at Queenstown. Third Class.
From: Carrowhawkin, Clonbur, County Galway.
Destination: 3434 Frazier Street, Oakland, Pittsburgh, Pennsylvania.

John Flynn came home to Ireland because he was promised the family farm by his sister Bridget. But when he arrived, she suddenly reneged on the offer and he was returning bitterly disappointed on *Titanic* to his wife and six children. He never arrived. The devastation for his children can only be imagined. One son, Ed, later committed suicide by jumping off a Pittsburgh bridge after his business failed.

Report of the American Red Cross (Titanic Disaster) 1913:
No. 142. (Irish.) The husband, returning from a visit to Ireland, was drowned. He had been a resident of this country 28 years and was a labourer, earning $2 a day. He is survived by a wife and six children, the eldest of whom is nineteen, and youngest three years of age. The two eldest girls, employed as housemaids, earn $4 and $5 a week. A cousin of the wife lives with the family and, beside her board, gives some small assistance.
The husband left $1,000 life insurance and a small piece of city property bought before his marriage, which promises to become valuable. The family own the house in which they have lived for twelve years. They saved enough money to buy the lot and borrowed $600 from a building and loan association, to which they paid $5 a month. At the time of the disaster, no payment had been made for three or four months, and $175 there was due … From relief funds other than the Red Cross, the widow received $3,697.28. ($1,700)

According to embarkation records, John Flynn had become a US citizen during his nearly three decades in America. He indicated that he was a 42-year-old agricultural labourer, but may have worked in open-cast mining in the Pittsburgh area.

Folklore in Clonbur, County Galway, states that John Flynn was not drowned in the disaster, but died from exposure on board a lifeboat. This conviction cannot be verified from any available sources. A sister of the deceased, Mary Gallagher of New York, wrote to Bridget in Ireland, claiming the body had been landed from the *Carpathia*. It was alleged to have been buried in Long Island.

His sister Bridget's decision to keep the farm meant that John's was not only a wasted journey, but also a deadly one. His return ticket was bought at the shipping agency of Joe Coyne in Clonbur.

A photograph of John was taken on the day he left to board the *Titanic*, but it has been lost.

JOSEPH FOLEY (19) LOST

Ticket number 330910. Paid £7 12s 7d, plus 5s extra.
Boarded at Queenstown. Third Class.
From: Mountplummer, Newcastlewest, County Cork.
Destination: Larchmont, New York.

There were two Joseph Foleys whose stories became merged with the *Titanic* disaster. One lived, the other died. The one who lived was a 26-year-old from Foulkesmill, County Wexford, who crossed the Atlantic on the White Star liner *Celtic*, arriving on 20 April 1912. However, a relative of this Joseph Foley spotted the name on a list of *Titanic* casualties, plunging a family into needless grief. But they had the joy of relief on learning he had arrived in America two days after the *Carpathia* landed the meagre number of *Titanic* survivors.

The Joseph Foley who died was aged only 19, the eldest in a small family and the first offspring to opt for emigration. Good-looking, and a gentle gardener on a landed estate, he was described as 'angelic and saintly'. Some newspaper reports linked the name of this *Titanic* casualty with the other Joseph Foley:

> *A Wexfordman's luck – did not sail in the* Titanic
> In connection with the *Titanic* disaster, which still continues to occupy the public attention, we are reminded of the luck of a young Wexfordman, Mr Joseph Foley, Carrigbyrne, who had booked his passage for America on the ill-fated liner, but waited over for some comrades sailing on the *Celtic* some days later, and so escaped most probably death.
> Mr Foley's friends at home, and his brother, Mr Thomas Foley of Chicago, well known to many Wexford Gaels, were naturally very anxious as to his fate, and had begun to fear the worst, especially the latter, who communicated to his brother, Mr John Foley, of Carrigbyrne, the sad intelligence that it was almost a certainty that Joseph had been lost.
> With reference to the fears entertained by Mr Foley in Chicago, we cull the following from the *Daily Tribune* of that city, of Saturday April 20th:

> *Thomas Foley's brother gone*
> Thomas Foley, 3157 Harrison Street, a street car conductor, a well-built young man with

an unspoiled Irish burr in his speech, called to ask if the morning newspapers had correctly included the name of Joseph Foley, his brother, in the list of those missing.

At first Chief Clerk Holstrom failed to find the name of Joseph Foley in the passenger list, and the Chicago brother heaved a sigh of relief.

But the clerk scanned the list once more and found the name this time. The White Star accounts for Joseph Foley the same way as it does for 1,595 other passengers.

'I guess he is gone,' said Foley, pulling excitedly on his pipe. 'Poor lad, he was a fine, clean-cut young fellow, 26 he was. The last letter I wrote I told him to stay at home on the farm with the old folk. Joe is the first to go. There were twelve of us children, eight boys and four girls. They are all in the old country except myself and Nick, who is a fireman for the Chicago and Northwestern in Chicago'.

The Foley family at home have since received a letter from Joseph informing them of his safe arrival off the *Celtic*, and so all anxious fears are allayed.

(*Enniscorthy Echo*, 18 May 1912)

The *New Ross Standard* had this report on 3 May 1912:

A fortunate young man
Rumour gained credence around some time again when it was floated around that Mr Joseph Foley, Barmony, was numbered among the missing on board the ill-fated *Titanic*. He was booked to travel on the *Titanic*, but fortunately changed his mind, and his name appeared in the daily papers as one of the Third-Class passengers.

Luckily indeed for himself and his family that he took a berth on the *Baltic* [sic]. Mr Foley is a fine type of young Irishman, and when at home was a keen Gael. We wish him every good luck in the land of his adoption, and congratulate him on his lucky escape.

The Joseph Foley who died was travelling out with his girlfriend Bridget O'Sullivan, who was from the same parish. Joseph (19) worked as a gardener on the Hearnsbrook estate close to his home, but was hoping to achieve something different in life.

The families of both seemed hopeful the couple would make a go of things in America and get married. Instead Bridget and Joseph died at sea. *The Cork Examiner* wrote on 2 May 1912: 'As they were both deservedly popular, their untimely fate has evoked universal regret …'

Joseph's parents were David, 45, an agricultural labourer, and his wife, Julia, 40. 'His mother was heartbroken when he was going, he was such a devoted son.' Joseph was travelling out to his uncle, John Hickey, in Larchmont, NY.

WILLIAM FOLEY (20) LOST

Ticket number 365235. Paid £7 15s.
Boarded at Queenstown. Third Class.
From: Commeen, Donoughmore, County Cork.
Destination: 252 West 115th Street, New York city.

William was not wanted in America. He desperately wanted to go and had begged his sister Julia in New York for the passage money. But she was finding it hard to make ends meet, and consulted their brother Jeremiah as to what she should do. America-based Jeremiah made a succinct reply: 'Don't send him the fare. We're not doing so well ourselves, why would he come over?' This story was related by William's niece Nora Mullane, who adds that a sympathetic Julia said nothing, but raised the money herself and sent it secretly.

Travelling in steerage on the *Titanic*, William blithely believed he was on his way to his brother Jeremiah (33), who had pioneered the emigrant trail to America's east coast. He stated as much on official records. He certainly knew more about it than Jeremiah did: 'He only found out when the *Titanic* went down. There was a lot of bad feeling about it, and what had happened. Julia came home to Ireland on her own a little later.'

Report of the American Red Cross (Titanic Disaster) 1913:
No. 143. (Irish.) A farmer, 20 years old, was lost while coming to join his sister and brother in New York. The sister claimed to have sent $60 for his passage and, because ill and out of work for several months, to need this money. She was asked to secure a receipt for the draft sent to her brother. Nothing further was heard from the girl. The family in Ireland were not dependent.

William Foley, left at home in Ireland for weeks amid confusing signals, at length began to plan his one-way trip to the United States. He would travel with his fellow parishioner, Hannah Naughton, a trained schoolteacher, and a third person was due to join them on the way to a new life in 'the Land of the Free'.

The day they were due to travel, William called to the house of Hannah Maria Cremin (18) to accompany her to Mallow and the train for Cork. The girl was distraught, however, because a last-minute hitch meant her papers were not in order. Hannah Naughton and William had to leave without her. Hannah Cremin arrived in the United States a year later aboard the *Titanic*'s sister ship, *Olympic*.

Donoughmore victims, Donoughmore, Wednesday
It is regrettable to have to record that among those who lost their lives in the historic *Titanic* disaster were Hannah Naughton, daughter of John Naughton, and William, son of John Foley, Commeen, both of this parish.

The greatest sympathy is felt for the parents of both for the sudden and tragic way in which they lost their lives. Hopes were entertained that their names would appear in some lists of those saved, but it is now certain that both were lost.

Nearly three-quarters of a century after William Foley was lost on the *Titanic*, a nephew named after him, 57-year-old William Foley, was drowned in waters from whence the White Star liner sailed, when he had a heart attack at the wheel of his car, which veered off an unprotected quay into Cork harbour in 1986. The victim's sister had foreseen William's death by drowning in a dream the previous night.

1901 census:
Parents: John Foley (65), farmer, Ellen (55), mother.
Children: Mary (24), Jeremiah (22), Julia (20), John (17), Dennis (11), **William (9)**.

PATRICK FOX (28) LOST

Ticket number 368573. Paid £7 15s.
Boarded at Queenstown. Third Class.
From: Killaroo, Streamstown, Mullingar, County Westmeath.
Destination: 123 West 80th Street, New York city.

It was said that Patrick Fox could easily clear a five-bar farmyard gate in one flying leap. A famed high-jumper, he had claimed victory in a local sports event intended purely as an exhibition occasion for a big city champion. The ability to clear locked gates could have been an advantage on the *Titanic* were it not for the fact that there was little headroom below decks. In fact, Pat was such an all-round athlete – having been offered a kind of sports scholarship in Dublin after demonstrating his prowess – that people in his locality refused to accept his death. They felt sure Pat would have been able to swim to safety, pull himself aboard a raft, or cling to floating wreckage until rescue arrived. Neighbours were thoroughly shocked when confirmation arrived of his demise.

Patrick had spent much of 1911 at home with his family in Killaroo, having spent a few years in the United States, originally journeying out in 1906 to join his sister Bridget. In his home place he was remembered as being happy-go-lucky and 'as wild as a goat'.

He had returned in part to repay the original passage money to America to a wealthy acquaintance from whom he had borrowed the fare. But the generous gentleman refused to accept repayment, saying it was reward enough to see how well Pat had turned out. Suddenly therefore, Pat had extra money and he began to think about making his future in Ireland. A neighbouring family, the Conlons, were selling a five- or six-acre parcel of land which would double the Fox holding if they could make the acquisition.

Pat's father was nearly 80 years of age and since Pat was the only son of the household it would have made sense for him to take over both his own farm and the Conlon ground. He could have afforded it if he disposed of some assets in the US. The night before he was due to return to settle his affairs by the *Titanic*, Pat Fox told neighbour John Conlon (35) that he was not to sell his widowed mother's holding until he came back. Conlon readily agreed and a deal was struck. But the point of no return arrived unforeseen a few days later.

> A gentleman from the Streamstown district, a Mr Fox, was also a passenger on board the ill-fated vessel. The *Titanic*, which had been described as a 'floating palace', and has been declared to be practically unsinkable, was built in Belfast by the great shipping firm over which Lord Pirrie presides.
> The loss of the great Atlantic liner is a tragic reminder that man has not yet conquered the deep, and that there is, after all, something in what is regarded as the ignorant fear of 'old fashioned' people about the dangers of travelling.
>
> (*Westmeath Examiner*, 20 April 1912)

Fox was described as a 26-year-old general labourer on Board of Trade embarkation records, but was in fact born on 15 July 1883, making him two years older.

1911 census – Killaroo, Streamstown.
John Fox (78), farmer, and wife Bridget (60). Married 39 years, nine children, five living. **Patrick (27)**, farmer's son; Katie (23), dressmaker; Christine (18).

MARTIN GALLAGHER (25) LOST

Ticket number 36864. Paid £7 14s 10d.
Boarded at Queenstown. Third Class.
From: Currafarry, Caltra, County Galway.
Destination: East 143rd Street, New York city.

Martin was travelling with four other Galway people: Thomas Kilgannon, Thomas Smith, Ellen Mockler and Margaret Mannion. He appears to have been their inspiration for the journey. He was originally from Ballina and had returned to Ireland having made good in the United States. Mockler was his next-door neighbour at home in Currafarry and Kilgannon lived just two smallholdings away. Smith he knew from his schooldays and Mannion was the reason he had come home in the first place. It was thus natural that Gallagher should become the leader of the little group of five that set out from Caltra parish for pastures new.

Martin's brother Michael had years ago preceded him to the USA, becoming a rancher in Wyoming. But he himself became successful in Rye, upstate New York, building up a healthy business from about 1908 onwards to become relatively well-to-do. It was then his thoughts turned to the girl he left behind. The dream of returning to make Margaret Mannion of Loughanboy, Caltra, his bride had long sustained him in the United States. They had corresponded frequently, and now Martin was home to collect her and make her his wife.

Martin Gallagher died on the *Titanic*, having saved his love and helped to steer other girls to safety.

> Some stayed in their cabins – that's where Mary Agatha Glynn and four discouraged roommates were found by young Martin Gallagher. He quickly escorted them to boat No. 13 and stepped back on the deck again.
>
> Walter Lord, *A Night to Remember*

Nephew Paddy Gallagher says Martin Gallagher led a party of desperate steerage passengers through the ship and up to the boat deck, brooking no opposition along the way. Of the five in the Caltra party, only the two girls – Ellen and Margaret – survived, and both later paid tribute to Gallagher's leadership. Margaret's last glimpse of Martin was as her lifeboat was lowered. He was on deck, Rosary in hand. He was down to his shirt in the bitter cold, having stripped off a top layer of clothing to give extra warmth to Miss Mannion.

According to White Star records, Martin Gallagher planned to stay at 296 East 143rd Street, New York. He had bought his own ticket, and most likely Margaret's too, in Ryan's pub and shipping agency in Ballygar, County Galway. Gallagher, Kilgannon and Mannion had sequential tickets. For the steerage men, these were counterfoils to an icy grave.

Seven years after the tragedy that took her sweetheart, Margaret Mannion returned to Ireland. A year later she married and had three children. Her husband was another Martin.

The five Caltra passengers who boarded the *Titanic* are commemorated in a plaque in their home village. Martin Gallagher's name will thus be remembered for decades to come.

WILLIAM GILLESPIE (31) LOST

Ticket number 12233. Paid £13.
Boarded at Southampton. Second Class.
From: Abbeyleix, County Laois.
Destination: Vancouver, British Columbia, Canada.

Carpets in the *Titanic* were made by an Abbeyleix firm with whom William Gillespie was associated. He seems to have been travelling to Canada to drum up more business, while having the useful calling card of being able to boast about Abbeyleix finery on the floors of the luxury new liner.

Born in County Carlow, William was the fourth son of Abbeyleix gentleman Richard Gillespie, who died aged 74 in 1908, when William was 27. William became a law clerk in Dublin, and his mother, Eliza (1851–1914), ran a coffee shop in the town in a bid to deter alcoholism. Among the other children, according to the 1911 census, were Emmanuel, a 27-year-old druggist, sisters Esther Deborah (24) and Ida Ruth (22), and Matthew Humphrey Gillespie (17).

It appears William was working in 1912 for Viscount De Vesci of Abbeyleix, who ran an award-winning carpet factory in the town. The Kildare Carpet Company supplied four carpets for staterooms, including the wardroom, on the White Star's magnificent new vessel. Order books were full and the United States and Canada were among the export markets.

After William's drowning, a number of contributions were made in his name to the *Irish Times* relief fund. W. A. Robinson and the staff of James Pim & Co., Mountmellick, contributed £3 10s, while the Abbeyleix Choral Society donated £5 5s – an astonishing figure given that basic wages in the factory amounted to only three shillings a week.

William's mother died within two years of his loss, and the carpet factory closed within the year. His name is memorialised on a tablet at the graves of his parents in Abbeyleix Church of Ireland graveyard: 'And their fourth son, William Henry, lost at sea in the *Titanic* disaster, 15 April 1912'.

KATIE GILNAGH (17) SAVED

Ticket number 35851. Paid £7 14s 8d.
Boarded at Queenstown. Third Class.
From: Rhyne, Esker, County Longford.
Destination: 230 East 55th Street, New York city.

Katie Gilnagh survived because of a white lie. When she finally gained the upper deck, she was told that lifeboat No. 16 was too full and she could not go. As the boat began to descend, Katie cried: 'But I want to go with my sister!' The crewman hesitated and suddenly relented. She could get in.

'God help me, I told a lie,' she told the New York *Daily News* on the fiftieth anniversary of the sinking in 1962. 'At first they didn't want to let anyone else into it because it was overcrowded. I said that I wanted to go with my sister. I had no sister aboard. They let me get in, but I had to stand because we were so crowded.'

Katie did have a sister in New York – who was inconsolably arranging for a Requiem Mass when Katie walked through the door.

Besides the lie, Miss Gilnagh had also lived because of her beauty and the effect it had in winning sympathy and securing help. On two separate occasions men acted to ensure that Katie made progress to the upper decks.

During the crossing she had occupied compartment Q161 on E deck, all the way aft on the starboard side, five decks down from the boats. Her cabin partners are believed to have been sisters Margaret and Kate Murphy, and Katie Mullen, all fellow County Longford travellers. All four were saved on boat No. 16, launched from the port side.

Relatives tell that a week before sailing, a gypsy woman called to the Gilnagh house and was being turned away by her father, Hughie, when Katie demanded that her fortune be read. She was told she would soon be crossing water and there would be danger, but that she would come to no harm. The palm reading cost her sixpence.

Author Walter Lord, in *A Night to Remember*, described how years later Gilnagh told of attending a party in steerage on the Sunday night of the disaster. At one point a rat scurried across the room. The boys gave chase and the girls squealed with excitement. Then the party was on again. Lord describes what happened for Katie after the berg impact:

> Katherine Gilnagh, a pert colleen not quite sixteen [*sic*], heard a knock on the door. It was the young man who had caught her eye earlier that day playing the bagpipes on deck. He told her to get up – something was wrong with the ship …
>
> At another barrier a seaman held back Kathy Gilnagh, Kate Mullins and Kate Murphy. (On the *Titanic* all Irish girls seemed to be named Katherine.)

The report goes on to recount the story of how James Farrell got them through the gate (see James Farrell) and then continues:

> Even then, Kathy Gilnagh's troubles weren't over. She took a wrong turn … lost her friends … found herself alone on the Second-Class promenade, with no idea how to reach the boats. The deck was deserted, except for a single man leaning against the rail, staring moodily into the night. He let her stand on his shoulders, and she managed to climb to the next deck up. When she finally reached the boat deck, No. 16 was just starting down. A man warned her off – there was no more room. 'But I want to go with my sister!' Kathy cried … 'All right, get in,' he sighed, and she slipped into the boat as it dropped to the sea – another Third-Class passenger safely away.

Katie (seated) with her sister Molly, New York, 1912

Gilnagh described James Farrell as her 'guardian angel'. He appears to have reached the upper decks, according to an *Irish Independent* report of 15 May 1912, about a letter written home by Katie concerning the 'sad fate of fellow-passengers from her district':

> (She) states that James Farrell of Clonee was very kind to her and another girl. As they were leaving the ill-fated vessel he gave her his cap to cover her head, and shouted 'goodbye forever'.

An *Irish Post* article from 25 May 1912 records:

> *A County Longford survivor*
> Among the passengers who were saved from the ill-fated *Titanic* was a young lady named Miss Katie Gilnagh, of Killoe, County Longford, whose photo we reproduce. She has written to her parents in Longford giving a graphic narrative of her experience.
>
> In her letter she states that she and another girl named McCoy were the last two girls taken on the last boat, and a young man who had previously got into the boat was taken out of it. She further states that she was wearing a small shawl on her head which got blown off, when a person named Mr James Farrell of Clonee, gave her his cap.
>
> As they were being lowered, he shouted: 'Goodbye for ever' and that was the last she saw of him.

Katie may have been identified aboard *Carpathia* by fellow survivor Lawrence Beesley in his 1912 book *The Loss of the SS Titanic*:

> Among the Irish group was one girl of really remarkable beauty, black hair and deep violet eyes with long lashes, perfectly shaped features, and quite young, not more than eighteen or twenty; I think she lost no relatives on the *Titanic*.

Joyously welcomed by sister Molly in New York, Katie was photographed to reassure the family back home. She sat on a chair, smiling sweetly, as Molly stood protectively alongside.

Katie was born in Rhyne, County Longford, on 13 October 1894, appearing in the 1901 census as the second eldest child of parents Hugh (35) and Johanna (33) Gilnagh. Katie was aged just six, and had an elder sister Mary (7), the selfsame Molly who was waiting anxiously in New York eleven years later. Four other children listed were Ellen (5), Thomas (3), Bridget (2) and one-year-old Elizabeth.

Katie was initially assisted by the Jewish Emigrant Society in New York and was aided to the tune of $100 by the American Red Cross, which described her as an Irish domestic servant, 17 years old. She later married John J. Manning from Roscommon. Heartbreak came to Katie with the death of her brother William in 1917, while her adoring sister Molly died in 1933. Katie also lost her husband before they could grow old together. He died in April 1955, not yet 60.

She went back to Ireland only once, in 1962, on the fiftieth anniversary of the sinking, and crossed the Atlantic for only the second time in her life – this time on an airliner. Her nephew Johnny Thompson recalls that a soothing voice which came over the intercom had the opposite effect on Katie: 'Good afternoon, ladies and gentlemen, this is Captain Smith …' Horribly alarmed and distressed, Katie had to be brought to the cockpit to verify that it wasn't the same Captain Smith who was in charge on her first Atlantic journey.

Earlier that year, as a 67-year-old grandmother, Katie had attended a 50th anniversary memorial service at the Merchant Marine Institute in South Street, Manhattan. She told the *Daily News* of her memories of the sinking:

When we had gotten away from the ship I could see its lights but it was so dark I didn't know what was happening. The man in the boat kept saying 'I can see it sinking'. Then I did see it sink. It went down bow first. The water crept up to the portholes, extinguishing the lights. When it went under it made a loud frightening noise. About eight hours later we were rescued by the liner *Carpathia*. My relatives thought I was dead, and when I got to my sister's house they were preparing for my funeral.

She told her family that there had been epithets about the pope on steel girders about the *Titanic*, written by the 'Orangemen' among the Belfast builders, but made no claims about seeing them herself.

Unlike other Irish survivors, Kate was not haunted by memories of *Titanic* and talked freely to those interested. She believed that she was spared for a reason and was intent on enjoying the years given to her after 1912. However, she never set foot on a ship again. Even when seeing off friends and family she would only ever go as far as the gangway. She died on 1 March 1971, aged 76. Her death certificate gave a date of birth at odds with Irish records (29 October 1895), making her 75 years old.

1911 census – Rhyne, Killoe, County Longford.
Hugh (46), farmer. Wife Johanna (44).
Married 18 years, ten children, nine surviving.
Mary (18), **Kate (17)**, Ellen (15), Thomas (14), Bridget (12),
Elizabeth (11), Margaret (9), Johanna (7), Hugh (5).

MARY AGATHA GLYNN (18) SAVED

Ticket number 335677. Paid £7 15s.
Boarded at Queenstown. Third Class.
From: Slievenore, Killaloe, County Clare.
Destination: 715 North Capital Street, Washington DC.

The *New York Herald* photographed Mary eight days after the disaster, attending a reunion of the rescued at the Irish Immigrant Aid Society on Seventh Street. She looked rather more dishevelled than her perfectly composed studio portrait.

In an interview at that time she declared:

Everybody on the vessel seemed to be interested in the fact that the *Titanic* was going to make the distance across the Atlantic in a fast time. Sunday night, only a few hours before the collision with the iceberg, it became very warm in the steerage, so warm that we asked the sailors what was wrong. We were told the ship's engines and boilers were being pushed for all they were worth and that the ship was making the best time of her maiden voyage.

Her room was below decks, close to the engine room, and earlier in the voyage she had sat in her cabin with her coat on for warmth. But on the Sunday evening it was so warm that she and her companions discarded every piece of excess clothing they could.

Mary Agatha roomed aboard the vessel with Julia Smyth, the younger Kate Connolly and Mary McGovern, all of whom may have been rescued in the same boat, believed launched from the starboard side dangerously late in the night. Accounts from the three other women seem to put them in a starboard boat, probably No. 13. Mary Agatha Glynn was certainly saved in No. 13 and she remembered pulling in one of her companions. She also remembered a man standing up to urgently cut the lifeboat falls as another boat (No. 15) threatened to come down on top of them. Their boat landed 'flatly' on the ocean, and they got away. Mary had an added reason for the terror felt by almost everyone – she was acutely conscious that she could not swim.

She and her cabin mates were among a group saved by Martin Gallagher. He had rushed from his own quarters at the bows of the ship to alert the ladies at the stern. Unlike Mary Glynn and the other women, however, Gallagher was fated by his sex to drown. Mary said that she and her friends had knelt on the steerage deck and begun to pray before Gallagher had found them there and took them up a private stairway to the second cabin. Here he ushered them to No. 13. Mary said she saw Martin fingering his Rosary beads in prayer as the boat was lowered. She also heard barking dogs, 'neighing horses' and the sweet strains of the orchestra rising above an overpowering soundscape.

Mary remembered pulling at an oar in the boat and later claimed a man had been found hiding below who was wrapped in a cloth and wearing 'articles of clothing sufficient to pass himself off as a woman' – a suggestion echoed by Julia Smyth who was in the same

boat and felt him to be an Irishman. The man, claimed Mary subsequently, had a towel wrapped around his head and had used nail scissors in an optimistic or desperate bid to help sever the lifeboat falls. It seems this 'woman' of No. 13 might have been Edward Ryan, who admitted to using a towel like a shawl.

One of the crewmen in No. 13, she said, at one stage asked a woman with a baby to keep the infant warm under her coat while giving him the baby's woollen garment so it could be set alight as a flare for keeping the boats together.

She always believed she had heard 'Nearer My God to Thee' and recalled that as the long hours of darkness gave way to dawn she saw proof that the world was round by smoke appearing over the horizon, followed by stacks, and then the entire form of the *Carpathia*. Bizarrely, she also claimed in later years to have seen whales blowing spray in the area where the *Titanic* foundered, as well as sharks feeding on bodies and deckchair pillows alike.

On her safe arrival in New York, Mary was aided by the American Red Cross to the tune of $50 (case No. 156), and also received a gratuity of $125 from the immigrant aid society.

Clare girl saved
A telegram received in Ennis on Friday states that the girl, Mary Glynn, who was a passenger by the *Titanic*, has been saved.

(*Clare Journal*, 22 April 1912)

Mary continued her journey to Washington DC after its unexpected interruption. following her convalescence in hospital. She left behind in the wards a woman named Margaret Mannion, the deeply shocked fiancée of Martin Gallagher.

In 1914 Mary met a 26-year-old Washington streetcar conductor named Patrick O'Donoghue from Knocknagoshel, County Kerry, who had come out a number of years earlier. They were married in 1917 and remained in the capital for many years.

Mary Agatha Glynn O'Donoghue died in St Petersburg, Florida, on 26 February 1955. She was 61 and is buried in Fort Lincoln Cemetery, Washington DC. Husband Patrick died a year later.

KATE HARGADON (17) LOST

Ticket number 30631. Paid £7 14s 8d.
Boarded at Queenstown. Third Class.
From: Ballisodare, County Sligo.
Destination: 133 West 126th Street, New York city.

Suffering from seasickness the whole voyage, Kate Hargadon died because she did not feel strong enough to climb a vertical crew ladder to the boat deck. Kate's friend Mary Burns stayed to help her and was also drowned.

Margaret Devaney later provided two different versions of what happened that night to Kate Hargadon. One version stated that the three girls were with Margaret, making their way up from the lower decks, when the latter went ahead to find a boat at about 1 a.m. She was pushed into lifeboat No. 12 and never got a chance to go back for her friends.

Devaney later told a slightly different version to the *Irish World* newspaper of 4 May 1912:

There were four of us from Knocknarae, County Sligo – Mary Burns and Kitty Hargadon and a boy we knew. We were all up on deck, not thinking it was serious, when the boy comes along and said: 'You girls had better get into a boat.' Then he held out his hand saying, 'I hope we'll meet again'. I got into the boat, but Mary Burns and Kitty Hargadon held back, thinking it was safer to remain on the ship. I never saw them again.

Seventeen-year-old Kate had been going to America to stay with a sister in New York. The American Red Cross, in its 1913 report on aid to those affected by the disaster, reported case No. 174:

Irish Girl, 19 years of age, coming to a sister in New York and to work at domestic service, was lost, leaving dependent parents and two delicate sisters in Ireland. The sister in New York had provided $63 for the passage, expecting to be reimbursed and to have help in supporting the family in Ireland. The committee gave the sister $100, of which $40 was sent to Ireland for emergent relief. The English committee later gave £40 to the family.

1901 census – Hargadon, Ballintogher West, Ballisodare. Patrick (37), farmer; Mary, wife (40). Children: Mary Ann (11), Bee (11), Maggie (8), **Kate (6)**.

HENRY HART (28) LOST

Ticket number 394140. Paid £6 17s 2d.
Boarded at Queenstown. Third Class.
From: Drumiskabole, County Sligo.
Destination: West Newton, Massachusetts.

Henry Hart had already made it big in the United States. He had a comfortable job as coachman for shipping and sugar magnate E. F. Atkins of Concord Avenue, in Belmont, Massachusetts. Henry's wife was Bridget (Delia) McGillycuddy, another servant at the Atkins estate in Massachusetts, who was originally from Killorglin, County Kerry. The two employees were married in America on 30 July 1911, in a ceremony at the town clerk's office. When Bridget fell pregnant, the couple decided to travel home to Ireland for the birth.

Henry was originally from Drumiskabole, Sligo, but the expectant couple moved in with Bridget's parents, Dennis and Bridget (née Fahy), on their arrival back in Ireland in spring 1912. It appears that Henry was subsequently summoned back to America before the birth could take place. After he was drowned on the return journey, Bridget gave birth to a son whom she named Henry after the father he would never know. They lived in Killorglin, where Henry Jnr is now buried.

According to the report of the American Senate into the disaster, Henry was travelling to join one John Hart, likely a brother, with an address at PO Box 307, Marion, Massachusetts. He had been originally booked on the *Celtic*, which arrived on 20 April 1912, with his name scored out in the passenger manifest. In this listing, he gives next of kin as his sister Marie in West Newton, Massachusetts.

On board the *Titanic* Henry appears to have joined up with a group including Margaret Devaney, Mary Burns and Kitty Hargadon. Devaney told the *Irish News* that the women and 'a boy we knew' made up four passengers from the same area of Knocknarae, County Sligo.'

The *Belmont Tribune* of Massachusetts declared on 4 May 1912:

Bridget and Henry Jnr

> It is reported on good authority that Mr Henry Hart, formerly employed by Mr E. F. Atkins of this town, was one of the unfortunates who went down in the ill-fated *Titanic*. Mr Hart was married while residing in Belmont and went to Ireland with his young bride.
>   He was returning to this country alone, according to the report, and was unlucky enough to take passage on the *Titanic*'s first trip.

Could there have been a serious marital disagreement that resulted in Henry leaving before his child was born? It seems unlikely given the devotion which saw Henry Jnr named after his father. Henry Snr was born in 1883 to Michael Hart and his wife Mary (née Cunningham) of Sligo.

NORA HEALY (34) SAVED

Ticket number 370375. Paid £7 15s.
Boarded at Queenstown. Third Class.
From: Greethill, Athenry, County Galway.
Destination: 284 St Nicholas Avenue, New York city.

Nora Healy went insane from her experiences on the *Titanic*. Although saved, a slow descent into madness began to claim her life and within a short time she could not even recognise her own father. Her rational, sentient existence was over long before her death on 11 March 1919, less than seven years after the sinking.

It seems Nora was saved on lifeboat No. 16, the last means of escape on the port side for the steerage passengers struggling to board the craft. In fact there were two boats yet to leave, unseen in the darkness at the far end of the forward deck. Boat No. 16 appears to have been a site of trouble, yet escaped any real focus at both the American and British inquiries. Some of its occupants were severely traumatised, including Nora Healy and Annie Kate Kelly.

Nora had been on her way to an aunt, Mrs W. Robinson, but there is no evidence she ever got there. Taken off the *Carpathia* in a state of deep shock, she was in no position to meet her aunt or her waiting cousin Anne Kearney from 4324 Broadway. Immigration officials, attempting to somehow conform to normal procedures, recorded her as a 24-year-old maid, although she was in fact ten years older. Mysteriously, her landing details were later expunged from the records, indicating that she might not have had any official status during her stay in America.

There is evidence that she was treated for some time before being transferred back to Ireland. Taken back to her home place, her unbalanced senses became gripped with some kind of recognition, until she ran to the arms of a well-wisher neighbour, pronouncing him to be her father.

Nora, whom neighbour and fellow *Titanic* passenger Andy Keane had always regarded as 'slightly touched', even before she boarded the White Star leviathan, showed no signs of familiarity with her old homestead, nor any spark of empathy with her family. The shattered Healys initially hoped that all she needed was love and time for healing, but instead she grew more withdrawn and darkly suspicious that tricks were being played upon her. The family finally bowed to the inevitable and she was admitted to St Brigid's psychiatric hospital in Ballinasloe on 9 July 1914.

She ended up a forgotten victim of the *Titanic*, one of the 'living dead', with something in her brain having broken forever on that icy night in April. On her death in 1919 her remains were taken from the echoing wards of Ballinasloe to lie in Wilmount Cemetery in Athenry with other members of the family.

Nora was born Honor Healy on 6 February 1883. Her parents were Thomas and Mary. In the 1901 census, the family is shown as follows:

Thomas (60), farmer. Mary (52), wife.
Children Margaret (29), Mary (27), John (25), **Honor (23)**, Catherine (18), Patrick (16), Ellen (14).

NORA HEGARTY (20) LOST

Ticket number 365226. Paid £6 15s.
Boarded at Queenstown. Third Class.
From: Killavallig, Whitechurch, County Cork.
Destination: 41 Washington Street, Charlestown, Massachusetts.

Nora and her cousin Jeremiah Burke were both due to stay at the rooming house of a Mrs Burns in Charlestown. But although they were travelling to a new life together, they were shortly due to separate as Nora had decided to join an order of nuns in Boston. In fact it may have been her religious devotion that inadvertently led to her death. Many Third-Class passengers understandably sought the succour of prayer and the protection of

priests during the terrible moments as the *Titanic* descended into a Dante's Hell.

Nora and Jeremiah travelled to Queenstown together and died together in the bone-piercing cold of the North Atlantic. Neither body was ever found. The couple had both been due to sail to America on the 7 April crossing of the *Cymric*.

Nora was the third eldest of seven children. Her parents, Laurence and Mary, were not well off, and when her father was granted administration of his late daughter's estate on 18 September 1912, the remaining effects of poor Nora were worth just £10.

More Cork victims
The sympathy of the people of Cork will go out in full measure to the parents of Miss Nora Hegarty of Killavallig, Whitechurch, and Mr Jeremiah Burke, of Upper Glanmire, both of whom were only 19 years of age and who lost their lives in the *Titanic* disaster.

(*The Cork Examiner*, 27 April 1912: for the full story see Jeremiah Burke)

1901 census – Hegarty, Killaverrig.
Parents: Laurence (50) and Mary (41).
Children: Kate (13), Willie (11), **Norah (19)**, Mary (8), Hannah (6), Maggie (5), Timothy (2).

DELIA HENRY (21) LOST

Ticket number 382649. Paid £7 15s.
Boarded at Queenstown. Third Class.
From: Togher, Clonown, Athlone, County Westmeath.
Destination: Boston.

Drowning ran in the Henry family. Delia's father, Patrick, died in the same manner as his daughter, three years before the *Titanic* sailed. He lost his life in the River Shannon a little distance from the family home in Togher, Athlone, in circumstances that are now unclear. The loss of a husband and daughter in such a short time for Margaret Henry can only have been devastating.

Delia, baptised Bridget, was one of eight children. She appears to have been aged around 21, but was entered as age 23 on the *Titanic* manifest, having joined a large group from the Athlone area who were travelling out together. But she appears to have had severe misgivings about the trip, according to a letter sent to her aunt, Ms M. S. Curley, in Boston:

Friday 5th. Clonoun, Athlone, Ireland.

My Dear Aunt,

Just a line to let you know that I am to leave Athlone, Wednesday 10th April. Will be sailing 11 April. I hope to God that we will get there all right. The ship is supposed to go in four and a half days. I hope you do have this small note, hoping to meet soon with God's help.

It was a great disappointment over that Miss Mee, as she could not get to come, but there is some people going from Athlone. We must put our trust in God, he is the best.

Dear Aunt, I know sister Lizzie will feel bad to know that I did not pick up with anyone from home, for the way it is at home with the people is all to Boston they do go to. But I hope to God I do get there all right.

Well Dear Aunt, this is the name of the boat, *Titanic*, I am going on. I hope you do meet. I will wear a black coat and skirt and black hat with black and white ribbon on it.

I close with best love to you all from your fond niece,

Delia Henry.

Delia never wore her distinctive arrival bonnet with the black and white ribbon. Maggie Daly, one of her Athlone companions, later wrote in a letter home: 'That little girl from Summerhill (Delia Henry) and that Connaughton boy (Athlone), and I think Mrs Rice and her five boys perished.'

Delia appears to have been small in stature, for the same phrase of 'the little Summerhill girl' is also used in describing her in another letter home by an Athlone survivor, Bertha Mulvihill. Bertha wrote to her sister Maud from the *Carpathia*: 'The little Summerhill girl is gone down, unless she is picked up by some ship that we don't know of.' Delia appears to have been something of a mascot among the Athlone contingent.

Irish passengers, Athlone, Tuesday
The loss of the *Titanic* has created consternation in this district. Inquiries at the booking office supply the information that there were more local bookings for the *Titanic* than on any other occasion this season. These were all steerage passengers, from Mayo and Roscommon. From Athlone town there were eleven passengers.

(*The Cork Examiner*, 17 April 1912)

Delia's letter to her aunt was brought back to Ireland in 1912 by her sister Lizzie who had been staying in Boston when it arrived. Lizzie also returned with a suggestion that Delia had been seen on deck saying the Rosary at the time of the sinking.

1901 census – Cloonown, just inside County Roscommon.
Patrick (40), farmer. Margaret (38), housekeeper.
Eliza (15), Edward (14), Mary (12), **Bridget (Delia, 10)**, Margaret (9), Thomas (8), Nannie (5), Patrick (2).

'JOHN HORGAN' LOST

Ticket number 370377. Paid £7 15s.
Boarded at Queenstown. Third Class.
From: Cork/Limerick?
Destination: New York.

The 'Quiet Man' could be applied to John Horgan, whose name appears on the embarkation records for the *Titanic*, but whose disappearance led to not a single newspaper reference, nor any legal action against the Oceanic Steam Navigation Company, nor any charitable disbursement, nor even a death notice nor a legal move for administration of his estate.

John Horgan certainly existed – but whether he embarked on the *Titanic*, or was replaced by someone using his ticket, is another matter. It will remain a mystery while Horgan's own origins remain unclear.

What is known is that John Horgan was listed to sail on the *Cymric*, from Queenstown, on Easter Sunday, 7 April 1912. He did not board that vessel – instead all of those booked aboard were transferred to the *Titanic* when the *Cymric* did not sail.

A man called 'John Horgan' did board the *Titanic* on Thursday 11 April 1912. Later, in listing the Irish victims, the *Irish World* in New York referred to Horgan as being from County Limerick. It is also true that he came to the *Titanic* at Queenstown in the company of six other passengers from County Limerick. They were among the last to board, and it is known that the connecting train from Cork to Queenstown was late arriving at Deepwater Quay on that day. But it is also possible that John Horgan might have sold his ticket and this would explain the lack of newspaper references to anyone mourning his passing.

It is known that William O'Doherty, a Cork publican, bought the ticket assigned to a James Moran, and died in the disaster in the latter's name. O'Doherty was friends with another tavern worker, 19-year-old Timothy O'Brien, whom the Cork newspapers also insisted had gone down on the *Titanic*. But Timothy O'Brien does not appear on the list of passengers. Is it possible that he followed his friend O'Doherty's example and bought his ticket from John Horgan? *The Cork Examiner* of 17 April 1912, in a section headed 'Believed Passengers', referred to 'William Doherty [*sic*], 12 Old Market Place, employed by Messrs W. F. O'Callaghan, Daunt's Square, and Timothy O'Brien, billiard marker at the Oyster Tavern'. The rival *Cork Constitution* newspaper made the same pairing in the same day's edition.

The Mansion House relief fund does not list John Horgan among its Irish cases in a March 1913 report, but mentions a claimant mother of the surname Landers. It may be that Horgan sold to O'Brien, who in turn sold to Landers, but the case is mysterious. Daniel Landers of Castletown Conyers, County Limerick, is a likely candidate – most of his siblings had preceded him to New York.

ANNIE JERMYN (26) SAVED

Ticket number 14313. Paid £7 15s.
Boarded at Queenstown. Third Class.
From: Dereenaclough, Ballydehob, County Cork.
Destination: East Lynn, Massachusetts.

Assisted into collapsible D, the last boat to be launched from the davits at around 2 a.m. on the morning of 15 April 1912, Annie Jermyn must have been terrified by the swamping sea now visibly dragging the *Titanic* nose-first to her watery consummation.

Amidst the green glow of the water swallowing rank on rank of portholes, the fury of men's desperate last actions and the tumult of grief and panic, Annie Jermyn may not even have known that her saviour was Bridget Driscoll, who eased her into the boat to safety. Bridget and Annie had travelled together from Ballydehob, County Cork, to the Devil's Hole off the Grand Banks of Newfoundland, but instead of cementing their comradeship, the *Titanic* drove them apart.

Bridget Driscoll never saw Annie Jermyn again after the numbed and bedraggled survivors landed at New York three days later like so much storm-tossed flotsam. Both were treated by the American Red Cross, but Annie's movements later faded into obscurity – cloaked by her abrupt decision to disappear from her family in the United States with a man they regarded as an unsavoury character.

The entire family emigrated to the United States in the immediate aftermath of Annie's brush with death. Thomas Jermyn, her brother, died in Massachusetts in October 1965. Annie had been travelling to stay with her married sister, Mary Grace Draper, who was aged 29 and already living in Lynn, Massachusetts, where a local newspaper reported:

Survivor of Titanic *in Lynn Home*
Miss Annie Jermyn, sister of Mrs May Draper, of 21 Webster Street, and who is a survivor of the ill-fated steamer *Titanic*, arrived in this city Monday evening in company with Richard W. Draper, her brother-in-law … Mrs Draper had given up all hope of ever seeing her sister again. News came Saturday that she had been saved and was in St Vincent's Hospital, New York city.

Sunday, Mr Draper left for New York, met Miss Jermyn at the hospital and assisted her to this city, where she is to make her home with her sister, at 21 Webster Street. This was the first time that they had met each other in many years, and the meeting was a happy one. Miss Jermyn was in a very nervous condition.

Only immediate relatives of the young woman were allowed to see her. She immediately took to her bed and will probably be confined there for a week or so.

Mrs Draper says that her sister made but little talk of the disaster, evidently wanting to forget the terrible scenes of the night of horror when she made her hasty escape from the vessel. Miss Jermyn is unable to account for the exact cause of the injuries she received to her stomach, but believes that they must have been caused while getting into the lifeboat. She comes from County Cork, Ireland.

Annie Jermyn, back row, third from left

Audrey Carlton Sampson tells the subsequent story of this survivor. Audrey says her mother, Susan Sophia, known as Sophie, worried for years about what ever became of her sister Annie – whom the family always called 'Nancy'. Sophie told her daughter that 'Nancy' had lived with her own parents, Henry and Susan Jermyn, for a short time after they came to settle in the US, immediately after the disaster. But Annie – or 'Nancy' – became involved with 'a character the family didn't like' and suddenly vanished with him, losing all contact with the family.

The estrangement was a lasting one, and it is not known if Nancy later married her unsuitable suitor. Henry and Susan settled in Peabody, Massachusetts and lived in a big house on Carlton Street. Henry died there in 1930. Four years later, his widow, Susan Connell Jermyn, went for a one-day visit to the home of her son Harry in Lynn, Massachusetts, only to fall ill and die suddenly.

It was at this time that another of the sisters, Elizabeth Jermyn Hurd (also called Bessie or Betty), decided to try to find 'Nancy'. She went to great effort and was successful in locating Nancy, who at that time, 1934, was living in New Jersey. But Nancy, perhaps still smarting from the sting of parental disapproval, refused to return for her mother's funeral and was never again seen by the family. Alienated in turn, some members of the Jermyn family told their children that their Aunt Nancy had been drowned on the *Titanic*. It was easier than telling them the painful truth.

Annie Jermyn had been born on 13 July 1885 into what appears to have been a prosperous Church of Ireland family – one that brought forth ten children over twenty years. Aged 26 when the *Titanic* sailed, she was in the company of Bridget Driscoll and Westmeath woman Mary Kelly, the trio buying sequential tickets at the Ballydehob shipping agency in West Cork.

1901 census – Jermyn. Dereenaclough, Ballydehob, County Cork.
Parents: Henry (45), Susan (44).
Children: Mary Grace (19), Richard (17), **Annie Jane (15)**, James (14), Henry (11), John Willie (8), Lizzie (6), Thomas Michael (3), Susan Sophia (1).

HENRY FORBES JULIAN (50) LOST

Ticket number 110344. Paid £26.
Boarded at Southampton. First Class.
From: Torquay, Devon.
Destination: San Francisco.

A thoroughly English gentleman, Henry Forbes Julian happened to have been born in Cork city on 9 May 1861. He was the son of a coachbuilder and his wife, Marie. He began his schooling in Cork, but the family soon relocated to Little Bolton, Lancashire. There is no evidence that Henry spent any time in Ireland for more than thirty years before the *Titanic* sailed.

He married in 1895, by which time he was a metallurgical engineer and a consultant to mines in South Africa and Germany. He was an extensive traveller, having also visited the West Indies, Mexico, Canada and the United States, having crossed the Atlantic thirteen times in the process.

Trip number fourteen was the unlucky one. His wife, Hester, was saved by a bout of flu which meant she could not join him on his journey to do business in California. The couple lived at 'Redholme', 62 Braddons Hill Road East, Torquay. Henry was a founder of the Royal Automobile Club.

ANDY KEANE (23) LOST

Ticket number 12460. Paid £7 15s.
Boarded at Queenstown. Third Class.
From: Tobberoe, Derrydonnell, Athenry, County Galway.
Destination: 162 Melrose Street, Auburndale, Massachusetts.

Andy Keane was one of three brothers who were local sports stars. He and his brothers, Pat and Mike, were the backbone of the Derrydonnell hurling team, winners of the club championship for all of County Galway in the years 1909 and 1911. A former treasurer of Derrydonnell, Andy played in the championship final at Tuam on 26 November 1911, when special trains were laid on to carry supporters to the venue. Derrydonnell scored three second-half goals to beat Claregalway by a good margin.

Andy decided to leave Ireland and the team just months later, because his two sisters, Mary-Anne and Ellie, who were already in the United States along with his brother John, sent over the money for his passage. Both girls returned home for good in the wake of the sinking. Buying his ticket at Mahon's shop in Athenry, Andy signed aboard the *Titanic* as an agricultural labourer, giving his age as 23. He knew a near neighbour, Nora Healy, was also travelling on the vessel but was anxious to avoid her. He considered Nora 'a bit touched'. He joked with his brothers that if he met her on board he would pretend he had never encountered her in his life before.

Andy packed his championship hurling medals, a dozen hurleys and a melodeon in his baggage. He was due to stay in America at the address of his brother John Keane, two years older, who had established his home in the small town of Auburndale, Massachusetts. Andy might also have decided to become an emigrant because his father had recently died, leaving older brother Patrick (26) to inherit the family farm.

There were eleven children in the family, six boys and five girls, and while the 120-acre farm was large, Andy evidently decided his fortune lay elsewhere.

Report of the American Red Cross (Titanic Disaster) 1913:
No. 232. (Irish.) A farmer, twenty years of age, was drowned, leaving dependent his widowed mother and four younger children in Ireland. This Committee gave $100 to the mother for emergent relief. The case was referred to the English Committee, which made a grant of £25. ($100)

A solemn Requiem Mass was said in Andy's honour in the parish church, Athenry, in July 1912, celebrated by Canon Canton, PP, and attended by Gaelic games enthusiasts, team mates, and representatives of clubs from all over County Galway. At the county convention later in the year, the board presented a portrait of the deceased to his brother Patrick.

1911 census – Keane family, Tobberoe, Athenry.
Head: Norah Keane (61), widow.
Children: Patrick (26), labourer, **Andrew (22)**, labourer, single, Michael (20), Mary Anne (18), Martin (15), Thomas (9).

DANIEL KEANE (35) LOST

Ticket number 233734. Paid £12 7s.
Boarded at Queenstown. Second Class.
From: Gallowshill, Cratloe, County Clare.
Destination: St Louis, Missouri.

One of the few Irish Second-Class passengers, Daniel Keane clearly decided to travel in comfort on his voyage to America. Indeed, he was considered rather rich in his home place

and eyebrows were raised at the abandonment of a valuable bicycle, which he had grandly left behind at his sister Bridget King's house. It was not the only commodity he forswore in Ireland, for his estate subsequently amounted to £145, a large sum indeed when many of the Irish victims of the disaster left only a handful of pounds.

'He was going to America to get a job. He had a belt around his stomach made of all sovereigns,' said his grandniece Ita Cusack. 'The night before he left, he attended a farewell party and dance at his sister's house.'

Before he decided to seek pastures new, Keane had been living in Dublin and working as a tram conductor on the Donnybrook–Phoenix Park line. He lived in lodgings in Marlboro Road, Donnybrook, close to the terminus of the No. 59 tram. He appears in No. 4 Marlboro Road in the 1911 census, where he is described as a 34-year-old tram conductor, single, from County Clare. Keane was boarding with the Gaffney family, and his fellow tenants include a motor man, a carpenter and a lacemaker.

Dublin Passengers
It is stated that there were four Second-Class passengers booked from Dublin at Messrs Cook's offices. Two women who called at noon yesterday to make enquiries bore marked traces of the grief and anxiety that they were suffering.

One of the four passengers booked from Dublin was Daniel Kane [*sic*], who, up to the time of his leaving Ireland, was employed as a tramway car conductor on the Donnybrook line.

He is a County Clare man and lived in lodgings in Marlborough Road, Donnybrook.
Irish Independent, 18 April 1912

Daniel was born on 25 June 1876, and was aged 35 when the *Titanic* sailed. Administration of the estate of Daniel Keane, late of 4 Marlboro Road, Donnybrook, Dublin and Gallowshill, Cratloe, County Clare, tram conductor, who died on 14 April 1912 at sea off the coast of North America, was granted at Limerick to Honoria Keane, widow.

The papers show that Mrs Keane could neither read nor write. Solicitor R. Frost wrote that her affidavit had been 'first read and explained, she being illiterate, and she seemed to understand same and made her mark thereto'.

NORA KEANE (46) SAVED

Ticket number 226593. Paid £12 7s.
Boarded at Queenstown. Second Class.
From: Gardenhill, Castleconnell, County Limerick.
Destination: 167 Paxton Street, Harrisburg, Pennsylvania.

A corset nearly got in the way of Nora Keane saving her own life. She was wasting so much time as she fumbled to put it on and lace it up that it became the object of a dispute with her travelling companion, Edwina Troutt. When Edwina returned to her cabin, one woman, Susie Webber, had already left. The other, Nora, was still dressing. Having replaced her dressing-gown with a warmer coat, Edwina dealt with the nervous Irishwoman. When Nora insisted on trying to put on a corset, Edwina grabbed it from her and sent it flying down the narrow passage leading to the porthole. Interestingly a similar confrontation over a corset is played out in the James Cameron movie *Titanic*. Edwina could not believe that Nora could put her life at risk over a foolish item of clothing at the height of a sinking.

The three women had been sharing compartment 101 on E deck aft. Edwina Celia Troutt (27) was from Bath, heading back to a sister in Massachusetts. Susie Webber (37) was from Devon, bound for Hartford, Connecticut. Both also survived. Edwina lived to be 100, dying in December 1984, while Susan Webber died in 1952 at the age of 77.

Edwina later recounted how their Irish companion, Nora Keane from Castleconnell, had undergone a sudden premonition that the *Titanic* would sink when boarding at Queenstown, speaking openly of her fears when the vessel was barely underway. It is one of a number of verified incidents of foreboding and one of the most chilling – Edwina later claimed that Nora told her she was so overcome with sudden dread as she tottered towards the towering *Titanic* that she dropped her Rosary and prayer book into the water as she was going up the gangway from a tender that had brought mainly Third-Class Irish passengers from Deepwater Quay.

Another member of the women's cabin had a story of foreboding to share: Nellie Hocking, a 21-year-old girl from Cornwall. Edwina later recounted how Nellie put the fear of God into Nora Keane by telling her how she had heard a cock-crow on the *Titanic* at dusk on the fateful Sunday. Hearing such a cry while travelling on a journey is viewed as an ill omen in Cornish custom. Nora told the unnerving story to Edwina, who laughed it off. But Nellie had not been imagining things – there was a live rooster and other poultry on the *Titanic*. First-Class passengers Marie Grice and Ella Holmes White were importing a clutch of French chickens to the United States.

Nora was on her way back to Harrisburg, Pennsylvania, where she and her brother ran the Union Hotel on Paxton Street.

She told her story to a local paper:

MISS KEANE HOME; HER COMPLETE STORY
Survivor of Wreck tells how Ship Sank as those in Boats looked on – Drifted Eight Hours in
Darkness and Cold before Aid Came

Miss Nora Keane, the only resident of this city who was aboard the *Titanic* when it was wrecked off the Newfoundland banks, arrived home at 7.10 o'clock last evening. She was accompanied by her brothers and their wives who met her at the Cunard line pier where the *Carpathia* docked Thursday evening at 9.15. Last night she told to *The Patriot* all the details of her terrible experience, from the time the giant ship first struck the iceberg until she was gathered into the arms of her four big brothers on the New York dock.

'It was terrible that wreck … I felt a slight shock a little time before they came. I thought nothing of it. No person had any idea that the vessel was hurt. Even after we were told to get ready we didn't think there was any danger, for we had been told that the ship could not sink – that it was unsinkable. People had told me that it was an impossibility for it to go down. I went on deck with other persons. The officers had perfect control of everything. There was some excitement amongst some of the people but not what you would expect under the circumstances.

'Officers called out just who were to go in the boats. I was fortunate to get out in the fourth or fifth boat that left. The crew showed every courtesy in lowering the women and children into the boats. The men passengers stood back. Without doubt, they sacrificed their lives to give women and children the preference … There was a foreigner of some kind ran from some part of the ship and jumped into our boat. No one saw him go. When we got into the boat, we tramped over him for some time but didn't see him or even know we were stepping on a human form.

'Later he proved of great use. He could handle the boat. After we rowed away from the ship, we learned that he was in the boat and asked him if we hurt him when we walked over him. He said, "No, still living." The boat had but one sailor in it and this man came in very useful in helping us work the boat. He did good work … Two men floated by us. Both of them had life preservers. One of them drooped low in the water. He did not call. The other called to us: "Take me on." It was almost an impossibility to do anything. Our boat barely floated. "Goodbye," the man in the water called. Then his head went down a little later. He disappeared out of sight. That was the case with many others. It was [a] terrible sight to witness. It cannot be forgotten. The sight of men in the sea was awful.'

From the lifeboat, Nora saw the *Titanic* go down. 'The ship seemed to go down forward and raise to an awful height, all at once. There was a roar and a deafening sound. The cries and moans of those passengers and crew in the water were awful. Very soon there was nothing seen or heard. The ship went down about 100 yards from where our boat was. Bodies drifted past us. Pieces of the wreck were around.

'And that band played, I don't know how the men did it, while we were getting on the boats. It played when we drifted away. Men jumped into the sea but the band played. Some of them must have stood in water that was then over that part of the deck while they played, for we were on nearly the same level with the deck then.

'They played *Nearer My God to Thee* till the ship rose and they went out of sight. They must have been playing when it went down,' said Nora.

Nora and the 704 other survivors were picked up by the *Carpathia* about daybreak. And it was *The Patriot* which told her brothers in Harrisburg that she was safe, having previously reported their anxiety about her.

At 9.15 a.m. on 18 April, the *Carpathia* docked in New York where Nora was met by her brothers, Dennis, William, Patrick and John Keane.

Nora then returned to Harrisburg where she had made her home with another brother, Michael, who had a hotel there.

(*The Patriot*, 20 April 1912)

The same newspaper the day before quoted Nora, in an account dictated to her brother Dennis, as saying that 'some shots were fired on the ship. People said men had been shot. I don't know who they were … it is so awful I cannot think of all that happened.'

Nora, who discreetly carved eleven years off her age when signing aboard the *Titanic*, had been born in 1866 to John Keane (1819–1885) and his wife Nora Fee (d. 1916) of Gardenhill, Castleconnell, Limerick. Nora later bought and managed a pub in Harrisburg, using money she received from an inheritance. The American Red Cross assisted her to the tune of $100.

Nora told her family back in Ireland little about the disaster. She said the other women in her cabin were woken up by stewards and told to leave the ship immediately. She was in the lifeboat all night, dressed only in her nightgown – *sans* corset of course – and strictly enjoined her nephews and nieces in later life: 'When they tell you to get off the boat, do what they say!'

She eventually returned to Ireland and died on 20 December 1944, at the County Infirmary in Limerick, aged 78. The cause of death was complications from a broken leg.

ANNIE KATE KELLY (20) SAVED

Ticket number 9234. Paid £7 15s.
Boarded at Queenstown. Third Class.
From: Cuilmullagh, Addergoole, County Mayo.
Destination: 303 Eugenie Street, Chicago.

Annie Kate made a pact with God. If He would save her from the apocalyptic slaughter about to be visited on the *Titanic*, she would dedicate her life to His service. Annie was saved, and, true to her word, became a Dominican nun.

Weeks earlier she had no such intentions, writing to her cousin in the Windy City: 'I am coming to America on the nicest ship in the world. And I am coming with some of the nicest people in the world, too. Isn't that just splendid? They live in Chicago and I shall be able to make the entire trip with them. They have told me all about Chicago, and I know I shall like it much better than I do Ireland.' But she was not able to make the entire trip with her friends.

Annie's account, as related to an American newspaper in 1912, is important because it contains a claim that steerage passengers were 'held back until the last moment'. Annie was one of a party of young people from the Lahardane area of County Mayo, and appears to have been one of the very last Irish passengers to be rescued:

The young girls would talk about what they would do in America before they were married. That is, they would talk about it when they were not scurrying around the deck laughing and making friends here and there with everybody and joking with the stewards, and it's a God's mercy that Annie Kelly did joke with one of the stewards or he take notice of the girl, or she would not have been alive this moment.

The weather was grand and the waves that washed against the great boat were smooth as smooth could be, and the night it all happened was a grand night, with the stars as bright as moons and the water as if oil had been poured over it.

It was cold, to be sure, but they were always warm because their hearts were gay, dancing and singing. In that part of the boat everybody must be in bed early. There was a grand ball upstairs in the first cabin, and that was why when the call came so many of the women up there had all their jewels on.

The call came to them, but late. I do not know how it was with the others, but Kate Burke could not sleep after the steward opened the door, nor could John her husband; nor Kate McGowan, nor Annie, her niece; nor Annie Kelly, nor nobody at all of those that came from Mayo, though they talked and talked and said to each other it was nothing.

Then somebody said, 'Let us tell the beads,' and they all got up and said the Rosary and their fear fell from them, and they went to bed again. The steward came again to them and said, 'All hands on deck. For God's sake, hurry if you would have a chance for your lives,' and then they went in their nightgowns, just as they were. The first thing they saw was the people being held back from going up the stairs to the second deck.

You see, it was feared, for the excitement they would cause to the people up there who were getting away in the lifeboats, and they held them back to the last moment.

About half an hour before the boat went down was the time they called the Burkes and the others from Mayo from their berths.

And here it was that the steward, to whom Annie Kelly had been talking so often, saw her running with the Burkes and Mary Mannion and the others towards the ladder that went up to the second deck. For then they were not letting the steerage passengers up the stairway, and he screamed, 'Miss Kelly, here's a chance for your life,' and took her by the hand and ran up the stairs without anyone stopping him, because then they were for letting all the people come up the stairs, and he called out to a boat that was just being sent away. 'Let this young girl go with you. You've got room. Let her in,' and they shoved Annie Kelly on the boat, in her nightgown …

Not a thing did Annie Kelly know when she was pulled over the side of the other boat, the *Carpathia*, at 5 o'clock in the morning, though they poured hot whiskey and raw brandy into her and buried her in blankets and hot water bottles, she was that frozen. It was noon before she came to herself and found herself in the hospital, with Annie McGowan there too, though how Annie McGowan came to be saved, she herself could not tell. She was young and swift as a deer, and when the call came for all to go on deck, she ran among the first to see what was the matter, and thus was saved.

But of poor John Burke and Kate, his wife, and jolly Kate McGowan and all the other light-hearted lads and lasses that started that day from Castlebar, save Annie Kelly and Annie McGowan, there will never be any more of them in this world, and may God rest their souls.

(*Chicago Record-Herald* interview with Annie Kate Kelly. Reprinted in the *Irish Independent*, May 1912, 'The Story of how fifteen Girls and Boys from the West of Ireland started for America on the *Titanic*, and how two of them arrived'.)

Annie was born on 14 January 1892 in Castlebar, and was 20 when the *Titanic* sailed, although she preferred to view herself as 17. Her parents were John Kelly and Ellen Flaherty, and despite her age appearing as 10 on the 1901 census, Annie told US immigration she was a 17-year-old 'helper'. She had been on her way to join her cousins Anna and Mary Garvey, who lived in Chicago.

Annie Kelly and Annie McGowan were released from St Vincent's Hospital in New York wearing the nightgowns in which they had escaped, donated shoes and coats. Dr Mary O'Brien, Porter of the Catholic Women's League, met them at Chicago train station and later appealed to that city's mayor to disburse some of the appeal funds to the pair.

The American Red Cross noted in relation to Annie Kelly:

No. 235. (Irish.) Girl, 17 years of age, lost clothing and $200 in cash and suffered permanent injury. Arrangements have been made for the suitable training of this girl, when health is sufficiently restored. ($400)

In 1922, having been unable to forget the anguished screams which accompanied the departure of the boats, before the screaming of the drowning had even begun, Annie Kelly took the veil and became a Dominican nun. Her nephew Paddy Flanagan said, 'She had made a pact with the Man above.' On her rare visits to Ireland, Paddy says, Annie always talked about the *Titanic* on the night before she had to cross the Atlantic again. She recounted how there had been dancing every night in Third Class, and she had gone to bed exhausted that Sunday night. She would have slept forever had her cabin not been roused by a steward.

Sister Patrick Joseph, Annie's religious name, taught in St Phillip Neri Grammar School at 72nd and Clyde Streets in Chicago. In later life, she suffered from arteriosclerosis, or hardening of the arteries, and died from this disease on 28 December 1969, in Adrian, Michigan. She was 78 years of age.

JAMES KELLY (45) LOST

Ticket number 330911. Paid £7 12s 4d, plus 4s extra.
Boarded at Queenstown. Third Class.
From: Leixlip, County Kildare.
Destination: New Haven, Connecticut.

Hardworking James Kelly had found it impossible to provide for his family by dint of the piecemeal agricultural labouring he could only occasionally come by in Ireland. In desperation, he and his wife, Kate, formed a plan – to evacuate the family to America. It would have to be done by degrees because of the family's finances, but the beginnings had already been made. Their eldest daughter, Margaret, emigrated to the United States in early 1911. Now she was paying the fare for her father to join her. His sweat in turn would pay for succeeding members of the clan – or that was the intention.

It all came to nought when James Kelly's body was taken from the unforgiving ocean by the *MacKay-Bennett* search vessel on 23 April. He was buried at sea in canvas sacking the following day.

Body No. 70. Male. Estimated age 34. Hair and moustache light.
Clothing – Dark suit, vest and trousers; white socks; black boots.
Effects – Beads, left on body; comb; knife.
No marks. Name – James Kelly.

Immediately after the sinking it had been reported:

New Haven girl's father on the Titanic; *may be among the lost*
Relatives of this city of James Kelly today fear that Mr Kelly is among the passengers who were lost by the sinking of the *Titanic* Sunday night. The fears regarding Mr Kelly are founded on the fact that in the list of passengers reported saved Mr Kelly's name does not appear. They are, however, hanging to a thread of hope that Mr Kelly has been saved.

James Kelly is a brother of John Kelly who is a machinist and works in the repair shops of the New Haven road in this city. A daughter … Margaret Kelly, employed at Strouse-Adler's corset shop … The rest of her immediate family are in Leixlip, County Kildare, Ireland.

Miss Kelly came to this country ahead of them. She went to work in the corset shop and when she saved up enough money … she bought a steamship ticket and forwarded it home to her father. The ticket called for Mr Kelly taking passage on the *Titanic* on 11 April. That is why Miss Kelly thinks that her father was on the ill-fated ship when she struck the berg and went down. The man supposed to have been lost is 40 years of age …
One ray of hope that Miss Kelly clings to is that the reports show that a greater number of people were saved from the steamship than was reported in the earlier news of the day.

The Kellys are certain that James Kelly took passage on the *Titanic*, for they received a letter from him saying that he received the tickets for his transportation and that he was coming over on the *Titanic*.

(*New Haven Register*, 16 April 1912)

The *New York Herald* reported on 24 April 1912:

> *New Haven Friends of James Kelly – Believe His Body is Found*
> New Haven, Connecticut, Tuesday – The James Keely, whose body was picked up at sea, and whose name appears in today's list of the *Titanic* victims, probably was James Kelly, who was on his way here to join relatives. He was in the steerage.

The death plunged the family at home into financial crisis as well as the deepest grief. Now Mrs Kelly had no breadwinner to enable her to feed the children, whereas before the family had just been able to manage. The Kellys were thrown 'onto the parish', as the following newspaper excerpts show:

> One of the applicants for relief at the Celbridge Guardians meeting yesterday was Mrs Kate Kelly of Leixlip, whose husband perished in the disaster. She has six young children. The application was referred to the treasurer of the relief committee.
> (*Irish Independent*, 4 May 1912)

> Husband Drowned in *Titanic*
> Mr Ronaldson again drew attention to the case of Mrs Kelly, Leixlip, whose husband was drowned in the *Titanic*. She was badly in need of relief. She had three children under age, who were doing nothing, and pending the receipt of some money from the Distress Fund she should get relief …
> Mrs Kelly came before the Board and said her husband was not working on the *Titanic*. Her sister [*sic*] was taking him out to America and he was a passenger on the boat.
> It was decided to give Mrs Kelly the sum of 4s per week as relief.
> (*Kildare Observer*, 18 May 1912)

The entire family later emigrated to America to join daughter Margaret and other relatives:

> *Report of the American Red Cross (Titanic Disaster) 1913:*
> No. 237. (Irish.) The husband, a steerage passenger, was drowned. He was coming to this country for the first time to join his eldest daughter Margaret, 20 years of age, who had been here two years working in a factory in a New England town. He planned to send for his wife and five younger children within a few months. The family had sold their possessions in Ireland, were in readiness to come to this country, and so decided to carry out the original plan. Margaret's employer volunteered to be responsible to the immigration authorities that the family should not become public charges, and they were admitted upon their arrival in June. This Committee advanced $625 to pay for the passage and to meet the expenses of establishing the new home. The two girls next younger than Margaret, aged 16 and 18 years, are now employed in the factory with their sister. The other three children, 13, 12 and 8 years old, are in school … From other relief sources the family received $2,718.58. ($2,150)

Margaret wept when her mother and five siblings finally arrived at Union Station, New

Haven. A huge crowd greeted the family, with banners saying 'Welcome – *Titanic* Kellys'. They had become unwilling celebrities.

Eldest son, Tom, a sergeant with the Connaught Rangers in India at the time of his father's death, described his grief in a 1915 letter to his sister May. Aged 26, he reflected that he had been in the army and away from home for eight years:

> Eight years ago, May, we were together – all of us happy, even tho' the times were bad. Now there is a vacant chair & the one we all loved so well is gone. But that is God's will; nevertheless the memory of our dearly beloved father is still fresh & we can't help but dwell on the time that he used to sing for us. How I remember those days & all the stories he used to tell us & how he loved us all.
>
> Tho I have refrained very much in my letters to Mother & Maggie from saying anything about our dear father, my grief was something beyond description. I was in India thousands of miles from my own people, but I had to bear up. But times I broke down & had to at last give away to my grief. You dear sisters are the first I have told this to, but I know I should have said something to Maggie. But poor Maggie. She was worse than I was & what could I say at the time to soften the grief that all of you must have been going through. No, I was too far away from you all to do any good, so I bore my grief alone …
>
> I am always your
> Loving Brother
> Thos. Kelly

Further anguish visited the family, however, when Tom was killed a year later without ever coming back to them. He died of wounds suffered in battle on Sunday 23 January 1916 in Mesopotamia. A military memorial in Basra, Iraq, bears his name.

At home in Ireland, in the absence of the Kellys, a grant of administration was made for the estate of the late James Kelly on 14 December 1912. He left effects worth just £10. A legal instrument noted:

> He owned no property at the time of his decease and the only claim which survives to his administrator, when appointed, is the claim against the owners of the *Titanic* for damages resulting from his death which must be prosecuted in the American courts.
>
> He left surviving the undersigned, his widow, and the following children, whose names and ages are hereto appended:
>
> Widow Kate Kelly, Age 44. Children Thomas Kelly, 22. William Kelly, 11. James Kelly, 8. Margaret Kelly, 20. Kate Kelly, 18. May Kelly, 16. Bridget Kelly, 14.

MARY KELLY (22) SAVED

Ticket number 14312. Paid £7 15s.
Boarded at Queenstown. Third Class.
From: Castlepollard, County Westmeath.
Destination: 113 West 15th Street, New York city.

Orphans saved from the *Titanic* by Mary Kelly created one of the abiding sensations of the tragedy. They were the '*Titanic* Waifs', two curly-haired French boys named Lolo and Momon, who found themselves alone and adrift in an open lifeboat with only a young Irish girl to comfort them with her crooning foreign tongue. The children were parentless only because their 32-year-old father, Michel Navratil, had stolen them from their mother Marcelle in a tug-of-love snatch from the south of France. Toddler Michel was aged three and his brother Edmond Roger only two. They were smuggled to Southampton where their father signed aboard under the name of Louis Hoffman.

When disaster struck, 'Hoffman' handed his two boys lovingly into the arms stretched out to receive them from collapsible D, the last boat lowered. It was near two o'clock now, and close to the end. Mary Kelly helped take them into the boat and then soothed them in their uncomprehending distress.

Mary Kelly was uniquely qualified to do so. A young girl who loved children, she was planning to have many of her own and was on her way to New York to marry the man of her dreams – boyfriend John Heslin from her home place who had travelled over to America some months earlier to prepare a place for them both.

Mary was a domestic and she hoped to get work in the big houses in New York, possibly as a nanny caring for the children of the gentry. With the French boys pressed tearfully to her skirts and bosom, she may have thought it was a little early to begin her calling, but that she needed the practice. When the children were landed safely aboard the *Carpathia*, a determined effort was made to discover who they were. But the shocked tots were incapable of telling. Eventually passengers who had known the father on board – he now floating dead in the Atlantic with a loaded revolver in his pocket – identified them by their false name, Hoffman.

Mary Kelly cared for her charges until they landed in New York, when the press had a field day. Eventually the tots were claimed as a near-trophy by First-Class passenger Margaret Hays, while feverish attempts were made to reunite them with their family. Eventually Marcelle Navratil came forward and the boys were on their way home.

Miss Kelly meanwhile had moved quietly on and into the arms of John Heslin, with a housewarming gift of $100 from the Red Cross. Not that it compensated for the loss of

Mary's wedding trousseau – the slew of beautiful presents from family and friends – which now lay at the bottom of the Atlantic. Mary and John went on to marry within a year and to have six children. Mary told them that she escaped from steerage because a crewmember showed her a way to the upper decks through an airshaft or ventilation chamber. She died in her home at Coney Island Avenue, Brooklyn, two days after Christmas 1950. She was 60 years of age.

> 1911 census – Kelly, Packenhamhall Street, Castlepollard.
> Mary (48), mother, widow.
> Children at home – John (16), Edward (14), Bridget (11) and Margaret (9).

JOHN KENNEDY (20) SAVED

Ticket number 368783. Paid £7 15s.
Boarded at Queenstown. Third Class.
From: 1 Rosemary Place, Limerick city.
Destination: 29 Perry Street, New York city.

John Kennedy survived a brush with death on the *Titanic*, only for a shaving brush to bring him death six years later. He succumbed to deadly anthrax poisoning in 1918, having been drafted into the United States Army for the First World War. The highly communicable bacillus, which lives in the hair and hide of animals, was believed to have been picked up from his shaving brush while in basic training in Camp Hancock, Georgia. He had been in boot camp for only a few weeks when boils surrounded his mouth and face. Within days he was dead, expiring on 9 June 1918, one month and four days after his induction. The remains of machine-gunner Kennedy were placed in a sealed coffin and sent home to his brother in Brooklyn.

It was not what Kennedy had envisaged for himself on his twentieth birthday, 11 April 1912, when he boarded the *Titanic* at Queenstown. He had been a humble picture framer by occupation in Ireland, and hoped for new opportunities through emigration to the United States. His brother Michael had already transplanted himself there and had written glowingly of the chances for improvement to be found in the United States. So John bade farewell to his ageing parents, Thomas (64) and Mary (61), kissing his 21-year-old sister Ellen goodbye as he packed for the trip to Queenstown by rail. The train from Limerick, via Cork, brought him to the very water's edge at Deepwater Quay, where tenders were waiting to take this latest herd of humanity to their emigrant vessel.

How John Kennedy escaped from the *Titanic* remains a mystery, although he somehow gained access to one of the early lifeboats – probably one of those on the starboard side (one of the odd-numbered boats) where men were allowed board when no further women came forward. We know he was a pipe smoker – perhaps the decision to go for that last puff on deck before bedtime helped save his life.

The American Red Cross relief report, case No. 239, notes his occupation as a picture framer. Uninjured, Kennedy was awarded only $50 compensation.

John Kennedy moved in with his brother Michael at 29 Perry Street in New York and lodged a claim for compensation with the US District Court. His losses included Irish whiskey and Limerick hams and bacon.

1 Blue coat – £5 10s; Freeze overcoat – £3 10s; half doz. suits underwear £2 2s; 1 blue serge suit – £3 10s; 1 suit clothes – £2 5s; 1 English cover watch & chain – £3 10s; half doz. pairs socks – 12s; 1 brooch – 10s; Miscellaneous: Shawls, clothing and underwear for three children – £3 10s; 1 pair shoes – 16s; 1 pair shoes – 10s; 1 set china and fancy ornaments – £1 16s; religious articles, prayer books, rosaries, etc. – 16s; 1 Meerschaum pipe, 1 lb mixture – £1 2s; articles for presents: Irish whiskey, Limerick hams and bacon – 18s. Currency – £2 10s. TOTAL £33 7s.

Exhibit A.

List of Personal Property lost by John Kennedy, 29 Perry Street, New York City.

	£	2	d
1 Blue Coat	5...10		
Freeze Overcoat	3...10		
1/2 dozen suits Underwear	2... 2		
1 Blue serge suit	3...10		
1 suit clothes	2... 5		
1 English cover Watch & chain	3...10		
1/2 dozen pairs socks	12		
1 Brooch	10		
Miscellaneous:			
Shawls, clothing and underwear for 3 children	3...10		
1 pair shoes	16		
1 pair shoes	10		
1 set china and fancy ornaments	1...16		
Religious articles, Prayer Brooks, Rosaries, etc.	16		
1 Meerschaum pipe, 1 lb. Mixture	1... 2		
Articles for presents:			
Irish whiskey, Limerick Hams and Bacon	18		
Currewey	2...10		
	33... 7		
Personal Injuries	500....0		
Total	533... 7		

But Kennedy was even more enterprising – he also submitted an arbitrary £500 bill for unspecified personal injuries. His final compensation claim therefore came to over £533, at a time when the pound sterling was equivalent to five dollars. By such standards, Kennedy's claim was the largest by far of any submitted by an Irish survivor, amounting to $2,665. When the final payout came, it was limited in liability and represented only three cents to the dollar.

It is doubtful he benefited, because May 1918 brought his call-up to serve his adopted country's cause and proved fatal:

HANCOCK SOLDIER SUCCUMBS TO MALIGNANT CASE OF ANTHRAX
Private John Kennedy, of Machine Gun Company 21, Has Cheek Infected by Use of Shaving Brush and Hasty Death Results.
After an illness of four days, Private John Kennedy, age 25 years, of machine gun company no. 21, a draftee coming to Camp Hancock from his home, Brooklyn NY, 5 May, died Sunday afternoon at the Base Hospital from malignant anthrax.

The death of Kennedy from this cause is the first case of this nature to develop in any cantonment of the United States and the only case of a like nature ever known in this city or vicinity, according to physicians.

Anthrax is the most infectious disease known to medical science. From the standpoint of infection and immunity the disease is of particular interest. It is the first disease of which the bacterial etiology was proven, that is, the first case where disease by germ was proven beyond question.

It is particularly applied to cattle and sheep and prevails in certain European countries, especially Russia and Australia. That it is peculiar to animals was possibly the reason for its early discovery in Kennedy's case, the lieutenant-physician pronouncing the case anthrax coming from northern New York, where the disease is not such a rarity, and where tanneries are many.

The examining physician, recognising the symptoms of anthrax, had Kennedy immediately taken to the Base Hospital where a spear was taken from the pus and sent to the University Hospital for analysis. The answer came back positive. The disease started on the right cheek of the deceased and is believed to have been communicated by a shaving brush. It is known that bacillus anthrax has survived from 10 to 12 years on dry hair.

The remains of Private Kennedy were forwarded from the R. E. Elliott funeral home Monday afternoon, the casket being hermetically sealed, and sent to the home of Michael Kennedy, the only living relative, at No. 7, Fourth Place, Brooklyn, NY.

(*Augusta Chronicle*, 11 June 1918)

1911 census – Kennedy.
Thomas (63) labourer; wife May (61).
Married 42 years, 13 children, five alive.
John (23), shop porter. Ellen (19), domestic servant.

JOHN KIERNAN (25) LOST
PHILLIP KIERNAN (22) LOST

Ticket numbers 367227 and 367229. Paid £7 15s each.
Boarded at Queenstown. Third Class.
From: Fostragh, Aughnacliffe, County Longford.
Destination: Grove Street, Jersey city, New Jersey.

Brothers John and Phillip went down to their deaths together – their loss all the more poignant because John had returned from America to bring Phillip to a new life across the sea. John Kiernan was an attractive personality, good-looking and charming. He had prospered in New Jersey, having originally crossed the Atlantic to work as a bar tender in a premises run by his uncle, Phillip Kelleher, a beer distributor in Jersey city. He lived at an address at the junction of Grove and 20th Streets.

Among a number of Kiernan children already in America was John's older sister Margaret, who was three years his senior, and the natural progression of their young sibling Phillip to his own beginnings in the 'Land of the Free' seemed assured. Indeed John Kiernan had returned to Ireland in the spring of 1912 with the express intention of 'bringing the young lad over'.

John's magnetic personality made him an object of female fascination in the tight-knit locality. He had apparently been courting a neighbouring girl, Margaret Murphy, for some time before he emigrated, and certainly saw her again on his return home. He may only have been indulging in renewing an old flame, but unbeknownst to him, Margaret had her own plans. She hoped to marry John and intended to travel with him back to America – bringing her sister Kate as well.

On the night of the Kiernan brothers' American wake, the Murphy girls came to the going-away party. At some stage, Maggie confided her real purpose and in her account of John's reaction, she told how he 'reluctantly agreed' that she and her sister could join them on the long journey the next morning. He may not have known that the Murphy family knew nothing of the planned disappearance of both their daughters.

Also in the emigrant party was Thomas McCormack, aged 19, another bar trade worker. A cousin, Thomas, roomed with the brothers on

Phillip Kiernan

board the mighty vessel, while the Murphy sisters occupied a cabin at the other end of the ship for single women. McCormack told the *Jersey Journal* of 23 April 1912:

When the *Titanic* first struck the iceberg I was in my stateroom preparing to retire. I heard the crash as the ship struck the ice and at once hurriedly dressed and ran on deck, followed by my cousin, Phillip Kiernan, of Jersey City.

It was brotherly love that cost Phil his life. As he was hurrying toward the deck his brother John called to him to go on, that he would be there in a minute. As we reached

John Kiernan

the stairs Phillip looked around, and not seeing his brother, started to return to look for him. I kept on and did not see either of them again.

An *Irish World* account of 4 May 1912, discloses Maggie Murphy's description of the last moments of the Kiernan brothers, with all the emphasis on her favourite, John:

I was trying to get to a lifeboat when John shouted to me and came running up. 'Here, take my lifebelt,' he said, seeing I did not have one. He made me put it on and put me in a boat. He and his brother Phillip were drowned.

John's chivalry at the time of his own imminent demise is indeed admirable, but the next account shows that he was also beaten by sailors, who believed his delivery of the lifejacket to be a ploy to allow him near to the boats. The Murphys are believed to have been saved in either boat No. 14 or boat No. 16, all the way aft on the port side. Note, however, in this extract that Margaret Murphy goes on to make specific charges against members of the crew:

A Brave Irish Youth
Having related how a brave young Irishman, John Kiernan, who was lost, gave her his lifebelt, she said –
    'A crowd of men were trying to get up to a higher deck and were fighting the sailors; all striking and scuffling and swearing. Women and some children were there, praying and crying.'
    'Then the sailors fastened down the hatchways leading to the Third-Class section. They said they wanted to keep the air down there so the vessel would stay up longer. It meant all hope was gone for those still down there.'
    John Kiernan, she said, helped her into the boat and said 'Goodbye' – as he had said it a hundred times at the door of her father's store. She knew he did not intend to get in himself, but the sailors drove him away. She added – 'Just as the davits were being swung outward, a Chinaman pushed a woman out of the boat and took her place. Sailors grabbed him and handed him back to the deck. Then some one shot him and his body tumbled into the water. It was terrible.'
                                                                    (*Irish Independent*, 9 May 1912)

Margaret's account is similar to other descriptions of shootings in this left-rear quadrant of the *Titanic's* boat deck – whereas the official inquiries were only told that warning shots were fired to dissuade jumpers as the boats were lowered. Fifth Officer Harold Lowe admitted that he shouted at passengers that he would shoot the first leaper 'like a dog'. Lowe also said he both heard shots and fired them.

J. P. Farrell, MP for Longford, tried to raise the 'Brave Irish Youth' newspaper report with Lord Mersey, chairman of the British inquiry which called no steerage passengers to testify during its proceedings. Lord Mersey rejected the application and asked Mr Farrell to confine himself to what were 'proper issues'.

It appears that John Kiernan may have become separated from Phillip during the sinking, since the latter receives scant mention in eyewitness reports. Local folklore in Fostra is that John went on deck while Phillip was asleep – and was later unable to retrace his steps to find his brother because the steerage passengers were kept back and he couldn't breach the cordon.

Margaret Murphy referred in one interview immediately after the sinking to a crowd fighting with sailors for access to the boat deck. She added: 'John Kiernan and the other lads grabbed some chairs and piled them on top of each other so they made a sort of a scaffold. They helped us girls on top of the chairs so that we were above the crowd fighting all around us and not in such danger of being hurt.'

The *Jersey Advocate* printed a tribute to John Kiernan soon after the sinking:

Two of the Longford boys lost on the Titanic *– the brothers John and Philip Kiernan*
Several readers of the *Advocate* in Jersey city and natives of County Longford wish to send their deepest sympathy to the relatives and friends of the two brave youths, John Joseph and Philip Kiernan, who, it seems, lost their lives by trying to save others. I have heard that some of the survivors say that they owe their lives to them. I have known John Joseph since he first came to this country about seven years ago. He was then a mere boy … Well may the saying be applied to him, no one saw him but to respect him, or knew him but to love him. On 12 August 1911, he sailed for Ireland to visit his parents and friends there. On the eve of his departure, he was given a grand send-off party by his friends and acquaintances, and was presented with a solid gold signet ring and many other presents, and it was a most unusual sight to see the number of people, men and women, and even different nationalities, that accompanied him to the pier on the morning of his departure, and all stood with heavy hearts and streaming eyes watching the boat that bore him away as long as a glimpse of it could be seen – as if they all knew he would never return. Everyone was watching and waiting for him to return when the sad news came that he was on the fatal ship, the *Titanic*. He had his younger brother, Philip, with him whom he was bringing back to this country. They had acted like heroes and went down with the doomed ship and to their eternal reward.

1901 census:
Parents John Kiernan (60), farmer, wife Catherine (50).
Children Bernard (20), Margaret (17), **John (14)**, **Phillip (11)**, Ellen (6).

THOMAS KILGANNON (22) LOST

Ticket number 36865. Paid £7 14s 9d.
Boarded at Queenstown. Third Class.
From: Currafarry, Caltra, County Galway.
Destination: 444 West 59th Street, New York city.

Tom Kilgannon wrote a letter to his widowed mother, Mary, on his last day in Queenstown. He boarded the *Titanic* the next day after a long journey from his home place, via Ballinasloe and a train from Athlone. He complains about the extortionate charges for bed and breakfast accommodation in Cork and possibly mirrored by Queenstown's twenty lodging houses for intending emigrants.

His punctuation has been changed for clarity, but his original spelling remains:

Queenstown
April 10, 1912

My Dear Mother
Just a few lyons to let you know how we got on we did not get in here untill half past tin this moring. We had to stay in Cork last knight and we reached that about half past twelve and our knight stay was seven and six on us apeace.

We expect to sail ought a bout tin on tomorrow morning. I am sending a ring to Maria and one to C Fallon hoping ye will get them alright. Write today or tomorrow and let me know how ye got home.

To J wife.

We have great fun all dancing I will finish now. Excuse the writing. For I am in a great hurry. Goodby, yours faithfully

T. Kilgannon.

The worry over expense can be readily understood when it is realised that the Kilgannons were among the poorest of the emigrants, 'living on the dirt under their fingernails' as the local phrase has it. They had just a five-acre holding with a tiny cottage distinguished by its dunghill in the front garden. The large pile of manure, built up of household waste, was used as compost fertiliser on their meagre plots.

Tom must have saved up for many years to buy his passage, which he eventually managed at Ryan's travel agency in the town of Ballygar, a little distance from his home. Not that his precarious finances made him parsimonious. The parting gifts to his older sister Maria and Miss Fallon, a girl from his neighbourhood, disclosed in the above letter, show how kind-hearted Tom Kilgannon was – kindness that even found expression in the midst of horror in mid Atlantic.

The reference 'To J wife' tells his family to write to his brother John's wife in America, his destination, to let him know how they got home from seeing him off at Athlone railway station.

Thomas Joseph Kilgannon was last seen kneeling on the deck of the *Titanic*, saying the Rosary with two Galway companions, Martin Gallagher and Thomas Smith. The trio were watched by Helen Mockler – to whom a courageous Kilgannon had earlier given his Aran sweater, seeing that she was shivering – as she descended in what may have been lifeboat No. 16 on the aft port side of the *Titanic*. For her countrymen left behind it seemed there were no more boats.

Kilgannon was one of five Galway people who formed their own distinct group on the *Titanic*, made up of the three young men and two women from the same parish, the latter pair being Mockler and Margaret Mannion. All five made their way to the *Titanic*'s open decks after the young men apparently came to the women's room at the stern to escort them to the upper decks during the evacuation. The quintet reached the open air and saw the distress rockets streak up to an empty sky. When Miss Mockler was suddenly seized by a desire to return to her room for a forgotten bag, it may have been Tom Kilgannon who told her frankly: 'Forget about your bag. If you save yourself, you'll be lucky.'

Mockler was referring to Kilgannon when she told a New York newspaper after the tragedy:

A young man who was in steerage with us helped me into the boat. It was cold and I had no wrap. Taking off the shirt he was wearing, he put it around my shoulders and the suspenders to keep it from blowing undone, and then stepped back into the crowd.

Helen Mockler later returned to Ireland and presented the sweater given to her by Kilgannon to his elderly mother, Mary. It must have been an emotion-charged moment. Mrs Kilgannon was a widow. After the *Titanic* tragedy, she was left with three hungry mouths in the form of two young daughters and a boy. Local lore tells that Mrs Kilgannon learned of the loss of her son in a cablegram delivered to her home from the post office in Ballinamore Bridge on 17 April 1912. The cable was put into her hand as the sky darkened and the sun was blotted out. It may sound portentous, but in fact there was an eclipse of the sun on 17 April 1912, visible all over Ireland and the British Isles, which lasted from 11 a.m. until 1.30 p.m. For Mrs Kilgannon, the astral blackness meant the loss of her son's life.

Report of the American Red Cross (Titanic Disaster) 1913:
No. 242. (Irish.) A farmer, 21 years of age, was lost, leaving a dependent mother in Ireland. The case was referred to the English Committee, and emergent relief was given. The English Committee gave £50.

Tom had been travelling over to join his brother John, a tram driver in Queens, New York. After the drowning, Tom's elder sister Maria emigrated to the United States, but Mrs Kilgannon refused to let her last remaining boy take a boat to the new land.

Instead William joined the Royal Irish Constabulary, serving during the worst years of the Irish troubles until 1922, when he left the force after nine years. His membership continued to cause the family many years of bitterness and division within their local community – whereas police work in America would have been a badge of pride for any Irish clan.

A lock of Thomas Kilgannon's hair is all that survives of the ill-educated but selfless man who went down in the North Atlantic. The family has preserved the blond cuttings in an oval frame, knitted to a linen garment that might have been his christening gown, surrounded by prayer cards and surmounted by the plain word 'Thomas'.

1911 census – Kilgannon, Currafarry, County Galway.
Michael (80), farmer, widower. His daughter-in-law Mary (60), widow.
Her children Maria (23), **Thomas (21)**, William (18).

JOHN JAMES LAMB (30) LOST

Ticket number 240261. Paid £10 14s 2d.
Boarded at Queenstown. Second Class.
From: Old Boleys, Wicklow.
Destination: Providence, Rhode Island.

John James Lamb appears to have worked in the world of theatre. He had emigrated from relatively wealthy origins in Ireland. He was from Old Boleys, County Wicklow, and was 30 years old. John James was the eldest son of prosperous farmer Martin Lamb, who was aged 70 by the time of the 1901 census. But the old man still had plenty of life in him – his wife, Catherine, John's mother, was three decades his junior and had borne him several children.

Catherine (41) was mother to five other children besides John, who was already in America by 1901. That year's census shows the other offspring at home in Ireland to be Martin (17), Edward (15), Catherine (12), Theresa (8) and Mary Anne (6).

Providence, R.I., April 16 – Four Providence residents are known to have been passengers on the ill-fated *Titanic*. They include … James Lamb, a theatrical man, who had been returning from a three-month tour abroad …

(*Brooklyn Daily Eagle*, 16 April 1912)

John James Lamb was born in 1881, had been living with his sister Catherine in Providence, Rhode Island, and was returning to the US after a visit home.

PATRICK LANE (16) LOST

Ticket number 7935. Paid £7 15s.
Boarded at Queenstown. Third Class.
From: 8 Clare Street, Limerick city.
Destination: West 45th Street, New York city.

'Poor Paddy Lane,' murmured the girl after a pause. 'He was a fine young fellow, a little younger than I am, and when we were leaving the other side, his folks asked me to please look after poor Paddy in America. When the boats were being lowered, Paddy knelt on the deck and prayed. Then he began to run around calling for the priest. And he started for the other side of the ship. I never saw him again. Paddy went down with the ship,' said survivor Nellie O'Dwyer, also from Limerick city, in an interview with the *Brooklyn Daily Times* in May 1912.

Paddy was the eldest son in a family of six children. He had been working as an assistant in a marine store and perhaps it was constant contact with affairs of the sea that drew him to consider crossing the Atlantic to seek his fortune. However, he was listed as an agricultural labourer aboard the *Titanic*, with a given age of 17. Nellie O'Dwyer was 23, but with cabins for single men and women at opposite ends of the 882-foot ship, there was a limit to how much she could look after the young man.

Feared loss of Limerick passenger
We have received, this evening, a communication from Messrs M.P. Riordan & Co., George Street, White Star Agents, stating: 'It is our painful duty to inform you that we have just received an official telegram that poor Patrick Lane of Clare Street, the young fellow whom we booked on SS *Titanic*, has to be definitely considered as lost.'
(*Limerick Chronicle*, 23 April 1912)

1911 census – Lane, Clare Street, Limerick.
Parents James (46), factory labourer, Margaret (38).
Children Bridget (18), **Patrick (15)**, Michael (12), Mary Kate (10), Theresa (4), James (1).

DENIS LENNON (20) LOST
MARY MULLIN (18) LOST

Joint ticket number 370371. Paid £15 10s.
Boarded at Queenstown. Third Class.
From: Lennon was from Curraghcreagan, Ballymahon, County Longford; Mullin was from Clarinbridge, County Galway.
Destination: New York city.

Denis and Mary are the star-crossed lovers of the Irish *Titanic* story. They ran away to sea together, an elopement that offended both families. When Mary's brother found out, he chased them with a loaded gun, but failed to catch the couple at the quayside. The lovers' satisfaction was short-lived, however, and they died together when the ship went down.

In their own minds, they were already married. They worshipped each other even though they knew their love would be frowned upon, and it must have been mostly as a sign of commitment – although perhaps partly in jest and partly for secrecy or mystery – that they signed aboard the *Titanic* as 'Denis and Mary Lennon'. There was no Mary Lennon. Her real name was Mary Mullin and she was the daughter of the family who ran the prosperous pub and thriving general store in Clarinbridge, County Galway, where Denis Lennon – from Longford – was working in 1912.

The first indication that all was not well was when Mary Mullin, aged 18, failed to disembark from a train in Dublin after the Easter holidays at home in Galway. Brother Bart had been due to meet her, ready to take her to Loreto Abbey boarding school in Rathfarnham.

Frantic communication with Clarinbridge subsequently revealed that Mary had left at the appointed hour, but now the barman was also missing. Her sister Bridget later gave this account: '[We] went up in the trap to Oranmore. At the station I saw a lad on the train, his name was Lennon, looking at me. Then later we got a wire from the school saying she had not arrived.'

It turned out that Mary had indeed gone to the station, but had caught a train for Cork in the company of the barman. They were eloping.

For years the mystery as to the identity of Mary Lennon was unsolved. Denis Lennon's origins were established: he was born in Longford on 9 December 1891, but had left the family home. He had no sisters called Mary. In 1901, nine-year-old Denis was living at Currycreaghan, Doory, with his parents. Father William was a 55-year-old farmer, with mother Bridget considerably younger at 38. Denis was the third eldest of six children, a seventh child having died in infancy.

Ten years later, Denis had left the three-room, three-window house, which was always severely cramped by the number of inhabitants. By 1912 he had made his way to the *Titanic* with a mystery woman, declaring himself a 21-year-old labourer, with 'Mary Lennon' stating that she was a 20-year-old spinster. For years, researchers pondered whether they were really man and wife, or somehow related. The answer lay in a single news paragraph from *The Connacht Tribune*, 27 April 1912:

> There were on board many Galway people, including a few from Ballymoe, and (sad to tell) an eloping couple from Clarinbridge. It is thought that the lady was saved while her lover perished.

It was pure conjecture whether Denis Lennon could have migrated from his home place of Longford to travel well over 100 miles in a south-westerly direction across Ireland to the famous oyster festival village of Clarinbridge, outside Galway. But that is exactly what happened, as a search through the 1911 census returns for Clarinbridge established the presence of Denis Lennon at a public house in the village.

> 1911 census – Hillpark, Clarinbridge, County Galway.
> Head of household – Delia Mullin (49), widow, publican. Husband Redmond deceased.
> Children Owen Mullin (22), shopkeeper; Joseph Mullin (25), bookkeeper; Bridget Mullin (19), spinster.
> Other occupants – **Denis Lennon (19)**, shop assistant, born in County Longford. Thomas Fleming (18), shop assistant, Galway; Margaret Killian (22), servant and cook, Galway.

There it was – but no sign of Mary. Careful inquiry in Clarinbridge yielded up the folk memory that there was indeed a Mary Mullin who had run away with a store-hand on the *Titanic*. She had been away in boarding school when the census was taken. She appears in the 1911 census as a pupil in Loreto Abbey, Rathfarnham.

Her quick-tempered brother Joseph was a carter on the Galway run for Guinness, and a regular inspector of the product in his off hours. The horse would be left between the shafts for hours as sessions developed – and folklore to this day tells of Joe coming out of pubs at night to throw his spare change in the air, just to enjoy the spectacle of an undignified scramble for the coins among the locals.

Such impulsiveness ran in the family: Joe's father and uncle split their wealthy inheritance in the previous century by tossing a coin to decide which got the pub and which one the farm. Yet the staff of the tavern had been considerably whittled down by 1912, and it must have been a whirlwind romance that Easter holiday with handsome Denis from the exotic location of Longford. But love took its course and the young couple stole away from home:

> A young couple who were attached to each other from early youth and who came to Queenstown by appointment and secured tickets in the name of brother and sister, intending to marry in America, are both apparently gone.
> (*The Cork Examiner*, 19 April 1912)

They were actually booked to travel to America on the White Star Liner, *Cymric*. Its cancellation was merely paradise postponed – for the couple managed to embark four days later, and this time to their delighted self-congratulation, they were travelling on the largest and most luxurious steamer in the world.

Meanwhile, unbeknownst to them, Joe Mullin had discovered the seduction of his sister. He rushed home, loaded a revolver, swore he would shoot her defiler dead on sight, and set out for Queenstown in hot pursuit. When he arrived, he found that the tenders for the *Titanic* had just cast off and he pounded the barrier in frustration. Some garbled hint of such a pursuit seems to be implied here:

> Both [elopers] were travelling under false names, and the passenger list to hand bears this out … they were seen in the tender leaving Queenstown and spoken to when aboard the

ill-fated vessel. The parents of the bride arrived in the city yesterday evening, and their grief can very well be imagined. Still there is hope that the youthful bride might be one of the female passengers aboard the *Carpathia*.

(*Cork County Eagle*, 20 April 1912)

Jimmy Lennon of Longford remembers sitting in his grandmother's kitchen as a small boy, warming himself beside an open hearth, listening to John Lennon – Denis Lennon's 17-year-old sibling of 1911 – tell of how his long-dead brother ran away with a girl to sea. As John told it, the lovesick young traveller was planning to marry the girl, but the couple feared disapproval and the denial of their desired nuptials. There may be an explanation for this. Denis' mother's maiden name was Mullen (and census returns collated by a colonially-imposed constabulary were notoriously prone to misspellings) and it might be that she and Delia Mullin were sisters-in-law. It is quite possible that one relative might have sent her boy to help out another wing of the family weakened by widowhood. If such is the case, then Denis and Mary would have been cousins and their relationship would have been likely to meet with deep disapproval.

If they were cousins, it would explain *The Cork Examiner* report, four days after the sinking, that a couple who signed themselves on board as brother and sister had managed to form an attachment to each other from early youth. Such a liaison could never have been permitted to develop. The couple might have hoped to put an ocean between themselves and such attitudes, but the ocean took their lives. There is no evidence to support *The Connacht Tribune*'s rather wistful hope that young lady might have been saved.

The family tale was that Denis had been stealing from the till in the Mullin pub in preparation for their new life together in America. If they were running away, it could also mean that young Mary might have been pregnant. Joe knew where the couple were likely headed – to Queenstown, to join a transatlantic liner for a new life, but by the time he reached Queenstown, the liner – the RMS *Titanic* – was already heading out to sea. On board were a couple subsequently said by White Star in error to be the 'Lemons'.

Family lore is that the police at Queenstown confirmed to Joe that there were two 'who looked like runaways, but we hadn't been told to look out for any runaways then'. The family solicitors, Blake & Kenny, engaged agents to question survivors in New York, and a tale emerged of a couple of the description who had either a lifebelt or a lifeboat place only for one, 'and she said that if he couldn't have one, she wouldn't have one either'.

Another story says Mary was brought alive into a lifeboat and died of exposure, but neither body was recovered.

After the tragedy, Joe returned to the bottle, while Mary's distraught sister Bridget (Sissy) immediately joined the Sisters of Charity and became Sister Mary Lourdes. The family eventually went bankrupt, while the brother due to meet Mary off the train, Bartholomew (Bertie), joined the British army as a field surgeon and lost an arm in the First World War.

An 80-year-old former Loreto pupil, Carmel McKeown, remembers that as late as 1949 prayers were still being invoked every April for Mary, the lost former pupil, and her tragedy held up as a warning against elopement or any form of premature entanglement. 'We were fascinated by it.'

Joe Mullin drank himself to an early death – yet his sister's 'deceiver' paid a speedier price.

MICHAEL LINEHAN (21) LOST

Ticket number 330971. Paid £7 12s 7d, plus 5s extra.
Boarded at Queenstown. Third Class.
From: Freeholds, Knocknageeha, Cullen, County Cork.
Destination: Shakespeare Avenue, Bronx, New York city.

Michael's death was worth just $444 and thirty-six cents. And an American lawyer grabbed more than half that final sum. Here is the text of the lawyer's letter, dated 6 May 1918, addressed to Bartholomew Linehan, the 77-year-old father of farm labourer Michael, the victim of a disaster six years earlier, who died aged just 21. The letter was addressed to Mr Linehan at Knocknaveeha, Cullen P.O., County Cork, Ireland:

Dear Sir:

I have collected for your account for the death of your son Michael, from the Oceanic Steam Navigation Company, as owner of the Steamship *Titanic*, the sum of $444.36, and have this day turned over to the United States Fidelity & Guaranty Co., of #47 Cedar Street, New York city, who executed the bond of your son Jeremiah, as administrator, for transmission to you, $206.36, being one-half of the amount received by me in settlement of said claim, less $5 paid by me as premium on the bond of your son, as administrator, and the sum of $10.85, administrator's commissions, the other one-half having been retained by me under a written retainer of your son, of 50%, or one-half of the recovery, for services rendered by me in the matter.

The United States Fidelity & Guaranty Company will, in a few days, transmit said amount to you by draft on the Monster & Linster Bank [*sic*], of Newmarket, which will notify you to call therefor when received by it, and to sign whatever papers are required of you, or the United States Fidelity & Guaranty Company may send the amount to you direct by Postal Money Order.

Regretting the loss of your son Michael, my inability to get you any more money therefor, and with very best regards, I am

Very truly yours,
JRJ/FEB

So much for the 'Monster' of the Munster & Leinster Bank. More than half as much money, in real terms, had already been provided from the emergency relief funds established immediately after the tragedy, as revealed in the American Red Cross report of 1913:

No. 267. (Irish.) Young man was lost, leaving dependent father and younger children in Ireland. Emergent help was given and the case referred to the English Committee, which later made an appropriation of £45.

Money had always been tight – which was why Michael was on his way over to America in the first place. The Jeremiah named above, who approached the lawyer to fight for compensation, was Michael's older brother, aged 23 in 1912. He had been working in a brewery in New York, and as soon as he was able, sent funds so that 'strong, well-built' Michael could come over and join him in the work.

The first news of Michael being lost came in a plaintive reference in a letter home composed by fellow Cork passenger Daniel Buckley on the rescue vessel *Carpathia*. Buckley told his mother:

> There is no account of … Michael Linehan from Freeholds.
> (Letter printed in *The Cork Examiner*, 13 May 1912)

Linehan roomed with Buckley, Pat Connell and Pat O'Connor on board the *Titanic*. The other men were at first reluctant to believe Buckley when the latter jumped out of bed and felt the splash of water on his feet after the collision. They were finally roused to the real danger and began hunting for lifebelts, yet Buckley never saw any of them again.

> 1901 census – Linehan. Knocknageeha, Cullen, Millstreet.
> Head of Family – Bartholomew (60). Widower.
> Children Margaret (15), Jeremiah (12), **Michael (10)**, John (8), Bart (5).

JOHN LINGANE (61) LOST

Ticket number 235509. Paid £12 7s.
Boarded at Queenstown. Second Class.
From: Ballyshonack, Quitrent, Kildorrery, County Cork.
Destination: Sylvan, Chelsea, Michigan.

Home on a holiday to visit friends and old neighbours, John Lingane knew he was paying probably his last visit to his native country before his death – even if he didn't expect the grim reaper for many more years yet. Mr Lingane was 61, had amassed a fortune in America and wanted to see old Ireland again. It would be nice too, if his acquired wealth could be the subject of congratulation among some of the people he grew up with, that their children might see what a man could aspire to through hard work and enterprise.

But such notions were incidental to his real purpose, because John Lingane was coming home to what remained of his family in Cork for much-needed solace and solidarity following the death of his wife, Ellen, in March 1911. He intended too, to visit

Ellen's family, the Savages, who still lived in the Kildorrery area where the couple had been married on 16 May 1876.

John was aged 25 when he married (b. 1851), and his bride was eight years older. When she died at the age of 68, he was inconsolable. Together they had forged a new life in Michigan, buying land they turned into a thriving farm, and having five sons together: Jeremiah, Patrick, James, Vincent and William.

Michael, six years younger than John, took over the family farm at Ballyshonack, Kildorrery, when John abdicated his prevailing right to inheritance by opting for America. Michael was the perfect host when John returned, and as the weeks passed into 1912, John's spirits began to revive. He had booked a return passage by the White Star's *Celtic*, but was persuaded to await instead the sailing of the luxurious new *Titanic*. The coal strike, in any case, had thrown everything into confusion, and John's family and friends in Michigan had no clear idea as to his intentions.

After the sinking, the nagging doubts began. His local newspaper in Chelsea reported the fears on 25 April, ten days after the disaster:

May have been on board Titanic
The friends of John Lingane are in grave doubts as to his whereabouts. According to letters he sent to two of his friends here, he stated that he expected to leave on his return journey from Ireland about April 1st.

It is possible that he may have sailed on the *Titanic*, which sailed from Queenstown, one of the principal seaports of Ireland, on April 10 [sic]. Mr Lingane was visiting at Kildorrery, County Cork …

Among the names of the Second-Class passengers appears the name of John Legame, and his Chelsea friends fear that the name is spelt wrong. Last Saturday, W. B. Waltrous telegraphed to the White Star Line office in New York making an inquiry in regard to Mr Lingane, but received a reply that there was no such name on the passenger list.

The uncertainty continued, until the *Cork Constitution* newspaper reported categorically on 11 May 1912, more than two weeks later:

Kildorrery man amongst the victims: John Lingan [sic]
Our Mitchelstown correspondent adds – There is not the slightest doubt about the unfortunate man's fate. He was born at Quitrent, Kildorrery, and a relative of his, Mr W. Kennedy, RDC, Kildorrery, informed me on Wednesday that he was home on a visit, returning by the ill-fated steamer. It is believed that he was possessed of a considerable sum of money.

Local lore says Johnny Lingane was carrying a quantity of ash plants (walking canes) to America when he lost his life on the *Titanic*.

MARGARET MADIGAN (21) SAVED

Ticket number 370370. Paid £7 15s.
Boarded at Queenstown. Third Class.
From: Church Street, Askeaton, County Limerick.
Destination: 338 East 155th Street, New York city.

Margaret is believed to have been rescued in lifeboat No. 15, launched from the starboard side of the stricken *Titanic*. Born on 11 August 1890, Maggie was only 21 when she boarded in the company of brother and sister Daniel and Bertha Moran, also from Askeaton, who were home in Ireland on a holiday. Maggie was leaving an aged and widowed mother helplessly alone because of emigration.

Missing County Limerick people
Amongst the passengers who embarked on the ill-fated steamer *Titanic* on last Thursday at Queenstown en route to New York were Mr P. Ryan, Mr J. Moran, Miss Bridget Moran, and Miss Maggie Madigan, who belonged to Askeaton, County Limerick.

On their arrival at Queenstown they were received at the boarding house of Mr McDonnell, The Beach, where the first-named met his cousin, Mr [Michael] O'Mahoney, HM Customs, who interested himself on their behalf, saw the whole party on board the great ship, and introduced them to one official on board who promised to look after their comfort and otherwise make them feel at home on the passage. Needless to say, he was shocked to hear of the disaster, and is still more grieved to find that their names are not given amongst those who have been saved.

(*Cork Free Press*, 18 April 1912)

The *Titanic* official to whom they were introduced could well have been Reggie Rice of the Purser's department. He was the son of the Board of Trade's principal officer at Queenstown. Rice, 25, born in Hull, was 'an exceedingly affable young fellow and greatly liked by all his associates', *The Cork Examiner* noted when reporting the recovery of his body.

Margaret Madigan was originally booked to travel on the *Cymric* on its Easter Sunday sailing from Queenstown, but was transferred like many others on its cancellation. She was heading over to join her 34-year-old brother, Simon, who lived at 338 East 155th Street, New York, with his wife and child. Under landing records from the *Carpathia*, Maggie stated that she was a servant, hoping, no doubt, to find work among the brownstone mansions of the east coast elite.

A telegram has been received at Askeaton by Mrs Madigan from her daughter Margaret, who was on board the *Titanic*, stating that she and Bertha Moran, also from Askeaton, are safe.

(*Irish Independent*, 20 April 1912)

Report of the American Red Cross (Titanic Disaster) 1913:
No. 287. (Irish.) Domestic servant, 21 years old, injured. ($150)

District Court of the United States. In the matter of the Oceanic Steam Navigation Company, Ltd:

> I, Margaret Madigan, residing at No. 221 Fourteenth Street, in the city of Troy, N.Y., do hereby make and present my claim for damages, loss and injuries sustained by me by reason of the collision of the steamship *Titanic* with an iceberg in the Atlantic Ocean on April 14–15 1912, and the subsequent sinking of the said steamship.
> I was a passenger on said steamship and had in my possession the following property, of the value of three hundred and seventeen dollars and fifty cents, which was lost when said steamship sank on the day last aforesaid:
> 3 tailored suits – $45; 4 pairs of shoes – $12; 1 gold watch – $50; underwear and stockings – $15; 2 odd skirts – $7; 2 hats – $15; 1 silk dress – $8; 6 shirt waists – $9; 4 pairs of gloves – $4; 1 toilet set – $15; 1 pocket book – $2.50; 1 satchel – $5; cash – $105; 1 gold ring – $25. Total – $317.50.

In 1913 Maggie Madigan married William Kane and moved to Glen Falls, New York. She had escaped from the horror of the *Titanic*, but six years later the great flu epidemic of 1918 took both her young husband and their only child from her. She lived for another sixty years, dying in January 1978 in her 88th year.

1901 census – Madigan; Church Street, Askeaton, County Limerick.
Parents: James (50), general labourer; Margaret (50).
Children: Simon (23), Mary (15), **Margaret (12)**.

DELIA MAHON (19) LOST

Ticket number 330924. Paid £7 12s 7d.
Boarded at Queenstown. Third Class.
From: Derrymartin, Addergoole, County Mayo.
Destination: 438 Franklin Avenue, Brooklyn, New York.

The fate of the *Titanic* was read in tea-leaves at the home of Delia Mahon. She lived with her widowed mother, Anne, and three other children in a tiny cottage in remote Derrymartin. Her brother Pat was 20 years old and a sturdy pair of hands on the meagre farm, and they managed, despite the loss of Delia's father, Michael, many years before. Pat claimed to be able to read the leaves at the bottom of a drained cup of tea, and there was consternation on Delia's last night at home when he predicted a mishap on the way to America. The uncomfortable atmosphere was soon punctured by hilarity when a neighbour at the hearth suggested she might arrive in New York pregnant! The immediate anxiety thus evaporated in laughter, and although Pat was scolded for alarming his sister, something stronger than tea was duly produced and the party fell to more convivial themes.

The family were very poor, and Delia's death did much to further dishearten them all. The American Red Cross in its 1913 report on relief cases provided a picture of their plight:

No. 289. (Irish.) A housemaid, 19 years of age, was lost. She left a widowed mother and three younger children in Ireland, and was coming on a ticket purchased by a girl friend, hoping to be able to do more for her mother when at work here.

The Committee paid the cost of the ticket to the friend, who could ill afford to lose the amount, as she was herself assisting her family. English Committee gave £60 to the mother. ($40)

Delia Mahon was born in 1892, and was baptised Bridget on 6 March that year. She was always known to the family as Delia, a familiar name for Bridget. Besides herself, her widowed mother and hard-working Pat, there were two youngsters in the house: Michael was aged 15 and Kate just 12, the latter crying her eyes out when Delia chose to leave.

1901 census:
Parents: Michael Mahon (60), farmer. Wife Anne (45).
Children: Patrick (11), **Bridget (Delia, 9)**, Maggie (7), Michael (4), Kate (2).
Mother-in-law Bridget Cawley, widow, 82.

MARY MANGAN (31) LOST

Ticket number 364850. Paid £7 15s.
Boarded at Queenstown. Third Class.
From: Carrowskehine, Lahardane, County Mayo.
Destination: 1848 Lincoln Avenue, Chicago.

Someone may have stolen a diamond ring from the body of Mary Mangan after it was recovered from the cruel sea. It disappeared from her listed effects. Mary had been due to be married on her return to Chicago as she had been on a trip home to County Mayo to see her elderly widowed mother and to receive the congratulations of friends and neighbours anxious to wish her well for her forthcoming wedding.

Of course they all wanted to see the ring. As the envious young girls crowded around Mary's outstretched left hand, the older married womenfolk smiled indulgently and made jokes at those same fingers soon being worn to the bone by doing all his mending and housework. When Mary sailed from Queenstown for a new life, she left not only with the earnest good wishes of all from her home place, but an extensive trousseau of wedding gifts. Most precious of all, however, was still the ring, symbol of love eternal.

When Mary's body was recovered floating in the sea on 22 April 1912, the ring was still bright on her finger. But although it was carefully noted and logged by the crew of the *MacKay-Bennett* search vessel, it was missing later from possessions due to be handed over to her family as last mementoes. A note in the public archives of Nova Scotia on a list of Mary's belongings states simply: 'No ring in effects'. Either it had been misplaced or pocketed by a person unknown:

No. 61: Female. Estimated age: 30. Hair light
Clothing – Green waterproof; black coat; skirt; blouse; red cardigan jacket; black button boots with cloth uppers.
Effects – One gold watch, engraved inside 'M. Mangan', and photo, and outside 'M. Mangan'; gold locket with hair and photo as in watch, engraved 'Mary'; gold chain; beads in pocket; brass belt buckle; medallion round neck; diamond solitaire ring; gold bracelet 'M.M.'; wire gold brooch.
No marks on clothing. Probably Third Class. Name – Mary Mangan.

Mary's body was buried at sea on the same day as its discovery. Only the effects were retained and later passed to Bridget Mangan, the deceased's 70-year-old mother, and Ellen Mangan, her 29-year-old sister. Mary and Ellen had returned to Ireland from America together, but Mary was returning to Chicago with the Bourkes – who lived in the next-door homestead in Carrowskehine – and Ellen was expected to follow; she never risked the Atlantic again, later marrying a neighbour, Pat Walsh.

The items sent home by the coroner's office in Halifax remained in the family. Mary's nephew Anthony Mangan still has her water-damaged watch, carrying the inscription that made her identification so easy, but now missing its hands. But the clasp containing her photo and a lock of hair has been lost.

Mary's mother later fielded a claim for $10,000 for the loss of her daughter against the White Star Line. She received just a pittance when the corpus of claims was finally settled under limited liability. In the meantime she had been granted administration of Mary's assets in Ireland, which came to a not inconsiderable £92 10s, in a judgement given at Ballina court on 10 August 1912. And then there was assistance from the American Red Cross:

No. 292. (Irish.) Domestic servant, 30 years of age, lost; left mother, brother and sister, not dependent upon her. Body recovered and part of burial expenses paid, the brother requiring this amount of help. ($50)

The surname Mangan is pronounced 'Mannion' in the local Mayo dialect and this explains why a description of a passenger named Mary Mannion (instead of another woman named Margaret Mannion, who was on board) may refer to Mary Mangan. Another Mayo survivor, Annie Kate Kelly, spoke of running towards a ladder to the Second-Class area of the *Titanic* in the company of the 'Burkes and Mary Mannion'. Annie goes on: 'For then they were not letting the steerage passengers up the stairway.'

There is no further mention of Mary Mangan after she is placed at the bottom of a vertical ladder, denied the chance of safety, peering fervently upwards at the stonily-set faces of the crew, her diamond ring possibly glinting in the near darkness as she brings her hands above her head, like so many others condemned to earnest entreaties.

1901 census – Bridget Mangan (55), widow.
Mary, daughter, farmer (20), John Mangan (22), Ellen Mangan (18).

MARGARET MANNION (28) SAVED

Ticket number 36866. Paid £7 14s 9d.
Boarded at Queenstown. Third Class.
From: Loughanboy, Caltra, County Galway.
Destination: 314 West 127th Street, New York city.

Saved in boat No. 16, which cast off from the port side of the *Titanic*, Margaret Mannion had to watch in agony as her sweetheart stepped back on deck and went to his death. Martin Gallagher had returned to Ireland from Rye, New York, to bring back the girl to whom he had written fond love letters from the United States.

According to the story told in her home place, Margaret Mannion was saved by being swung over into the boat by a man's braces that Martin Gallagher, her fiancé, divested himself of to provide the crude rope for escape. Another member of this group of Galway passengers, Ellen Mockler, who also survived, later wrote home and declared: 'The boys were magnificent.' Certainly their assistance saved Margaret Mannion – even as she was robbed of the man who was due to become her husband. Margaret lived another fifty-eight years, but only stayed seven in the United States.

More than a decade after her death, her grandson Michael Hopkins wrote his recollection of Margaret's account:

Down below, the Third-Class passengers began to get very panicky, especially as water started to rise about their feet. At last one brave Irishman jumped up and said, ''Tis do or die' and the rest of the men agreed and they stormed down the corridors followed by the ladies in their night clothes. Suddenly a large barrier at the foot of a stairway stopped them, but a few strong fellows managed to smash it down. They moved on with all their might. At one stage a sailor tried to stop them, but they took care of him. They soon reached the top where there were two more sailors standing with guns. They tried to threaten the passengers by firing shots in the air but this did not frighten the men. They just threw the sailors out of the way and rushed to the lifeboats. Men from all three classes tried to get onto the boats but some were shot down due to their actions.

In the only newspaper comment she ever made, Margaret merely told *The Connacht Tribune* in 1963 that the three men she had been travelling with from her parish had helped to secure places for her and her companion, Ellen Mockler: 'I never saw Ellen Mockler after we were landed in New York.'

On board that vessel as it inched into New York harbour on 18 April 1912, Margaret told immigration that she was a 24-year-old domestic from Loughanboy, County Galway. Identifying herself as a 24-year-old domestic to the American Red Cross in the same fashion, she was aided to the tune of $100. Her case was numbered 294 in the 1913 report of that organisation on assistance to survivors of the wreck.

Margaret Mannion booked her passage in Ryan's agency in Ballygar, County Galway and was one of five people from the hamlet of Caltra on board the *Titanic*. The two women were saved, their young male escorts drowned, victims of their sex as much as an iceberg. The two women appear to have been rescued in lifeboat No. 16, while the men were forced back and fell to their knees in prayer. Margaret blotted out the terrifying experience and Ellen Mockler found solace later by joining a convent.

Margaret found work as a domestic. She returned to Ireland in 1919, and a year later married Martin Hopkins from her home place. They farmed a smallholding until a Land Commission settlement prompted them to move in 1959 to a new farm in Laurencetown, some distance away. She had three children, but almost never spoke to them about the *Titanic*. She had a phobia about discussing the shipwreck, relenting only once when she agreed to do an Irish TV interview in the 1960s. But she never turned up at the appointed hour, pleading illness, and refused to reschedule.

Margaret Mannion Hopkins died on 15 May 1970, in her 86th year. She had been widowed four years earlier. She is buried in Chapelfinnerty Cemetery, County Galway.

1901 census – Mannion, Loughanboy, County Galway.
Parents: Laurence (65), farmer; Margaret (60).
Children: Bridget (20), Laurence (18), **Margaret (17)**, Celia (15).

KATE McCARTHY (24) SAVED

Ticket number 383123. Paid £7 15s.
Boarded at Queenstown. Third Class.
From: Ballygurtin, County Tipperary.
Destination: Guttenburg, New Jersey.

Bansha lady's escape – second last to leave the ship
Interesting Letter
Clonmel, Friday –
Miss Katie McCarthy, daughter of Mr Patrick McCarthy, farmer, Ballygurtin, County Tipperary, midway between Cahir and Bansha, has written to her father stating that she was the last to leave the *Titanic* on the night of the memorable tragedy.

It will be remembered that Miss McCarthy left home in company with Miss Kate Connolly of Tipperary, Miss Katie Peters, Ballydrehid, and Mr Roger Tobin, Ballycamon, the latter three being near neighbours.

Miss McCarthy's letter, which is written from New Jersey where she is now with her sister, is as follows:

'About 12 o'clock on Sunday night, Roger Tobin called us to get up, but told us not to be frightened as there was no danger. To make sure however of our safety, he told us to get lifebelts. There were three of us in the room, Katie Peters, Katie Connolly and myself. When Roger Tobin called me I wanted them to come up on deck, but they would not come. They appeared to think there was no danger. That was the last I saw of them.

'I then left the room, and on going out I met a man from Dungarvan who took me up to the Second-Class deck where they were putting out the boats. I was put into one boat, but was taken out again as it was too full.

'I was in the last boat to leave the ship and was the second last person put into it. This was a short time before the ship went down. We were only just out of the way when the ship split in two and sank.

'We remained in the boat all night until near eight o'clock the following morning when we were rescued by the *Carpathia*. Our boat was so full I thought it would go down every moment and one of the boats capsized when we were leaving the sinking ship.

'I did not however feel at all frightened and did not fully realise the danger and the full nature of the awful tragedy until I was safe on board the *Carpathia*. When we were put on board the *Carpathia*, we were immediately given restoratives and put to bed.

'I slept for an hour and then got up, feeling all right. When we landed in New York on Thursday night at eleven o'clock we were met by a number of Sisters of Charity nurses who took us up to St Vincent's Hospital where we were treated with the greatest kindness.'
(*The Cork Examiner*, Saturday, 11 May 1912)

Patrick McCarthy, who had been waiting in New York for the *Carpathia* to dock, wired home a telegram received on 19 April. It declared with economy: 'Katie is saved'.

Report of the American Red Cross (Titanic Disaster) 1913:
No. 276. (Irish.) Unmarried woman, 23 years old, coming to live with her sister in New Jersey, was severely injured. ($50)

According to the US Senate inquiry report, Katie had been due to stay at the rooming house of Mrs P. J. Murray at 231 East 50th Street in New York before continuing on to New Jersey. She told US immigration she was a 23-year-old domestic.

Soon after arriving in New York, Katie met a man, John Croke, from her home place of Bansha, County Tipperary, and they were married on 2 September 1914, at St Francis de Chantal Church. She was 26, while the groom, whose occupation was given as a watchman, was aged 30. Katie and John stayed a further seven years in America. In 1921 they decided to return home, and lived quietly in Tipperary for many years afterwards, running a shop in the village of Dundrum. They had no children.

Kate McCarthy Croke died at home on 12 November 1948. Cause of death was cited as 'essential hypertension with some coronary thrombosis and cerebral thrombosis':

> Mrs Catherine Croke, whose death occurred at her residence on 12th inst., was wife of Mr John Croke, farmer and merchant, Ballintemple, Dundrum.
>
> A descendant of a fine old Tipperary family, the McCarthys of Springhouse, she was a very kindly lady, held in affectionate regard in the district, where her passing, after three months' illness, is sincerely mourned.
>
> She was one of the survivors – believed to be the last in Ireland – of the ill-fated liner *Titanic*, wrecked by an iceberg in 1912.
>
> The remains were removed on 13th inst. to Donaskeigh Parish church and interment took place on Sunday in St Michael's Cemetery, Tipperary, in the presence of a very large assemblage.
>
> (*The Nationalist*, Clonmel, 20 November 1948)

1901 census – McCarthy, Ballygurteen, County Tipperary.
Parents Patrick (54), farmer; wife deceased. (Née Mary Boyle)
Children Patrick (23), John (21), Michael (17), Johanna (19), **Katie (14)**.

THOMAS McCORMACK (19) SAVED

Ticket number 367228. Paid £7 15s.
Boarded at Queenstown. Third Class.
From: Glenmore, Ballinamuck, County Longford.
Destination: 36 West 20th Street, Bayonne, New Jersey.

Thomas Joseph McCormack was 19, and in Third-Class passage to New York, returning to New Jersey after a visit home to his parents. He and Bernard McCoy – whose story follows immediately – alleged they were beaten off when they tried to clamber on board lifeboats as they struggled in the sea.

Extract from the British inquiry:

Lord Mersey to W.D. Harbinson: 'Who are the people you want to represent here?'
Harbinson: 'One is Thomas McCormack, who alleges in a statement –'
Mersey: 'Never mind what he alleges.'
Harbinson: ' ... the other person is Bernard McCoy.'
Mersey: 'Where are they now?'
Harbinson: 'America.'
Mersey: 'Are they coming here?'
Harbinson: 'No, but if your Lordship permits it, we propose to have their evidence taken on commission.'
Mersey: 'I think we are very unlikely to do that.'

Mr J. P. Farrell, MP for Longford, home county of both McCormack and McCoy, then stood up and mentioned the fact that he and his lordship were former colleagues in the House of Commons (he was then accorded some breathing space):

Farrell: 'Thomas McCormack alleges that when swimming in the sea after leaving the *Titanic* and while endeavouring to board two boats, he was struck in the head and hands and pushed back into the sea and an endeavour was made to drown him.'
Mersey: 'The man who did it may be guilty of manslaughter for all I know.'
Farrell: 'No my Lord, for McCormack was saved.'
Mersey: 'Well he may be guilty of an attempt to commit manslaughter, and I cannot try that issue.'
Farrell: 'Is it not a matter for investigation by this court? The same charge is made by McCoy.'
Mersey: 'I do not think it comes within my jurisdiction. This is an issue which must be tried by somebody else.'
Farrell: 'We have gone to a great deal of expense with the view of having it investigated.'
Lord Mersey told Mr Farrell to confine himself to what were proper issues.

McCormack had been working as a bartender in Bayonne when he decided to return home to visit to his parents, Bernard and Maria of Glenmore. In New Jersey, young McCormack lived with his sister, Mrs Catherine Evers, who was five years older. 'He jumped from the ship as it was sinking and was twice repulsed by lifeboats,' said the *Irish Independent* on 4 May 1912. 'Thomas McCormick [*sic*], one of the four male survivors,' added the *Irish World* of New York the same day, 'jumped overboard just as the ship was sinking and swam to a life raft.'

Mr McCormack often recalled that he was asleep in his compartment below decks when the mishap occurred. He was awakened after the collision by two cousins who died in the disaster. After dressing, he made his way to the main deck and jumped into the ocean. He was taken aboard a lifeboat an hour later.

(*Daily Journal*, New Jersey, 4 November 1975)

According to the *Western Nationalist,* 27 April 1912:

> Thomas McCormick [*sic*], who was rescued from the *Titanic* as he was returning from a visit to his parents in Ireland, is now in hospital suffering from shock and exposure, in addition to bruises on the head, which he declares he received at the hands of officers of the *Titanic*. He was accompanied on his voyage by two cousins, John and Philip Kieran [*sic*], who were lost. McCormick says that when the ship was sinking, he jumped and swam. He got his hands on the gunwale of one lifeboat when members of the crew of the *Titanic* struck him on the head and tore his hands loose from the boat.
>
> After repeated efforts to enter the boat he swam to another boat and met with the same reception.
>
> Finally however, two sisters in the boat, Mary and Kate Murphy, pulled him on board in spite of the crew's attempts to keep him out.

McCormack told the *Jersey Journal,* 23 April 1912:

> After being beaten severely by sailors with oars I managed to get into one of the lifeboats … After a while one of the sailors saw my legs protruding, and seizing them asked me 'what in ___ I was doing in the boat'. He dragged me out and tried to throw me into the water. I grabbed him by the throat and said if I went overboard I would take him with me. When he saw that he could not throw me over he finally desisted and I was allowed to remain.

Thomas with his sister Catherine

The *New York Herald,* 22 April 1912 noted:

> *Girls saved youth*
> Thomas McCormick [*sic*], nineteen years old, of No. 36 West Twentieth Street, Bayonne, N.J., who was a passenger on the *Titanic*, and is a patient in St Vincent's Hospital, this city, suffering from exposure, says that his life was saved by two sisters, Kate and Mary Murphy, who picked him up from the water, dragging him into a lifeboat and sitting on him after sailors manning the boat had struck him on the head and tried to drive him from clinging to the sides of the boat.

A body of opinion considers McCormack to have been saved not by the Murphy sisters, but by the McCoys, who were also from the same locality. McCormack himself named Alice and Kate McCoy in his early *Jersey Journal* account.

The *New Jersey News* recorded:

Memories of a Titanic *night – he recalls sinking 62 years ago*
The Easter season is never a completely happy time for Tom McCormack of Elizabeth, N.J. It always brings memories of his frantic, leaping escape from the sinking *Titanic*, which went down in the freezing Atlantic sixty-two years ago today.

McCormack is one of only thirty living survivors of one of the worst sea disasters in history, and throughout his life he has had nightmares about that night when more than 1,500 people died as the supposedly unsinkable ship hit an iceberg and sank on her maiden voyage.

'I try not to think about that night, but I can't help it,' McCormack said yesterday. 'It's a memory I'll always have with me.'

The 81-year old man has lived in retirement in a small apartment at 120 Madison Ave., Elizabeth, for 16 years. He is bedridden, but remains in generally good spirits under the care of his nephew, Barney Evers.

Sixty-two years ago, McCormack was a 19-year old with the same sense of adventure that drew the other passengers to the *Titanic's* trip. McCormack was returning to America with two cousins from a visit to his native Ireland.

Just before midnight, 15 April 1912, the indestructible sailing fortress smashed into an iceberg and began to sink. 'I was sound asleep at the time,' McCormack said. 'I jumped out of bed and ran into the hall with my two cousins when we hit. Everyone was crazy and running, screaming. My cousins and I separated in the confusion. They eventually drowned. I kept running toward the deck.'

When he got on deck, there were thousands of people pushing and shoving each other. 'They were crying, yelling. I didn't know what was going on. I panicked and ran to the rail. I never stopped to look how far from the water I was. I just jumped over. It felt like a mile down to the ocean, and it was freezing water. All I had was my lifejacket,' he said.

McCormack spent 80 minutes in the water before one of the *Titanic's* lifeboats picked him up. He spent another three hours in the lifeboat before he and the other survivors were picked up by the rescue ship *Carpathia*.

'The *Titanic* sank into the ocean while I watched from the lifeboat. It was a terrible sight … all those people screaming and moaning on the decks as it went under the waves …' McCormack said.

The young McCormack was brought to New York and spent four days recuperating at St Vincent's Hospital from exposure. Then he went to Bayonne, N.J., where he bought a tavern and operated it for fourteen years. Then he spent many years as a guard at a Bayonne factory before his retirement.

The sinking of the *Titanic* has always had some effect on his life. Afterward, he was afraid of sailing, and the only other ship he ever boarded was the troopship that carried him to the shores of France to fight in the First World War. McCormack had nightmares for years, and almost all of his conversations would somehow get around to the *Titanic*.

'When I was running up to the deck in the confusion that night, I did not think I was going to live. Maybe if I didn't jump into the ocean right away I would have died. I owe my life to God's kindness, nothing else,' McCormack said.

(*New Jersey News*, 15 April 1974)

He later filed a claim for his losses against the Oceanic Steam Navigation Company through Broadway solicitors Hunt, Hill & Betts:

1 blue suit – $25; 1 grey suit – £25; 1 brown suit – $25; 2 pair of cuff links – $5; shirts and underwear – $15; collars and neckties – $7; golf scarf-pin – $5; gold watch and fob – $35; 3 pairs of shoes – $15; 12 pair of socks and one sweater – $8; 1 leather bag – $12; penknives, razors and pipes – $10; 3 hats (1 soft hat, 1 derby and 1 cap) – $6; Money £18 Sterling (at $4.85 @ lb) – $87.30. Total – $280.30.

McCormack later married a Mary Donovan in New Jersey, who predeceased him by thirteen years. Born on 11 December 1892, Thomas died in Elizabeth, New Jersey, on 4 November 1975 aged 82. He was buried in the Holy Name Cemetery in Jersey City.

1901 census – McCormack. Glenmore, County Longford.
Parents Bernard (55), farmer, Maria (50), née McKenna.
Children John (20), Catherine (13), **Thomas (8)**.

AGNES McCOY (29) SAVED
ALICE McCOY (26) SAVED
BERNARD McCOY (23) SAVED

Joint ticket number 367226. Paid £23 5s.
Boarded at Queenstown. Third Class.
From: Carrickatane, Granard, County Longford.
Destination: 358 Madison Street West, Brooklyn, New York city.

Agnes, Alice and their brother Bernard were heading to New York to join their sister, Mrs Mary Heckel, at the above address, and to seek their fortunes.

Three Irish Survivors
Sisters' Thrilling Story – Saved Their Brother
The *Morning Leader*'s New York correspondent wires –
    Three steerage survivors who were at St Vincent's Hospital were Agnes, Alice and Bernard McCoy. They said that when the first shock came to the *Titanic* they were asleep. They dressed and hurriedly went on deck. There was an officer there who quickly reassured them.
    They returned to the steerage quarters and found men and women rushing about. They noticed stewards going through the berths, telling passengers to dress and put on lifebelts. They donned lifebelts and went on deck.
    They saw a boat half-filled with members of the crew and about to be lowered away. An officer came up pointing his revolver at the men and told them to get out or he would shoot. The men climbed out slowly.
    Then the officer turned to the two young women and their brother and told them to get back downstairs as there was no immediate danger. Miss Agnes said they started

down but drew back when they saw the water rushing into the steerage quarters.

By the time they got back to the officer, he was directing the placing of women in the lifeboat vacated by members of the crew and the women got in. Their brother, who is younger than either of them, watched as the boat was lowered.

That was the last they saw of him until they had been in the lifeboat half an hour. Then they saw him struggling in the water. One of them grabbed for him and missed, and a sailor told her he would throw her out if she did it again.

Their brother swam towards the boat and was shoved away with an oar. The third time he came, they grabbed him. A sailor with an oar hauled their brother into the boat.

(*The Cork Examiner*, 27 April 1912)

Sisters save drowning brother

Another dramatic story was told by two sisters, the Misses Agnes and Alice McCoy, who saved their brother, Bernard, after the seamen at the oars fought him off as he struggled in the water when the *Titanic* was sinking. Between sobs, Miss Agnes McCoy recounted the harrowing experiences. She said –

'Both my sister and I wanted to remain on shipboard when they would not allow poor Bernard to come into the lifeboat with us. He told us to go ahead, but we thought that if one was going to drown we might all go down. We were literally thrown into the lifeboat and while we fought and cried, it was lowered over the side. The boat bobbed around in the water for some time before the men got at the oars, and the first thing I knew, I saw a form whirl through the air and splash into the water near our boat.

'When the form came up, I recognised it as Bernard. I cried to my sister, who was nearer to him than I, to help him. The poor boy took hold of the side of the boat and I staggered to his rescue. Several persons pushed me back and I saw a seaman strike Bernard's hands with an oar. Then he tried to beat him off by striking him on the head and shoulders.

'It was more than I could stand, and calling for Alice, I made for the seaman. With more strength than I thought I ever possessed, I threw the man to the bottom of the boat and held him there fast. Yes, maybe I did hit him once or twice, but I think I was justified under the circumstances.

'In the meantime, Alice helped the poor boy over the side and lifted him to safety. I think everyone on board the lifeboat was highly elated and perfectly satisfied that our brother was safe with us. We need him here with us as any two sisters do.'

(*New York Herald*, 29 April 1912)

Fr Michael Kenny, spiritual counsellor to a number of survivors, gave an interview to the *Brooklyn Eagle* on 23 April 1912, in which he was evidently confused about who had rescued whom:

I also learned at the hospital that Agnes and Alice McCoy, who escaped in a lifeboat into which they were pulled by their brother Bernard, together with their brother lost their life savings, amounting to £180, leaving the sum in a pillow slip when they deserted the ship.

Report of the American Red Cross (Titanic Disaster) 1913:
No. 278. (Irish.) Two girls, 28 and 22, and their brother, 21 years old, suffered severely from shock and exposure, and lost $500 in cash besides all their effects. ($300)

Agnes McCoy later paid tribute to Fr Thomas Roussel David Byles, who stayed with the steerage passengers as the *Titanic* slipped to oblivion:

> I saw Fr Byles when he spoke to us in the steerage; and there was a German priest with him there [Fr Josef Peruschitz]. I did not see Fr Byles again until we were told to come up and get into the boat. He was reading out of a book, and did not pay any attention. He thought, as the rest of us did, that there wasn't really any danger.
>
> Then I saw him put the book in his pocket and hurry around to help women into the boats. We were among the first to get away, and I didn't see him any more …
>
> I learn from several passengers that Fr Byles and another priest stayed with the people after the last boat had gone, and that a big crowd, a hundred maybe, knelt about him. They were Catholics, Protestants and Jewish people who were kneeling there. Fr Byles told them to prepare to meet God, and recited the Rosary. The others answered him. Fr Byles and the other priest were still standing there praying when the water came over the deck.
>
> (*Irish World*, New York, 27 April 1912)

Agnes became a servant employed by wealthy New Yorkers, and in time became housemaid to Hollywood stars Douglas Fairbanks and Mary Pickford, who were married in 1919 but divorced in 1935. One of her treasured possessions was a photograph of Fairbanks inscribed 'to Agnes'.

Agnes never married, and died from heart failure on 14 January 1957, which some have suggested was due to shock from a break-in at her Brooklyn apartment. She was 74.

Her sister Alice was twice divorced in her later life. She then co-habited with a third man, considering herself excommunicated from the Catholic Church. She used the name Gardner from a 1962 marriage. A daughter, Colleen, survived her.

Bernard McCoy, known as Barney, developed a permanent stutter from his terrifying experiences as he struggled for survival. Like other male survivors, he was later drafted into the US army and fought in the First World War. He worked as a laundryman in New Jersey after demobilisation, never married, and died from spinal cancer in a veteran's hospital at the end of the Second World War in July 1945.

1901 census – John McCoy, farmer (60), wife Bridget (55).
Children: Margaret (28), Patrick (23), **Alice (15)**, **Bernard (13)**, John (10), Luke (7).

DELIA McDERMOTT (28) SAVED

Ticket number 330932. Paid £7 15s 8d.
Boarded at Queenstown. Third Class.
From: Knockfarnaught, Lahardane, County Mayo.
Destination: 404 Henrietta Street, St Louis, Missouri.

Although one of the first to find a place in a lifeboat, Delia insisted on climbing out of the early boat to insist on recovering a prized possession. She had bought a new hat in Cawley's shop, Crossmolina, the nearest big town to her home place in a remote part of County Mayo, just before she travelled to America.

Journalist Tom Shiel told her story in *The Connaught Telegraph* of February 1998:

Nephin Mór had been snowcapped on a number of occasions during the winter of 1912 and the people in the valleys below were longing for Spring. Even when only the boggy summit of Mayo's highest mountain was mantled in white, the people of Addergoole parish (Lahardane), indeed the whole of Ireland, had a cold time of it.

Many times that long ago spring of 1912, Delia McDermott looked westwards from her parents' thatched cottage at Knockfarnaught at the great majestic bulk of mountain. When the hedgerows were greening and only a few tiny stripes of snow remained on the upper reaches, Delia knew the time was fast approaching when she would be uprooted, perhaps forever, from her birthplace.

As part of her preparations for the great journey to America, she travelled one day to Crossmolina to buy new clothing. One of her purchases was a smart new hat. She liked the hat so much that weeks later she risked her life to recover it from her cabin in the ill-fated *Titanic*.

Delia was one of 14 people from Addergoole preparing in spring 1912 to travel on the White Star liner. Only three of the group survived. Delia, despite dicing with death on the double in order to retrieve her cherished millinery, was one of the lucky ones.

There was great activity in Addergoole as sailing time approached. Those not travelling were out and about on the land and in the bog, or perhaps taking the odd trip to Castlebar where the women sold eggs and the men purchased grain and farm implements.

Thoughts of turf-cutting and harvesting were far from the minds of those who were about to emigrate as they travelled by pony and trap over the steep Windy Gap and then at a smart gallop into Castlebar. By the time the scythes had felled the first grass of that year's hay harvest, they planned to be carving out new lives in Chicago or other bustling industrial cities in the industrial United States.

In March, ten of the intending passengers, including Delia McDermott, then 28 years old, booked their passage with Thomas Durcan of Castlebar. Three others booked with another travel agent, Mrs Walsh of Linenhall Street.

The days before they were due to travel for Queenstown were extremely busy ones for the Addergoole contingent. They visited neighbours most would never see again and there were tearful embraces on the doorstep of many a thatched cottage.

Delia McDermott's niece, now Delia Melody of Lord Edward Street, Ballina, tells the story of a strange and chilling encounter between her aunt and a mysterious man in black in Lahardane village the evening before she left for Cobh.

'She was in Lahardane with friends when suddenly a hand tapped her on the shoulder,' Mrs Melody explained. 'She turned around and there was a little man there whom she thought was a traveller. My aunt went to give the man a few pennies and he told her he knew she was going on a long journey. "There will be a tragedy, but you will be saved," the little man said before disappearing.'

When Delia mentioned the little man to her friends, they said they hadn't seen anybody. Thus Delia McDermott began her long and eventful journey to the New World filled with some foreboding …

Luck was also in Delia McDermott's favour. She was one of the first to find a lifeboat but returned to her cabin for the new hat she had bought before the journey. Says Delia's niece, Mrs Melody: 'It was perhaps a foolish thing to do, but luckily she managed to get a place in a boat. She had to jump fifteen feet from a rope ladder onto the lifeboat. At this stage the *Titanic* was sideways. It was going down.'

Delia indeed survived and later prospered in the United States. She never returned to Ireland.

Report of the American Red Cross (Titanic Disaster) 1913:
No. 323. (Irish.) Servant, 25 years of age, injured very severely, and long unable to work. ($200)

On 25 April, Delia McDermott received $150 from the Women's Relief Committee, formed in New York to aid survivors. She had intended to travel to her cousin, Mrs Celia Syson, at Henrietta Street, St Louis, but never left the east coast. She moved from New York to New Jersey, marrying a fellow countryman, John Joseph Lynch of Galway. He served in the First World War and spent his working years on the Jersey city docks. They had three children – Julia, Margaret and Tommy. Delia never spoke about her *Titanic* experiences and the children were forbidden to ask her about it. It appears however that Delia was rescued in lifeboat No. 13, launched from the starboard side of the ship relatively early in the night.

Her daughter, Julia Danning, remembers Delia's later life:

She was a quiet, home-loving housewife, devoted to her family. She was very devout, with daily Mass and nightly Rosary. Her one and only vice was a weekly Euchre game with friends. She rarely spoke of her experience aboard the *Titanic* except for having left a lifeboat to go back and retrieve her new hat. Hats being what they were in those days, it was no doubt a huge expenditure for her family and it was a going-away gift. Otherwise I believe the ordeal was so traumatic that she closed her mind to it.

Delia died in Jersey City, N.J., on 3 November 1959. She was believed to have been aged 75 – a figure supported by the 1901 census which put her age at 17. However, if an age of

32 from the 1911 census is correct, she would have been 33 when the *Titanic* sailed, and 80 when she died.

> 1911 census – McDermott, Knockfarnaught.
> Parents: Michael (77), farmer, Bridget (73). Married 40 years, seven children, four living.
> Children in house: Thomas (35), **Bridget (Delia, 32)**.

MICHAEL McEVOY (19) LOST

Joint ticket number 36568. Paid £15 10s.
Boarded at Queenstown. Third Class.
From: Farraneglish, Glebe, Ballycolla, County Laois.
Destination: 231 East 50th Street, New York city?

Eloping Michael McEvoy seems to have become infatuated with a woman nearly twice his age. The callow teenager was travelling on the same ticket as an intriguing female, fifteen years his senior. Norah Murphy, a 34-year-old nanny, already had one broken marriage behind her. How she became embroiled with 19-year-old Michael – and he with her – remains uncertain.

Norah was originally from Sallins, County Kildare, while Michael was born in County Laois. They may have met in Dublin as their ticket was bought in the capital and Norah had an aunt living close to the centre of the city. It seems the couple may have abandoned their home places to carry on an unapproved liaison in the city. Michael's family later airbrushed him out of their history, while Norah seemed to have left her own family trailing far in her wake, specifying only an aunt as her next of kin.

What is known is that Michael paid for both of their tickets and that the White Star Line subsequently misreported his name as 'McElroy', an error that has persisted to this day and which might be partly explained by the fact that there was a purser of this surname on board.

The money for Michael's passage was sent to him by his sister Annie Deegan, a 30-year-old maid in Norristown, near Philadelphia. The family in Ireland disapproved of what little they could discover, and relatives at home later shunned Annie because of Michael's death, according to grandniece Elizabeth Mary Haruch. They may have believed the drowning was heavenly retribution for his embrace of sin and Annie had encouraged him in this.

> Anxious inquiries are being made at the various offices of the White Star in Ireland by friends and relatives of passengers on the ill-fated liner.
> One of the callers at Messrs Cook's offices in Dublin yesterday was Constable P. McEvoy from the RIC Depot, whose younger brother Michael McEvoy of Kilmacanogue, is believed to have sailed in the *Titanic*.

They could not trace the latter's name at Messrs Cook's offices, but he may have boarded at Queenstown. His name appears in the passenger list as Michael McEvoy, Dublin.

(Irish Independent, 18 April 1912)

[Constable Patrick McEvoy, aged 45 in 1912, was from Mountrath, County Laois, and served one-third of a century with the DMP from 1890. He retired in 1923, and died at the end of the Second World War on 23 May 1945 at the age of 78.]

Michael McEvoy died in the disaster. His body was never recovered. He was the youngest of eight children, the baby of the family. Norah Murphy, however, was saved. Their parting on the decks of the *Titanic*, after only a few days earlier darkly delighting in parting from past lives on boarding the ship at Queenstown, can only be imagined. For 19-year-old Michael, alone on a sliding deck, the loneliness must have been absolute.

1901 census – McEvoy, Farran, Ballycolla, Abbeyleix. Aghaboe parish.
Parents: John (56), farmer. Bridget (50).
Children: Martin (22), ploughman, Mary (20), Anne (18), Thomas (16), James (14), Kate (12), John (10), **Michael (8)**.

JAMES R. McGOUGH (35) SAVED

Ticket number: 17473. Paid £26 5s 9d.
Boarded at Southampton. First Class.
From: Mandistown, Slane, County Meath.
Destination: 708 York Street, Philadelphia.

Born close to the Boyne river battle site of 1690, James Robert McGough is believed to have emigrated to the United States with his family while a young boy. By 1912 he was a buyer with Strawbridge & Clothier department store, and was enjoying enormously the regal comfort of the *Titanic* as he returned from a business trip. Life had never been better. So it seemed when he and four friends signed the back of their Sunday dinner menu, which featured a choice of lamb, roast duck or sirloin of beef, in celebration of good times together.

McGough was at the table in the First-Class dining room on D deck in the company of four other commercial buyers. They were Spencer Silverthorne of St Louis, George Graham of Winnipeg, Canada, Edward Calderhead of New York city and John Irving Flynn of Brooklyn. Only Calderhead had turned forty, the other four were still in their thirties.

At the bottom of the menu, someone noted that they were only 1,760 miles from landfall. But just three hours later, James McGough experienced a huge iceberg crunching by his starboard stateroom, dropping chunks of ice onto the carpet through his open porthole. And within a few hours, one of his table companions, 38-year-old George Graham, was dead.

McGough was in E-25 with Flynn, and Calderhead and Silverthorne were in the adjoining E-24. Graham may have died because he was sleeping in cabin C-42, two decks away, out of sight and out of mind.

James McGough submitted an affidavit to the US inquiry into the disaster:

I, James R. McGough, do depose and say that I was a passenger on the steamship *Titanic* …

I was awakened at 11.40 p.m. ship time; my stateroom was on the starboard side – deck E – and was shared with me by Mr Flynn, a buyer for Gimbel Bros, New York, at Thirty-third and Broadway. Soon after leaving our stateroom we came in contact with the second dining room steward, Mr Dodd, in the companionway, of whom we asked the question, 'Is there any danger?' and he answered, 'Not in the least,' and suggested that we go back to bed, which we did not, however, do.

It was our intention to go up on the promenade deck, but before doing so I rapped on the door of the stateroom opposite mine, which was occupied by a lady, and suggested to her that she had better get up at once and dress, as there was apparently something wrong.

Mr Flynn and I then ascended to promenade deck A, and after being there about ten minutes were notified to put on life preservers as a matter of precaution. We then had to go all the way from the promenade deck back to our stateroom, which was on E deck. After procuring our life preservers we went back again to the top deck, and after reaching there discovered that orders had been given to launch the lifeboats, and that they were already being launched at that time.

They called for the women and children to board the boats first. Both women and men, however, hesitated, and did not feel inclined to get into the small boats, thinking the larger boat was the safer. I had my back turned looking in the opposite direction at that time and was caught by the shoulder by one of the officers, who gave me a push, saying, 'Here, you are a big fellow; get into the boat.'

Our boat was launched with 28 people; we, however, transferred 5 from one of the other boats after we were out in the ocean, which was some time after the ship went down.

When our lifeboat left the vessel, we were directed to row away a short distance from the large boat, feeling it would be but a short time until we would be taken back on the *Titanic*. We then rested on our oars; but after realising that the *Titanic* was really sinking, we rowed away for about half a mile, being afraid that the suction would draw us down.

Although there were several of us wanted drinking water, it was unknown to us that there was a tank of water and also some crackers in our boat, having no light on our boat; and we did not discover this fact – that is, as to the tank of water – until after reaching the *Carpathia*.

McGough was saved in lifeboat No. 7, the very first launched from the *Titanic*, at 12.25

a.m. He heard no shooting during the unfolding crisis, but became aware of moaning and groaning after the sinking. Some of the women passengers in No. 7 objected to making the effort to go back for survivors.

In the aftermath, McGough went back to work. He lodged an insurance claim for lost property and was paid $612.90. He married and was eventually widowed. When the Wall Street Crash happened in 1929, McGough, then 53, found himself out of a job as his employers battened down the hatches. Unemployed during the Great Depression, McGough was living in Philadelphia in 1935 when he developed cancer. He died on 24 July 1937. His death certificate stated that he was born in Mandistown, Ireland, on the hundredth anniversary of the original American Independence Day. His parents, Thomas McGough and Catherine Dowdell, had both also been born in Ireland.

MARY McGOVERN (22) SAVED

Ticket number 330931. Paid £7 12s 7d.
Boarded at Queenstown. Third Class.
From: Clarbally, Bawnboy, County Cavan.
Destination: 435 56th Street, New York city.

Dry land was hundreds of miles away for the trapped passengers and crew of the *Titanic* on the icy blackness of the Atlantic, but Mary McGovern attributed her survival to a handful of soil. Mary was a 22-year-old steerage passenger, on her way to stay with a cousin, Mrs Greeves, in New York and work as a domestic, and the arrangements for her going had long been in place. She booked her ticket in Ballinamore, County Leitrim, the nearest big town to her home in Clarbally, Corlough, in west County Cavan.

She told of the *Titanic* tragedy in a newspaper interview forty years later:

We left Cobh on Wednesday for New York, and everything was grand. I was fast asleep in my cabin, a three-tiered affair, which I shared with two others from Virginia, County Cavan. On Sunday night we were awoken and thrown out of our bunks by the shock of the collision.

But we were not at all afraid, for everything was silent. The lights burned brightly. In fact we had no cause for alarm. But outside our door we heard a rising clamour and we went out and found the passages and corridors full of running people.

That was about midnight if I remember right, and we went up onto the boat deck, pushing our way through lines of linked sailors and armed men who were shouting 'Women and children first'.

Somebody told us to go back for our lifebelts, and with difficulty we went back to our cabin, found them over the door, put them on, and fought our way back again.

We went from lifeboat to lifeboat, all of which were packed, and which one by one, were being lowered away down into the water. I knew how near the water was, for I had actually seen it washing down the corridor as we went down for our lifebelts.

We were shoved into the last of the lifeboats to leave and had to watch drowning men being beaten with oars to prevent them from overturning the boat we were in.

We watched the lights go out one by one in the huge ship sliding to her grave on the starlit water and saw the last, long, slow death struggle of the pride of Queens Island, the greatest and newest ship in the world.

Next day we were picked up by the *Carpathia*. I am one of the 712 people saved out of a total of 2,201. Sewn in my clothes from the time I left my native Corlough here in Cavan, I have carried a little locket of St Mogue's clay. I still have it hidden in the rafters of my home.

(Sunday Independent, 21 September 1952)

Mary's locket of St Mogue's clay was soil taken from the grave of a Leitrim man of God, which the faithful believed would protect her from death by drowning, fire, or in an accident.

Her parents were John and Bridget, and Mary was born in 1890. When news of the disaster reached them, it was followed a few days later by a telegram and they dreaded its possible contents. A younger brother was dispatched to collect the cable from Corlough post office and the returning teenager came back into view from the post office and waved the telegram over his head, signalling that it was obviously good news. Bridget McGovern fainted with relief.

Mary's account of drowning men being beaten with oars to keep them from entering her boat is eerily reminiscent of the accounts of the Murphy sisters, the McCoy family and Thomas McCormack, although this is probably coincidental.

Report of the American Red Cross (Titanic Disaster) 1913:
No. 282. (Irish.) Girl, 20 years old, injured. ($100)

Mary McGovern is believed to have shared the same compartment on the *Titanic* as Mary Glynn, Julia Smyth and Kate Connolly. Mary Glynn was from Clare, but the other two were fellow Cavan girls and all four became instant friends. They all survived. It seems likely that they entered a boat together. Julia Smyth followed Kate Connolly into lifeboat No. 13 and both had to jump, indicating the boat was already lowered some way. Mary Glynn also seems to have been in No. 13, and Mary McGovern's use of the word 'we' indicates she too may have made it into this vessel.

When she arrived in New York, Mary McGovern was ferried to St Vincent's Hospital in a Gimbel's truck along with some other Third-Class survivors. Private trains met some of those rescued from First Class. Eight months later, she filed a claim against White Star for $50 and after a few weeks topped it up with a $20 loss to cover the cost of two crocheted collars given to her by her mother.

A year or two went by and Mary McGovern returned to Ireland. In 1921 she married her namesake Peter McGovern. They lived in Tullytrasna, Corlough, close to her home place. She had a son, Hugh, and a daughter, Mary Kate. Mary died on 24 August 1957, aged 67.

1901 census – Clarbally, Corlough, County Cavan.
Parents: John (50), Bridget (35).
Children: Patrick (11), **Mary (9)**, John (7), Thomas (5), Francis (2).

ANNIE McGOWAN (17) SAVED

Ticket number 330923. Paid £7 15s 7d.
Boarded at Queenstown. Third Class.
From: Massbrook, Lahardane, County Mayo.
Destination: 3241 North Ashland Avenue, Chicago.

Annie made the most of her ocean reprieve, living into her mid-nineties. When she died in the last decade of the twentieth century, nearly 78 years had passed since the *Titanic* went down.

The terror of that night affected her memory, and when she met fellow survivor Annie Kate Kelly – herself a teenager – in the sickbay of the *Carpathia*, she had no idea of how she had escaped from the stricken steamer:

Not a thing did Annie Kelly know when she was pulled over the side of the other boat, the *Carpathia*, at 5 o'clock in the morning, though they poured hot whiskey and raw brandy into her and buried her in blankets and hot water bottles, she was that frozen.

It was noon before she came to herself and found herself in the hospital, with Annie McGowan there too, though how Annie McGowan came to be saved, she herself could not tell.

She [Annie McGowan] was young and swift as a deer, and when the call came for all to go on deck, she ran among the first to see what was the matter, and thus was saved.
(*Chicago Record-Herald* interview with Annie Kate Kelly, reprinted in the *Irish Independent*, May 1912)

Annie was travelling with her aunt Catherine, who had come home from America on a holiday intending to take Annie over on her return. They were due to stay in Chicago at the home of another aunt, Catherine's sister Mary, who had become Mrs Thomas McDermott and who lived at North Ashland Avenue.

Catherine was lost in the disaster, and Annie survived wearing only her nightgown. She cannot be attributed to any lifeboat, since she refrained from all later comment about the *Titanic*, even when pressed by her family. Her daughter Mary Kapolnek said after Annie's death in 1990: 'She wouldn't talk about the sinking. She refused to return to Ireland to see her parents because she was afraid of both the water and flying. She would be scared if we children even went in a rowboat.'

When Annie left hospital, she was wearing a donated coat and a pair of old shoes over her nightgown. She and Annie Kelly travelled together to Chicago, where Dr Mary

O'Brien of the Catholic Women's League met them. The League sought money for the two destitute teenagers from a relief fund established by the mayor.

Report of the American Red Cross (Titanic Disaster) 1913: No. 283. (Irish.) A girl, 17 years of age, travelling with her aunt, who was lost, left without funds or friends, suffered seriously for many months, from shock and exposure. She lost all her belongings, and received, immediately, clothing and $125 from other American sources of relief. She went to Chicago with some girl friends. This Committee interested a Chicago Society in making plans for the girl's training. She is now in a boarding school where she will remain for a year to be fitted for self-support. ($575)

She lived with her two aunts, Margaret McDermott and Sarah Gollogly, after the sinking, attended a Chicago business school and worked for several years before meeting Raymond Straube, a plumbing contractor, whom she married. Annie had by now reverted to calling herself Ann, her given name. They had three daughters – Jackie, Mary and Frances.

Ann Straube finally broke her silence on the tragedy in an interview with grandson Kris Kopp in 1984. It appears Ann, then in her eighties, had imported learned material into her own account, edited here. Yet she also states clearly that the ship broke in two. A year later the *Titanic's* discovery confirmed the fact, and confounded the conclusions of two official inquiries that she sank intact.

After 72 years, Titanic survivor talks
For 72 years she has kept her memories of that miserable night to herself, always refusing to tell reporters what she saw, what she felt.

'When I came to Chicago they would pester me and pester me,' she said of the aggressive reporters who pursued her (in 1912). 'My aunt just wouldn't permit it.' The only people who could coax any information out of her at all were grandchildren writing book reports about the sinking of the *Titanic*.

But now one of her grandchildren is a reporter and 87-year-old Anne McGowan has agreed to make an exception. She emerges from her bedroom carrying a package wrapped in orange tissue paper. Inside are yellowed and ragged newspapers from 1912 with screaming headlines such as 'Liner *Titanic* Sinks – 1,300 drowned, 866 saved'. The clippings arouse the memories she has struggled to repress all these years, and as she slowly begins to speak, her eyes grow teary.

McGowan was 15 at the time and travelling with her Aunt Margaret [*sic*] McGowan from Ireland to New York on the newest luxury liner. 'I felt so sure of the safety – everybody did,' McGowan said. 'Wealthy people had waited on lists to get on the ship.'

McGowan remembers enjoying the lovely flower gardens and other luxuries on board. She also took part in the activities, even the adult dance on Sunday, April 14. (The memory of her naughtiness makes her giggle.) That's where she was when the confusion began.

'I was at the party, and there were a bunch of drunks there. My aunt wanted me away from the party, but everyone was having so much fun,' McGowan said. She doesn't recall feeling any jolt or bump, but suddenly officers and crew were rushing around and the word spread quickly that the ship had hit an iceberg. She asked a crewmember if the ship could be saved, and he assured her there was no chance of that.

She was in one of the first lifeboats to be lowered. '"You take her, you take her" – they just grabbed me the way I was, wearing just a dress and shoes; they would not even let me take my purse,' McGowan recalled. 'I was just numb and it was so cold out on the ocean.

'The whole time in the lifeboats the crew just kept telling me, "Don't worry, your aunt is in a lifeboat on the other side, and she'll be all right."

'Women wouldn't leave their husbands,' McGowan said. 'They were screaming, and I could hear gunshots in the background. Apparently, some of the men had tried to dress like women in order to be rescued, and they were shot.'

Even in her lifeboat, men were begging to get in. 'Let me in or I'll tip the whole lifeboat, is what one man said,' McGowan said. 'Of course, we had to let him in.'

While bobbing up and down in the waves, the survivors still could see the ship, and they heard the band still playing. 'They just kept playing *Nearer My God to Thee*,' McGowan recalled. 'Then the ship just busted in half, and that's when all the screaming started. It was just so terrible; I guess a boiler had busted.'

By the time McGowan's lifeboat was hoisted aboard the *Carpathia*, her eyes had begun to bleed, apparently from the salt water and wind, and she was shivering violently.

'By morning we were dripping wet,' she said. 'We were chilled, but the fright alone was enough to chill our bodies. I didn't know if there was any chance. One ship had already refused to acknowledge the signals before the *Carpathia* came through. You don't know how awful it was.'

Hesitating for a few moments, McGowan brings up the most painful memory of all. She never saw her aunt again. She believes her aunt's lifeboat was sucked into the whirlpool created when the *Titanic* finally sank.

'I am still upset because I don't know what happened to my aunt,' she said calmly. 'In the newspapers, when we got back, they had her listed as a survivor, but I can't believe that.'

(*Chicago Sun Herald*, 15 April 1984)

Ann died on 30 January 1990, finally succumbing to liver cancer at her home in Chicago. She was buried in All Saints Cemetery in Des Plaines, Illinois. Only Ellen Shine Callaghan, aged 101, outlived Annie McGowan Straube as the last living Irish connection to the *Titanic* disaster. Her family believed Ann to be aged 92 when she died. Her death certificate shows a birth date of 5 July 1897, which placed Annie at only age 14 when aboard the *Titanic*, easily the youngest of the Irish passengers.

It seems instead that she was definitely aged 17, and about to turn 18. The *Titanic* passenger manifest shows her as 18, but the figure of 17 is quoted elsewhere. It thus appears that she was actually aged 95 when she passed from this life.

1901 census – Terry, Massbrook, County Mayo.
Anthony (grandfather), widower (71).
John (30) and wife Maria (30), née McGowan.
Children: **Annie (7)**, Anthony (6), Maria (4), Margaret (2), Thomas Henry (seven months).

CATHERINE McGOWAN (42) LOST

Ticket number 9232. Paid £7 15s.
Boarded at Queenstown. Third Class.
From: Terry, Massbrook, County Mayo.
Destination: 3241 North Ashland Avenue, Chicago.

A letter sent from Ireland by her young niece Annie McGowan, in October 1911, could have sown the seeds of Catherine McGowan's death. It inspired the idea of Catherine coming home to Ireland to see her family for Christmas, at a time when she was readjusting to life in Chicago after several years working in Cleveland, Ohio, and Annie intended to return with her.

The *Chicago Record-Herald* explained what happened in a piece contributed by Mary O'Connell Newell soon after the disaster:

Little Annie McGowan, who was Kate McGowan's niece, wrote to Kate way out in Chicago last October, saying she would be coming over in a month. Now Kate hadn't thought for a moment of going back to Ireland. But she said to herself: 'If Annie comes out, it may be that I'll never be going back to Ireland again, and what need indeed would she have of it, with her favourite sister in Chicago and her father and mother being dead?'

So, without thinking for as much as one day about it, she sat down and wrote to Annie: 'Wait. I'll be back in Ireland in three weeks, and we'll come together in the spring.' Then she sold her boarding-house on the North Side, bought a ticket, and was soon back on the Green Isle.

Unsettled Kate may have been feeling her biological clock ticking. Unlike her sisters, she was still unmarried, and her best friend had gone home to Ireland in 1910 – and had walked up the aisle the same year. Kate McGowan's dearest confidante had been Kate McHugh – the pair had spent many years in America together – but the latter had gone home to Mayo to become Mrs John Bourke, a farmer's wife in her home place.

Let the 1912 *Chicago Record-Herald* take up the story again:

> It came about this way. When Kate McHugh went back to Ireland over a year ago, it was little anyone knew that she would soon be changing her name to Burke. Not a word did her sister Ellen in Chicago know of what she meant to do, and there's no telling that she knew herself indeed, but be that as it may, she married John Burke, whom she had known all her life, and never thought to leave Ireland again. Nor would she, but for Kate McGowan's coming home.
>
> Not a thought did Kate Burke and her husband John have of coming to America, not then nor all winter through. But what with the talk of Kate McGowan's sailing and the thoughts of it, and the excitement of it, and all that – Kate and John sold the farm and started with the others from County Mayo.

Catherine's arrival home in Mayo certainly seems to have provided the impetus for many others to join her on the return journey:

> From Queenstown, in the Bay of Cork, they sailed the other day, John Burke and his bride of a year, and their hearts were as light and as happy as ever hearts were in song and story.
>
> And with them sailed a jolly crowd of other young folks from County Mayo. Fifteen in all there were that went that day from Mayo … all bound for America to make their fortunes, or finish making them.
>
> For many of these were 'Yanks'. 'Yanks' are the Irish lads and lasses who have been to America and come back to Ireland for a look at the old place and the blessing of the old father and mother, before they go back to America to stay for good and all.
>
> Kate Burke, she that was McHugh, was a Yank. So too, was Kate McGowan.

Both Kates must have been seen as good advertisements for that booming country. Catherine was indeed a 'Yank', having by then become a full citizen of the United States. She had been born and baptised on 30 September 1869 in Terry, Massbrook, the daughter of Anthony McGowan and Bridget Mayock, both dead by 1912. She had made her own way in America and had become a successful property owner. Her relative wealth was indicated by the fact that after her death a $10,000 claim for the loss of her life was lodged with the White Star Line, along with another $900 compensation demand for the loss of her property.

Kate McGowan, her very best friend, and her best friend's husband and sister, all drowned in the freezing Atlantic on 15 April 1912. Niece Annie survived.

MARTIN McMAHON (20) LOST

Ticket number 370372. Paid £7 15s.
Boarded at Queenstown. Third Class.
From: Cragbrien, Ennis, County Clare.
Destination: 415 West 53rd Street, New York city.

A strange coincidence hangs on the name of Martin McMahon – because two men of this name, from the very same locality, drowned in the sinkings of separate White Star liners within three years of each other.

Martin McMahon of Derragh, Cragbrien, County Clare, died on the *Titanic* on 15 April 1912. Martin McMahon of Ballyveskil, Termaclane, County Clare, died when the White Star's *Arabic* was torpedoed on 19 August 1915. Like the *Lusitania* the same year, the *Arabic* was sent to be bottom within fifteen minutes by a submarine, in this case U-24. The *Arabic*'s Martin McMahon was one of forty-four fatalities out of 434 on board.

> *The* Titanic *disaster: young Clare man lost*
> A telegram received in Ennis during the week confirmed the worst fears that had been entertained as to the safety of a young man named Martin McMahon, from the Cragbrien district, about five miles from Ennis.
>
> It was known that he was a passenger on the ill-fated boat, and though his name did not appear in the list of survivors, it was hoped he might have been rescued, but it is now definitely stated that he has been lost. He was a fine athletic young man and very popular in his local district.
>
> (*Clare Journal*, 29 April 1912)

Martin was an agricultural labourer. He had originally booked to sail on the White Star liner *Cymric*, which was due to depart for America on Easter Sunday, four days before *Titanic*. But the service was withdrawn, and the *Cymric* instead slipped her moorings a few days after her brand-new sister.

> *Report of the American Red Cross (Titanic Disaster) 1913*:
> No. 285. (Irish.) A farmer, twenty years of age, was drowned, leaving a dependent mother in Ireland. Emergent relief was provided and the case referred to the English Committee, which later made an appropriation of £25. ($50)

1901 census – McMahon. Cragbrien, Clondagad parish, Lisheen.
Parents: Anthony McMahon, farmer (57); Honour McMahon (46).
Children: Michael (15), Edmond (11), **Martin (7)**, Margaret (5).

NEAL McNAMEE (27) LOST

Joint ticket number 376566 (with his wife Eileen). Paid £16 2s.
Boarded at Southampton. Third Class.
From: Rooskey Lower, Castlefinn, County Donegal.
Destination: 1609 Winter Street, Philadelphia.

Neal and Eileen McNamee were newlyweds – and young go-getters. Their lives were taking off, and their move to New York was the latest confirmation of their upward progress in the world.

Neal McNamee was born in Lower Rooskey, County Donegal, on 29 August 1884. Neal's father, William, was a road worker and had married his wife, Catherine, when both were teenagers. They had two children before either was out of their teens, and two more in their early twenties. The cottage containing the six of them had two windows and three rooms. The family later left the little house in Rooskey, but while some stayed elsewhere in Donegal, Neal was already on his way to Britain, determined to succeed.

Donegal man and wife among the victims
Amongst the passengers who sailed on the ill-fated *Titanic* were Mr and Mrs Neil [*sic*] McNamee, the former being the son of Mr William McNamee, Ruskey, Convoy, County Donegal.

He entered the service of Lipton, Londonderry branch, about nine years ago, being then seventeen years of age. He remained in Londonderry for a little over two years, when he was transferred on promotion to London, and was ultimately appointed to the management of several of Lipton's district branches throughout England.

Recently he was appointed to an important position in connection with Lipton's business in New York. He got married to a Miss O'Leary just a few weeks previous to leaving. Both he and his wife sailed in the *Titanic* and their names do not appear in the list of survivors.

The greatest sympathy is felt for his father and mother, and for other members of the family in the Convoy district.

(*Tyrone Constitution*, 26 April 1912)

The woman who became his bride was Eileen O'Leary, who met Neal when he moved to England. Eileen had previously been involved in a crisis at sea. At the age of two she was aboard a vessel with her parents when it was struck by a cyclone in the Bay of Biscay and left without power or rudder. It was adrift for some time before being taken under tow. Her father, Richard O'Leary, had been on his way to Malta 'to take charge of the electric light at the fort'.

Eileen worked in a Lipton's provisioning branch in Hounslow, and seems to have known Neal for some little time. He had become the manager of Lipton's grocers in Silver

Street, Salisbury. The couple had been married only a few months before sailing, tying the knot in Pokesdown, Devon on 17 January 1912.

The couple moved in with the bride's parents at Kingston House, Walton Road, Salisbury. By now Richard O'Leary was a clerk in the War Office. Within weeks, the McNamees were offered a glittering new life with an important and guaranteed job in booming America. Neal had been asked to take control of the company's first venture into the United States, a Lipton's Export store on the east coast. He carried with him to America a letter of recommendation from Sir Thomas Lipton himself, and the *Titanic* carried 917 lbs of Lipton's tea in freight.

Neal had a relative in America, Jeremiah McNamee, who was due to meet the couple on their arrival. It has been suggested apocryphally that Eileen was offered a place in the boats but was one of the women who chose instead to stay with their husbands. Her body was recovered by the *MacKay-Bennett* on 22 April, and she was buried at sea the same day in a weighted canvas bag. Her effects were listed and some returned to relatives.

It was recorded that body number 53 had an estimated age of 23 (she was 19) with brown hair. She wore a brown velvet coat and a white blouse with a blue anchor on the front. She had a blue flannel petticoat with the embroidered initials 'E Mc' and blue corsets, a blue skirt, black stockings and shoes. Her effects included a wedding ring (turquoise and diamond), and she had a gold bracelet on her right wrist, with two Third-Class tickets in her pockets. A purse containing the sum of one shilling and eleven pence was found on the remains. So too were a fountain pen, keys, cosmetics, and cards with her name and address imprinted.

> Jeremiah McNamee, of No. 1609 Winter Street, will go to Halifax to claim the bodies of Mr and Mrs Neil McNamee, of Queenstown, who were on their way to this city to reside with him.
> (A rather inaccurate report from the *Evening Telegraph*, Philadelphia, 25 April 1912)

There is the story that after the disaster two portraits were commissioned of the young bride and groom by their sorrowing families to mark their love for each other, and these same works were the only reminders of a charismatic couple for their grieving kinfolk in Ireland and Britain. The portraits are now with family members in Bangor, County Down.

A plaque and tree exist in memory of Eileen and Neal at Churchill Park, Salisbury, Wiltshire. The inscription reads: 'In Memory of the young Salisbury couple, Eileen and Neal McNamee, who perished on the RMS *Titanic* on April 15th 1912'.

> 1901 census – McNamee, Rooskey Lower.
> Parents: William (36), Catherine (32) née Gordon.
> Children: Ellen (18), woollen weaver, **Neal (17)**, scholar, Catherine (12), Mary (10), Andrew (8).

BRIDGET McNEILL (27) LOST

Ticket number 370368. Paid £7 15s.
Boarded at Queenstown. Third Class.
From: Treen, Castlerea, County Roscommon.
Destination: 200 Sherman Avenue, Elm Park, New York city.

Titanic *Victim*

Amongst the missing passengers on the ill-fated *Titanic* was Miss Bridget McNeill of Treen, near Castlerea. Miss McNeill had been four years in America, and came to Treen some time ago for a month's holiday.

Her name does not appear in the official list of those who have been saved. Much sympathy is felt with the relatives in their great sorrow.

Mrs Beirne, of Drimdoolin, Castlerea, was to have sailed on the *Titanic* also. She had her passage booked with a local agent and accompanied Miss McNeill from Castlerea to Queenstown. Both were to have sailed together from that port, but at the last minute, owing to a providential mishap, Mrs Beirne did not go.

(*Westmeath Independent*, 27 April 1912)

On 13 May 1912, James Scott & Co., the Queenstown agents for the White Star Line, wrote to Maurice Staunton, solicitor for Bridget's family. Using paper with a letterhead that insensitively still boasted that the *Titanic* was one of the 'two largest steamers in the world', the company wrote:

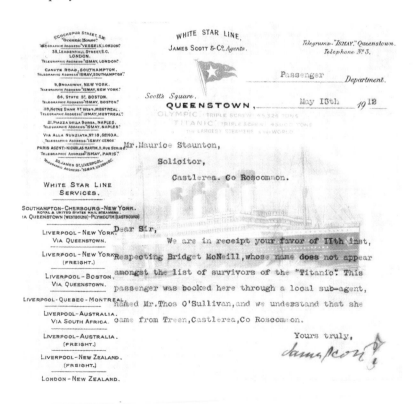

Dear Sir,
We are in receipt your favor of 11th inst, Respecting Bridget McNeill, whose name does
not appear amongst the list of survivors of the "Titanic". This passenger was booked here
through a local sub-agent, named Mr. Thos O'Sullivan, and we understand that she came
from Treen, Castlerea, Co. Roscommon.
Yours truly,
James Scott & Co.

McNeill, Bridget (case 77), 11 June 1912.
Administration of the estate of Bridget McNeill, late of Treen, Castlerea, County
Roscommon, spinster, died 15th April 1912, granted at Tuam to Michael McNeill, farmer.
Effects £100.

From Mansion House *Titanic* Relief Fund Booklet, March 1913, Case Number 484: 'McNeill:
Two Brothers, Grant £20 and £10'.

1901 census – McNeill. Treen, Castlerea.
Parents: Michael (58), farmer. Rose (52).
Children: Martin (18), **Bridget (16)**, James (12)

JOHN MEEHAN (22) LOST

Ticket number 3130. Paid £7 15s.
Boarded at Queenstown. Third Class.
From: Currowhunane, Curry, County Sligo.
Destination: 4745 Indiana Avenue, Chicago.

John was a 22-year-old general labourer who hoped to make a better life for himself in
America. He was travelling out to Chicago to join his sister Nora, two years his junior.

John belonged to that group in which death was most likely – male steerage passengers.
He joined the depressing statistics of the lost, for if chivalry was against him in 1912 it was
outright class discrimination which copper-fastened his fate. Steerage passengers appear
to have been deliberately held back in some areas because of fears that a mass surge to
the boats could jeopardise the lowering of escape craft. Thus First- and Second-Class
passengers were accorded the preferential treatment for which they had paid premium
fares and this extended to avoidance of a meeting with the grim reaper. It was simply the
scheme of things.

The casual dismissal of a whole swathe of humanity extended beyond the watery tomb.
No one in the White Star Line was terribly concerned with getting John Meehan's name
right. He was variously and sloppily reported as Mechan, Mahan, or some other variation.

Very little is known about John Meehan except what can be gleaned from the
American Red Cross report on aid to victims, published in 1913:

No. 304. (Irish.) Young man, 21 years of age, was drowned, leaving dependent parents in Ireland. This Committee gave emergent help and referred the case to the English Committee, which later made an appropriation of £80. ($100)

Folklore in his district says that John Meehan was a powerful swimmer and 'a big strong fellow'. The tale has grown up, more wishful thinking than reality, that he clung to a piece of wreckage for hours, before finally succumbing to exhaustion. This tale seems grounded in stories that John, in times past, often won impromptu swimming races with his pals in the River Moy in the heart of summer after long hours toiling in the fields. But the Atlantic in April is an altogether different proposition.

1901 census – Meehan. Curraghhoonaun, County Sligo.
Parents: Thomas (42) farmer; Honora (39).
Children: Bridget (14), Margaret (18), **John (11)**, Honora (9), Ellen (6), Thomas (3).

ROBERT MERNAGH (28) LOST

Ticket number 368703. Paid £7 15s.
Boarded at Queenstown. Third Class.
From: Ballyleigh, Ballywilliam, New Ross, County Wexford.
Destination: West Street, Chicago.

Quiet, decent and industrious. Three adjectives used to describe another of Ireland's *Titanic* dead, another steerage male whose fine qualities were never going to be enough to advance him up the queue for salvation dictated by cruel variables.

Robert was travelling to Chicago, his home of two years, having originally emigrated from Queenstown aboard the *Celtic* on 8 May 1910, as seen from extant Ellis Island records, which show him to be 5 feet 8 inches, with brown hair and blue eyes. He boarded the *Titanic* in the company of his cousin Elizabeth Doyle, 24, from Bree, near Enniscorthy. Both were drowned. It appears that Mr Mernagh may have gallantly delayed his own return to the United States to accompany his younger relative.

It is rumoured that Mernagh had intended going to America a year ago, but waited for Miss Doyle, who, it is stated, was a sweetheart.

So reported the *New Ross Standard*, four days after the sinking. The erroneous sweetheart reference can only have caused more distress to both families – and this is apparent in an effusive apology and correction printed later by the same newspaper.

Errors were common. The final White Star Line list of all victims referred to Robert by the preposterous surname of 'Nemaugh', a further careless, almost random, discourtesy.

The mistake came from a misreading of the handwritten entry of names in the passenger manifest.

County Wexford passengers
Two County Wexford passengers, Robert Mernagh, Ballyleigh, Ballywilliam, and his first cousin, Elizabeth Doyle, Bree, Enniscorthy, were on board the ill-fated *Titanic*, having booked the passages with the New Ross agent, and embarked at Queenstown.

So far no account as to whether they were saved or otherwise has been received, but it is feared that they have been drowned. Mernagh, who was 28 years of age, a labourer, and unmarried, was two years in America previously and only came to see his parents last winter. He was a very quiet, decent and industrious young man. His companion, who was also unmarried, was 24 years of age, and had been in America two years previously and was only a short time home. Several people from the New Ross district intended travelling by the *Titanic*, but luckily delayed their journey to a later date.

(*Enniscorthy Echo*, 20 April 1912)

MERNAGH & DOYLE – Robert Mernagh, aged 28, Ballyleigh, Ballywilliam, New Ross, and Elizabeth Doyle, Bree (first cousin), aged 24, lost in the *Titanic*. High Mass and Office at Bree Catholic church on Thursday. May their souls rest in peace.

(*New Ross Standard*, 17 May 1912)

The same newspaper later reported of the event:

The relatives of the deceased man who were present are – Mr Matt Mernagh, father; also deceased's mother, his brother Mr James Mernagh, and his sisters, Miss Mary Mernagh and Mrs John Molloy, Wexford. He was going to his brother Mr Matthew Mernagh, Chicago.

Robert Mernagh had been born as one half of male twins. His brother Moses died in infancy.

1911 census:
Matthew (78), cannot read; farm labourer. Wife Mary (70).
Married 45 years, nine children born, of whom five are living.

Matthew Murphy Snr died four years and one week after his son Robert, on 23 April 1916, aged 86 years. A memorial tablet containing both their names, bordered by angels, hangs in a descendant's home.

ELLEN MOCKLER (23) SAVED

Ticket number 330980. Paid £7 12s 7d, plus 5s extra.
Boarded at Queenstown. Third Class.
From: Currafarry, Caltra, County Galway.
Destination: 412 West 17th Street, New York city.

'Sister Mary Patricia is a delight,' wrote John O'Connor in the 15 April 1982 edition of the *Worcester Telegram*, Massachusetts:

> Her 93 years have not robbed the sparkle from her eyes or her quick smile and brogue as she talks of the past …
>
> Hard of hearing, she leans forward to listen to questions but can give minute details of an event that happened 70 years ago today.
>
> At the age of 23, Sister Mary Patricia, then known as Helen M. Mockler, left her home town of Currafarry, Ireland, with two other young women and three men of the village to begin a new life in the United States.
>
> They had no idea they were soon to be involved in one of the greatest civilian disasters at sea. Bound for New York the 'unsinkable' *Titanic* struck an iceberg 800 miles off Cape Race, Newfoundland, and sank, taking 1,517 men, women and children with her. The 46,328-ton ocean liner crashed into the iceberg at 11.40 p.m. By 2.20 a.m. the next morning the ship had sunk. Only 705 people survived.
>
> Helen Mockler was on deck that night 70 years ago when suddenly the whole ship shook. 'We knew something was wrong, but no one told us what.'
>
> She remembers that chickens escaped from the kitchen and began running around on deck.
>
> 'No one seemed to be worried,' she said. 'I remembered one woman was playing the piano.'
>
> At one point Miss Mockler decided to go back to her room and get her bag, which contained all of her belongings. But a man stopped her and said, 'Forget about your bag. If you save yourself you'll be lucky.' At another point, she remembers that she and her five companions knelt on the deck and said the rosary.
>
> 'Everyone was calm on the ship,' she said. 'No one knew what was happening.' Finally someone told her and the two women to get in a lifeboat. About 20 minutes later 'we saw the ship go down.'
>
> The three men with her did not survive. 'The three boys went back downstairs.'
>
> Why was Sister Mary coming to the United States? She chuckled. 'I was coming here to make my fortune.'
>
> The youngest in a family of four, Sister Mary's Third-Class passage was paid by her two sisters who were already in New York.
>
> She spent five years working for the National Biscuit Company in New York ('the best place in the country') before joining the Sisters of Mercy on Sept. 8, 1917, and being assigned to Worcester, where she later served as sacristan at St Paul's Cathedral for 30 years.
>
> Sixty-four years later, Sister Mary admits that her calling to religious life was probably always there. Recalling the night of the sinking, [she] said, 'There were only seven in our lifeboat. Many passengers stayed below deck. No one told them to come up. We probably would have gone to our rooms if the three boys with us didn't tell us to stay on deck.'

She spent the frigid night in the lifeboat wearing only a dress and her lifejacket. 'It was a very cold night,' she said. She was in the lifeboat from 2 to 9 a.m. until rescued by the *Carpathia*.

'We watched the *Titanic* sink until the last light went under water. Then everything was calm and smooth. You wouldn't even have known there was a ship.'

The two men in the lifeboat rowed during the night. 'We didn't see any other lifeboats.'

Is the tale true that the band played 'Nearer My God to Thee' until the ship went under? 'If they did, I never heard it,' she said.

The survivors were taken to New York. 'We were taken to a hospital and given an examination before we were able to see our families.' She said: 'I remember that Sunday, the New York police gave a party for the survivors after Mass.'

Two years after the above interview, Helen Mary Mockler, the name on her death certificate, passed away. She was aged 95 and it was 1 April 1984. In an obituary, the same newspaper reported another nun recalling that she had been initially reluctant to go over the side of the ship into a lifeboat. 'She asked, "Is there a bottom to it?" She was fearful. She didn't want to step into the water.'

Later, when away from the ship, the sister recalled her fellow religious saying that the lifeboat began to leak. 'They were scooping it out with their hands when they saw the *Carpathia*.'

The newspaper further noted:

'When the news of the *Titanic's* fate reached New York [Ellen] was listed as missing and presumed drowned,' the sister said. 'Of course the first news got was that she was drowned,' so they sent for the parish priest.

'He said, "I don't believe that we're going to pray. Get your coats and come with me",' the sister said. So the priest and the sisters went to the New York hospital where survivors were held overnight for examinations.

'The priest stood on a chair and he shouted her name out and said, "If you're there, stand up and wave." She stood up and waved,' the friend said. And one of her sisters immediately fainted.

Sister Mary did not talk willingly about that cold April night, the sister said. 'It was such an experience, she never really talked about it much. You had to probe her.' Even then, 'she only answered the questions that you asked her.'

Her experience aboard the *Titanic* and just after 'had nothing to do' with her decision to enter the Sisters of Mercy, her friend said.

Perhaps – but consider this contemporary report from the *New York Herald* of April 1912, quoting Ellen Mockler and two other Irish female survivors:

A priest's heroism – Rev. Thomas R.D. Byles
Three of the survivors who vividly remember the last hours of the heroic English priest are Miss Ellen Mocklare [*sic*], a pretty dark-haired young girl from Galway, now at her sister's home, number 412 West Seventeenth Street, Miss Bertha Moran, who had gone to Troy, New York, and Miss McCoy who is in St Vincent's Hospital.

These told their story in concert at the hospital.

'When the crash came we were thrown from our berths,' said Miss Mocklare. 'Slightly dressed, we prepared to find out what had happened. We saw before us, coming down the passageway with hand uplifted, Fr Byles.

'We knew him because he had visited us several times on board and celebrated Mass for us that very morning. "Be calm, my good people," he said, and then he went about the steerage giving absolution and blessings.

'A few around us became very excited,' Miss Mocklare continued. 'And then it was that the priest again raised his hand and instantly they were calm once more. The passengers were at once impressed by the absolute self-control of the priest.

'He began the recitation of the Rosary. The prayers of all, regardless of creed, were mingled and the responses "Holy Mary" were loud and strong.

'One sailor,' said Miss Mocklare, 'warned the priest of his danger and begged him to board a boat, but Fr Byles refused. The same seaman spoke to him again and seemed anxious to help him, but he refused again. Fr Byles could have been saved, but he would not leave while one was left, and the sailor's entreaties were not heeded.

'After I got in the boat, which was the last one to leave, and we were slowly going further away from the ship, I could hear distinctly the voice of the priest and the responses to his prayers.

'Then they became fainter and fainter until I could only hear the strains of "Nearer My God to Thee" and the screams of the people left behind. We were told by the man who rowed our boat that we were mistaken as to the screams and that it was the people singing, but we knew otherwise.'

'Did all the steerage get a chance to get on deck?' she was asked.

'I don't think so because a great many were there when our boat went out, but there were no more boats and I saw Fr Byles among them.

'A young man who was in steerage with us helped me into the boat. It was cold and I had no wrap. Taking off the shirt he was wearing, he put it around my shoulders and the suspenders to keep it from blowing undone, and then stepped back into the crowd.'

(*New York Herald*, 24 April 1912)

The man who gave Ellen his shirt was Thomas Kilgannon, and nine years later, on a visit home to Ireland, Ellen presented the garment to the dead man's mother.

There are contradictions and implausibilities in some areas of the above interviews. Ellen Mockler said she was on deck and in her berth when the iceberg struck. She said there were only seven in her lifeboat, while the least-full lifeboat contained twelve occupants, all of whom are known. And being in an under-populated lifeboat is not consistent with it being one of the 'last to leave', nor being able to see both Fr Byles and the *Titanic*'s last moments, while paradoxically not being able to see any other lifeboats all night.

Sister Mary Patricia's very advanced age must be considered at the time of the later interviews, while the 1912 account seems to include much that belongs exclusively to the journalist – such as the strains of 'Nearer My God to Thee', when the survivor herself later said she never heard the hymn.

Ellen told US immigration on arrival that she was to join her sister, Bridget Lynch, at West 17th Street. She also told the Red Cross that she was 19, and received a $100 relief payment. The organisation noted that Ellen, case number 315, had been injured during her ordeal.

Meanwhile word had been sent back to Ellen's elderly father in Ireland soon after the sinking that his daughter had been lost. As a result he had a heart attack and died. Sister Mary Patricia sometimes reflected sadly to her family in subsequent years how sad it was that he never knew she had survived.

Ellen Mockler was born on 1 April 1889 and died on 1 April 1984, her 95th birthday. She is buried in St Joseph's Cemetery in Leicester, Massachusetts.

1911 census – Mocklare, Currafarry.
Parents: Andrew (72), Catherine (70). 35 years married.
Children: Michael (29), **Ellie (20)**.

DANIEL J. MORAN (27) LOST
BERTHA MORAN (28) SAVED

Joint ticket number 371110. Paid £24 3s.
Boarded at Queenstown. Third Class.
From: Toomdeely North, Askeaton, County Limerick.
Destination: 22 Dow Street, Troy, New York.

The night before Daniel and Bertha left home to board the *Titanic* all the dogs in the house began howling, making them both distinctly uneasy, as Bertha later told her children.

New York policeman Daniel Moran was 27, his sister Bridget, known as Bertha, a year older. He drowned and she survived. Both were originally from the Askeaton area of County Limerick, although each had been living in America for some time, Bertha working in the Peabody Shirt Factory in Troy, New York. They travelled with Patrick Ryan.

The *New York Sun* reported on 22 April 1912, that Daniel, a New York city precinct officer, had been home to claim an inheritance of $12–15,000 from the estate of his deceased father. Daniel's own life, by contrast, was worth only £100 in a 1913 London High Court ruling. He had first emigrated at age 17 aboard the Cunard Line's *Etruria*, from Queenstown in 1901. In 1912:

Mr [Michael] O'Mahoney, a Customs officer at Queenstown, saw off three Limerick friends of his safely on board the *Titanic* and saw them settled down very comfortably. They were Mr D. J. Moran, a New York policeman, his sister Margaret, and Patrick Ryan.

I can find no evidence of either having been saved, but the lists received here are very incomplete.

(The Cork Examiner, 19 April 1912)

Daniel and Bertha appear to have been held back in steerage at the stern. Bertha told her family in later life that they were 'barred from getting up to the lifeboats until some managed to break through', finally reaching the boat deck when all but the most aft lifeboats appeared to have left. Bertha was spoken to by the *New York Herald* in St Vincent's Hospital as she recovered from her ordeal. She told how she was in the company of English priest Fr Thomas R. D. Byles from Ongar, Essex, who had been acting as a kind of chaplain to the steerage passengers the entire voyage, saying Mass for them that Sunday when the vessel struck. 'Continuing the prayers, he led us to where the boats were being lowered. Helping the women in, he whispered to them words of comfort and encouragement.'

Daniel was left behind. The boats were full of women, and as a policeman, it is likely that he relied upon instilled discipline to suppress his own fear and help others as best he could. His body was not recovered.

Bertha is thought to have been saved in lifeboat No. 15. Bertha said half a dozen of the fifty passengers on the boat died before the *Carpathia* came to the rescue.

Report of the American Red Cross (Titanic Disaster) 1913:
No. 319. (Irish.) A policeman, 27 years old, was lost, while returning from a visit to Ireland with his sister, a laundry worker, 28 years old. She lost baggage valued at $300, and was ill from shock and exposure and unable to work for several weeks. An invalid sister was dependent upon her and the deceased brother. Hospital care and clothing and $650 was provided from other American sources of relief. The Committee gave $300 for emergent relief, and later set aside $600 to be used for the benefit of the invalid sister. ($900)

The invalid sister was 33-year-old Mary, known as Minnie Moran. She also applied for funds from the *New York American* newspaper, which had held a disaster appeal. Money seems to have been a recurring motif in the Moran saga, with the likelihood that a huge amount of inheritance cash was lost when the *Titanic* went down. Bertha launched her own claim for compensation in the American courts, while an action for the loss of Daniel's life resulted in the derisory £100 award by Mr Justice Bailhache in June 1913, following a five-day trial.

From the papers of the US District Court, Southern District of New York:

I, Bertha Moran, residing at No. 22 Dow Street, in the city of Troy, N.Y., do hereby make and present my claim for damages, loss and injuries sustained by me by reason of the collision of the steamship *Titanic* with an iceberg in the Atlantic Ocean …

Cash – $360; 8 suits – $250; 3 dresses – $84; shoes and slippers – $20; 4 hats, plumes, feathers &c. – $135; silk petticoats – $18; 7 tailored shirt waists – $14; 4 fancy shirt waists – $20; underwear – $39; 4 pairs of gloves – $4; 12 pairs of stockings – $12; 1 diamond studded watch – $65; 1 diamond ring – $200; 1 locket and chain – $15; 2 gold bracelets – $36; 1 mesh bag – $15; 1 pair eye glasses – $5; fur coat – $50; 1 set furs – $80; 1 trunk and suit case – $23. Total $1,445.

Bertha only received payment at the rate of a few cents in the dollar due to the court's finding of limited liability. She stated that she received just $92, enough to replace her dresses and gloves, but nothing else. It may have rankled in later life – in 1956 an article in the *Detroit News* indicated that Bertha would not discuss the *Titanic* with reporters unless she was paid. The newspaper declined to do so. But Bertha did comment forcibly that steerage passengers were not allowed on deck until almost all the lifeboats were gone.

Bertha married Irishman Richard Sinnott in 1913. They moved to Detroit, Michigan, where Richard worked for the Timken Detroit Axle Company. A son was born on 29 August 1914, whom Bertha named Daniel, presumably after her lost brother. Yet further pain was not far away – her husband was killed in an industrial accident in November 1917 when Daniel Jnr was just three years old, and baby Eileen only a year and a half. A third child was born almost nine months after Richard's death. Named after the second man to be untimely wrenched from Bertha's life, Richard Jnr arrived on 6 July 1918.

With three young children in tow, Bertha's prospects did not look good. But her fortunes changed, she took work as a beautician, and a new relationship developed within just a few years. By the beginning of the 1920s she was married again, to George C. Cooper, and the family of five became six when little Bertha entered the world on 22 February 1923. In fact there were more – Cooper, a butcher from England, had three children of his own from a previous marriage, but they did not live with them.

This husband too died young, leaving Bertha widowed again, but now with five children to raise on her own through the hungry years known as the Great Depression. She coped well, and all five of her children later went on to marry and have children of their own.

In 1953 Bertha Cooper was photographed by the *Detroit Free Press* at a special showing of the movie *Titanic*, featuring Clifton Webb and Barbara Stanwyck. Her family said she wept through much of it.

In later years she retired to tending her garden at 2236 23rd Street, and looking after her soul with daily Mass and Tuesday night novenas. She taught her grandchildren the sign of the cross in Gaelic, Irish lullabies and the proper way to make tea.

Bertha Moran died on the forty-ninth anniversary of the *Titanic*'s sinking and her younger brother's death. She is one of five survivors to die on an anniversary. She finally joined her brother Daniel in death at Mount Carmel Hospital, Detroit, on 15 April 1961. The cause was heart failure, the culmination of the effects of colon cancer which she had suffered for two years. She was 77 years old and was buried in the Holy Sepulchre Cemetery in Oakland, Michigan.

1901 census – Moran. Toomdeely North, Askeaton.
Parents: Patrick (50), boatman. Wife Bridget deceased.
Children: John (24), Mary (22), **Daniel (18)**, Patrick (16), Thomas (12).

THOMAS MORROW (31) LOST

Ticket number 372622. Paid £7 15s.
Boarded at Queenstown. Third Class.
From: Drumlough, Rathfriland, County Down.
Destination: Gleichen, Alberta, Canada.

An Orangeman, Tommy Morrow was leaving Ireland just as the Home Rule Bill was being put to the British parliament. He did not live to see the measure passed that same month of April 1912 – only for the implementation of 'Rome Rule', as the Orangemen called it, to be later suspended for the duration of the First World War and eventually forgotten.

Thirty-one years old, Tommy was going to Canada, still a loyal dominion, to join his brother Waddell, who owned a ranch close to the industrial town of Gleichen, way out west in Alberta.

He had been persuaded to try his luck in the New World by a boyhood friend, Robert John Bell, who had returned to County Down to visit his dying uncle. Bell, who now lived in Chicago, talked Tommy into crossing the Atlantic with him when he went back.

But while both men travelled to Queenstown together, fate intervened. Bell couldn't get a ticket and Morrow sailed alone.

Newry man amongst the victims

Information has just been received that one of the ill-fated passengers on board the *Titanic* was Mr Thomas Rowan Morrow, of Drumlough, Rathfriland. The news has been confirmed by the officials of the White Star Line, London.

The deceased was a young man of much promise, and his tragic death has aroused widespread feelings of sympathy in Newry, Rathfriland, and district. He was a prominent Orangeman, and had been Worshipful Master of the Drumlough L.O.L. for many years past.

(*Belfast Newsletter*, 27 April 1912)

Thomas Morrow was a Presbyterian. His mother had been widowed since the turn of the century, and was aged 61 by the time he embarked on the White Star liner. His sister Sara, aged 25, was by then the only other child left in the house. He had a brother George, who owned a confection shop in Belfast, and Thomas had previously given his occupation as a grocer in the 1901 census.

Thomas Morrow must have been lonely as the sole passenger from Ulster in the Third-Class section of the *Titanic*. The English-speaking steerage was made up of many of his southern countrymen who were ardent Home Rulers. He appears to have kept himself to himself, and no survivor speaks of him on board.

A great grandnephew in California, Robert S. Morrow, says Thomas 'had with him two or more rifles, which required special handling, among other pieces of luggage'.

Lawrence Beesley, writing in his book *The Loss of the SS Titanic*, illustrates the isolation of an unknown passenger who seemed strangely at odds with his steerage shipmates, standing on the poop deck, above the after well deck, where the Irish held dances and games:

> Standing aloof from all of them generally on the raised stern deck above the 'playing field' was a man of about twenty to twenty-four years of age, well dressed, always gloved and nicely groomed, and obviously out of place among his fellow passengers; he never looked happy all the time.
>
> I watched him, and classified him at hazard as the man who had been a failure in some way at home and had received the proverbial shilling plus Third-Class fare to America: He did not look resolute enough or happy enough to be working out his own problem.

This passenger seems too young to have been Thomas Morrow, whom we know was successful and socially well connected. But it suggests perhaps the loneliness that Morrow could have felt amid all the gaiety – and his regret at the failure of his friend to board.

While Morrow was the worshipful master of an Orange lodge rather than a masonic lodge, it is interesting to note that one of the survivors in a boat spoke of hearing, after the sinking, when hundreds were struggling in the water, the coded calls of fellow-masons in distress.

KATIE MULLEN (21) SAVED

Ticket number 35852. Paid £7 14s 8d.
Boarded at Queenstown. Third Class.
From: Rhyne, Killoe, County Longford.
Destination: 231 East 50th Street, New York city.

It was the worst shipping disaster the world had known, but Katie Mullen was saved. Thirty years later her own boy was not so lucky – son John drowned when a US vessel he was aboard as a soldier was torpedoed off the North African coast during the Second World War.

Catherine Mullen was born on 29 May 1890, the daughter of Thomas and Mary Mullen, who farmed a smallholding in a poor area of County Longford. She boarded the *Titanic* claiming to be 20 years old and signed aboard as 'Mullin'. She roomed with her close neighbour Katie Gilnagh, with whom she had set out for Queenstown, and also with the Murphy sisters, Margaret and Catherine. They occupied cabin Q161 on E deck.

Katie's daughter Peggy recalled:

> She used to say that they were having a party in the [Third-Class] lounge and then she and the other girls went down to their room. A man from their county, Jim Farrell, then knocked on their door and told them 'something must be up' because the engines had stopped.
>
> One of the girls then said 'Maybe we've landed' and they had a little laugh. But then when they tried to go up on deck they found they were blocked. They couldn't get through.

Walter Lord, author of *A Night to Remember*, wrote of Katie being prevented by a crew-member from ascending to the upper decks and the prospect of a lifeboat. She was with her friend Katie Gilnagh and Catherine Murphy when a seaman refused them further progress:

> Suddenly steerage passenger Jim Farrell, a strapping Irishman from the girls' home county, barged up. 'Great God, Man!' he roared. 'Open the gate and let the girls through!' It was a superb demonstration of sheer voice-power. To the girls' astonishment, the sailor meekly complied.

However, Katie's grandnephew Brian Wall insists the story is rather different. He says she told him that Farrell used an axe, intended for firefighting, to smash the barrier and then fought with the crewmember.

It is most likely that Katie was rescued from the *Titanic* in the company of Katie Gilnagh, who was the last person admitted to lifeboat No. 16 by her own account. Katie Mullen told her daughter that the last she saw of James Farrell was of him 'kneeling beside his suitcase saying the Rosary'. Rosary beads were later found on his body.

Longford folklore tells that Katie was most reluctant to enter a boat and had to be pushed in, while one version has her actually thrown into the water and later picked up, but this is embroidery. Her daughter declares: 'They had to jump into the lifeboats. Some missed it and fell into the sea.'

> Titanic *survivor: another Longford survivor relates her experience*
> Miss Kate Mullen, daughter of Mr T. Mullen of Rhyne, has written to a friend in this country the following account of her experiences in connection with the dreadful *Titanic* disaster:
> 'Don't you think I went through enough on my first trip across the Atlantic? I was the last person put into the last boat just fifteen minutes before the *Titanic* disappeared. I saw her going down. It was dreadful to see and hear the cries of the poor people on board after the last boat had left. When the funnels disappeared beneath the waves, the ship rose up a tremendous height, and with a roar like thunder disappeared forever in the depths of the sea. There were fifty people in our boat. We were like eggs in a box, but felt glad we had escaped with our lives. We tried to warm ourselves as well as we could, but it was difficult owing to the boat being quarter-full of water and ice. We got into the boat at 12.30 at night and until 9 next morning we were surrounded by huge icebergs, with hardly anything but light clothes on.
> 'The cold was intense, and when the *Carpathia* arrived we were in a dreadful way from exposure and hunger. We were well treated on board the *Carpathia* and supplied with clothes.'
> (*Longford Leader*, 18 May 1912)

In later life Katie remarked on the calm of the sea, although reluctant to discuss the tragedy in any detail. 'The sea was like glass. There wasn't even a ripple on it.' The American Red Cross later aided her with a payment of $100, listing her as case No. 321.

She had intended to work as a domestic in New York, but soon met Martin J. Kearns, the Galwayman who later became her husband. They married on 2 January 1916, at Our Lady of Good Counsel on East 90th Street in Manhattan. Their daughter Margaret (Peggy) was born before the end of that year. John was next to arrive, followed by Mary and Eileen. A lasting sorrow came with the Second World War and son John's drowning with 496 others in the sinking of his troopship on 20 April 1944. A member of the Medical Air Corps, he lost his life exactly thirteen months after he had entered service, aged only 19. No remains were ever recovered.

In later years, the family moved to an apartment building at 65th Street, Woodside, Queens, NYC. They were happy but John's death had taken much out of Katie. She became especially alarmed when her daughter Peggy took a trip to Ireland aboard the *America* in December 1948. 'She was in an awful state,' said her daughter. 'But she let me go.'

Photographed by the New York *Daily News* in 1962 for a feature commemorating the fiftieth anniversary, 'Mrs Katherine Mullen-Kearns' declined to comment on the calamity except to thank God for her survival. She didn't want to be reminded of what had happened that night, she said. She died at the age of 80 on 1 November 1970, and was buried in St Raymond's Cemetery, the Bronx.

1911 census – Rhyne, Killoe.
Thomas (65), farmer. Wife Mary (64). Married 40 years, nine children, seven surviving. Thomas (23), Bridget (24), **Kate (19)**. Granddaughter Lizzie K. Murray (5).

MARY MULLIN – SEE DENIS LENNON

BERTHA MULVIHILL (25) SAVED

Ticket number 382653. Paid £7 15s.
Boarded at Queenstown. Third Class.
From: Moydrum, Coosan, Athlone, County Westmeath.
Destination: 12 Inkerman Street, Providence, Rhode Island.

Bertha was one of the most colourful characters on board the world's most luxurious liner. She was returning to Providence to get married, and was weighed down with wedding presents – including one unusual item, a portrait of the Irish patriot Robert Emmet. She told the *Daily Sketch* of 4 May 1912 that she watched from a lifeboat as the Atlantic finally closed around the doomed leviathan. 'As the ship went down, all she said was "Goodbye Robert".'

This report came from the *Providence Journal*, Saturday 20 April 1912:

Bertha with husband Henry Noon

Miss Bertha E. Mulvihill of this city, among the survivors of the *Titanic* tragedy, told a thrilling story of the last moments aboard the great stricken liner yesterday at the home of her sister, Mrs E. J. Norton at 12 Inkerman Street.

Miss Mulvihill, who was in a state of hysteria when she landed at the Cunard Line pier in New York on Thursday night, had regained a certain measure of composure when she reached her sister's home here, but she gave way to sobs as she recalled some of the more tragic scenes of the great disaster.

Among the very last to leave the ship, Miss Mulvihill's story of the disaster was a vivid one. She heard the shrieks of the steerage passengers, saw the armed officers of the ship keep the men back from the lifeboats until the women had been saved and watched as if fascinated the lights of the *Titanic* as the water crept higher and higher and then went out.

Then came the explosions, she said. The big vessel quivered, careened slowly to starboard and sank to her deep ocean grave. The nervous stress of the hours in the lifeboats among the ice cakes, the sobbing of the women in the boats of the little fleet and then the life-giving sight of the Cunarder *Carpathia* as she loomed up in the morning's mist all made a deep impression on Miss Mulvihill.

'It was about 11.45,' she said. 'I was just in bed and was just getting to sleep. Then came a heavy jar. I lay still for several minutes, not knowing what was the matter. Then I slipped on a heavy coat over my nightgown, pulled on my shoes and went out into the passage.'

Fighting in steerage
'The people were rushing up the stairways, and way down in the steerage I could hear the women and men shrieking and screaming. The women called for their children. The men cursed.

'Then I hurried back to my room, stepped up on the washstand and took down a life-belt. This I adjusted about me and then hurried out into the passage.

'At the top of the passage I met a sailor with whom I had become acquainted on my passage across. I later learned that his name was Robert Hickens [Hichens] of Southampton, Eng. I asked him what the matter was.

'"There is no danger, little girl," he replied to me. "We have hit an iceberg."

'"We're lost; we're lost," I cried, but he took me by the arm and told me to follow him. Some of the Italian men from way down in the steerage were screaming and fighting to get into the lifeboats. Capt. Smith stood at the head of the passageway. He had a gun in his hand.

'"Boys," he said, "You've got to do your duty here. It's the women and children first, and I'll shoot the first man who jumps into a boat."'

Priests brave to the last
'There were two Catholic priests aboard. They were coming to America from Ireland. After we got off, I was talking with Eugene Ryan [*sic*], a boy from my home town in Athlone, and he told me the priests were among the men on the *Titanic* as the vessel was sinking and administered the last rites of the church. And they stuck to it, too, until the water was up about their knees.

'To go back, my sailor friend told me to follow him and he would try to get me into a lifeboat. We climbed up bolts and cleats until we got to the next deck. Nearly every woman had left the ship then, I guess, and only two boats remained.

'Beside me there was a family named Rice, consisting of the father and mother and six children. The father was not permitted to leave the ship, but the mother and her six children could leave if they wished. The mother was crying and weeping. She wouldn't go into the lifeboat and leave her husband to perish. "I can't go and leave my husband," she cried to the officers. "Let him come with me, oh please let him come with me," she pleaded. "I don't want to live if he can't come, there will be nobody to earn bread for my little children," she wailed. But the officers wouldn't let the father go. "I'll stay with my husband then," the woman cried. I saw her clinging to her husband and children just before I left the vessel. That was the last I ever saw of her. The whole family went down together.

'Only two boats remained. One of these pushed off. I stood directly over the other. "Jump," said the sailor. I jumped and landed in the boat. Then a big Italian jumped and landed on me, knocking the wind out of me.

'We pushed off among the ice cakes. It was a beautiful starry night. You could see the poor *Titanic* sinking. She was surely going down. The women in the boats were screaming. They cried for their husbands. Every once in a while a cake of ice would crash into our boat. The men on the *Titanic* were all gathered about the rail. They were singing. It sounded like "Nearer, My God, to Thee".'

Fascinated by sight
'The *Titanic* was going down slowly, yet surely. I had marked in my mind's eye two portholes on the vessel. I watched the water come to them, pass them and swallow them up from sight. I was fascinated.

'Then the lights on the *Titanic* began to glimmer and go out. A few minutes later there were two heavy explosions. The big vessel quivered and seemed to settle. Then she leaned over on the other side a little and slowly sank to her grave. I think I heard the band playing.'

Miss Mulvihill stopped. Her hand trembled and her whole frame shuddered. Her sister stroked her brow and sought to calm her. 'But it was a good ship – a good ship,' stammered Miss Mulvihill insistently. 'And they went down bravely. They were good to us – good to us,' she sobbed.

'There, there, dear, calm yourself,' murmured her sister soothingly.

After a pause of a few minutes, Miss Mulvihill continued.

Pull away from ship
'The sailors rowed hard, thinking the suction from the big vessel would pull us down. But the explosions threw the water away from the vessel so the small boats were able to get away all right.

'Then began the long vigil for the rescuing ship. All night we bumped among the ice cakes, out there on the Atlantic. From 11 o'clock until about an hour later – that is, I think it was an hour, although it seemed but an instant to me, we had fought and struggled on the *Titanic*. From midnight until dawn the next morning we wept and moaned on the face of the ocean.

'All the boats that had left the port side of the vessel had clustered together, and all the boats that had left the starboard side clustered in another little bunch, a little distance away.

'It was awfully cold. The water every once in a while slapped up over the bow of the boat and covered us with spray. None of us had on more than nightclothes, with a scant covering over those.'

Star shine over all
'The sailors silently pulled their oars, the oarlocks creaked, the ice bumped against us. We could hear the women in the other cluster of boats sobbing and crying for their husbands. And the stars shone bright above.

'Dawn was just breaking when I saw a light way off in the distance. I spoke to the nearest sailor about it, and asked if it possibly could be a vessel coming to help us. He said it must be a ship's light, but someone spoke up and said it was probably a boat's light.

'Then two big green lights broke through the mists above it, and we knew it was a ship coming to rescue us. We cheered and cheered and cheered. Some cried. I just sat still and offered up a little prayer.

'Slowly the mist cleared and the big boat pushed toward us. This was about 5 o'clock in the morning. From then until 8 we drifted about, waiting for the *Carpathia* to pick us up. It was bitter cold, and the only thing I can remember very distinctly about those hours is a white cake of ice, which bumped and bumped and bumped against the boat near me. I watched it, and once I remember, I laughed when another cake of ice pushed between it and the boat. I think I must have been ill then.'

Great kindness shown

'At about 11 o'clock the *Carpathia* took us aboard. Everybody was so kind to us. They had hot whiskey and brandy for all of us. They wrapped us up in blankets and gave us food. A physician came and visited all of us. Then the other passengers let us sleep in their bunks. Everybody was kind, and everybody helped us.

'After that night – Tuesday, was it – the *Carpathia*'s captain told us we were obliged to look out more for ourselves. The First-Class passengers aboard the *Titanic* had First-Class accommodation on the *Carpathia*, as near as possible. I was in the Third Class, because I decided on the spur of the moment to visit my sister here and it was impossible to get anything else until June, so far ahead were the passages booked.

'So we herded in the steerage until we crept up New York harbour. I sent a wireless message off to my mother in Ireland to reassure her.

'You see, I had lived for the last few years with my sister, Mrs Norton, here in Providence. Last Labour Day I went back to Ireland to attend the wedding of my sister, Kittie. I intended to stay over there longer, but one day last week, Friday it was, I think, I was returning from a funeral in my home town at Athlone, when I passed the steamship company's ticket office.

Gets ticket for death boat

'I went in and bought my passage for America without saying a word to anybody. Then Friday I told my [family? Illegible] that I was going back to America to my sister, and was going to Queenstown the next morning to go aboard the boat.'

'Oh, Bert, why couldn't you have told them?' interrupted Mrs Norton, addressing her sister by a familiar name. 'Bert' laughed.

'She didn't know I was coming at all on this boat, my sister didn't; I was going to surprise her,' she said.

'No, we didn't know she was aboard at all until Henry read her name among those saved in the *Evening Bulletin* Tuesday night,' said Mrs Norton.

'Henry?' it was asked.

'Yes, Henry Noon – he is her sweetheart,' responded Mrs Norton. 'He was reading the list of those on the boat when his eye came upon Bert's name. He nearly fainted. Then he rushed over here to my house – he lives at 76 Lisbon Street – and told my husband and me that Bert was on the *Titanic*.

'So yesterday my husband and Henry went over to New York to wait for the *Carpathia* to come in.'

Plenty of aid offered

'Yes, and they were so kind to us in New York,' Miss Mulvihill hastened to say. 'We were met down the bay by tugs and all kinds of vessels. The officers told us they were newspapermen and we mustn't talk to them then. And then at the dock we were met by lots and lots of people who wanted to help us. There were priests and sisters and doctors. They gave us food and clothing and medicine.'

She laughed. 'See that hat over there? That was given to me in New York and I wore it over here to Providence.' The hat was a light pearl grey felt.

'When I got onto the dock,' resumed Miss Mulvihill, 'I met Henry and Mr Norton and they rushed me over to the Grand Central Station and took me to Providence.'

'She was hysterical on the train,' explained Mrs Norton. 'She kept thinking of the disaster and the scenes she had witnessed. She laughed and cried and threw her arms about her.'

'I nearly swooned with joy,' continued Miss Mulvihill, 'when I got off the train here in the Providence station and saw my sister.'

'The doctor told her she must eat sparingly and only of liquid foods,' said Mrs Norton. 'He said he wouldn't let her go to sleep right away for fear that during her sleep she would review the scenes of the disaster, and upon waking, would not be in her right mind.'

Dreamed of disaster

'It was a funny thing,' said Miss Mulvihill. 'There was a boy named Eugene Ryan from my town who was with us. When we left Queenstown he told us that he had dreamt that the *Titanic* was going to sink. And every night we were at sea he told us he had dreamt that the *Titanic* was going down before we reached New York. On Monday night just before he went to bed, he told us the *Titanic* was going to sink that night. It was uncanny.'

Miss Mulvihill is 24, an apple-cheeked Irish lass, with bright blue eyes, which yesterday were deeply ringed with suffering, privation and terror.

Bertha's hometown newspaper, the *Westmeath Independent*, reported in their edition of the same day on the other side of the world:

Cablegram received today 3.40 – 'Providence R.I. – Mrs Martin Mulvihill, Coosan, Athlone. Bertha safe – Mary'. Mary is her sister.

A few days earlier, the newspaper had been optimistic in a piece entitled 'Local Passengers':

Amongst the list of survivors issued on Thursday evening are the names of Marsala Daly and Bertha 'Malliedell'. This latter is probably a blundering attempt at Mulvihill and hopes are entertained that other Athlone passengers may be among the survivors.

Miss Bertha Mulvihill, of Coosan, was crossing to the States for the second time. She had spent six years in America and came home last August to spend the winter with her friends. She was going back to get married, and for this event she had made very elaborate preparations by bringing with her a large amount of furniture, etc. She has lived to enjoy the home, but she must be satisfied with Yankee furniture since all her luggage and effects are buried deep in the Atlantic. There was great relief and joy in Athlone and Coosan when it was made known she had escaped.

While she was at home she made a host of friends, who were greatly relieved by news of her escape. She was a most amiable and energetic lady, of a bright and lively disposition, liked and appreciated by all who know her. Among her other accomplishments, she was an expert swimmer.

(*Westmeath Independent*, 27 April 1912)

Miss Bertha Mulvihill of Coosan, Athlone, one of the survivors of the *Titanic*, has sent a letter to her sister, written on board the *Carpathia*, in the course of which she relates her experiences and how she was saved: 'I had a prayer-book, a watch and a little money in my pocket,' she says. 'But all the rest went down. I never saw such a sight as when the *Titanic* struck the iceberg.

'She broke in two. The scene was awful. The picture I had of Robert Emmet has gone down with the ship … I had an oar in the small boat and it warmed me and kept me from sticking to the ship.'

Miss Mulvihill intends coming back to Ireland in the autumn.

(*The Cork Examiner*, 4 May 1912)

Grim humour: another survivor and her patriot picture
It went down and she said 'good-bye Robert'
Miss Bertha Mulvehill [*sic*], one of the survivors of the *Titanic* disaster, has written to her sister at Coosan. Her letter – written on board the *Carpathia* – betrays the grimmest of humour. The text of the letter is as follows:

On board the Cunard RMS *Carpathia*

Dear Maud
Experience is great … I am fine and dandy – never better. What time did you hear of the dreadful disaster?
I AM SO GLAD I WAS IN IT. I shall never forget it. We are just in New York. Having a jolly time. Don't worry. How is father? Nothing like a bit of life. Don't worry for me. I am O.K. We lost 2,472 passengers and saved 710. I was a hero to the last. We were picked up after eight hours by a ship bound for Naples, everyone was very good to us, and then transferred to the *Carpathia*. The passengers on the *Carpathia* gave us clothes. I had a prayer-book, a watch and a little money in my pocket. All the rest lost. I never saw such a sight as when the dear old *Titanic* sank. She broke in two pieces. The scene was awful … Don't think me mad for being so happy to witness the sight … I am with a jolly crowd in this old ship [the *Carpathia*] … I am awfully happy – like the night I was born – never felt happier in my life. I have nothing to worry … I can imagine, mother dear, that when you heard the news you felt for your lost daughter, but she is the safest one you have got. I shall be a millionaire when I arrive in New York. I shall go back this summer, it may be on my honeymoon, but let's keep that quiet. My watch was saved, but a picture I had of Robert Emmet has gone down. 'Good-bye Robert', said I as the ship went down. Poor lad, he was drowned. Sarah Curran, I am sure, felt terribly sorry at being left alone … Pray for me, I am so happy; console all my friends. There is no place like the sea … I am writing this in a hurry, for I want my supper … The little Summerhill girl went down, unless she is picked up by another ship that we don't know of … we struck the iceberg at ten minutes to

twelve and the ship sank at two. We were launched in small boats at one … I am a d--il or an angel – I don't know which … Tell Pat I had his pen in my petticoats, and that it gave me fifty sticks in my legs …

(*Westmeath Independent*, 4 May 1912)

Bertha undoubtedly appears to be in clinical shock and trauma from the above letter, even confabulating a double transfer to a Naples ship and then onto the *Carpathia*. In fact, the *Carpathia* was bound for Naples.

Report of the American Red Cross (Titanic Disaster) 1913:
No. 322. (Irish.) Girl, 22 years of age, returning from a visit to relatives, suffered very severely from shock and exposure, and it is feared, may be permanently disabled. She lost clothing and jewellery valued at $665 and $140 in cash. Relatives are unable to give financial assistance. ($950)

Niece Maura Fox, who was born on 1 December 1911, to Bertha's sister Kitty, maintained that Bertha's trip home to Ireland was to tell her parents that she intended to marry Henry Noon. Maura adds that Bertha chose to return on the *Titanic* having heard about the maiden voyage of such an impressive ship:

She just had to be on that ship. She was very adventurous. She jumped onto a lifeboat and landed awkwardly and then someone jumped on her back. In latter years Bertha suffered from back pain because of the injury picked up on that night.

She jumped off the ship wearing an old frieze coat over her nightdress and with a sock on her head. She also clung to a tattered damp bible which she had recently been given by my father.

It also appears the picture of Robert Emmet had been acquired having seen a play about the dashing Irish rebel during her trip home, performed by an amateur cast that included many family friends of the Mulvihills.

Bertha filed the following schedule of losses as part of a class action in the US District Court:

One trunk, new – $15; One suit case, new – $12; One leather hand bag and one mesh bag – $30; One case of photographs and portraits – $30; Two costumes, tailor made suits – $70; Four dresses – $65; Two hats – $45; Eight sets of underwear, crocheted and embroidered – $100; Sundries, shoes, stockings, gloves, umbrellas, hatpins – $150; Jewellery, diamond pin, lockets, bracelets, two rings, brooches – $200; Two toilet sets – $35; One manicure set, sterling silver – $70; Baskets and linen – $150; Sofa pillow – $40; Table linen – $25; Books – $15; Albums – $10; Cut glass, butter dishes, fruit dishes, etc. – $100; Silver ware – $75; Four suit lengths – $65; Souvenirs – $100; Weather guide, barometer – $5; Crocheted collars – $45; Irish linen waists – $50; Pieces of hand embroidery – $100; Money in hand bag $140; Two brass candlesticks – $12; Amethyst Rosary beads – $10; Other small articles, valuable papers and receipts. Total $1,774.

Bertha married her sweetheart, Henry Noon, a master welder with Brown & Sharpe, a short time after the tragedy. They had a daughter, Helen, who died four days before Christmas 1928 at the age of just nine. Four other children lived to adulthood.

Interviewed in 1956 on the forty-fourth anniversary of the sinking Bertha declared: 'I don't know where they get all that women and children first business. I never saw it! I'll tell you what I saw. I saw a mother and her five children standing there on that ship. When the ship split in half, I saw the mother and five children drown.'

In 1958, she refused an all-expenses-paid trip to England offered by the production unit of the movie *A Night to Remember*, pleading that her memories were too painful.

Bertha died from cancer at the age of 73 in North Providence on 15 October 1959. The following obituary appeared two days later:

> Mrs Noon, formerly of 28 Windham Ave, lost her trousseau when the *Titanic* hit an iceberg and sank in 1912.
>
> A resident of the Mt Pleasant section most of the last 33 years, she came to this country from Ireland at an early age and later became engaged to Henry F. Noon of Providence. Before the marriage, she returned aboard the *Lusitania* to County Athlone [*sic*] for a last visit with her parents and relatives. During the nine months' visit, she collected hand-stitched Irish linens and laces for the trousseau, and a chiffon gown for the wedding, and carefully packed them for the return voyage.
>
> When the ship hit the iceberg, the girl, a steerage passenger, rushed up on deck and never gave a thought to the trousseau. She managed to get in one of the last lifeboats with 75 other survivors, and suffered several broken ribs in the crush. She wore shoes on bare feet, a coat over her nightgown and, as she waited for rescue, used her prayer book. The only other article she saved was a watch, a gift of her fiancé, which she had pinned to her nightgown.
>
> Mrs Noon died Thursday at Our Lady of Fatima Hospital after a short illness. Mr Noon died about thirteen years ago.

MARGARET MURPHY (24) SAVED
KATE MURPHY (17) SAVED

Joint ticket number 367230. Paid £15 10s.
Boarded at Queenstown. Third Class.
From: Fostragh, County Longford.
Destination: 2238 Fairhill Street, Philadelphia.

Maggie Jane and Kate were sisters who ran away from home to join the *Titanic*. Margaret told of an emotional last kiss with her male companion, who pledged he would see her soon.

Locked in steerage: Irish girl's terrible story
A terrible story of women and children locked in the steerage of the sinking *Titanic* is

told by Miss Margaret J. Murphy of Foster [*sic*], County Longford, who, with her sister, Miss Katherine Murphy, was saved from the wreck.

Interviewed by a representative of the *New York American* at the residence of their sister, Miss J. Toomey, the Bronx, Miss Murphy stated –

'Before all the steerage passengers had even a chance of their lives, the *Titanic*'s sailors fastened the doors and companionways leading up from the Third-Class section. That meant certain death to all who remained below.

'And while the sailors were beating back the steerage passengers, lifeboats were putting away, some of them not half-filled.'

Kate and Margaret

A Brave Irish Youth

Having related how a brave young Irishman, John Kiernan, who was lost, gave her his lifebelt, she said –

'A crowd of men were trying to get up to a higher deck and were fighting the sailors; all striking and scuffling and swearing. Women and some children were there praying and crying.

'Then the sailors fastened down the hatchways leading to the Third-Class section. They said they wanted to keep the air down there so the vessel would stay up longer. It meant all hope was gone for those still down there.'

John Kiernan, she said, helped her into the boat and said 'Good-bye' – as he had said it a hundred times before at the door of her father's store. She knew he did not intend to get in himself, but the sailors drove him away. She added –

'Just as the davits were being swung outward, a Chinaman pushed a woman out of the boat and took her place. Sailors grabbed him and handed him back to the deck. Then someone shot him and his body tumbled into the water. It was terrible.'

(*Irish Independent*, 9 May 1912)

This report, with its 'Brave Irish Youth' headline was raised during the British inquiry by counsel for the Third-Class passengers. But inquiry chairman Lord Mersey ruled it out of order.

The Murphy sisters are reported to have saved the life of their fellow Longford passenger Thomas McCormack after their boat had been lowered and he swam to its side to beg to be taken aboard. This is his tribute:

Girls saved youth

Thomas McCormick [*sic*], nineteen years old, of No. 36 West Twentieth Street, Bayonne, N.J., who was a passenger on the *Titanic*, and is a patient in St Vincent's Hospital, this city, suffering from exposure, says that his life was saved by two sisters, Kate and Mary Murphy, who picked him up from the water, dragging him into a lifeboat and sitting on him after sailors manning the boat had struck him on the head and tried to drive him from clinging to the sides of the boat.

(*New York Herald*, 22 April 1912)

A week later, the same newspaper reported on the Murphy links with the Kiernans:

Eloping girl tells story
Perhaps the most interesting story was that told by Miss Margaret Murphy, a pretty girl with rosy cheeks and Irish blue eyes, who left her home in Fostra, County Longford, unknown to her parents and relatives, with the intention of marrying here John Kiernan, a neighbour, who was in her party.

When the critical moment on shipboard came, Kiernan gave up his life for her when he surrendered his lifebelt to her and saw her safely into a lifeboat. She said:

'The night before the little group in our village was to leave to go aboard the *Titanic*, together with several other young women and men, I slipped away from my home, carrying all the clothes that I could, and went to the Kiernan home, where a farewell party was being held. At that time, I had promised to wait at home until Mr Kiernan would come to this country and make a place. Then I was going to join him. But the thought of being separated from him was too much for me and I decided to run away from home.

'At the Kiernan house I was received kindly, as we were all neighbours. At the first opportunity I told Mr Kiernan of my purpose. He reluctantly agreed. He was twenty-five years old and I am nineteen.

'When we heard the *Titanic* was doomed, we left our berths and rushed on deck. I saw boat after boat being loaded with passengers while I stood trembling at the side of Mr Kiernan. He tried to cheer me, and the truth of the matter is that I never thought for a moment that the steamship was going down.

'When both of us realized it was sinking, Mr Kiernan took a lifebelt off himself for me and assisted me in one of the last lifeboats. We kissed each other goodbye and he promised to see me soon.'

Miss Murphy could not restrain herself longer and she told this story and broke into tears. When she regained her composure she said:

'I saw the poor fellow go down with the *Titanic* soon afterward, and I felt mighty mean to know that I had a lifebelt around me which might have saved poor John.'

Miss Murphy is here at the home of her sister at No. 3649 Olinville Avenue, the Bronx.

From *The Irish Post*, 11 May 1912:

Longford girls' experiences: interview with their mother
Letters describing the disaster
The house where the Murphys were born is a thatched farm house approached by a narrow lane from the main road, leading to Aughnacliffe and about a mile and a half from the village. Mrs Murphy, the mother of the girls, a comparatively young woman, with hair turning grey, produced the letters written by her daughters, to our representative.

The letter from Miss Kate Murphy in reference to the disaster ran as follows:

'It was a terrible disaster which happened the ship which was to bring us here. I suppose you have heard a good deal about it. It was a terrible place when the ship was going down to hear the cries of the poor passengers who were drowning.

'We were in bed, and were the first to hear in our rooms, for the water came rushing into our room, so we got up and called the other girls. Everyone was up in a few minutes, and rushing on deck for the lifebelts.

'You know we had no hopes of being saved, and the stewards were telling everyone to go back to bed, that there was nothing the matter. They didn't care, I suppose, for they knew that they would be saved themselves. The crew are saved but a few, and nearly all the passengers we knew were drowned, and poor John and Philip Kiernan are lost too.

'It was they got the lifebelts for us, and there were five girls and seven boys that we knew in Queenstown who were with us, lost.

'My name was on the papers for being lost and poor Patrick (her brother) was nearly dead with grief when we met him after coming off the *Carpathia*, which picked us up. After landing, we got money to buy clothes, &c., in place of what we lost, as we only had a light garment on.'

The writer of the letter is only seventeen and never travelled on sea before. Her sister, Maggie, was returning to the States after a holiday with her relatives. She did not write much about the disaster and most of what she wrote was similar to the other letter:

'We were awake after two o'clock. I was first to waken after the accident, and I saw the water coming into our room. I woke Katie, and we then called the other girls. Having first put on some little clothes, we ran up on deck. We were told by an officer there that nothing was the matter, though.

'Lots of people were there looking for lifebelts. Philip Keernan [*sic*], who is lost, put on my lifebelt. We were taken into one of the boats and were eight hours in it, famished, before a ship that was going to California picked us up.

'We could see poor John Keernan and his brother Phil on deck when the ship was going down. That was the last I saw of them, and a boy named James Farrell, of Clonee, Killoe, who was lost too. It was terrible to hear the cries of the poor creatures when they were going down, and I can't just bear to write about it, so I will send you the papers with all about it. We were brought to St Vincent's Hospital and feel all right again.'

(*The Irish Post*, 11 May 1912)

Family accounts tell that the girls' widowed and elderly mother, Maria, refused to entertain the idea of her two daughters emigrating and insisted that they both stay on the farm. She said she did not rear her children for them all to go to America and abandon their last parent. It is difficult not to have sympathy with Mrs Murphy's position – she had given birth to twelve children in all, five of whom died in infancy, and by 1912 she had but a quarter of her offspring at home. Her husband had died from a heart attack a year previously.

Margaret and Kate decided that they were going to go to America anyway, despite their mother's refusal, and began hiding trunks in the barn and taking items out to the trunks. Both ran away to the Kiernan home just before the departure for Queenstown.

Kate brought her violin aboard the *Titanic* and played sets with other musicians in the Third-Class party on the night of the collision. She left behind her instrument in the chaos of trying to get to the boat deck and remembered John Kiernan building a makeshift ladder out of deckchairs for the girls to clamber to the safety of the Second-Class deck.

Anne McCabe, daughter of Margaret Murphy, says she does not believe her mother was engaged to John Kiernan, despite mysterious mention of a $100 diamond ring in Margaret's claim for lost personal effects.

The Murphy girls were met on arrival in New York by brother Patrick and the three other sisters – Annie, Bridget and Rose.

Barely two weeks thereafter, Kate met the man who was to become her husband. Romance blossomed at the wedding of her sister Annie to Dennis Guilfoyle, when bridesmaid Kate became entranced with the groom's brother Michael and later married the 19-year-old postman at Corpus Christi Church in New York in 1913. Two sisters were now married to two brothers.

In that same year of 1913, fellow *Titanic* survivor Margaret Murphy met and married mortician and sometime ballroom promoter Matthew O'Reilly from Cavan. This couple returned home that year on honeymoon to see Margaret's mother, the bride deeply ashamed that she had never said goodbye properly. Kate, however, could not be prevailed upon to make a return visit, and in fact never did so, retaining 'an extreme fear of water and flying'.

It is reported that Mrs Murphy was relieved to see at least one of her daughters, having originally believed that neither Margaret nor Kate had been saved, but rather drowned as punishment for defying their mother.

Both Catherine and Margaret had children, three each, and both families were brought up for a time in the same four-storey building in Manhattan.

Report of the American Red Cross (Titanic Disaster) 1913:
No. 323. (Irish.) Two sisters, domestic servants, 21 and 16 years old. ($200)

The sisters were also each given $25 in cash from Fr Michael J. Henry of the Irish Immigrant Society. Perhaps believing that free money was easily obtained in the United States, both Margaret and Kate filed hugely exaggerated claims for compensation for property lost on the *Titanic*. The extended clan now insists the sisters were acting under instructions from an older brother. Together they sought more than $1,800 for their few belongings, as follows:

Schedule of Margaret Murphy:

1 cloak, $30; 3 suits, $80; 10 gowns, $150; 6 shirtwaists (2 lace), $35; 4 skirts, $25; 1 set of furs, $50; 6 hats, $60; ½ doz. pairs silk stockings, $6; 1 doz. cotton stockings, $6; undergarments, $50; 6 pairs shoes, $24; 2 albums, $12; 12 yds linen, $30; 5 Irish lace collars, $125; 6 prs gloves, $9; ½ doz. lace handkerchiefs, $3; 1 doz. linen handkerchiefs, $3; 1 silk umbrella (gold handle), $15; 1 parasol, $5; 1 diamond ring, $100; 1 locket and chain, $25; 1 bracelet, $10; 2 hand knit sweaters, $10; 1 raincoat, $7; 1 silver mesh bag, $10; 1 leather bag, $4; 1 silver toilet set, $10; 2 sets combs, $4; 2 trunks, 2 dress suit cases. Total: $901.

Schedule of Katherine Murphy:

One gold watch, $30; Two rings, $20; One gold bracelet, $5; Two gold breast pins, $8; One set of Rogers' silverware, $15; One assorted lot of linen, towels, table cloths, $25; Two long coats, $50; One set of mink furs, $50; Four embroidered dresses, $60; Two silk dresses, $40; Four tailor-made suits, $100; Two hats with plumes, $25; Three Irish linen dresses, $40; One gent's suit, $35; Twelve pairs of hand-made stockings, $12; One shawl, $2; One lot of underwear, $23; One half-dozen pairs of shoes, $20; One lot of family relics, $40; Cash, U.S. currency, $300. Total: $900.

Margaret Murphy O'Reilly died of a heart attack in Slate Hill, New York, on 29 September 1957. Aged 68, she had been a widow for nearly twenty years.

Katherine Murphy Guilfoyle died at Swan Lake, New York, her home of thirty-seven years, on 24 September 1968. She was aged 73, and had been a widow for six years.

1911 census – Murphy. Fostragh, County Longford.
Parents Michael (70), farmer, and Maria (66).
Married 40 years, with 12 children born, of whom seven were then living.
Children in house: John (38), **Maggie Jane (21)**, **Kate (16)**.

NORAH MURPHY (34) SAVED

Joint ticket number 36568. Paid £15 10s.
Boarded at Queenstown. Third Class.
From: Sallins, County Kildare.
Destination: 231 East 50th Street, New York city.

Norah was travelling with Michael McEvoy, a 19-year-old workman with whom she had taken up following the ending of her own marriage, details of which remain obscure.

She was 34 years old, and had been working as a nanny in her home town of Sallins, County Kildare. In the 1911 census, she is found to be a domestic working in the household of John and Mary Healy and their family of six children in Sallins.

Norah and Michael were travelling on the same ticket, but were accommodated at opposite ends of the *Titanic*. Norah had signed aboard as a spinster, but local folklore in her home village suggests she had a chequered past.

In the chaos of the early morning of 15 April 1912, Norah was bundled into a lifeboat, possibly No. 16 on the port side, while Michael accepted the fate ordained for him as a man of low social standing.

Ms Murphy had initially stated a boarding house address as her intended destination, at 231 East 50th Street, but following her rescue by the *Carpathia* she indicated to customs and immigration officers that she now intended to seek refuge at the Irish Immigrant Girls Home at 7 State Street. It is known that she did go there and received a small amount of assistance from the religious administrators of the home. She was also given relief by the American Red Cross, in the amount of $100. Listed as case number 324, an Irish nursemaid, she said she was 32 years old.

Not a single detail is known of Norah Murphy's later life in the United States. One report was that she became a domestic for a *Titanic* survivor from First Class – a woman she met on the *Carpathia*.

THOMAS MYLES (62) LOST

Ticket number 240276. Paid £9 13s 9d.
Boarded at Queenstown. Second Class.
From: Fermoy, County Cork.
Destination: Cambridge, Massachusetts.

Thomas Myles was an adventurer who had worked for the White Star Line – owners of the *Titanic* – for nearly half a century. But he had also been able to assemble an independent fortune, having arrived in America in 1875 at the age of 26 with just £1 in his pocket.

From a wealthy landed family who lived in Brook Lodge, Fermoy, he had nonetheless roved off to sea, joining the original White Star company. He sailed to India from Liverpool on a freighter skippered by his cousin, and visited Bombay and Calcutta. Later he sailed the length of the mighty Mississippi. He began acquiring land and eventually became a real estate tycoon, owning a string of properties. By the turn of the century, he lived in a splendid mansion named 'Idlewild' in Cambridge, Massachusetts.

He had reached his later years when a family death brought him back to Ireland to sell part of the family's holdings to provide for the future well-being of his severely mentally handicapped brother James, now the only family member in Ireland. In packing for the return journey, he made sure to bring with him fifty pounds of pure Irish creamery butter, together with ten pounds of tea, valued at $15. Clearly he was a man who liked his comforts from the old country. Myles was the only passenger booked aboard with an address at Cambridge, Massachusetts, and he is clearly the man described by his fellow Second-Class passenger, Lawrence Beesley, on the afternoon of Sunday 14 April:

> Close beside me – so near that I cannot avoid hearing scraps of their conversation – are two American ladies, both dressed in white, young, probably friends only: one had been to India and is returning by way of England, the other is a school-teacher in America, a graceful girl with a distinguished air heightened by a pair of pince-nez.
>
> Engaged in conversation with them is a gentleman whom I subsequently identified from a photograph as a well-known resident of Cambridge, Massachusetts, genial, polished, and with a courtly air towards the two ladies, to whom he was known but a few hours; from time to time as they talk, a child acquaintance breaks in on their conversation and insists on their taking notice of a large doll clasped in her arms; I have seen none of this group since then.
>
> (*The Loss of the SS Titanic*, Lawrence Beesley, 1912)

From the *Clonmel Chronicle* of 24 April 1912:

> Among those who, it is feared, perished in the disaster was Mr T. F. Myles of Boston, who had just visited Fermoy, of which he is a native, and intended returning with his family next year.

He left a widow, Mary, and sons Leo and Frederick (who coincidentally lived beside John Kiernan, another Irish *Titanic* passenger, in Grove Street, Jersey city), along with daughters Gertrude, Agnes, Elizabeth and Eileen.

The family were visited three weeks after the tragedy by a passenger who told them he had seen Myles in a lifeboat – but the old man had stepped out again, saying 'Women and children first'. He was also seen in a group kneeling on the deck of the *Titanic*, saying the Rosary.

Lawrence Beesley, who had falsely been reported lost, had met the family, and commiserated with them on the false reports that their Papa had been saved:

> The name of an American gentleman – the same who sat near me in the library on Sunday afternoon and whom I identified later from a photograph – was consistently reported in the lists as saved and aboard the *Carpathia*: his son journeyed to New York to meet him, rejoicing at his deliverance, and never found him there. When I met his family some days later and was able to give them some details of his life aboard ship, it seemed almost cruel to tell them of the opposite experience that had befallen my friends at home.

HANNAH NAUGHTON (21) LOST

Ticket number 365237. Paid £7 15s.
Boarded at Queenstown. Second Class.
From: Kilcullen, Donoughmore, County Cork.
Destination: 433 West 33rd Street, New York city.

Hannah was going to America to take up a job as a schoolteacher in New York, but she became a victim of arithmetic and was just another of the steerage women to die. Nearly half of all adult females in Third Class lost their lives – 87 out of 178 – compared with just thirteen per cent of the women in Second Class and a minuscule three per cent of those in First.

Hannah was born on 10 April 1891, exactly twenty-one years before the *Titanic* began her maiden voyage from Southampton. She was named after her grandmother. Her family had a sheep farm of forty acres, which is still owned by descendants. One older brother,

25-year-old Paddy, had emigrated to New York a few years before, was working on the railroad, and had patiently put prospects in place for Hannah.

Donoughmore Victims, Donoughmore, Wednesday
It is regrettable to have to record that among those who lost their lives in the historic *Titanic* disaster were Hannah Naughton, daughter of John Naughton, and William, son of John Foley, Commeen, both of this parish.

The greatest sympathy is felt for the parents of both for the sudden and tragic way in which they lost their lives. Hopes were entertained that their names would appear in some lists of those saved, but it is now certain that both were lost.

(*The Cork Examiner*, 22 April 1912)

Hannah's father, John, and his wife, Ellen, had suffered the death of another daughter, Bridget, when she was only a few months old, and Hannah's loss seemed to renew and magnify that earlier pain. John died within three short months of her loss. He was shattered at the extinction of his only surviving daughter among six strapping sons. She had been the apple of their eye – the parents had paid for expensive boarding school tuition for Hannah at Crosshaven Convent, many miles away along the coast. When Hannah qualified with a certificate of merit in English, arithmetic and geography, they were extremely proud. But the news that she next wanted to teach in America came as a blow. Her brothers Martin and Paddy were already 'over there', but somehow John Naughton had always clung to the belief that his closeness to his beloved daughter would keep her close to home. However, John and Ellen told her to follow her dream, swallowing their own sense of loss. A short time later the reality of that loss overwhelmed them.

1901 census – Kilcullen, Donoughmore. Naughton.
Parents: John (50), agricultural labourer; Ellen (40).
Children: Martin (16), Patrick (14), John (12), **Hannah (10)**, Cornelius (8), Michael (6), William (2), Bridget (two months).

DENIS O'BRIEN (21) LOST

Ticket number 330979. Paid £7 12s 7d, plus 4s extra.
Boarded at Queenstown. Third Class.
From: Caheragh, Drimoleague, County Cork.
Destination unknown.

Denis O'Brien was a postman. Within a short time of his departure from the quay at Queenstown, his father, Michael, a rural postmaster, received a letter that didn't need onward delivery. A grim White Star Line confirmation hit home.

Although he had been working as a letter carrier, Denis was signed on board the *Titanic* as a 21-year-old farm labourer, according to available embarkation records. Work as a postman would have been extremely limited in his quiet townland in those days – probably not sufficient to sustain a living wage.

Denis was diminutive in stature – 'a tidy size' according to folk memory – and earned a reputation as a talented jockey in his district. He had won a number of races locally and further afield. He began to dream of working full time with horses in America. It is believed he was travelling to New York to join his sister Margaret who had emigrated a short time before.

The 1901 census establishes that his parents were Michael and Mary O'Brien, aged 50 and 51 respectively at that time, eleven years before the *Titanic* sailed. In various family reports and other censuses Michael listed his many and various occupations as boot and shoemaker, postman and publican. The children named on the 1901 census form are Bridget (24), Catherine (21), assistant postmistress, Margaret (18), seamstress, Michael (16), rural postman, Mary Ellen (14), and Denis (10).

Another brother, who did not appear in that census, was 'Batt', a nickname for Bartholomew. A carpenter, he joined the Royal Navy and fought at sea in the Great War. The area has a strong connection with seafaring, linked to a lack of economic opportunity in the hinterland.

THOMAS O'BRIEN (26) LOST
HANNAH O'BRIEN (26) SAVED

Joint ticket number 370365. Paid £15 10s.
Boarded at Queenstown. Third Class.
From: Grean, Pallasgreen, County Limerick.
Destination: 638 Sherman Place, Chicago.

Tom and Hannah were one of just two married couples to embark among the 113 Third-Class passengers at the *Titanic*'s final stop – or were they? They signed aboard as husband

and wife, yet there is no record of the O'Briens ever having married in Ireland according to the scrupulously kept civil registers. Also, none of Tom's family in the United States had ever heard of his having a bride and were thoroughly shocked when such a claimant presented herself.

What complicated the story further was that Hannah was more than two months pregnant on the *Titanic*. She was the only Third-Class passenger who was in the family way when aboard that is known to have survived the sinking. Hannah is believed to have been saved in lifeboat No. 16, while the unborn mite's father – if he knew she was pregnant – must have known in his heart that he would never see his new son or daughter draw breath. Thomas O'Brien, who had worked in a creamery at home, died in the sinking – sundering the soon-to-be family whose welfare might have prompted his moving to the United States in the first place.

The couple may have met during milk deliveries from Hannah's parents' farm in Kilduffahoo, Doon West, County Limerick. But folk memory tells of love blossoming on a train to Limerick months before the *Titanic* sailed. Michael gallantly gave up his seat for the fresh-faced young beauty, and seized his chance to strike up a conversation. It is said that the couple eloped and were married by a priest in Limerick related to Hannah. No official record exists.

Their passionate involvement could have led to their elopement. If Hannah realised she was with child – a shameful condition for a single girl in those days, one that invariably involved giving up the child for adoption and never seeing it again – a joint decision to disappear forever could have become the only option.

They first booked themselves aboard the *Cymric* for passage to America – just like Denis Lennon and Mary Mullin, another runaway couple who were fleeing to the United States. Both couples were cruelly disappointed that the White Star vessel's Easter Sunday sailing was cancelled. But they were elated to be transferred instead to the mighty *Titanic*. These seem to be the only two Irish couples that could be referred to in the following newspaper reports of eloping lovers:

> The most pathetic feature of all is that of a young couple, a prepossessing and well-connected girl, aged about 20, and her husband, who is about the same age, who were turned away from the parental home when it first became known that they were married, and who took the first chance of leaving for the Land of the Free by the *Titanic*. It is known that both were travelling under false names, and the passenger list to hand bears this out as no such names as those borne by the parties appears on the list, though they were seen in the tender leaving Queenstown and spoken to when aboard the ill-fated vessel. The parents of the bride arrived in the city yesterday evening, and their grief can very well be imagined. Still there is hope that the youthful bride might be one of the female passengers aboard the *Carpathia*.
>
> (*Cork County Eagle*, 20 April 1912)

Tom O'Brien had four sisters living in the Chicago area who knew he was coming out to join them. One married sister, Mrs Mary Hunt (38) of Sherman Plaza, was named on official documents as his sponsor for accommodation. But the sisters had no idea that Tom might be accompanied, and the news that Hannah Godfrey had become his wife sent their senses further reeling after the shock of realising he was dead. Nonetheless they were determined to do 'the right thing'. They offered Hannah a place to stay.

When the survivors landed in New York, however, Hannah did not travel on to Chicago. Instead she stayed with a friend in Brooklyn. She told immigration that she was 26, from Limerick, and that her next of kin was Mrs Eliza Godfrey of Cappamore. She later lodged a claim for compensation for her husband's drowning, a legal move that clashed with similar papers seeking financial assistance filed by his sisters. This is how the American Red Cross reported the developments and dilemmas in its 1913 revelations about aid to survivors:

No. 346. (Irish.) The husband was drowned. His bride, who was saved, was placed in a hospital in New York city to await confinement, which occurred in September. She is unwilling to return to Ireland, because her family cannot support her, and unwilling to go to her husband's sisters, who have offered a home although they cannot assist her financially, because she is an entire stranger to them and association with them would only keep her husband's death constantly before her mind. She now has employment where she can have her baby with her. She was given $500 by this Committee for her own use upon leaving the hospital, and the remainder of the appropriation has been placed in trust for her child. The Society of St Vincent De Paul is interested and will keep supervision over her affairs. From other relief sources she has received $2,282.38. ($1,500)

Hannah gave birth to Tom's daughter, Marion Columba O'Brien, on 3 September 1912. The following March she wrote to his sister Mary, whose home had been Tom's nominated destination, in the following brusque terms, which caused a stir when it was sent home to Ireland for perusal:

My dear Mrs Hunt
I have just received your letter this morning. You need not bother yourself about that law-suit. I have all that fixed long ago. I settled with them, you needn't worry about me. My baby and myself will be all right.

I knew ye were all trying to get some money. I produced my marriage certificate, and I had the nearest claim. So you nor the lawyer needn't bother.

With love from baby and myself your fond Sister

Hannah O'Brien.

Hannah next met and wooed James Quinn, a New York fireman born in Kilkenny, and they were wed in New York in November 1916. She then had a second child, James Jnr. But within a few hard years Hannah had joined her first husband in death. She passed away just six years after arriving in New York in the great influenza epidemic of 1918. When she died from pneumonia on 17 October that year, daughter Marion had just turned six, while James Jnr was a toddler.

Her hard-drinking husband returned from the burial three days later and immediately burned all Hannah's documents and private papers, including her marriage certificate to Thomas O'Brien.

Marion, a latter-day orphan of the *Titanic* disaster, grew up to marry Willie Hanlon, another Irish immigrant, a 'spoiled priest'. They lived in New Jersey and had three children – Margaret, Catherine and Billy. Marion's husband died of lung cancer in April 1975, and she then went to live with her daughter Catherine in Manchester, Tennessee, where she died on Independence Day, 1994. She was 81 years old and is buried in St Agnes' Cemetery in Albany, New York.

Catherine says her mother:

… sort of resented it all: the fact that she was left without anybody. She never knew her father and then her mother died when she was five or six. She had it tough when she was younger but her life was happy with my father. The only real sorrow she had was the death of my brother [from melanoma, at age 27].

She wouldn't go near water, she hated it. Even when we went to the ocean she stayed well back on the beach. She didn't like boats, she never went on one. She never spoke about the *Titanic*.

The first her children knew about her involvement in the disaster was when Catherine as a youngster went to see the 1958 movie *A Night to Remember* and came home to tell her mother about it. Marion then confessed that she had survived the sinking, carried into a lifeboat in her mother's womb.

1911 census – Kilduffahoo, Doon West, County Limerick.
Parents: Michael Godfrey (41), son, farmer. Eliza Godfrey (71), widow.
Children: **Hannah (32)**, Patrick (30).

PATRICK D. O'CONNELL (18) LOST

Ticket number 334912. Paid £7 14s 8d.
Boarded at Queenstown. Third Class.
From: Kingwilliamstown, County Cork.
Destination: New York city.

Patrick Denis O'Connell was unusual in that he had no need to emigrate to America. There was no economic engine driving his departure, since his family owned both a farm and a pub. But wanderlust and a craving for excitement drew him away. His parents were worried about his devil-may-care attitude. His father, Denis, thought his second son was too naive and impulsive to head off to America and believed he should stay at home. But Denis' wife, Hanna, thought that the US might be the makings of 'Patie', and that he would grow up quickly.

One day Hanna abruptly bought her son his ticket, so there was little Denis could do. Patie was intending to travel on another vessel, but the family were pleased when a large group of intending emigrants from Ballydesmond formed a group to go together. They were particularly happy that Nora O'Leary would be there: despite the fact that she was a year younger than Patie, they believed she acted as a calming influence upon him.

Patie's first bit of growing up came when he had to part with his dog. It was an emotional wrench, but he managed the leave-taking. The canine howled and mourned all night – and then repeated the anguish four days later, on the night when the *Titanic* was sinking.

Patie was a cousin of Daniel Buckley, and the family pub stood right next door to the Buckley home in the village centre of Kingwilliamstown. Both Dannie and Patie attended an American wake with other lads and lasses from the village and its hinterland on the eve of their embarkation journey to Queenstown. Much of the party likely centred around Denis O'Connell's pub and it is certain that Patie was prevailed upon for a song, as were all the would-be emigrants.

The four lads from the same area roomed together in a compartment at the bow of the ship. Short minutes after the first scrapings of disaster they had to evacuate their cabin urgently – although it seems they initially believed Buckley was pulling their legs about something being wrong with the ship. But then water came sliding onto the floor of their room in the aftermath of the ship's forward starboard plates being opened to the sea. Dannie had already fled, allowing the others space to tumble out of their bunks and organise themselves. He never saw them again.

Buckley, in a letter home composed on the *Carpathia* a few days after he had been saved and when he was still under severe psychological stress, deals with his friend, neighbour and cousin's death in these dissociated terms – 'There is no account of Patie Connell (25) ...' the age is wrong, and its inclusion seems inappropriate.

Although referred to colloquially as Patie Connell, there is no doubt that his surname took an O' prefix, as demonstrated repeatedly by class rosters from his earliest schooling in Kingwilliamstown. It is also clear from the passenger manifest, booking records and a White Star receipts statement that Patie liked to include his middle initial in his name – hence entries for both 'Pat D.' and 'Patrick D. O'Connell'.

He may have thought the inclusion of the 'D.' a very sophisticated, or American, thing to do. He was young, he was innocent and he had dreams. And then death got in the way.

1901 census – O'Connell, Kingwilliamstown.
Parents: Denis (42) and Hanna (42).
Children: Mary Anne (12), Timothy (10), Hannah (8), **Patrick (7)**, Catherine (5), Julia (3).

MAURICE O'CONNOR (16) LOST

Ticket number 371060. Paid £7 15s.
Boarded at Queenstown. Third Class.
From: Ballinloughane, County Limerick.
Destination: 539 East 72nd Street, New York city.

Maurice O'Connor was painfully young to die. He was travelling to New York to live with Michael O'Connor, who might have been a brother two years older who went by the name of 'Murt' to distinguish him from his father, also Michael O'Connor.

Maurice O'Connor was one of those who were transferred to the *Titanic* after the withdrawal of the *Cymric*'s intended transatlantic passage of 7 April.

1901 census – O'Connor, Ballinloughane.
Parents Michael (50), farm labourer; Kate (41).
Wife's child from a previous marriage: Margaret Regan (14).
Joint children: John (8), Murt (7), **Maurice (5)**, Ellen (3).

PATRICK O'CONNOR (23) LOST

Ticket number 366713. Paid £7 15s.
Boarded at Queenstown. Third Class.
From: Tureenavoscane, Boherbue, County Cork.
Destination: New York city.

Pat was the oldest among the group of men from the Duhallow area of Cork who roomed together on the *Titanic*. As such, his might have been the mocking voice that told the youngest occupant of their compartment, Daniel Buckley, when the latter reported something wrong with the ship: 'Get into bed. You are not in Ireland now.'

When O'Connor and the others – Michael Linehan and Patie D. O'Connell – were finally alerted to the danger of the situation, they sprang out of the bunks in their narrow cabin, located right at the bows where the ship had struck. To make room for them as they jumped into their clothes and hunted for lifebelts, Dannie Buckley stepped out into the corridor. He declared that he never again saw Michael and the two Pats, one of whom had uttered the laughing put-down.

It appears Pat O'Connor did make it to the upper decks, however. One of the party travelling from Kingwilliamstown was his cousin Hannah Riordan, who survived. She told her own children years afterwards that her cousin was one of the men left on board as her boat was lowered.

She added that he had called out to her, and others with her, as their lifeboat pulled away: 'Goodbye, girls. I'll see you in New York.' Self-assured and confident to the last, Pat O'Connor may have convinced himself that twinkling lights of a mystery ship seen off the port bow represented sure-fire rescue. His cockiness, if such it was, could not have lasted long.

Patrick O'Connor had been one of only two children left behind at the family homestead from a brood of eight surviving children born to his parents. It must have been unusual for him to find himself the oldest among his *Titanic* cabin companions because he had always been the baby at home, the very youngest of all. This was a likely factor in his emigration. The family farm was due to be inherited by his older brother Michael.

Duhallow men amongst the missing
Our Duhallow correspondent writes – There now appears to be little doubt that three young men of the farming class from the Boherbee and Williamstown districts have perished in the *Titanic* disaster.

Their names are Patrick Connell, Kingwilliamstown, and Michael Lenihan and Patrick Connors, Boherbee … The deepest sympathy is felt for the friends and relatives of the young men who left the green shores of Ireland only to meet with such a tragic end.
(*The Cork Examiner*, 25 April 1912)

Patrick O'Connor seems to be the person referred to mysteriously as 'Jim Connor, Hugh's son, from Tureenavonacane' by Buckley, the only survivor of this group, in a letter home composed on the *Carpathia*. Buckley had a neighbour named Hugh Connor who had a son named Jim, but this man had remained at home. Buckley was certainly still in shock when writing the letter and also recording that there was no account of his companions and that he hoped they were 'taken into some other ship'. But there was no hope for Patrick O'Connor.

What is clear are the Board of Trade records for this passenger, which show him to be a 24-year-old farmer named Pat O'Connor. This surname also accords with his baptismal records and the census returns, so there is no room for doubt. Patrick O'Connor was due to sail on the *Cymric*, four days before *Titanic*, but was transferred to the latter.

He was born on 30 May 1888, in 'Tureenavuskane', and was a just over month short of his 24th birthday when he died. His nephew, also named Pat O'Connor, later emigrated to the United States and became a famous boxer in the 1940s and 1950s.

Mansion House *Titanic* Relief Fund Booklet, March 1913:

Case number 494. O'Connor, P., parents. Grant £20.
1911 census – Tureenavoscane, County Cork.
Parents: James (69) and Abina (65). Married 41 years, eleven children born, eight alive.
John (28), farmer's son, **Patrick (23)**, farmer's son.

WILLIAM O'DOHERTY (22) LOST

Ticket number 330877. Paid £6 19s 2d.
Boarded at Queenstown. Third Class.
From: 12 Old Market Place, Cork city.
Destination: c/o G. P. McDonough, Ellis Island, New York city.

William O'Doherty died in another man's stead. O'Doherty's name does not appear on the official passenger list. Instead it is certain that he died under another name, as O'Doherty had purchased his passage from one James Moran, and embarked and was lost under this name. (A James Moran from Annabrack, County Offaly, aged 20, emigrated to the USA on the *Titanic's* sister ship *Olympic* in September 1912.) As William O'Doherty was a barman, the transaction might even have taken place in a pub, the slip passing over the counter in exchange for a discount price.

Fate of a young Corkman
The first name on the list of passengers represents a young Corkman who travelled under the name of James Moran. The real name is William Doherty [*sic*], a young man, aged 22 years and nine months, whose relations live at the Old Market Place, Blarney Street.

Mr Doherty was, up to the eve of his sailing, employed at Mr W. O'Callaghan's (vintner), Daunt's Square. In an interview with the father, he stated that his son had purchased the ticket off an acquaintance some time since.

He had very little hope as to his son's safety, for he had failed to get any information. The fate of the young man caused the greatest anxiety, not only among his relations, but also among his acquaintances.

(*Cork Free Press*, 17 April 1912)

The 1911 census reveals that William John O'Doherty was a 21-year-old barman, living at home with his father, William Snr, 55, a retired RIC officer, railway policeman and grocer, and his mother, Anne (53). Among other children in the family were Thomas Peter (23), railway porter, Annie (18); John James (16), another barman; and Bartholomew (15). The family had lived in Cross Lane, Rosscarbery, in 1901.

James Moran, Cork, sold his ticket to Willie Doherty, Cork, who was lost under name 'James Moran'.

(*Irish World,* New York, 11 May 1912)

There is no 'James Moran' of any age in either Cork city or county in the 1911 census. And despite references to Doherty, the name used in census returns, descendants today are adamant the name was O'Doherty.

A number of newspaper reports indicated that O'Doherty could have been on board the *Titanic* in the company of another barman, Timothy O'Brien. But O'Brien's name does not appear on the passenger list.

O'Doherty's niece says William's mother, Anne, gave her son £5 towards his passage, despite her husband not wanting him to go. In a family memoir Philomena Cobley wrote that the mother 'was suicidal and racked with grief and had to be locked in her room for three days when confirmation came there were no more survivors. I can just imagine the suspenseful vigil that they endured and the torment at their loss.'

According to folklore, the family of his mother (née Golden, of Donoughmore, Co. Cork) was blighted by a disgruntled tenant with a *piseóg*. Drowning would dog the family, the curse vowed. And so it turned out. A brother and a nephew of Anne's were later drowned, along with three of her own children, including William.

Peter Crowley, William's grandnephew takes up the story:

When William bought his *Titanic* ticket he would join the list of those cursed to die by water. William's uncle James had drowned in a stream having fallen from a horse. Of William's five siblings, Michael had already drowned in a cauldron of hot water on the family farm, aged three, when supposed to be under the supervision of Anne's sister Mary.

There is a certain amount of mystery concerning William's decision to travel to America. The story is that William was going with a girl of whom his mother disapproved. So, to break the relationship, she opted to pack her son off to America where her brother William, and sisters Teresa and Frances, would look after him.

The family believe the vital ticket, counterfoil number 330877, was sold because Moran was ill. It was snapped up for £5 – a bargain, since the original cost was nearly £7.

NELLIE O'DWYER (26) SAVED

Ticket number 330959. Paid £7 12s 7d, plus 5s extra.
Boarded at Queenstown. Third Class.
From: 33 High Street, Limerick city.
Destination: 13th & East 3rd Street, Brooklyn, New York city.

Limerick girl's thrilling narrative

The *Brooklyn Daily Times* contains an interview by one of its representatives with Miss Nellie O'Dwyer, High Street, Limerick, who was a passenger on board the ill-fated *Titanic*, having booked her passage with Mr Ludlow, emigration agent, Glentworth street. Miss O'Dwyer had been six years residing in Brooklyn, ever since she came from her native city. She was returning to New York after a visit to her father. The interview proceeds to say –

'I was about dozing off to sleep when the big ship seemed to jar,' she began. 'I was not frightened; but got up to ask the other girls what made the vessel act so. Then it was still. You know, all day and all night there was a whirr of machinery and then when it stopped it was queer. For the longest while, none of us could find out what was the matter, but then some young men who were on the vessel with us from Queenstown, told us to go back to sleep, it was nothing.

'"Ye foolish girls, go back to your beds," they said to us; "sure the ship struck an iceberg, but it would take a power of icebergs to harm her." So we – well, most of us – started to go back, but the boys said they were going up on deck to see the berg, for the Captain was going to bring it aboard. Of course, 'twas fooling us they were. Some time later we could hear folks running around above, and we went up the stairway to the upper steerage deck. Something was wrong, we could see that, but we were not frightened, really.

'But then we heard them shouting to get the lifebelts. We knew then something must be wrong. We girls and some of the women with us knelt down on the deck and said the Rosary. Some ladies and gentlemen passed us from cabins and they looked at us curiously. Boats were being lowered and people were being helped into them. Some were almost thrown in.

'Poor Paddy Lane,' murmured the girl after a pause. 'He was a fine young fellow, a little younger than I am, and when we were leaving the other side, his folks asked me to please look after poor Paddy in America.

'When the boats were being lowered, Paddy knelt on the deck and prayed. Then he began to run around calling for the priest. And he started for the other side of the ship. I never saw him again. Paddy went down when the ship sunk.

'Then there was a sweet little boy. Oh! the grandest and most beautiful prayers that one could hear from a child, do you know. I think he was lost, for I don't remember seeing him the next morning in any of the boats.

'The captain treated everyone alike, whether they were from the first cabin or the steerage. He acted angry only towards the men that were rushing forward. He kept us from the panic, so he did. The Italian men were the worst. There was a poor fellow near where I was, and they could not get him back, and an officer shot him and he fell at my feet. I never heard the ship's band playing louder. Men were shouting, women were crying for their husbands and children to stay with them. I don't know how I got to the cabin above.

'I was among the last, and there was only one boat left. Yes, it is true about the old couple. I could hear her husband bidding her to get into the boat, and the last I heard her say was "No, no, no!" As we came along, the last thing I saw was the priest, waving his hand towards us, like as if it might have been absolving all. The poor man was going towards the steerage.'

Afraid to go into the boats

'Do you know, we still had no notion the ship was going down? We were a little afraid about going into the boats. That is, all of them, men or women, were afraid, except the stewards. There was a queer look on their faces as they helped us along. I didn't understand then – none of us did. Now we who were saved know what that look meant.

'There was some trouble with the nurses [stewardesses]. They were supposed to place lifebelts on the people. A few of them tried to escape. But the officers shouted at them, and they came back to their work.

'The poor girl that was to go into the boat just before me was afraid. She jumped and missed the boat, all but one ankle, and a man at the oars grabbed her. She slipped from his hold and was drowned. I got afraid and an officer lifted me. Some one said "Careful there", and I was dropped into the boat. She pulled away, and I sat up to look at the big ship. It could not have been more than seven minutes before there was a terrible explosion. O God, be merciful to us all! The cries that came from the ship I'll never forget. I could see before the explosion just dimly the face of a woman who had six children with her on board. I think none of the little ones got up soon enough to be saved. The poor mother never left the ship.

'Then those in charge began to give orders, keeping the boats a little apart. A little while after, we could see one boat with a green light on it. Some man was giving orders in it. In our boat was a tall man with a moustache, and he seemed to have some giving of orders. We had sixty-five in the boat, and they started taking people out and putting them in boats that had very few in them.

'Five or six Chinamen were found in the bottom of one boat. The way they were saved was by fixing their hair down their backs, and putting their blankets about them. They were taken for women when the boats were leaving the ship. When they took some of the people from our boat we had a sailor and an Italian stoker to row us. It was awful, so it was. The Italian knew no English, and he didn't seem to understand the sailors telling him to "back water". There was no other man now. So, to try and save the people, I took the oar from the Italian and the sailor and I rowed about as best we could. Sometimes the green light I told you about on the boat made me think now and then a ship was coming, and we were afraid it would run us down before we could be saved. We would often mistake a bright star, do you know, for the top light of the vessel.

'Towards morning we rowed over the place where the *Titanic* went down, but there were only pieces of wreckage floating, except the new lifebelts that poor souls had adjusted the wrong way before they left the ship.'

There have been varying accounts as to the air that the ship's band played as the vessel was sinking, but Nellie O'Dwyer declares without hesitation that it was 'Nearer, My God, to Thee'. She declares that her boat was equipped with neither water nor provisions of any kind. She knew the names of none of the persons in her boat.

The awful period of sorrow aboard the *Carpathia* was relieved by Nellie O'Dwyer, who was an angel of mercy. Her robust constitution had been disturbed but little by the trying privations of the night on the open sea, and she went among the suffering survivors tenderly nursing them, making tea for them, and with the characteristic buoyancy of her Celtic heart, forcing a smile and cheering the forlorn with a word of comfort.

(*Limerick Chronicle*, 7 May 1912)

Nellie O'Dwyer could have been rescued in lifeboat No. 10, hanging at a gap of a yard or so from the deck because the *Titanic* was listing heavily to port. It also has an attested case of a woman jumper falling between the boat and the ship, but instead of plunging into the water and drowning, she was caught on the deck below and pulled in. First Officer William Murdoch was in charge of filling the lifeboat. No crewman later made any mention of shooting at this location. People were transferred from overcrowded boat No. 10, as reflected in Nellie's account, when Fifth Officer Harold Lowe formed a flotilla of lifeboats. The woman who had six children on board appears to have been Margaret Rice, who had five sons – one of whom may have been the child who was praying so beautifully.

Dining room steward William Burke put a man he believed to be an Italian at an oar after the transfer of seamen from boat No. 10 to boat No. 14, the latter craft going back to the wreck site to search for survivors. But the Italian confided he was actually Armenian when Burke tried to talk to him.

Nellie O'Dwyer was treated in hospital on landing, and later went to the home of her brother John at East 3rd Street in Brooklyn, where she gave her newspaper interview. She later attempted to get work as a domestic servant. Nellie was aided by the American Red Cross in case number 351, with a grant of fifty dollars.

List of personal property lost by Miss Nellie O'Dwyer, 138 East 3rd St., Brooklyn, NY: 2 ostrich plumes – $10; 2 sets of dishes – $15; 2 suits – $30; Irish lace – $25; 2 hats – $8; watch and chain – $50; set of furs – $20; 4 pictures – $10; white shawl – $5; silver mesh bag – $3.50; 2 pair shoes – $5; coat – $10; ring – $10; silk skirt – $8; underwear – $20; 2 Irish linen table cloths – $15; house dresses & aprons – $15; white dress – $10; music book, stockings, ties – $4; trunk – $10; suit case – $5. Total: $288.50.

PATRICK O'KEEFFE (30) SAVED

Ticket number 368402. Paid £7 15s.
Boarded at Queenstown. Third Class.
From: Spring Garden Alley, Waterford city, County Waterford.
Destination: 416 West 38th Street, New York city.

Patrick O'Keeffe had a dream the *Titanic* was going to sink. The vision came to him before he ever went on board, and he tried to sell his ticket for the crossing, but got no takers. He had been home to Ireland on holiday, visiting his father in Waterford, but as soon as he reached Queenstown for the return journey, he was filled with a sense of foreboding.

The *Evening Telegraph* of 20 April 1912 described his woe:

The principal topic of discussion in the city during the week has been the terrible ending to the maiden voyage of the *Titanic*. Amongst the passengers was Patrick O'Keeffe, son of Mr O'Keeffe, Spring Garden alley, who was returning to the States after a month's holiday in this city. As if the poor fellow had some premonition of what was to happen, the following postcard was received by his father prior to his departure from Queenstown:
    'I feel it very hard to leave. I am down-hearted. Cheer up, I think I'll be alright. – Paddy.'

And *The Cork Examiner* subsequently amplified the reasons for O'Keeffe's unease:

Waterford Survivor
Letters have been received by his father and friends from Patrick O'Keeffe, the only passenger from the city of Waterford on the ill-fated *Titanic*, and who was saved.

He says he dreamt before embarking at Queenstown that the steamer was sinking and would sell his steerage ticket for £7 if he got anyone to buy it. He says he escaped quite easily with two Londoners on a raft and attributes his luck to a cool head.

On 16 May 1912, the same paper printed his picture with the caption 'Another *Titanic* Hero'. It related:

An act of heroism was performed by Mr Patrick O'Keeffe, who, plunging into the sea from the steerage deck, managed to capture a collapsible raft on which he first pulled an Englishman from Southampton and then a Guernsey islander, and after that, with the assistance of those he had already rescued, some twenty other men and women who were finally landed safely on board the *Carpathia*.

The *Enniscorthy Echo* recorded:

Waterford Passenger's Escape
On Saturday Mr John O'Keeffe, Waterford, received a telegram from his son Patrick, who was on board the *Titanic*, stating that he was safe in the St Vincent Hospital, New York. Mr O'Keeffe, who was to have Masses said in the Waterford churches on Sunday for the repose of his son's soul, changed them to Masses of thanksgiving for his rescue.
(*Enniscorthy Echo*, 27 April 1912)

Hospital visitor Fr Michael Kenny told the *Brooklyn Eagle*, 23 April 1912, of the heroics of 'James O'Keeffe', a Waterford boy, whom he had met and spoken to. He told the newspaper: 'O'Keeffe's success in rescuing lives after he assumed absolute command on the raft was one of the many providential avenues of escape provided for the steerage passengers of which I heard many recitals during my visit to St Vincent's.'

Two collapsible boats floated off the *Titanic* in its final moments. Collapsible B remained upside down throughout the night, while A was low in the water and flooded. The use of the word 'raft' and some other details have led to it being considered more likely that O'Keeffe saved himself on capsized B.

Two things stood to O'Keeffe. One was the fact that he was

a strong swimmer, used to cold water because he swam in the sea each Christmas Day. Another was his occupation as a porter (although he had been signed aboard the vessel as an agricultural labourer), which meant he was capable of handling heavy weights.

Harold Bride, one of the ship's wireless operators, had been trapped under collapsible B, but swam out from below and tried to clamber aboard. He spoke fleetingly in testimony to the US inquiry about a passenger who seemed to be at the centre of assistance efforts:

> *Bride*: And there was a passenger; I could not see whether he was first, second or third.
> *Senator Smith*: What kind of looking man?
> *Bride*: I could not say, sir.
> *Smith*: Have you learned who it was?
> *Bride*: No, sir; I heard him say at the time he was a passenger.
> *Smith*: Was it Col. Gracie?
> *Bride*: I could not say. He merely said he was a passenger.
> *Smith*: Where did he get on?
> *Bride*: I could not say. I was the last man they invited on board.
> *Smith*: Were there others struggling to get on?
> *Bride*: Yes, sir.
> *Smith*: How many?
> *Bride*: Dozens.

O'Keeffe was registered on arrival in New York as a 21-year-old porter. In aid case number 352, in a report of the American Red Cross, he is also described as a 21-year-old porter, Irish, who was 'severely bruised and unable to work for several weeks'. He was given a grant of $102.

Pat remained in New York, moving to an address at Second Avenue, and then Eighth Avenue, Manhattan. He found work as a window dresser for a big store. On 19 September 1923, 41-year-old O'Keeffe married Anna Nolan. His Irish bride was aged only 18. A bookbinder by profession, she had an address just a few doors away from the home of the cousin with whom Pat had first stayed. The couple were immediately blessed with a daughter, Margaret, likely conceived on honeymoon, since she was born nine months and one week after their marriage on 26 June 1924. Margaret lived to be 63, and died in January 1988.

Within a few years the O'Keeffe marriage had hit trouble, due in part to the wide disparity in ages and Anna's difficulty in understanding the demons that still attended her husband. They reluctantly divorced. Several years later, however, Anna and Pat returned to each other's embrace. They decided to formalise their rekindled relationship and in 1936 they married each other again.

This time Pat was 54 and Anna 30 as they walked down the aisle at the Church of the Ascension on 8 February that year. Twelve-year-old Margaret may have acted as a page girl – and the couple covered up what would have been a deeply sinful charade in the eyes of the Church by claiming it was a first marriage for them both.

Another child was born, a son, Edward. He later had two girls.

Within three years of his second wedding, Patrick O'Keeffe was dead. He succumbed to a heart attack brought on by angina at the age of 57 – his heart possibly having been fatally weakened by his ordeal in the *Titanic* a quarter of a century before. The death certificate states that he was born in Ireland, the son of John O'Keeffe and Catherine Fitzgerald, and had been working as an elevator operator in an office building. He was a resident of New York for thirty-five years, placing his first arrival in 1904 when he was aged 13. He lies buried in Gate of Heaven Cemetery in Hawthorne, New York.

Just before he had sailed with White Star, Pat O'Keeffe had had his photograph taken at the Poole portrait studios in Waterford city. It is an image of an undoubtedly brave man who, within days, was put sorely to the test and triumphed magnificently.

NORA O'LEARY (17) SAVED

Ticket number 330919. Paid £7 12s 7d, plus 4s extra.
Boarded at Queenstown. Third Class.
From: Glencollins, Kingwilliamstown, County Cork.
Destination: 2873 Eighth Avenue, New York city.

Nora O'Leary was awakened by a crash. The teenager didn't know what it was – and even when water began seeping into her cabin she thought that a pipe had burst, according to the story she would later tell when safely back in her home town. She felt an uncomfortable atmosphere after being woken, although there was very little confusion. She decided to make her way on deck and when she got there asked crewmen what was the matter. She didn't get an answer.

Nora said a lifeboat was being filled and an officer was calling for people to get in. She decided to enter the craft as a precaution, believing it would soon return to the *Titanic*. As the lifeboat was being rowed away, she realised something dreadful was happening.

Someone started saying the Rosary and the large number of Irish who were in the boat – Nora mentioned a figure of eighteen – joined in. Mentally she thanked God that she hadn't decided to go back to her cabin for her case. She would also tell her family that she distinctly saw the lights of another steamer – the 'mystery ship', most likely the *Mount Temple*, reported by many off the port bow – and believed it was coming to rescue them. But it never did.

On board the *Carpathia*, fellow Cork passenger Daniel Buckley would write home to his family: 'Thank God some of us are amongst the saved. Hannah Riordan, Brigie Bradley, Nonie O'Leary ...'

When US immigration came aboard at New York, Nora said she was a 17-year-old domestic, the daughter of John O'Leary of Tureencrigh, Kingwilliamstown, County Cork. She said she was going to stay with her cousin, Mrs Margaret Olmberger, at Eighth Avenue. She also had a sister Catherine (Katie) living in the Bronx.

When allowed off the Cunarder with the other 711 survivors, Nora recalled seeing thousands waiting at the quayside in the stormy night. It was only then, she said, that she realised what had actually happened. She collapsed with delayed shock into the arms of her sister Katie O'Leary of 137 West 11th Street, who had journeyed to meet her. Together they sent a telegram to their parents in what is now Ballydesmond. 'Nora safe and sound', was the import of the message. The American Red Cross aided her: No. 353. (Irish.) Girl, 17 years old, injured ($100).

Nora would later tell of the heady social excitement that had been enjoyed in Third Class. There had been dancing and singing, she said, echoing many accounts of tremendous jollity in the steerage rooms. She had made friends with other Irish girls and lads. 'We had made plans to meet when we arrived – I know now that I will never meet most of them again.' But Nora did meet up with Dannie Buckley and some Irish survivors at a reunion a couple of months later. She herself would stay working in New York for nine years before feeling again the draw of home and returning to Ireland. And she didn't have to steel herself for the sea journey: 'It never cost me a thought.'

She married Tom Herlihy in the early 1920s. He was a veteran of the War of Independence and a former volunteer for the Old IRA. They had five children – Hannah, Sheila, Kathleen, Nora, and Timmy. Tom died on 23 November 1968, but Nora was to be allotted a span of another seven years. She passed away on 18 May 1975, and is buried in Ballydesmond Graveyard – just in front of the grave of fellow *Titanic* passenger Dannie Buckley, killed fighting in France fifty-seven years earlier.

1901 census – Glencollins Upper, Kingwilliamstown.
Parents: John (50), farmer. Johanna (45).
Children: Daniel (24), Catherine (17), Denis (15), Martin (14), John (11), Jeremiah (9), **Honora (6)**, Margaret (3).

BRIDGET O'SULLIVAN (21) LOST

Ticket number 330909. Paid £7 12s 7d.
Boarded at Queenstown. Third Class.
From: Dromdeveen, Glenduff, Broadford, County Limerick.
Destination: 290 Park Avenue, New York city.

'Wait!'

Bridget O'Sullivan made it onto the Third-Class deck space with others, according to folk memory. They were still a long way from the boat deck, but at least they were up and moving – when suddenly she was seized with the need to retrieve her handbag. Ignoring advice, she turned to go below … and suddenly her boyfriend, Joseph Foley, was with her, knowing her determination to save her clutch-bag from her cabin. They would never be seen again.

Bridget's sister Hanna was meanwhile working blithely in New York as maid to a Mrs Gilroy on fashionable Park Avenue. She had paid Bridget's fare, having previously brought over a third sister Nellie, and couldn't wait for all three to be together again.

Tales around her home place tell that Bridget could have travelled to America with an earlier party, but chose to wait for the man she had been courting for nearly two years, gardener Joseph Foley, who would act as protective companion on the first long journey of her life. The wait was fatal.

Hanna and Nellie went to the dock as the *Carpathia* berthed in New York, anxious to ascertain Bridget's fate for themselves. There, some charitable agency or do-gooder pressed upon Hanna a card of comfort, intended to ease the grief of both anxious relatives and bereaved survivors. It was a simple poem entitled 'Waiting', written by John Burroughs. Hanna would remain devoted to the contents all her life – and it seems the sentiments could have been specially written to suit the last remaining memory of her sister, a keepsake portrait stunning in its understated beauty:

Serene I fold my hands and wait
Nor care for wind, nor tide, nor sea
I rave no more 'gainst time nor fate
For lo! My own shall come to me.

I stay my haste, I make delays
For what avails this eager place?
I stand amid the Eternal ways
And what is mine shall know my face.

Asleep, awake, by night or day
The friends I seek are seeking me;
No wind can drive my barque astray
Nor change the tide of destiny.

What matter if I stand alone?
I wait with joy the coming years;
My heart shall reap where it hath sown
And garner up its fruit of tears.

The waters know their own and draw
The brook that springs in yonder heights
So flows the good with equal law
Unto the soul of pure delights.

The stars come nightly to the sky
The tidal wave unto the sea
Nor time, nor space, nor deep, nor high,
Can keep my own away from me.

The original card bearing the poem's treatment of the pain of separation – no doubt felt all the keener in sisters so close remains faithfully framed today in the home of relatives in Ireland. The sisters themselves have long been joined in death, but the echo of loss remains.

County Limerick Victims
From enquiries made, it appears that the names of Joseph Foley of Mountplummer and Bridget O'Sullivan of Glenduff, Ashford, two passengers on the ill-fated *Titanic*, do not appear amongst the lists of survivors and consequently the worst is now feared.

As they were both deservedly popular, their untimely fate has evoked universal regret, and the utmost sympathy is felt for their relatives in their very sad bereavement.

(*The Cork Examiner*, 2 May 1912)

The *Titanic* was not only the first trip abroad for Bridget O'Sullivan, but also her first journey outside her native county. She was very much a home bird. By the turn of the century, her father was dead and she was living at home with her widowed mother, Mary, three sisters and an older brother. She was just eleven years of age. A decade later, two of her sisters were living and working in New York. And to ease the pangs of their own separation, they sent for Bridget.

1901 census – Dromdeeveen, Glenduff, Ashford.
Mary O'Sullivan (48), widow.
Children: William (21), agricultural labourer, Hannie, daughter (14), Ellie (13), **Bridget (11)**, Mollie (7).

KATIE PETERS (26) LOST

Ticket number 330935. Paid £7 17s 9d, plus 5s extra.
Boarded at Queenstown. Third Class.
From: Ballydrehid, Cahir, County Tipperary.
Destination: 243 East 45th Street, New York city.

Miss Peters has been in America some four years and came home on a few months' stay. Miss Peters is a daughter of Mr William Peters, farmer, and was returning to America after a three month stay in her native land.

(*The Cork Examiner*, 18 April 1912)

In fact she had been nearly five and a half years living in the United States, having originally emigrated on the White Star Line's *Oceanic* from Queenstown in September 1906 when just 19. The manifest discloses that her hair was auburn and her eyes grey.

Katie, one of twelve children, roomed on board the *Titanic* with Kate McCarthy and Kate Connolly, both also of Tipperary. Katie Peters was a sweetheart of Roger Tobin, another Irish passenger, according to folklore in her native place. From surviving records, it is clear that both Katie and Roger separately gave the same destination – the address of Mrs John Egan at 243 East 45th Street in Manhattan. She was Katie's sister, who had paid her passage six years earlier.

Katie was five years older than Roger, who was just 21. If they developed a relationship, it can only have sprung up in the short time Katie was home. Yet it appears, from a *Cork Examiner* report, that Roger was just the kind of man a girl could easily fall for:

> Mr Tobin, son of Mr Patrick Tobin, farmer, was a young man of splendid physique and noted in the Gaelic field for his prowess as a hurler and footballer.

After the perishing cold of the North Atlantic stole the lives of Tobin and Katie, there was nothing left for her family to do but to tie up loose financial ends:

> *Report of the American Red Cross (Titanic Disaster) 1913:*
> No. 378. (Irish.) A housemaid, 26 years of age, returning from a visit to Ireland, was lost, leaving dependent parents in Ireland. This Committee refunded to a brother in New York $50 of the money advanced to his sister for passage, which he sent to his parents. The English Committee gave £15 to the family. ($50)

> Peters, Catherine (551), 15th October 1912. Administration of the Estate of the late Catherine Peters, late of Ballydruid [*sic*], Cahir, County Tipperary, spinster, who died 15th April 1912 on the SS *Titanic*, granted at Dublin to William Peters, farmer. Effects £64.

> 1901 census – Peters. Ballydrehid, County Tipperary.
> Parents: William (56), farmer. Mary (46).
> Children: Thomas (16), James (14), **Katie (15)**, Brigid (10), Margaret (7), Helena (6), Josephine (1).

MARGARET RICE (39) LOST
ALBERT RICE (10) LOST
GEORGE RICE (8) LOST
ERIC RICE (6) LOST
ARTHUR RICE (5) LOST
EUGENE FRANCIS RICE (2) LOST

Joint ticket number 382652. Paid £29 2s 6d.
Boarded at Queenstown. Third Class.
From: Athlone, County Westmeath.
Destination: 1922 Columbia Avenue, New York city, en route to Spokane, Washington.

Margaret Rice's death, and that of her five young sons, is the single biggest catalogue of loss endured by any Irish family. It is all the more tragic as she brought her sailing date forward by a month to embark in April rather than May.

It wasn't as if Margaret didn't have it hard enough herself. Aged 39, she had been widowed almost two years earlier when her engineer husband, William, was killed in a locomotive tragedy in America in late 1910. Originally from Athlone and home on a visit, she was returning to Spokane, Washington, with her five sons – Albert, George, Eric, Arthur and the baby, baptised Eugene, but whom she called Frank. All were drowned, and the destruction of the family is commemorated in the Cobh (Queenstown) memorial to the Irish passengers lost, which was unveiled in July 1998.

Mrs Rice's body was recovered, indicating that she managed to get on deck with her children – but the delay in organising them all probably cost the family a place in the boats. She was identified by a pill box she had on her person, which was dispensed to her by a chemist in Church Street, Athlone, two days before boarding. She is buried in Mount Olivet Cemetery in Halifax, Nova Scotia – on the opposite side of a continent to her husband.

Irish Passengers missing: some pathetic incidents Queenstown, Friday
As far as we can make out from the list of survivors to hand here so far, about one third of the 123 passengers who joined the *Titanic* at Queenstown on Thursday last have been saved. The percentage is not as long as was originally believed.

There are many pathetic incidents connected with those Irish passengers. We have turned in vain to every list for some trace of Mrs Rice and her fine young family of five children, with whom she had been in Athlone on a brief holiday, or what was more a rest after a great affliction, she having lost her husband recently.

Mrs Rice's fine handsome children evoked all round admiration. Two were quite young ones in arms and all seem to have perished.
(*The Cork Examiner*, 19 April 1912)

Nellie O'Dwyer from Limerick may have witnessed the last moments of Margaret Rice and her offspring:

The cries that came from that ship I'll never forget. I could see just before the explosion, just dimly, the face of a woman who had six children with her on board. I think none of the little ones got up soon enough to be saved. The poor mother never left the ship.
(*Irish Independent*, 7 May 1912)

Nellie also spoke of 'a sweet little boy' and of hearing 'the grandest prayers that one could hear from a child', before adding: 'I think he was lost. I don't remember seeing him next morning in any of the boats.'

Meanwhile Bertha Mulvihill also saw the Rices on the port side. She said she saw Mrs Rice with one child in her arms and the others clutching at her skirts, just before the end. Speaking on the forty-fourth anniversary of the sinking in 1956, she declared:

'I don't know where they get all that women and children first business. I never saw it! I'll tell you what I saw. I saw a mother and her five children standing there on the ship. When the ship split in half, I saw the mother and five children drown.'

Mrs Rice and her children are pictured in the *Irish Independent* of 19 April 1912. The caption reported: 'Mrs Rice and her five sons, who were returning to their home at Spokane, Washington. Mrs Rice is an Athlone woman. Her husband, who was an engineer, was killed last year on one of the American railways. She had been paying a visit to her uncle, Mr John Norton, Mardyke Street, Athlone.'

A short distance away from that address was Fleming's chemist on Church Street, where Margaret bought pills just before she left Athlone to bring her sons to Queenstown. The tablets were in a numbered container that was later to provide the identification of her body. It also declared: 'Two every four hours if pain severe.' The coroner's report recorded:

A Pathetic Picture:
The last photo of the Titanic, *taken by Mr John Morrogh at Red Bay, Crosshaven, after the vessel had left Queenstown*

> Body number twelve – Female. Estimated age 40. Hair, dark.
> Clothing – black velvet coat; jacket and skirt; blue cardigan; black apron; black boots and stockings. Effects – Wedding ring, keeper, and another gold; locket and photo; one jet, one bead necklace; gold brooch in bag; £3 in gold; £4 in Irish notes; gold brooch; plain gold wag earrings; charm around neck, B.V. M.; False teeth in upper jaw; £10 note; box pills. Probably Third Class.

The White Star Line in New York later sent home a gold locket taken from Margaret's body in Halifax (where it was buried), which contained 'photo and hair', believed to be from her deceased spouse. Accompanying it on the *Oceanic* in August 1912 was a letter noting that her remains had been interred without taking off the rings. The 'bead necklace' and 'charm' in her effects were clarified as a Rosary and Blessed Virgin Mary scapular. None of her children's bodies was ever found.

Athlone Victims

Mrs Rice (née Norton) and her five children were returning to their home in Montana. Mrs Rice, who was a native of Athlone, was a widow. A little over two years ago her husband was killed near their home in the States and in her great bereavement she came home to Athlone, bringing her five children with her.

She remained here just two years. She had intended to return in May, but the fact that other passengers were going from Athlone induced her to start earlier. Her husband left her ample means and a beautiful home, but in this disaster, apparently the whole family is wiped out. The eldest child was only eight years of age, and the youngest three. The home which Mrs Rice was returning to has been closed since her husband's death.

The Rice family – which was completely wiped out in the *Titanic* disaster – appears

to have been dogged by tragedy. Mrs Rice's first baby was choked by a 'comforter' teat, her husband was killed, and now she and the remaining five children are buried in the ocean.
(*Westmeath Independent*, 27 April 1912)

Margaret Rice, the daughter of James Norton and Mary Garty, was baptised on 6 October 1872, in St Mary's Church, Athlone. Almost twenty-six years later, she was married in the same church to William Rice, an Englishman, whose family, like her own, was involved in the railways. The couple wed on 18 June 1898. By this time Margaret's was already a family steeped in tragedy. Both of her parents were dead. Her mother had died in 1885 following complications of childbirth and her heartbroken father had opted to emigrate alone to America in 1891. From the middle of 1892 his letters stopped and the family became convinced that he had died. Thus it represented a new beginning and an end to despair for Margaret Norton when she married William Rice in the church of her childhood. They shared dreams of a better life, and a short time later they were off to the United States themselves to seek their fortunes, with William quickly finding work in Montreal with the Grand Trunk Railroad, whose president, Charles M. Hays, later died in the *Titanic's* foundering. William initially worked as a shipping clerk, but itched to get back to what he knew best – driving trains.

Two of the couple's children were born in Montreal – George Hugh on 30 November 1903, and Frederick (Eric) Thomas on 19 January 1908.

By 1910, William had broken free of the bonds of deskwork and was out on the rails. His work took the family to Spokane, Washington. Their last child, Eugene Francis, was born on 13 October 1909. Albert and Arthur completed the impressive five-son line-up, which always drew admiring comments when the family were out together.

Happiness was short-lived. William was crushed to death by a locomotive on 24 January 1910. He was buried in a plot paid for by the Grand Trunk, and Margaret was awarded $6,500 in compensation. She returned to Ireland.

She had $2,500 in bonds with her on board the *Titanic* when the vessel foundered. Her sister Norah Stetson and a surviving brother, Michael, eventually received only $200 each from her estate after all taxes, fees and debts were paid. Margaret had borrowed $500 against investments held in trust for her children in order to return to the United States. At that time, she was living above Bernard Finnerty's public house in Castle Street, Athlone. The 1911 census identifies her and the children as boarders there, with Margaret describing herself as a returned American widow. All of the five sons are identified as having been born in America, and their names and ages given as follows: Albert (9), George (7), Eric (5), Arthur (4) and Frank (1).

Living with them in these rooms was Margaret's niece, 15-year-old Catherine Norton, from County Sligo. Family folklore says Catherine journeyed to Queenstown with the Rices. It seems Margaret asked her to come over to America to help look after the children, but something prevented the teenager from taking the plunge – literally – and becoming the sixth member of one family to die.

HANNAH RIORDAN (22) SAVED

Ticket number 334915. Paid £7 15s.
Boarded at Queenstown. Third Class.
From: Glenalougha, Kingwilliamstown, County Cork.
Destination: 319 Lexington Avenue, New York city.

Hannah's story is one of crossed wires of communication that conspired to keep the joy of her salvation from keenly sorrowing sisters. She was 22 years old and one of a group that travelled from the small hamlet of Kingwilliamstown, County Cork, and would have enjoyed the emigrants' farewell party staged the night before the adventure began.

It was one long party in the steerage as the *Titanic* sailed, and Hannah might have been in no rush to arrive in America – although New York promised to be even more exciting and enthralling. She was due to be met at the pier in Manhattan by her sister Ellie and was looking forward to exploring the metropolis with her older sibling, who lived on fashionable Lexington Avenue.

Another sister in New York was Julia – and when she and Ellie learned of the calamity both were inconsolable. They had no expectation that a Third-Class passenger might live at a time when the American newspapers were reporting the heroic deaths of millionaires and military attachés. They forced themselves to search the columns of known survivors cabled by the *Carpathia*. But there was no sign of Hannah Riordan. Unknowingly, they passed over the reports of an 'Anna Reibon' among the escapees – garbled wireless transcriptions meaning they had missed the encrypted news that their sister had been rescued.

They went to the pier in any case to meet the 'Ship of Death', as it had been luridly described in the same newspapers. And when a stunned and shivering Hannah appeared in ill-fitting clothes down the gangplank, there were no words to convey their amazement and sheer relief. Tears and hugs said it all.

Hannah Riordan was one of the girls mentioned by Dannie Buckley of the Kingwilliamstown contingent in a letter home from the sanctuary of the *Carpathia*. She was later aided with a $100 gratuity dispensed by the American Red Cross. Her case was listed as number 393, and she pared her age a little to be described as a 20-year-old servant. She had in fact been born on 27 January 1890, and appeared in the 1901 census as an 11-year-old.

Irish Titanic *survivors meet*
34 Men and Women From Various Parts of the Old Country, Who Were Passengers on the Sunken Vessel, Aided by the Patriotic Pastor of the Irish Immigrant Home.

Last Sunday afternoon, Rev Michael Henry welcomed the Irish survivors of the ill-fated *Titanic* at their reunion at the Mission of Our Lady of the Rosary, the Irish Girl's Immigrant Home, 7 State Street, this city. Among the survivors present were Hannah Riordan …

(*Irish World*, New York, 4 May 1912)

Hannah returned home only once, in 1924, and told neighbours and relatives in Ireland that she really didn't know what had happened that awful night in mid-Atlantic. She had gotten such a fright that she had blotted it all out, she said. She only knew that it was terrible.

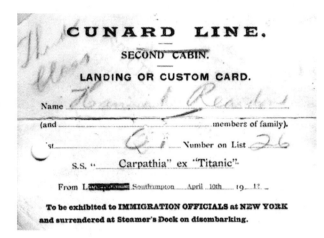

Returning to the United States, Hannah immediately applied to become a US citizen. The paperwork was carried out in 1925 in New York city and she was duly naturalised on 10 May 1928. The application forms indicated she was still unmarried by the age of 35.

She insisted on her declaration papers that she was only 29. The details also show her to have been a grey-eyed brunette, still working as a maid in New York. Hannah declared: 'I emigrated to the United States from Queenstown, Ireland, on the vessel *Titanic*.' The Department of Labour decided otherwise, certifying for bureaucratic purposes that she had arrived via the *Carpathia* on 18 June 1912 – the date the *Titanic* survivors' immigration papers were finally placed on record. Her sister Mary, then working as a cook in the city, witnessed her application.

Hannah married Irishman John Spollen at St Anselm's Church in the Bronx on St Patrick's Day 1936. Her husband was 36, and Hannah signed the register as the same age – the first white lie of the marriage. She was actually a decade older, and unsurprisingly, they had no children.

Hannah's niece Mary Edward of Cresskill, New Jersey, said her aunt hated mention of the *Titanic* and 'would even seem angry' if the topic was brought up. Hannah Riordan Spollen died in the Bronx, New York, on 29 September 1982, aged 92. Heartbroken husband John died seven months later, aged 82.

1901 census:
Parents: Peter (51). Wife Mary, née O'Connor, deceased.
Children: Ellen(13), **Hannah (11)**, Mary (9), Norah (7), James (5), Eugene (3).

EDWARD RYAN (24) SAVED

Ticket number 383162. Paid £7 15s.
Boarded at Queenstown. Third Class.
From: Ballinaveen, Emly, County Tipperary.
Destination: Troy, New York.

Eddie Ryan freely admitted impersonating a woman in his effort to escape the sinking. The ruse worked:

Irish Survivor's Experience – Tipperary Man's Escape
Mr Eddie Ryan, youngest son of Mr Daniel Ryan, Ballinaveen House, Emly, County Tipperary, was a passenger on the ill-fated *Titanic*. The following is an extract from a letter which Mr Ryan sent to his parents:

'Dear Father and Mother,
'I had a terrible experience. I shall never forget it. You will see all about it in the papers which I'll send on to you. I was the last man to jump into the last boat. I stood on the *Titanic* and kept cool, although she was sinking fast. She had gone down about forty feet by now.
'The last boat was about being lowered away when I thought in a second that if I could only pass out I'd be all right. I had a towel around my neck. I just threw this over my head and let it hang at the back. I wore my waterproof raincoat.
'I then walked very stiff past the officers, who had declared they'd shoot the first man who dare pass out. They didn't notice me. They thought I was a woman.
'I grabbed a girl who was standing by in despair and jumped with her 30 feet into the boat. An Italian and myself rowed away as fast as we could, and soon after the great liner sank.
'We were for seven long hours in the boat, and were nearly dead for want of a drink. I attribute my safety to Almighty God.
'We were treated fine on the *Carpathia* and landed in New York on Thursday. I was released from St Vincent's Hospital on Saturday, hale and hearty, even without having got a cold, and went to Troy on Sunday. I'll tell you more of my experiences in my next letter.'

(*The Cork Examiner*, 6 May 1912)

Ryan may have been in No. 14 lifeboat, launched amid some trouble from the port side. 'They were all women and children, bar one passenger, who was an Italian, and he sneaked in, and he was dressed like a woman,' Fifth Officer Harold Lowe testified to the American inquiry. 'He had a shawl over his head, and everything else; I only found out at the last moment.' Lowe later made it clear he was referring to after the sinking, when he was transferring passengers from boat No. 14 to a small flotilla assembled of other craft, intending to use his own to go back to search for survivors.

'It was at this time that I found the Italian. He came aft, and he had a shawl over his head and I suppose he had skirts. Anyhow, I pulled this shawl off his face and saw he was a man. He was in a great hurry to get into the other boat, and I caught hold of him and pitched him in – because he was not worthy of being handled better.'

The obvious problem with this account is that Ryan was not Italian – but speaks himself of being at the oars with an Italian. Lowe seems to have used 'Italian' rather freely in describing unedifying characteristics among foreigners in general.

Ryan's admission to impersonating a woman – reported publicly in Ireland – caused him embarrassment in subsequent years. Locals to this day say he was treated with a certain distance as a result on his trips home, and indeed he chose to live out his later years in England. Things had changed since the scenes that initially feted his survival:

> Mr P. J. Ryan, Croom, was one of the first to receive word of his cousin's safety, and he lost no time in wiring the good news to his relatives in East Limerick and Tipperary. When the news reached Hospital and Emly the people of those districts were wild with joy and excitement, for Mr Eddie Ryan was a favourite with all who knew him, and that night the hills of his native district were alive with bonfires and illuminations in celebration of his Providential escape.
>
> The youths of the district gathered at many crossroads, and dancing and singing were kept up in honour of their favourite Eddie until the early hours of Saturday morning, for all were greatly gratified at Eddie's safety, and the heroism he displayed shows that he is a worthy siren of the old clan O'Ryans, whose ancestry in his old home dates back for over fifteen hundred years.
>
> Numerous telegrams and letters of congratulation have reached the young man's parents from all parts of Munster, but particularly from East Limerick and Tipperary, where his relatives are so numerous and well-known, with all of whom we join in our congratulations for his escape and heroism.
>
> (*Munster News*, 11 May 1912)

Five years before he died, Ryan gave a different, rather self-serving, account of his escape that night. This time he airbrushed his earlier confession, but provided some startling new details while maintaining the assertion of a 30-foot descent in the company of a woman:

> On the *Titanic*'s last day at sea, a Sunday, I remember reading the last log report on the ship's progress. It said, 'A calm sea, 22 knots, icebergs ahead.' We didn't take any notice of this because none of us had ever seen an iceberg. That afternoon we had the usual games and on the Sunday night there was a concert in the dining room. About 300 people attended and I remember there were some very good turns.
>
> The two men in my cabin went to bed about 11 o'clock. I was still up at the time, looking for a piece of wire to free my pipe, which was stopped up. At that moment the ship struck the iceberg. Soon stewards came knocking on all the doors asking everybody to go on deck with their life jackets on. I woke up the men who shared my cabin and told them the ship had struck something, but they took no notice. I never saw them again.
>
> On deck the ship's sirens started to blow and distress signals lit up the sky. There were hundreds of people about, but no-one seemed to know what had happened. I had £300 in my cabin, so after half an hour I decided to go down and get it. But the water was already halfway up the stairs when I got there and I just couldn't get near the cabin.

All Prayed

On deck I told a sailor what I had seen but he told me to keep quiet in case of panic. I managed to get to the boat deck, which was barred to Third-Class passengers. There the order was 'women and children first', and the boats were being lowered.

Some of the women wouldn't get into the boats because of the distance to the water, while others wouldn't leave their husbands. All the men could do was watch, and things looked very grim. Everyone prayed. There were still about 1,500 people on board, including women and children, after the boats had left and the ship was sinking fast.

The angle of the deck became steeper and men started to climb the ropes supporting the masts. Everybody was making for the highest part of the ship. At this stage there was panic amongst the passengers because everybody knew there was little chance of being saved. When I heard some people shouting around the stern of the ship I made my way there, to see what was happening.

There was a woman looking over the side at a boat in the water. There was a rope hanging over the side – I think it must have been the ship's log cable – and it seemed to offer a chance. I said to the woman, 'It's only a matter of minutes before the ship sinks. I'll wind the rope around me, and we'll try to slip down to the boat below.' She agreed.

No Smoking

We could barely see the boat but we could hear the people in it. It must have been about 30 ft down. We went down the rope gently – our hands bled – and landed right in the centre of the boat. I took the skin off a woman's shin, but she didn't seem to mind. The boat had evidently left the ship a half an hour before, but they couldn't move away from the stern because the sailor in charge had broken his arm.

We managed to get a hundred yards away from the ship and out of immediate danger. I found I still had my pipe, so I scraped around in my pocket linings for some tobacco dust and then lit up. This offended a First-Class woman passenger who asked me to stop smoking. Possibly she thought I was too unconcerned, but the truth of the matter is I was scared stiff.

At this stage there were hundreds of people jumping overboard, some with life jackets on, and some without. The forward part of the ship was now submerged and the water was up to the bottom of the first two funnels. People were climbing up the slippery deck to get clear of the water.

As we rowed further away, the stern of the ship suddenly rose high up in the air and it went down. This was followed by two loud explosions. There were hundreds of people everywhere after the ship went down, all floating about. It was pitiful to hear mothers calling for their children and husbands. This lasted for some time and then everything went quiet. It meant that about 1,500 people had died in the icy waters.

Calm Sea

It was a starry night and a calm sea. We had seen several pieces of wreckage, including a keyboard of a piano. We rowed all the time and everybody was drenched with spray. The boat plug was leaking, and I plugged it with my shirt.

When daylight came we could see the smoke from the funnels of a ship. It was the *Carpathia*, and the most welcome sight I had ever seen. We rowed towards her for all we were worth and at last came alongside. We were hoisted aboard by bosun's chair and everybody on deck cheered as we came aboard.

They rigged us out with warm clothing and gave us hot food. Even the passengers on the *Carpathia* gave us their berths.

When I was bidding goodbye to my parents they lit a lamp beside the statue of Christ. The light was kept burning night and day for my safe crossing of the Atlantic. When the ship was actually going down, I thought of the statue. I have this statue still in my home in Hull today.

(*Evening Herald*, 14 April 1969)

The thrust of this account – given when Ryan was 81 – may still place him in boat No. 14, where there was a leak of about eight inches of water which men stopped with their hats. There was also a woman with a broken arm aboard, and some discussion of not using tobacco – Officer Lowe warning against it because it 'makes you thirsty'.

There seems a possibility that Ryan was by now mixing stories he had heard. Canadian Major Arthur Peuchen courageously clambered down a rope to boat No. 6, where coincidentally there was an Italian at an oar who was unable to row because of a broken arm. There were complaints about smoking in some boats.

Whether Ryan was the 'woman' exposed by Lowe in No. 14 remains arguable, but the likelihood exists. Nonetheless it also seems clear that a number of men impersonated women that night or were thought to be women – from Dannie Buckley having a shawl put over his head by a woman in one lifeboat, to Nellie O'Dwyer's description of Chinamen who had let their hair down their backs and put their blankets about themselves to resemble females, down to a story about John Jacob Astor putting a girlish hat on a 13-year-old boy and then declaring: 'Now he is a girl, he can go.' Ryan's comment about walking 'past the officers' and 'passing out' could be significant, however, since boat No. 6 departed early when such measures were not required.

The whole area of ascribing passengers to lifeboats is fraught with difficulty. The British and US inquiries disagreed on the timing and order of boat departures, while many survivors persuaded themselves theirs was the last boat:

Irishman's leap for life
Further details of what happened during the fateful half-hour before the *Titanic* plunged beneath the sea were furnished to the *Brooklyn Eagle* of April 23rd by Fr Michael Kenny, an associate editor of *America*, a Catholic weekly of New York, who questioned some thirty of the survivors of the *Titanic* at St Vincent's Hospital …

Edward Ryan, a Tipperary man, told me at the hospital of a remarkable leap for life he made with a fainting woman in his arms. Ryan was helping to fill the boats of the promenade deck when the woman, a first cabin passenger, became hysterical and fainted.

It had been his turn to enter the boat now being lowered. Ryan seized her and jumped into the boat after the officer in charge had ordered it to be lowered. Fortunately he landed in the boat without injury either to the woman or himself after dropping a distance of more than twenty feet.

(1912 *Irish Independent* reprint of a report in the *Brooklyn Eagle*)

Ryan was on his way to join his sister Mrs Bridget Welsh in Troy, upstate New York. On the *Carpathia*, Ryan told immigration officers that he was a 24-year-old chauffeur. He moved to Hull, England, after some few years in the US, and worked as a maintenance engineer with the firm of Rose, Downs & Thompson on Humberside.

Born on 28 January 1888, Edward Ryan died on Guy Fawkes Day, 5 November 1974. He was aged 86, and succumbed to a heart attack at his retirement home in Pearson Park, Hull. The only man to admit using the pretence of being a woman to get into a lifeboat, Ryan had wrung sixty-two years out of a single towel and a stiff walk.

1901 census – Ballinaveen, Emly.
Parents: Daniel (57), farmer. Alice (50), wife.
Children: Bridget (17), Lena (15), **Ned (13)**.

PATRICK RYAN (29) LOST

Joint ticket number 371110. Paid £24 3s.
Boarded at Queenstown. Third Class.
From: Toomdeely North, Askeaton, County Limerick.
Destination: 1503 Hoe Avenue, Bronx, New York city.

Cattle dealer Patrick Ryan must have been struck with awe by his old schoolfriend's description of life in the United States. He met with Daniel Moran when the latter arrived home to conclude some legal business following the death of his father. Dan's tales of life as a policeman in New York deeply impressed Pat Ryan, who may have impetuously desired to become a cop in the big city as so many Irish had done before.

Certainly the temptations were enough to persuade him to abandon what had been a good job by Irish standards of the time, one paying a decent wage of £2 a week – which was substantially more than some of the skilled crew on the *Titanic* were paid.

Pat resolved to travel to America with Daniel Moran and Dan's sister Bertha, and all three travelled on the same ticket. It would have cost each of them £8 1s, were it to be split three ways. Also in the group travelling from Askeaton to Queenstown was Margaret Madigan, who seems to have been a particular friend of Bertha Moran. The quartet found lodgings at Queenstown in the McDonnell rooming house at The Beach.

A customs official called to the address the next day to see his cousin – Patrick Ryan. Their cheerful reunion and backslapping was also a goodbye, however – for both knew they were unlikely to see the other again by reason of the vast, intervening Atlantic. The *Cork Free Press* of 18 April 1912 reported that Michael O'Mahoney, the helpful 24-year-old customs officer, originally from Limerick but now boarding at Roche's Row in Queenstown, had gone out of his way to accompany the Askeaton party onto the ship from a tender and had asked White Star officials for their very best treatment for these well-connected personages:

> Mr M. O'Mahoney, HM Customs, interested himself on their behalf, saw the whole party on board the great ship, introduced them to one official on board who promised to look after their comfort and otherwise make them feel at home on the passage. Needless to say, he was shocked to hear of the disaster, and is still more grieved to find that their names are not given amongst those who have been saved.
>
> (*Cork Free Press*, 18 April 1912)

Ryan's elderly father, Thomas, contacted solicitors soon after the disaster. He made a statement of claim and a writ against the Oceanic Steam Navigation Company was issued on 3 July 1912. Thomas alleged he had suffered damage from the defendants' negligence in carrying his son Patrick Ryan on their steamship *Titanic* on a voyage from Queenstown to New York in which the said Patrick Ryan was drowned 'in consequence of the said ship colliding with an iceberg and foundering in the North Atlantic Ocean on 15 April 1912'. Thomas deposed that his son was his sole support, and that by his death he had lost all means of support and living. The grounds of the alleged negligence included the improper speed of the *Titanic*, failure to heed ice warnings, failure to maintain a proper lookout or to supply lookout men with binoculars, and the failure to provide adequate lifeboat accommodation.

The Ryan lawsuit became the *Titanic* test case in Britain. It was amalgamated with a claim for the life of Daniel Moran – his fellow passenger from Askeaton, whose family had followed Thomas Ryan's example – and it went to trial before a judge and civil case jury in the High Court. The action was tried from 20 to 26 June 1913.

The jury found that the navigation of the *Titanic* had not been negligent in respect of proper lookouts, but that the speed had indeed been negligently excessive. They decided that there was not sufficient evidence that a crucial Marconi-gram, containing an ice warning from the *Mesaba*, had been passed to a responsible officer. The jury also found that the defendants had not done what was reasonably sufficient to give Ryan and Moran 'notice of the conditions' (alerting them to the real gravity of the situation, or the lack of boats).

The jury assessed damages at £100 per life – and Mr Justice Bailhache ordered this amount paid over, with full legal costs, to Thomas Ryan. It was the equivalent of one year's annual salary for his son.

Patrick Ryan was one of those booked to sail on the *Cymric* from Queenstown four days before he boarded the *Titanic*. That service was withdrawn – otherwise Pat Ryan might have been swinging a nightstick in New York for decades to come.

1901 census – Ryan. Toomdeely North, Askeaton.
Parents: Thomas (63), farmer. Ellen (56).

Children: Ellen (26), Johanna (24), Michael (20), **Patrick (18)**, Honora (16), Thomas (14), James (12).

MATTHEW SADLIER (19) LOST

Ticket number: 367655. Paid £7 14s 7d.
Boarded at Queenstown. Third Class.
From: Clooncoe, Lough Rynn, Mohill, County Leitrim.
Destination: Lakewood, New Jersey.

Matthew Sadlier's house was built on the stones of misery. It was little surprise, therefore, to some prognosticators of doom at least, when misfortune reached through the generations to inflict more anguish.

The Sadliers were land stewards on the Rynn estate in Leitrim, formerly the domain of a savage landlord. The notorious Lord Leitrim (William Sydney Clements) carried out a series of tyrannical evictions in the wake of the Irish Famine when his tenants could not pay punitive rents which had been arbitrarily increased. The new Sadlier house was built of the best stones of the knocked cottages, one cornerstone to this day bearing the initials and date of John Mulligan, a tenant who had built his frugal home in 1838, only to be forced into exile like thousands of others.

Lord Leitrim was finally assassinated – after many attempts – in 1878, and crowds in faraway Dublin, such was his infamy, would attempt to intercept the coffin and throw him in the River Liffey while on his way to the family vault. The estate then passed to a second cousin, since Leitrim hated his own kin, and by 1903 the Wyndham Land Act finally reformed tenant rights and dashed the old landlord system forever. The new owner, Henry Clements, left the one-time feudal seat and turned to book collecting in London.

Matt Sadlier, the youngest child of a family now turned to farming, also wanted to get away. The baby of seven children, he simply saw no future on the lake-dotted land around Mohill. But he had no future on the *Titanic* either. Matthew Sadlier was drowned before he could reach his twentieth birthday.

He was due to stay in Lakewood, New Jersey, with his brother Tom, eleven years his senior, whose address was only given as a *poste-restante* number. His parents didn't wish him to leave, his mother being particularly attached to her youngest, having already seen offspring William, Thomas and Fanny take the American boat.

On the morning he was to leave, a cockerel came to the doorstep and crowed three times. His mother, seizing on superstition for her own ends, declared, 'That's enough now!', grabbing Matthew's suitcase from his hand. It was unspoken knowledge that a cockcrow at the door meant sad news. Matthew patiently retrieved his case from his mother's grasp, said farewells and went about his journey.

Days later, according to oral tradition, a Mr Easterbrook was cycling home when he met the ghost of a sister of Matthew's, who had died before the *Titanic* disaster, walking along the estate avenue. Water was running down the hair of the ghost, which vanished with Easterbrook's balance as bike and rider crashed to the ground.

The worst feared
Up to the present no word has been received of the young man, Matthew Sadlier, of Cloncoo, Lough Rynn, Mohill, being saved.

Fears are now entertained by his parents and friends that he is amongst the seventeen hundred victims that perished in the wreck. He was going out to two or three brothers in the States, much against the wish of his parents, it is stated.

(*Longford Independent*, 20 April 1912)

1911 census:
Matthew (56), shepherd. Wife Catherine (59).
Married 30 years; nine children born, seven surviving.
Catherine (19), **Matthew (18)**, agricultural labourer.

JAMES SCANLAN (21) LOST

Ticket number 36209. Paid £7 14s 6d.
Boarded at Queenstown. Third Class.
From: The Bodhreen, Rathkeale, County Limerick.
Destination: The Plaza, New York city.

Reputed to have been born in a workhouse, James Scanlan had a tough start in life, even by the dirt-poor standards he saw all around him. His father, John, was a labourer, with a wife ten years older, and James was the second eldest of their offspring.

His sister Kate, two years younger than James, had been the first to emigrate to America. Now she had an impressive-sounding address at a place called The Plaza, and the streets seemed to be paved with gold in New York. She had sent home for James to join her in New York.

Boarding the *Titanic* at Queenstown, James described himself as a 20-year-old farm labourer. But he was fated never to see his sister at the pier on the Hudson.

County Limerick Victims: Abbeyfeale, Sunday
The list of survivors published Friday contains no reference to the names of Mr Patrick Colbert, Kilconlea, Abbeyfeale, Mr James Scanlan, Rathkeale, nor of other young men and women said to have been on board from East and North Kerry.

(*The Cork Examiner*, 22 April 1912)

1911 census:
John (45), labourer, Catherine (45).
Married 20 years, ten children, six alive.
William (24), labourer, **James (20)**, labourer, Patrick (11), Edward (9), Cornelius (7).

PATRICK SHAUGHNESSY (28) LOST

Ticket number 370374. Paid £7 15s.
Boarded at Queenstown. Third Class.
From: Tynagh, County Galway.
Destination: 1509 Lexington Avenue, New York.

'Pake' Shaughnessy was lost for the sake of a horse. He delayed travelling to the United States because he was owed money for a steed he'd sold. Pake was promised the cash – it could have been £10 – and decided to wait.

When he didn't receive the money after repeated assurances, he gave it up as a bad job and prepared to take the *Titanic*. His unhappiness at his lot in life was expressed in a letter written to brother Willie on the other side of the Atlantic divide. In it Pake complained that 'there is nothing around Tynagh' and that he had 'most of the fellows around here bet' – meaning beaten.

An Apparition in Galway

A young man named Tynagh, in the Banagher district, it is stated, decided upon emigrating to America in opposition to the wishes of his mother, whose only son he was, and on the morning on which he left home for Queenstown she refused to shake hands with him. The parting scene was a very sad one.

He perished in the disaster, and the moment the big ship went down Mrs Lynch heard a noise outside her house and saw the figure of her son approaching her in the same attire he wore the morning he left.

Thinking he had changed his mind, she rushed forward, exclaiming 'Have you come back again, Tom?' when suddenly the figure vanished.

(*Irish Independent*, 27 May 1912)

The family of Pake confirm the substance of the above error-strewn story. Ellen Shaughnessy did indeed have a vision of her son in broad daylight and knew at that moment he was dead. A namesake nephew, Pat Shaughnessy, declares: 'She didn't want him to go because he was the youngest and the favourite.'

A physically tough man, equine trader Pake was also described, somewhat paradoxically, as a stylish dresser, always concerned to cut a dashing figure. He was envied too for a new bicycle, the best in the village.

On the gravestone of his brother Thomas in Tynagh today is the inscription: 'His brother, Patrick 'Pake' who was lost in the *Titanic* Apr 14 1912 aged 28 years'.

Being the eldest, Thomas had stayed at home, as he would inherit the family farm. By the 1911 census, Tom is the farmer on the land, while mother Ellen is a widowed housekeeper. Tom's younger brother, Patrick, in a place of subservience, is described as a farmer's labourer.

Pake was initially travelling out to America to join his sister Bridget, who had married a man named Burke and had moved to New York. The Burkes lived on Lexington Avenue, and Pake was assured of a hearty welcome in his newly adopted home. He hoped to pick up some kind of manual work and had already lopped some years off his age to prepare for hiring-fair competition with younger men. He told the record-takers for the *Titanic* that he was 20, but had hit that mark at least six years earlier if the 1911 census or later grave inscription are to be believed.

Pake was one of those originally slated to travel on the White Star's *Cymric*, but transferred to the more luxurious *Titanic* by reason of the coal strike and crossing cancellations.

1911 census:
Ellen (65), housekeeper, widow.
Thomas (40), farmer; **Patrick (24)**, farmer's labourer.

ELLEN SHINE (17) SAVED

Ticket number 330968. Paid £7 12s 7d, plus 4s extra.
Boarded at Queenstown. Third Class.
From: Lisrobin, Newmarket, County Cork.
Destination: 205 Eighth Avenue, New York city.

The longest-lived Irish survivor of the *Titanic* was Ellen Shine. She reached the age of 98 (although she had convinced herself she was 101), dying in Long Island, New York, in 1993.

She told a story of the men in steerage being kept back and was quoted as witnessing actual killings.

Cork girl's story
A thrilling story was told by Ellen Shine, a 20-year-old girl from County Cork who crossed to America to visit her brother.

'Those who were able to get out of bed,' said Miss Shine, 'rushed to the upper deck where they were met by members of the crew who endeavoured to keep them in the steerage quarters.

'The women however rushed past the men and finally reached the upper deck. When they were informed that the boat was sinking, most of them fell on their knees and began to pray. I saw one of the lifeboats and made for it.

'In it there were already four men from the steerage who refused to obey an officer who ordered them out. They were however finally turned out.' – *Reuter*

That report, carried in *The Times* of London on Saturday 20 April, is exactly the same as quotes attributed to Ellen Shine and carried in the *Denver Post*, the *Daily Times*, and other US newspapers on the previous day, with one difference. The American reports continued:

> … in it were four men from the steerage. They were ordered out by an officer and refused to leave. And then one of the officers jumped into the boat, and, drawing a revolver, shot the four men dead. Their bodies were picked out from the bottom of the boat and thrown into the ocean.

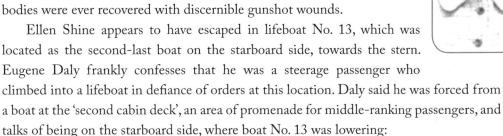

How can posterity reconcile these two versions? Were the claimed killings the product of a survivor's fevered mind or a journalist's reckless embellishment? Did Reuter deliberately choose to tone down the story in plucking it from another source, or was there simply no mention by Ellen of any killings in the first place? No other witnesses described four men being callously shot inside a lifeboat by an officer of the White Star Line, and no bodies were ever recovered with discernible gunshot wounds.

Ellen Shine appears to have escaped in lifeboat No. 13, which was located as the second-last boat on the starboard side, towards the stern. Eugene Daly frankly confesses that he was a steerage passenger who climbed into a lifeboat in defiance of orders at this location. Daly said he was forced from a boat at the 'second cabin deck', an area of promenade for middle-ranking passengers, and talks of being on the starboard side, where boat No. 13 was lowering:

> We afterwards went to the second cabin deck and the two girls and myself got into a boat. An officer called on me to go back, but I would not stir. Then they got a hold of me and pulled me out.

No one testified to any disorder at boat No. 13 at the two official inquiries. Steward Frederick Ray, who was in this boat, told the US Senate investigators, in reply to questions, that he saw no male passengers or men of the crew 'ordered out or thrown out of these lifeboats on the starboard side. Everybody was very orderly.' But Irish passenger Dannie Buckley declared: 'Time and again officers would drag men from the boats …' Resolution of the problem is elusive. Should one disregard the claims of men shot dead for staying stubbornly in a lifeboat? Someone somewhere is spinning pure invention.

Ellen Shine told her story once and would never be drawn on it again. According to the embarkation records, she was an 18-year-old spinster, but by the time US immigration had come aboard the *Carpathia*, she declared herself to be a 16-year-old servant from Newmarket, County Cork. She was actually aged 17 when she boarded the *Titanic* and from the small hamlet of Lisrobin (Buckley mistakenly referred to her as 'the Shine girl from Lismore' in a letter home composed on the *Carpathia*). She was on her way to join her brother Jeremiah in New York.

Ellen collapsed in hysterics when met by Jeremiah and other relatives at the Cunard pier in New York, according to the *Brooklyn Daily Eagle*. It reported the next day that she and other women had knocked down crewmen who tried to prevent steerage passengers from reaching the boat deck.

Ellen's was case number 418 to be dealt with by the American Red Cross. The notes from this report record her saying she was aged 16 and that she had lost clothing and a cash sum of $500. She was awarded $100 in aid.

In later years, Ellen Shine married and became Mrs John Callaghan. Her husband, a firefighter, hailed from Kiskeam, also in Cork, and they settled in New York. They first returned to Ireland only in 1959, on the *Mauretania*, but made a number of visits thereafter. The couple had two daughters, Julia and Mary, whom Ellen would be fated to outlive.

In 1976 she moved from Manhattan to Long Island to be with her family following the death of her husband. In 1982 she entered Glengariff nursing home where she celebrated her 100th birthday in 1991 – three years early. By this stage, however, Ellen was in the advanced stages of Alzheimer's disease. Never having discussed the *Titanic* disaster in nearly seventy years, she suddenly could not stop babbling about it. A torrent of *Titanic* revelations flowed from her loosened tongue, to the irritation of other residents. When Ellen finally wanted to talk about the disaster, no one was listening.

Ellen Shine Callaghan died on 5 March 1993, and is buried in St Charles Cemetery, East Farmingdale, New York.

A survivor of the Titanic *Dies: Glen Cove woman was 101*
Helen Shine Callaghan of Glen Cove, one of the last survivors of the sinking of the *Titanic* in 1912, died yesterday at North Shore University Hospital at Glen Cove at the age of 101.

Callaghan, who was a resident of the Glengariff Nursing Home in Glen Cove, was 20 when she left her native Cork County, Ireland, for a better life in the United States, according to her granddaughter, Christine Quinn [in 2011, the Speaker of the New York City Council].

'She was from a big family and her parents were deceased and her sister was head of the family and decided that some of the siblings had to go to America,' said Quinn.

Like many of the survivors, Callaghan rarely discussed the tragedy. 'I remember asking her questions as a girl. She never really answered them directly,' Quinn said. 'My mother only found out about it when she was in school and the teacher passed around a list with the survivors' names on it and she saw her mother's name on the list.'

(*Glen Cove Record-Pilot*, 6 March 1993)

1911 census – Shine, Lisrobin.
Mary, widow (55). Had been married 21 years, nine children, eight yet living.
Maggie (30), **Ellie (18)**, James (22), John (25), creamery manager.

JULIA SMYTH (17) SAVED

Ticket number 335432. Paid £7 14s 8d.
Boarded at Queenstown. Third Class.
From: Pottlebawn, Kilcogy, County Cavan.
Destination: 462 West 20th Street, New York city.

Julia credited her long legs with saving her – she was one of those who had to jump across a terrifying gap towards lifeboat No. 13 as the *Titanic* slumped deeper in her final death throes. In a letter home from New York to her family in Pottlebawn, written in a poorly educated hand, Julia described in a fleeting paragraph all the terror of the *Titanic*. She told how one of her shipboard companions, fellow Cavan passenger Kate Connolly, made the first leap of faith into a boat, prompting her to do the same:

> I am sure that there is not one in Pottle, boys or girls, would make the fight I made. There was thousands before me, and Katie jumped ought [*sic*] into the boat. Only my legs was long, I would never made it.

Julia later also attributed her salvation to having some clay from a saint's grave with her on board the *Titanic*, which was reputed to protect one from death by drowning. Mary McGovern, Julia's roommate, had obtained the sacred clay as a precaution before sailing.

> Mr P. O'Connor, agent to the White Star Line in Granard, has received a telegram stating that Miss Julia Smyth, Pottlebawn, was rescued. The passage issued to Miss Smyth was first issued to a Miss Lynch from Pottlebawn for the *Olympic* on the 21st September last, on which occasion the vessel collided with the *Hawke*.
> Miss Lynch changed her mind about emigrating, and a few weeks ago her passage was transferred to Miss Smith.
> (*Irish Independent*, 19 April 1912)

Julia was the daughter of Henry and Mary Smyth, of Pottlebawn, Kilcogy, County Cavan, one of seven children. She had been born in Dublin on 4 July 1894, the date perhaps a portent of her future emigration. When she chose to go, she was only 17 years old. She already had a brother in the United States, Henry, ten years her senior.

When she wrote home to her mother, Julia had already found work as a domestic in a house at 346 Lexington Avenue. The letter, undated but thought to have been composed in late May at the earliest, betrays her inadequate schooling:

> My Dear Mother,
> I suppose you thought you would never here tell of me again when the ship sank. I suppose youse were in a terrible fret. But if any of you see the site that we all had to go through your faces would never be seen again.
> I cannot always be explain of it, for I am sick and tired of it talking of it all the time.

Well mother I am not feeling so lonesome now because I have a good place for the start. I am learning everything. It is so hard to get a first-class place but I got it. But there is nothing but work. No matter where you go, every one say I am the luckeys one that ever struk New York to get in, because there is not a job to be got in the office. These people go to the country for the Summer. Nora Glean and me is left in the house for the Summer.

We will be doin nothing the holl Summer. I can have a good rest. I hope youse have all the work done home and not last. Hope youse have Larry McCoonarty again. Tell him for me I will send him what will give him a good wash down for the Summer.

I am so very lucky to be on the land of the living at all. Every says to me I was not on the *Titinice* at all I look so good. Every say I must get good times in the old Ireland. I suppose I would look if I never got much. I was pretty shuck coming over. I was sick all the time on the Ship.

I nearly fell into the big sea when I was going up they ladder to the *Carpatin* that morning. I got wake [weak]. I was a few steps up. I fell back again but I said to myself I might as well strive and get in. Everyone for themselves that moment, life or death.

I am sure there is not one in Pottle, boys or girls, would make the fight I made. There was thousands before me and Katie jumped ought into the boat. Only my legs was long I would never made it. Everyone seems very nice to me. Bridget Ballasty bought me a nice waist. Bridget the neighbour bought me a lovely present. I saw all from home.

James told me that a lot of people went from home. He never told me there names. Tell him write and tell me. I am finished cleaning. Resting all evening. Write me soon. Pray for me, mama. XX Julia

I get oatmeal sturboat in the morning to ate. Tell the cricket I was asking for him. Is the gang in Pottle again.

346 Lexington Ave. This is my adres. America is no jock. Ireland is the place for everyone that can stay home. I am sure Henry crys the day he ever left Pottle.

The 'start' is an Irish term for getting a job. Julia jokes that she hopes that her family at home have all the work done and are not last – a reference to saving the hay and local competition not to be the last family to have gathered it all in. Larry appears to be a hired hand for that purpose, and his promised good wash down has nothing to do with hygiene and everything to do with refreshment after labour. Her mention of the 'Titinice' is a wonderful, if Freudian, conjunction of a *Titanic* that seems to have become enmeshed in ice.

It is noticeable that her friends in America bought her presents to console her, including a waist, which was a cummerbund-type of female apparel. But it also seems that Julia was sick for some time after rescue – she was pretty shaken coming over and 'sick all the time on the Ship', being the *Carpathia*.

We know from American Red Cross records that Julia became more seriously ill upon landing, reason perhaps for her to receive sympathetic presents and plenty of visitors:

No. 428. (Irish.) Girl, 20 years old, soon developed scarlet fever, and needed hospital and convalescent care. ($150)

Julia seems to have later lost contact with her comrade-in-catastrophe Kate Connolly, whom she had met at the platform in Ballywilliam train station in Cavan and accompanied all the way to Queenstown, onto the *Titanic*, into a lifeboat, up the ladder to the *Carpathia*, and onto Pier 54 in New York. The pair had roomed together on the *Titanic*, along with Mary McGovern and Clare woman Mary Agatha Glynn. Julia later married twice, but never had any children.

Her first wedding was in 1917. On 30 November that year, she married US Army officer William Glover, a 26-year-old New Yorker. Julia was aged 23, and had been living at 97 Central Park West. The space for her occupation on the marriage licence was filled with a dismissive pen-stroke. How that marriage came to an end is not known, but Julia visited Ireland in 1962, fifty years after the sinking, as the wife of an Englishman named Thomas White. He was then aged 68, Julia a year younger. Thomas outlived her by six years, dying on 28 April 1983.

> A United States Navy chaplain held a memorial service in an aircraft over the North Atlantic yesterday to mark the 50th anniversary of the sinking of the *Titanic*.
>
> A wreath was dropped from the US coastguard plane on the icy waters where more than 1,500 people died after the liner hit an iceberg on its maiden voyage from Southampton to New York in 1912.
>
> Several survivors of the sinking attended another memorial service in New York Seamen's Church Institute. Among them was … Mrs Julia Smith White (64), who was 14-year-old Julia Smith [*sic*] at the time of the disaster.
> (*Belfast Telegraph*, 16 April 1962)

> Miss Julia Smith White … recalled the legend of the man in woman's clothing. She said: 'I remember him, he was a lad from Dublin, and he got into our lifeboat, No. 13, the last to leave the ship.'
>
> She remembered not being able to leave the vessel immediately. 'We went back and braided our hair, and said our prayers,' she said.
> (*Evening Press*, 16 April 1912)

Niece Diana Ylstra Maher, the two-year-old in the photograph, said: 'My memories of Julia are of a very strong, outspoken woman who always stood up for what she believed. When my mother or I had to handle a difficult situation, we used Julia as our model.'

Julia Smyth White died on 27 April 1977 in Manhattan, at the age of 82. She is buried in St Raymond's Cemetery, the Bronx. Her long legs and determination had saved her for over sixty-five years since the *Titanic*'s sinking.

1911 census – Smyth. Pottlebawn.
Parents: Henry (68) and Mary (50), married 30 years, 9 children, 7 surviving.
Children: Mary Anne (29), dressmaker; Henry (26), James (23), Agnes (20), Delia (19), **Julia (17)**, Maggie (12).

THOMAS SMYTH (26) LOST

Ticket number 384461. Paid £7 15s.
Boarded at Queenstown. Third Class.
From: Chapelfinnerty, Caltra, County Galway.
Destination: Long Island, New York city.

Thomas Smyth was a talented groom. He loved working with horses in the stables of Lord Clonbrock's estate close to his home. But slowly, the white horses of the sea began to exert their own beguiling influence.

Tom was 26 years old and was the last of the offspring left at home. He alone had to look after his widowed father, Patrick, who was aged 77 by 1912. He worked all day, coming home to cook, clean and wash for the pair of them, and a concern grew that the best years of his life were slipping away. He struck a remarkable pact with his older brother Patrick, an electric streetcar driver in New York, to come home to relieve Tom in the filial duties, allowing the youngest sibling to sample life in America.

Patrick, aged 30, bought Tom his ticket and received a promise that Tom would return after two years in America. Two sisters, Bridget and Margaret, were already in Long Island, and it was to these that he would initially journey as the bargain was put into effect.

Patrick came home to Ireland at the end of 1911 and the following spring an American wake took place for Tom and four neighbours with whom he made the long trip to Queenstown by train from Ballinasloe. At the end of the night he walked home with his close friend, fellow Clonbrock estate worker, Johnny Tully. As they parted, Tom told the labourer: 'I might never see you again, Johnny.'

Smyth had gone to school with Tom Kilgannon, and a letter from the latter, posted in Queenstown, showed that the group were having 'great fun' as they headed on their merry way to America – even if overnight accommodation in Cork had been expensive at seven and six apiece. Smyth signed aboard the *Titanic* as a general labourer and said he was 24 years old according to the embarkation records. His name has been mistakenly rendered Emmeth in some White Star records.

The two Toms shared a cabin with Martin Gallagher, separated by a ship's length for reasons of decency from the two single women in their group, Ellen Mockler of Currafarry and Margaret Mannion from Loughanboy. All five were from neighbouring townlands in the small parish of Caltra. The loss of the three men, ordained to die by their class and gender, is marked by a tablet at the Marian grotto in the village, unveiled in 1996.

One claim in this locality was that Tom made it into the water as the ship was sinking, and struck out for a nearby lifeboat. But he was struck with oars to prevent his boarding and, thwarted in his attempts for survival, gave up and died. This story is impossible to verify.

Word of the wreck reached his home place within a few days, but there was to be no firm news until the *Carpathia* docked. Patrick, the brother who had swapped places at home with Tom, told their father: 'Tommy is not lost. He's too clever for that. He's stuck somewhere in another boat.'

Grim confirmation came a short time later in the form of a White Star Line telegram to Noone's post office in nearby Ahascragh. Patrick would have to stay longer at home than his intended two years. He farmed the family's miserable 10 or 12 acres of land and rented another holding to make his work a paying concern. In 1918 he married Mary Kate Delaney and had three children, the first of whom he named Tommy after his lost brother. The last reminders of *Titanic* Tom were lost when the homestead caught fire and burned to the ground in 1952 after a mishap when trying to smoke out an unwanted crow's nest.

Tommy now says of the uncle he never knew: 'My father told me that Tom just wanted to see the world.' The *Titanic* victim's supposedly frail father meanwhile lived another twenty years, dying at the age of 97 in 1932.

1911 census – Killeen, Clonbrock.
Patrick Smyth (76), farmer, widower, cannot read.
Son: **Thomas (25)**.

ROGER TOBIN (21) LOST

Ticket number 383121. Paid £7 15s.
Boarded at Queenstown. Third Class.
From: Lisgibbon, Bansha, County Tipperary.
Destination: 243 East 45th Street, New York city.

A quantity of hurley-sticks was among the more arcane consignments of cargo stored in the *Titanic's* holds. The ash sticks were intended for hurling teams among the Irish amateur sportsmen on the other side of the Atlantic and were specially brought aboard by Roger Tobin. They may still be in good condition two and half miles under the ocean. Some wood inside the wreck has survived the attention of wood-boring organisms, and linseed oil-treated *camáns* (the Irish word for the sticks) may not have proved to their liking.

Roger Tobin was 21 and from Bansha, Tipperary, heading to New York. After the impact, he journeyed the length of the ship from his own quarters – he was in dormitory room 38 on F deck on the port side of the bow – to the aftermost accommodation designated solely for the single women. There he alerted Katie Connolly, Kate Peters and Kate McCarthy to the danger, telling them to get up and put on their lifebelts. All four were from Tipperary and now a long way indeed from their home place, or from any other land for that matter.

> The late Mr Roger Tobin, who was only in his 22nd year, was a splendid type of Tipperary man, and was a universal favourite. As already stated, he was famous in the local Gaelic fields as a hurler and footballer, and brought with him on his voyage a fine collection of camáns.
>
> (*The Cork Examiner*, 24 April 1912)

The same edition reported elsewhere in relation to the Tipperary party:

> At second Mass in Bansha on Sunday morning, the celebrant, the Rev D. Moloney CC, said it was feared that two of their parishioners were amongst the victims of the great catastrophe. One of the three had happily been saved.
>
> He was personally aware that in accordance with the customs of Irish Catholics, they had approached the sacraments before leaving. The rev. gentleman, who was deeply moved, asked the people to pray for their eternal rest. The congregation, amongst whom were the weeping mother and sister of young Mr Tobin, responded with a heartfelt prayer, and the scene was extremely touching.

Katie McCarthy, a Tipperary survivor, wrote home from New Jersey to tell her family of the tragedy. She said she had been called to get up by Roger. 'He told us not to be frightened as there was no danger.' He told the three Kates to get their lifebelts. Miss McCarthy wrote of her companions: 'When Roger Tobin called me, I wanted them to come up on deck, but they would not come. They appeared to think there was no danger. That was the last I saw of them.'

Local lore around Katie Peters' home place suggests she was a sweetheart of Roger Tobin and that the couple were hoping to make a future together in the New World. Certainly a girl might do worse:

> Mr Tobin, son of Mr Patrick Tobin, farmer, was a young man of splendid physique and noted in the Gaelic field for his prowess as a hurler and footballer.
>
> Their names do not appear amongst the list of survivors in this morning's papers and their relatives are anxiously awaiting tidings of their fate.
>
> (*The Nationalist*, Clonmel, 17 April 1912)

Roger had been working in Kelly's men's drapery in Tipperary, but decided he would be better off in America where some cousins lived. His family splashed out the considerable sum of £25, equipping him with a spanking new suit and overcoat they thought would help him land a good job in America. Roger was due to lodge at a New York rooming house initially. Interestingly, Katie Peters was due to stay at the same address, which tends to support an oral heritage that they were romantically involved.

Roger may have stayed behind to comfort Katie Peters in her compartment on E deck or F deck, while Katie McCarthy wisely chose to ascend at least five decks to where the boats were waiting. Roger's devotion may have led to his laying down his life.

His mother, Margaret, reputedly had a dream that he was in difficulty on the night he died and was awoken from her nightmare by ghostly taps on the window. She was convinced it was a final leave-taking.

Gael Lost in Titanic
On Sunday last, a meeting of the Galtee Rovers F.C. (Bansha) was held, and all the members attended. After some trivial business being transacted, those present spoke with deep emotion of the terrible disaster to the *Titanic* and the now certain fate of their late comrade and fellow-Gael, Mr Roger Tobin. It was with great regret that the Galtees suffered poor Roger to go away to seek his fortune in a foreign land, but with what sorrow did they learn of his untimely fate; yet from the times of first news of shipwreck up to a few days ago, everyone hoped against hope that this splendid young fellow would be saved by some means, but now all hope is abandoned, and another young life is added to the list of those lost. Heartfelt sympathy was expressed with the parents, brothers and sister of Mr Tobin in their sad bereavement. It was unanimously decided to have Masses offered up for the repose of his soul, and may that repose be a peaceful and everlastingly happy one.
(*The Nationalist*, Clonmel, 4 May 1912)

On 9 September 1912, his family received the grant of administration of his estate. His father, Patrick, received legal entitlement to the £40 6s left behind by 'Rodger Tobin, late of Lisgibbon, Bansha, County Tipperary, farmer's son, who died 15th April, 1912, at sea'.

1911 census:
Patrick (55), Margaret (52), married 24 years, six children, five alive; Patrick (22), Mary (20), **Roger (19)**, William (18), David (16).

ELLEN TOOMEY (48) SAVED

Ticket number 13531. Paid £10 10s.
Boarded at Southampton. Second Class.
From: County Cork.
Destination: 119 Bates Street, Indianapolis, Indiana.

Ellen Toomey was nothing like the swarms of young Irish girls who crowded into steerage. Although she had been born in Ireland, Ellen had been living in the United States for many years and was a domestic servant. She was unmarried and was returning to the house of Mrs Bridget Hannery, where she worked, after a blissful visit home to her mother and relatives in County Limerick.

Ellen had returned to Ireland in November 1911 and had tried to book her return voyage on four other ships before she finally found a berth on the *Titanic*. The coal strike had interfered with her plans, but she finally managed to send postcards to her sisters in Indianapolis saying she was sailing on the new White Star liner.

She may have been rescued in lifeboat No. 3, launched from the starboard side relatively early in the night. On 24 April 1912, she described what happened in an interview with the *Indianapolis Star*:

> The wreck was due purely to carelessness. It could not have been otherwise.
>
> I do not know whether the stories are true or not, but it was common talk among the survivors that the man in the lookout was asleep at the time and that the Captain and the other officers were not doing their duty, but that they were below at a banquet when the crash came.
>
> Oh those cries and screams of the poor, drowning people. The sound was awful. I shall never forget it. But we did not see any of them in the water. We were too far away from the *Titanic* when it went down to see those who had leaped or who had been washed into the sea. But we could hear them for some little time. Then all was still and we knew the last of them had perished.

Toomey shared a Second-Class cabin with two women and a child. Shortly after midnight a ship's steward told them to put on lifebelts and go on deck:

> There was no confusion or excitement. We were ordered to the side of the ship along with the other women. The men stood aside. They were brave, those men on the *Titanic*. They were real heroes. The order was given to lower the lifeboats, and one boat on our side of the ship was loaded with women and children and lowered to the water.
>
> An officer stood by with drawn revolver. I did not see him shoot. He threatened to shoot a man because he did not do what the officer told him to do, but finally the man obeyed. But I heard several shots on other parts of the ship. Who did the shooting I do not know.
>
> I was put into the second lifeboat on the starboard side and I think there were about 30 persons in our boat. In the number were three members of the crew who had been ordered there by the officers. When we were lowered to the water we found two other men in the boat who had sneaked in some way.
>
> There was room in our boat for more people, but the hurry of loading and the fact that people thought the boat could not sink probably accounted for the fact that there was not a full load. When we struck the water the men rowed our boat rapidly away from the *Titanic* because when we left the ship we could see that it was gradually lowering in the water. After we were at a safe distance we drifted about.
>
> We could see the *Titanic* was sinking little by little and it was evident that it would go down. When there was but little of the ship above the water there was a loud explosion.

We could hear it plainly. Then the *Titanic* stood on end and made a dive straight down and that was the last of it. Then it was that one heard those awful screams from the drowning people. We could not see them.

We drifted in the lifeboats for seven hours before being picked up by the *Carpathia* [pictured below]. Our boat was the second or third that was picked up. The night was not very dark. The stars were out, but there was no moon. The sea was smooth as a lake. As we drifted about we saw icebergs all around us. They were everywhere. Some were very large and high. The one which was pointed out to us as the one which the *Titanic* struck was not large, at least it was not high out of the water. The weather was bitter cold.

Most of the women in our boat were thinly clothed because some of them were told to go back to bed after the collision and had done so, only to be aroused later when it was too late to dress. The weather was bitter cold, and there was much suffering in the boat. One French woman who had lost her husband became frantic in her grief, but we calmed her. This was the only confusion in our boat.

When we saw the *Carpathia* coming towards us it was the grandest sight that mortal eyes ever witnessed. It meant our deliverance. There was a loud shout of joy as the ship approached. All of the lifeboats kept as close together as possible while drifting and seven of them were tied together to keep them from being separated and lost.

Once we were on board the *Carpathia*, we were treated with all the consideration that could be shown us. They were very kind and good to us. Men gave up their rooms and women passengers shared their rooms with the *Titanic* survivors. They gave us clothes. They gave us hot brandy and coffee and took the best of care of us. Five or six of the survivors, however, died on board the *Carpathia*.

I shall never forget the bravery and heroism of the men on the ship in the hour of despair. I tell you, they were brave men. They stood aside while the women were loaded into the boats, and only a few of them tried to get in a boat. Some of them did, but the officers drove them back.

Report of the American Red Cross (Titanic Disaster) 1913:
No. 453. (Irish.) A houseworker, 50 years old. Injured. ($100)

Ellen was born on 2 February 1864 to parents John Toomey and Mary Brandon. She died on 23 December 1933 in Indianapolis. She was 69 and had never married.

The Cunard liner Carpathia *rescued 712* Titanic *souls. Her captain and crew were presented by a committee of survivors with medals, now highly prized by collectors. The* Carpathia *was torpedoed and sunk in July 1918, some 120 miles from the Fastnet rock in the southwestern approaches.*

WHITE STAR LINE.

"OLYMPIC."
45,000 TONS.
AND
"TITANIC."
45,000 TONS.

THE LARGEST STEAMERS IN THE WORLD.

ALL STEAMERS BUILT IN IRELAND.

QUEENSTOWN—NEW YORK
ON THURSDAYS AND FRIDAYS.

QUEENSTOWN—BOSTON
ON WEDNESDAYS.

For Freight and Passage apply to

JOHN DENNEHY,

Insurance Agent, CAHIRCIVEEN, Co. Kerry

EMIGRATION STATISTICS,

IRELAND.

TABLE Showing the Number of EMIGRANTS (Natives of Ireland) in each Month from 1st January, 1895.

YEARS.	January.	February.	March.	April.	May.	June.	July.	August.	September.	October.	November.	December.	TOTAL
1895,	761	977	4,002	10,198	9,612	4,042	2,780	4,741	5,815	3,759	1,409	607	48,703
1896,	790	1,206	3,033	8,868	8,510	2,685	2,340	2,947	4,081	2,848	1,126	561	38,995
1897,	545	773	1,996	7,237	6,188	2,679	1,937	2,522	4,072	2,723	1,313	550	32,535
1898,	642	1,015	2,275	7,505	3,880	2,554	1,695	2,546	4,967	3,176	1,405	581	32,241
1899,	651	1,100	2,524	9,268	7,243	3,160	2,212	3,680	5,383	3,358	1,674	979	41,232
Average, 5 Years, 1895-9,	678	1,014	2,766	8,615	7,087	3,024	2,193	3,287	4,864	3,173	1,385	655	38,741
Average, 10 Years, 1890-99,	849	1,399	3,273	9,951	8,666	3,921	2,663	3,791	4,799	3,342	1,577	724	44,955
1900,	995	1,843	2,464	8,443	9,254	3,813	2,246	3,519	5,493	4,297	1,920	1,001	45,288
1901,	1,114	1,362	2,498	8,288	6,621	2,934	1,986	3,240	4,928	4,182	1,683	777	39,613
1902,	979	1,064	2,352	8,392	5,940	2,620	2,278	3,591	5,600	4,844	1,729	801	40,190
1903,	798	1,106	2,249	8,102	7,747	2,749	2,236	3,651	5,307	3,622	1,512	710	39,789
1904,	653	887	1,947	7,441	5,013	2,429	2,201	3,387	6,196	4,412	1,625	711	36,902
Average, 5 Years, 1900-1904,	908	1,252	2,302	8,133	6,915	2,909	2,189	3,478	5,505	4,271	1,694	800	40,356
Average, 10 Years, 1895-1904,	793	1,133	2,534	8,374	7,001	2,967	2,191	3,382	5,184	3,722	1,540	728	39,549
1905,	672	1,067	4,568	6,067	4,351	2,225	1,422	2,071	3,772	2,550	1,314	597	30,676
1906,	838	984	2,622	8,451	6,150	2,567	1,760	2,628	4,081	3,140	1,372	751	35,344
1907,	693	1,196	2,670	7,814	6,712	3,139	2,082	3,117	4,903	4,283	1,808	665	39,082
1908,	611	934	1,881	4,163	4,228	1,664	1,234	1,634	2,850	2,396	1,077	593	23,295
1909,	727	884	1,945	6,558	4,572	2,121	1,602	1,915	3,743	2,799	1,177	633	28,676
Average, 5 Years, 1905-1909,	714	1,013	2,737	6,611	5,203	2,343	1,620	2,273	3,870	3,034	1,349	648	31,415
Average, 10 Years, 1900-1909,	811	1,133	2,520	7,372	6,059	2,626	1,905	2,875	4,687	3,652	1,522	724	35,886
1910,	615	896	2,358	6,888	5,459	2,739	1,861	2,243	4,530	3,322	1,123	423	32,457
1911,	644	847	2,618	7,346	5,122	2,182	1,704	1,876	3,443	3,178	1,071	542	30,573
1912,	653	811	2,203	5,683	4,720	2,369	1,807	2,267	3,956	3,129	1,274	472	29,344
1913,	607	886	2,228	6,171	6,069	2,908	1,711	1,972	3,854	2,979	1,151	431	30,967
1914,	497	734	1,426	5,144	3,648	1,460	1,208	1,029	1,911	2,331	670	256	20,314
Average, 5 Years, 1910-1914,	603	835	2,167	6,246	5,003	2,332	1,658	1,877	3,539	2,988	1,058	425	28,731
Average, 10 Years, 1905-1914,	659	924	2,452	6,429	5,103	2,337	1,639	2,075	3,704	3,011	1,204	536	30,073

IRISH CREW RMS *TITANIC*

SELECTED CREW FROM IRELAND

HENRY ASHE (34) LOST

Steward.
From: Glenbeigh, County Kerry.

ASHE – Drowned while on duty on board SS *Titanic*, Henry Wellesley Ashe, second son of the late Wm. St George Ashe, and grandson of the later Rev. Henry Wellesley Ashe, Rector of Glenbeigh, County Kerry.

(Cork Constitution, 29 April 1912)

The body of steward Ashe was recovered by the *MacKay-Bennett* search vessel, chartered by the White Star Line for the purpose and dispatched from Halifax, Nova Scotia.

No. 34 – Male. Estimated age 34. Hair, dark. Moustache, light.
Clothing – Blue suit and green shirt.
Effects – Gold watch and chain; keys; knife; 2 books; Freemason's book; photos; papers; lodge badge 'Nat. Union Ship's Stewards, Butchers and Bakers'.
Name – H. W. Ashe, 15 or 17 Wysdale, Aintree.

His body was taken to the morgue and was buried in Fairview Cemetery, Halifax, on 8 May 1912.

Sad loss of a husband and father
Henry Wellesley Ashe, aged 40, of 15 Wyesdale Road, Aintree, was a steward on board the *Titanic*. He leaves a wife and three children, of whom the eldest is seven years old and the youngest one year and eight months.

(Liverpool Daily Post and Mercury, 20 April 1912)

RICHARD BAINES (54) LOST

Greaser.
From: Dublin.

Baines signed aboard the *Titanic* giving his local address as 9 Union Place, Southampton. But other records clearly show him to be from Dublin, although his exact Irish address is not known, nor any other details about him.

He may have been the owner of a gold telescopic pencil recovered from the wreck site and inscribed 'R.L.B. Xmas 1908'.

WILLIAM BURKE (30) SAVED

Dining-room steward.
From: Queenstown, County Cork.
57 Bridge Street, Southampton.

William Burke saved a woman from drowning when she jumped from the *Titanic* but missed the lifeboat. He caught her by the ankle and held fast in one of the most terrifying individual incidents of the whole drama. The woman was then taken back aboard the ship at the deck below.

A dining-room steward in First Class, Burke was assigned to Isidor and Ida Blun Strauss, the elderly founder of Macy's Department Store in New York and his wife, who chose to die together when the supreme test came. In his testimony to the American inquiry, Burke told Senator William Alden Smith how he was in his bunk, awake, in a dormitory of dining room stewards, when the ship struck:

'When I first felt the impact I did not know exactly what to make of it. I thought probably she had dropped her propeller, or something. I did not get up right away. I waited for probably a quarter of an hour. About a quarter of an hour or 20 minutes later the order came to get out lifebelts and get up on deck and take our overcoats.

'Mention was made of the fact that it was very cold. I immediately got up with everybody else. Everybody was taking a lifebelt. I did not at that time bother about a lifebelt. I put on my coat and dressed in the ordinary way. As we were going out one of the last men said, "There is a lifebelt near my bunk, if you want one." I went back and got this lifebelt, and carried it out and took it up on deck. I went to the boat deck on the starboard side.

'I went to my station from there and found my boat (No. 1) had gone. I thought the next best thing to do was to assist with some other boat ... As I got to No. 10 boat, the Chief Officer was there [Henry Wilde].

'I just heard him say, "How many seamen are in that boat?" The answer came back, "Two, sir." He turned to some man standing there and said, "Is there any man here can pull an oar?" Nobody answered, but a man who seemed to me like a foreigner got close to him, and I didn't hear what he said, but he simply pushed him aside, and said, "You are of no use to me." I went to him and told him I could pull an oar but was not anxious to go unless he wanted me to go. He said, "Get right in there", and he pushed me toward the boat, and I simply stepped in the boat and got in ...

'When there were no more women to be had around the deck the Chief Officer gave the order for the boat to be lowered. I might say that about the last woman that was about to be passed in slipped, and was about to fall between the ship and the boat when I caught her. I just saved her from falling. Her head passed toward the next deck below. A passenger caught her by the shoulders and forced me to leave go. It was my intention to pull her back in the boat. He would not let go of the woman, but pulled her right on the ship.'

Senator Smith: 'Do you know who the woman was?'

– 'No sir; I did not know her.'

Senator Fletcher: 'Do you know whether she succeeded in getting into another boat or not?'

– 'I couldn't say. I supposed she got into another boat.'

(US Inquiry, pp. 821–826)

Able seaman Frank Evans said that the woman wore a black dress, and suggested that perhaps her heel had caught in the *Titanic*'s rail as she jumped. He testified that after her rescue she came back up to the boat deck, jumped, and this time landed safely in lifeboat No. 10.

Burke later returned to England on the Red Star Line's SS *Lapland*. He stayed working on the sea and in related trades, and retired to Liverpool, originally White Star's home port.

The late William Burke, from Albert Edward Road in Wavertree, was a ship steward. He was woken by a fellow crewmember, who came up to his bunk bed brandishing a piece of ice which had sheered off the iceberg as it hit the ship.

In an interview with the *Echo*, he recalled: 'I was sent to lifeboat station number ten and when a woman passenger leapt to board it, she slipped and was about to fall into the sea when I grabbed her.

'I hung on to her, but it was a terrific strain. Then, just as I thought I must let go, we reached the level of the next deck and two sailors clasped her by the head and shoulders and hauled her to safety.

'Our boat was so full that everyone had to stand. At first we could not believe the *Titanic* would sink … but sink she did, and the hours from when I was roused from my bunk to the time we got picked up by the *Carpathia* are not ones which I am anxious to recall.'

(*Liverpool Echo*, 1956)

TIMOTHY CASEY (38) LOST

Trimmer.
From: County Cork.
Sailors' Home, Southampton.

Nothing much is known about Casey, apart from the fact that his death benefited relatives in the United States. His nephew, William James Casey, of Texas and five nieces received compensation payments after they were tracked down by a diligent lawyer and offered a deal. Relatives continue to live in Longview, Texas.

It appears he may have been an agricultural labourer from Rea, Castlehaven, near the small ports of Castletownshend, Union Hall and Glandore, all of which had strong seafaring traditions. Living alone with his elderly mother, Johanna, by the 1901 census, he may have gone to sea following her death.

WILLIAM CLARK (36) SAVED

Fireman.
From: Greenore, County Louth.
30 Paget Street, Southampton.

Clark had previously served on the sister ship *Olympic*. As a fireman, he was very lucky to escape the wreck of the *Titanic* (his means of doing so remains unknown), since only thirty-six out of a total of 167 stokers lived. More remarkably still, Clark also survived a proportionately greater maritime disaster just two years later, when the 14,000-ton *Empress of Ireland* was struck by the collier *Storstad* in the St Lawrence river, sinking in just a quarter of an hour and taking the lives of 1,014 of her 1,477 passengers and crew.

This is from *The Times* account of interviews with *Empress of Ireland* crewmen on their return to Britain aboard the *Corsican* in June 1914. It was submitted by the newspaper's Glasgow correspondent:

A Comparison with the Titanic
Much the most interesting of the personal statements given in answer to questions was made to me by William Clarke [*sic*] a fireman of Liverpool – actually a survivor of the *Titanic* disaster – a quiet, matter-of-fact old man with a grey moustache and kindly eyes, rather toil-worn. He said:

'I was a fireman on both the ships. It was my luck to be on duty at the time of both accidents. The *Titanic* disaster was much the worst of the two. I mean it was the most awful. The waiting was the terrible thing. There was no waiting with the *Empress of Ireland*. You just saw what you had to do and did it.

'The *Titanic* went down straight, like a baby goes to sleep. The *Empress* rolled over like a hog in a ditch. I was shovelling coals when the *Empress* was struck. I heard the engines stop. I ran up to my boat, No. 5. We swung her down, but the list of the ship threw her out from the side into the water, and then the hooks of the davits loosed off and she floated away.

'I had to dive into the water to catch her. By that time the ship was just going. I heard screaming and then helped to pull people out of the water. We were picked up by the *Storstad*.'

(*The Times*, 10 June 1914)

A major follow-up interview with Clark appeared less than a fortnight later in an Irish newspaper. It revealed amazing new details about how he had cheated death before. From the *Dundalk Democrat* of Saturday 27 June 1914:

> If ever a fireman bore a charmed life it is Fireman William Clark, of the ill-fated liner *Empress of Ireland*.
>
> An insatiable thirst for adventure has carried him all over the world. He has heard the thunder of big guns on the warships of Britain's fleet; he has been wounded by sniping Boers on the blood-stained veldt of South Africa; he has been given up for lost when suffering agonies on a sick bed in a military hospital; has been carried to almost certain death in the mighty *Titanic*; hurled from the torn deck of the *Empress of Ireland* when she plunged to her doom in the dark waters of the St Lawrence – and, fit and well in spite of it all, he still survives to tell the tale.

> *Flirting with death*
> Ever since he came to man's estate, William Clark, the quiet, unassuming fireman of the lost *Empress*, has flirted with death. Not once in generations is it given to a man to face peril after peril in this way and come practically unscathed through it all. Yet, if you ask William Clark whether he has not tired of adventure and intends to settle down to a quiet life, he will answer you quietly: 'I shall go down to the sea again when I am ready and as soon as I can get another ship!'
>
> I found Clark at his home in Bootle yesterday. Let me describe him to you. In appearance he is a typical Irishman, with the soft dark hair and big blue eyes which have earned for the lassies of his race a reputation for beauty that is known throughout the world. There is a look of fearless honesty in those blue eyes of his, and when you talk to him you get the impression of a calm, quiet man, calculated to keep his head and act with coolness even in moments of the greatest excitement and danger.
>
> A full dark moustache hides the lines of his mouth, and he strikes you as being too kindly of disposition to be what one would describe as a 'firm man'. But there is an air of quiet courage about him, and you feel instinctively that this is a man you could rely upon in any emergency involving danger. He is about 43 years of age and unmarried.
>
> When I saw him he was still wearing the clothes cut on the American style, which were supplied to him after the *Empress* catastrophe, in which he lost everything he had with him. He looks grotesque, and it is almost amusing to see him walking in the square-toed, dome-capped boots beloved of the Yankee – brown boots with soft felt uppers.
>
> They are very small, and it is a strange thing about this remarkable man that one of his few vanities is an abounding pride in the smallness of his feet.
>
> William Clark could tell of many hairsbreadth escapes on land and sea if he would, but though he has come safely through them all, the horror still clings to them and has left its mark upon him. He does not like to talk of these things, and it is with difficulty that one can persuade him to unfold the pages of the past.
>
> Except in his appearance one can hardly call him a typical Irishman. He lacks much of that spontaneous gaiety and vivacity of bearing – that quick impulsiveness which has set a kind of trademark on Irishmen all the world over. But his looks stamp him as Irish beyond question, and that craving for adventure may also be counted among the attributes conferred upon him by his nationality.

The lure of the sea

Clark was born at Greenore, County Louth, about 43 years ago. What he did as a lad, I do not know, but the love of roaming, coupled with a passionate longing for the sea, asserted itself early in life and before he was twenty he left his native land and came to Liverpool to seek his fortune.

As may be imagined, he found his way down to the docks. The big ships called to him and the restless tides of the Mersey sang an eternal song of invitation, luring him out to stormy seas and strange lands. But he loved the sea not only for its own sake, it was the adventure, the excitement, and the change of a seafaring life which called to him with an insistent attraction that would not be denied, and before long he found himself on a British warship.

But life in the navy nowadays lacks much of the charm of olden time, and for the bluejacket of today there are no wild adventures on the Spanish Main, no exciting chases after French privateers in the Bay of Biscay, no gold to be wrested from the Indies, and no prize money. All that sort of thing belonged to the days of the wooden walls now gone for ever, and now the navy man gets plenty of discipline, not a little monotony and no fighting.

It was hardly to be wondered at that Clark's restless temperament soon tired of the necessary restrictions of a modern warship and before long he made up his mind to quit. He deserted and got clear away, but the lure of the sea still held him and he shipped as a fireman on board a merchant steamer.

A knock-about time in many oceans followed, and eventually Clark found himself on a ship in Durban port when South Africa was seething with the unrest which culminated in the war.

The thirst for adventure and excitement was too much for him. There was going to be fighting, and men were needed. He left his ship, gave himself up to the naval authorities as a deserter, and in the height of the war fever was let off lightly when it was understood he was anxious to volunteer for the front.

Fighting the Boers

He went to the military riding school in Pietermaritzburg and learned to ride like a cowboy. Then he joined Brabant's Horse and went right through the war in the army of Lord Methuen.

He had many exciting adventures, but shot and shell and bayonet, which laid so many of his comrades low, left him for a long time untouched.

At last his luck changed a little. During a fierce scrap at Blackfontein, Clark was wounded; but here again he got off lightly. A bullet struck a bit of woodwork and one of the splintered fragments struck his arm and opened a nasty cut along the wrist. It was a little affair; Clark's time had not come.

The hardships of the campaign, however, did not altogether pass him by. Towards the end of the war he was stricken down with disease, and for eighteen months he lay in hospital hovering between life and death. But his splendid constitution stood him in good stead, and he was discharged from the hospital fit and well.

Again he took to seafaring, and eventually he shipped aboard the huge *Titanic* and helped to keep her fires going on that first and last voyage, the awful end of which remains one of the most terrible incidents in our history.

Clark went down in the ship when the mighty iceberg ripped her side open and hurled her to her doom.

How he escaped he does not know. He was caught in the swirl of waters as the vessel plunged down – dragged down into the ocean depths with the crippled leviathan as she sank to her last resting place. Even then his abnormal luck did not desert him. He never thought to come up again, but the force of the boiler explosion lifted him and rushed him up to the surface. He struck out vigorously; was pulled aboard one of the boats, and came home to tell the tale.

This awful experience did not cure him of his craving for the sea and he continued to serve in the stoke-hold of various liners, among which was the *Empress of Britain*, the sister ship to the one of which he has again had a miraculous escape from death.

Titanic *and* Empress *Compared*

It was his first voyage on the *Empress of Ireland*. When the crash came and the vessel's stokehold filled with water, his thoughts instantly went back to his awful experience of the *Titanic*.

The scenes on the *Titanic* were the worst, he said, because there was more time to realise the full horror of the situation. On the *Empress*, death came more swiftly.

Clark was on duty in the stokehold of the *Empress* when the collision came. The water came pouring in, driving the firemen higher and higher up the vessel, like rats trying to escape rising water in a well. His lifeboat station was No. 5, and somehow or other he got there, but he cannot remember how she was launched. His mind is a blank concerning some of those awful moments spent on the canting decks of the doomed liner.

They had to crawl on hands and knees on the sloping hull in order to get the boat clear, and then their best chance of escape was to plunge into the water in the hope of being able to scramble aboard. Clark was drawn under several times before he got into the boat, and afterwards, he said, they were able to pull about sixty men into her.

And so this man who has faced death time after time was again snatched from the grave. He came home in the *Corsican* and is now once more in Liverpool.

In spite of all he has passed through he is still well, although he complains that sometimes he cannot sleep for thinking of the terrible experiences he has just come through. He is grateful for his good fortune and realises how close he has come to death.

Had all the luck

'If there is any luck on the sea, surely I have had it all,' he says.

But he still intends to follow a seafaring life, and until he gets another boat he is spending his time ashore with old friends and comrades, in true sailor fashion.

Clark is a Roman Catholic and has a great regard for religious observances. Often after a heavy voyage he returns home late at night tired out; but he is up again first thing in the morning to attend Mass.

He is the luckiest sailor afloat.

He has come face to face with death on land and sea – but death has passed him by.

The 1911 census shows Clark living with a wife nine years his senior, the former Mary Jane Humpreys. A Somerset woman, she had six children, all born in Southampton, but all using her surname. His life subsequent to *Titanic* is unknown.

JOHN COFFEY (23) DESERTED

Fireman.
From: Cottrell's Row, Queenstown, County Cork.
12 Sherbourne Terrace, Southampton.

John Coffey was the last man off the *Titanic* before the ice hit the hull. Days after the tragedy, newspapers from the *Enniscorthy Echo* to the *Belfast Newsletter* reported: 'It is said that one fireman, who felt that something was sure to happen, deserted at Queenstown.' The first such report was on 17 April 1912. Two days later, *The Cork Examiner* ran the following:

> *Lucky stoker – quits ship at Queenstown.*
> A young man named Coffey had a lucky escape from being amongst those lost on the *Titanic*. Coffey joined the *Titanic* at Southampton and on the passage to Queenstown, decided to get out of her as he did not relish his job.
>   Accordingly, at Queenstown, he stealthily got on board the tender which took the passengers out, and secreted himself on board and got clear at Queenstown successfully, and remained here until Sunday morning last when he joined the *Mauretania*.

An account of the escape was given in May 1912 to the Southampton *Evening Echo* by his fellow fireman on board the *Titanic*, Jack Podesta.

> All the White Star boats and Cunard liners outward bound called here to pick up mails and passengers by tender and it was the custom for we firemen and trimmers to go up on deck and carry the mail from the tender to the mail room.
>   A fireman whom I knew very well, John Coffee [*sic*] – I was in the SS *Oceanic* and *Adriatic* with him – said to me, 'Ack, I'm going down to this tender to see my mother.'
>   He asked me if anyone was looking and I said 'No' and bid him good luck. A few seconds later he was gone!

The story has always been that Coffey hid himself under a pile of mailbags taken off the ship for Ireland.

He was equally adept at achieving what he wanted three days later – that fateful Sunday 14 April – when he persuaded the *Mauretania* to take him on board as a crewman despite not having an official stamp to his Book of Continuous Discharge. From the available evidence it seems clear that Coffey used the *Titanic* as a taxi – to obtain a free ride to his home port having been left penniless in Southampton by the crippling coal strike.

Coffey stood as the most famous deserter in maritime history – a footnote without a face, until the efforts of his grandson, Brian Payne, once again brought his likeness to light in 2001. Coffey was a careless, carefree man and a serial deserter. He had quit the similar-sounding RMS *Teutonic* at Queenstown almost exactly a year earlier (on 20 April 1911), his Royal Naval Reserve records show. It may not be a coincidence, for he was born in Queenstown on 3 January 1889. Coffey's father, David, was himself a fireman, and the family was living at Cottrell's Row in the town. When John was born there, his mother, Elizabeth, neglected to tell the authorities until St Patrick's Day, a delay that played havoc with the birth registration.

It may have been inevitable that he followed his father into the calling of marine fireman, joining the Royal Naval Reserve in 1909. Another rite of passage took place – he had his initials tattooed onto his right forearm, common among sailors in case they drown. *Titanic* Quartermaster Robert Hichens, for instance, had his entire surname etched into his flesh. Coffey later added a star in the same place, and the name of a girlfriend, Kate.

Kate was water under the keel by the time Coffey met one Louisa Trevor in Southampton. She was only 17, Coffey had just turned 20, but he was smitten. He added a year to his age so that he would not have to seek his parental permission for the match, and took his teenage bride to the altar on 1 March 1909.

By 1910 Coffey was a fireman on the mighty *Lusitania*, the famed ocean greyhound. Later that year he blotted his copybook by failing to join her sister ship the *Mauretania*, having signed ship's articles. That abortive voyage was his last association with the *Mauretania* until he used her as a meal ticket in 1912.

The mother he was supposedly going to visit according to Podesta's account, was no longer in the town by the 1911 census. Another woman was – widow Margaret Coffey, who also had a son called John. By further coincidence this John was also a marine fireman, evidenced by the certificate of his 1911 marriage in Portsmouth, leading to a misidentification in the first edition of this book. This family lived in Thomas Street, at the top of the town, where folklore said the deserter stayed. In fact, the John Coffey of the *Titanic*, by RNR records, in June 1912 gave an address next door to Margaret in Thomas Street, Queenstown. Perhaps she was his aunt.

Although *The Cork Examiner*'s article reported that he deserted because 'he did not relish his job' other newspaper reports said that Coffey deserted because he 'felt sure something was going to happen'. Family fragments now say Coffey, on arrival by the *Mauretania*, told New Yorkers that he had a dream of the *Titanic* sinking, so he left the ship: 'The Americans loved the story and wined and dined him, taking it all in.'

Coffey earned a caution for his desertion, family lore suggesting he spent a few days in jail at Liverpool on the *Mauretania*'s return. In any case, his survival allowed him to father two more children, in addition to a daughter, Louisa. Son John, born in 1915, was later father to Brian Payne, who initiated a mission to uncover his grandfather's past, one made more difficult by Coffey's divorce and subsequent disappearance from the family horizon, *c.* 1920. The records Brian discovered showed that Coffey continued to sail with White Star and Cunard, but deserted from the RNR in November 1914, shortly after the outbreak of the First World War.

After his divorce, Coffey stayed single, working as a merchant seaman for the rest of his life, finally stepping off the *Urmston Grange* in Newcastle on the day of his 65th birthday in 1954. He died three years later (on 12 June 1957, after a stroke), and was buried in a pauper's grave in Hull's Eastern Cemetery, where he lies with three other adults and four babies.

Brian says: 'Granddad's grave was much better kept than I had expected. Fate is a strange thing. I will never know what God intended, but I feel that an empty page in my life was written up and completed [by visiting it]. I feel a better person for it.'

John Coffey, the serial deserter, is once more back with his family.

JOHN COLEMAN (58) LOST

Mess steward.
From: Cork.
7 Mortimer Road, Woolston, Southampton.

John Coleman was born in Queenstown, County Cork, and claimed to be 55 when signing on to *Titanic*, having admitted to being 57 in the 1911 census.

Married for thirty-two years to Roseanne, from Dundalk, they had only one child, who had died in infancy. In his Southampton census entry Coleman proudly noted that he was a ship's steward employed by the White Star Line.

JOSEPH COLGAN (33) SAVED

Assistant cook/scullion.
From: Dublin.
27 West Street, Southampton.

Colgan may have found a place aboard lifeboat No. 8 on the port side. He was born in Dublin, and may have once been a private in the Irish Fusiliers. He gave his last ship as the White Star's *Majestic* when signing on to the *Titanic*'s articles on 4 April 1912. Colgan worked in the First- and Second-Class galley, on wages of £3 10s per month. A scullion's duties essentially consisted of washing up.

He survived the sinking and returned to Britain on the *Lapland*. He received the balance of his wages on 30 April. He did not give evidence at either inquiry, but returned to life at sea thereafter, serving on the White Star's *Cedric* and other ships. Mystery surrounds his later life.

DENIS CORCORAN (26) LOST

Fireman.
From: Thurles, Tipperary.
Sailors' Home, Southampton.

Four firemen were seen on the poop just before the vessel sank. They were Matty Black, [Frank] Mason, Denny Corcoran, and John Bannon.

One of the boys, named Dillon, said to Bannon: 'Johnny, there's a light over there; I'm going to strike out for it. Are you coming?'

'Not just yet awhile,' said Johnny.

Dillon went over the side in the direction of the light on the lifeboat and was picked up. The [remaining] firemen took off their shoes and were on a piece of grating when the final plunge came.

(Able Seaman George McGough in a New York interview,
quoted in Phillip Gibbs, *The Deathless Story of the Titanic*, 1912)

Corcoran's remains were not found or identified. Some battered bodies of unknown crew victims were buried at sea in weighted canvas after being recovered by the *MacKay-Bennett*, but these were in the tiny minority.

JOSEPH DAWSON (23) LOST

Trimmer.
From: Dublin.
70 Briton Street, Southampton.

Dawson's body was recovered by one of the search ships (No. 227) and he is buried in Fairview Cemetery, Halifax, Nova Scotia. The following appeared in the *Daily Mail* on 3 April 1998:

Teenage girls are flocking to a lonely grave to mourn the young man they believe inspired the character played by Leonardo DiCaprio in *Titanic*.

They leave flowers, cinema ticket stubs, and even love notes before the headstone marked J. Dawson. Dawson's body was fished from the Atlantic after the liner went down in 1912. In the Oscar-winning film, DiCaprio plays Jack Dawson, a passenger on the doomed liner. But Jack was a purely fictional creation.

The remains in the cemetery at Halifax, Nova Scotia, are of 23-year-old James [*sic*] Dawson from Southampton, a lowly trimmer in the ship's engine room. When the filmmakers chose their hero's name, they had no idea there was even a J. Dawson on the crew list.

'We've probably broken a lot of hearts by telling the true story of the body in the grave,' Richard MacMichael of the Marine Museum of the Atlantic in Halifax said. 'James Dawson probably never saw the upper decks, let alone any beautiful rich young ladies like Rose in the film. He would have been down in the engine room in 120 degree heat, stripped to the waist.'

When buried at Fairview Cemetery, the Dublin-born youngster who came to England to find work was unmourned, known simply as body number 227. It was years before he was identified.

In fact Joseph Dawson had been identified within a short time by the coroner's office of Nova Scotia through his union membership card, found on the remains. He was buried under his surname and first initial on 8 May 1912, but the name was not recorded on his gravestone until much later.

No. 227. Male. Estimated age, 30. Hair, light; and moustache.
Clothing – Dungaree coat and pants; grey shirt. No marks on body or clothing. Effects – N.S. & F. Union 35638. Fireman.
Name – J. Dawson, 17 Briton St., Southampton.

Joseph was born in the slums of inner city Dublin in 1888, but his birth was not registered. His mother, Catherine Madden, was a widow, and his father, Patrick Dawson, a widower, who had once 'jumped the wall' in family lore to escape a hasty decision to enter the priesthood, unlike his three brothers, who became Fr Thomas, Fr William and Fr Bernard.

Joseph's parents were not married, although Patrick had a previous wife, Maryanne Walsh, who had died in childbirth in 1883, aged only 30. The 1901 census shows the family living in a tenement in Rutland Street. Patrick is a joiner aged 44, Catherine is a

Stokehold of the White Star liner Justicia, *sunk off Donegal in 1918. A trimmer's job was to bring barrows of coal to the furnaces.*

year older, and eventual *Titanic* victim Joseph is aged 12, with a younger sister, Maggie, eight. The Dawsons occupied just two tiny rooms, but shared the four-storey tenement with eight other families, some of whom, with eight and nine members, made do with a single room.

He was aged 18 when his mother died and Joseph moved to England with his sister, who then trained to be a nun, studying for her vows with the daughter of poet Hilaire Belloc. She later abandoned this intended vocation.

Joseph joined the Royal Army Medical Corps (RAMC) and took up boxing, a sport of which his father Patrick strongly disapproved. He was eventually based in Netley, a few miles from Southampton, and left the army in 1911. He moved into the family home of John Priest, a White Star fireman, who introduced him to life at sea. He first signed on as a coal trimmer aboard the *Majestic*.

Dawson began courting Priest's sister Nellie. Both men signed on for the *Titanic*, and the *Southampton Pictorial* later reported that Mrs Priest had 'one son restored to her, but her daughters Nellie and Emmie both lost sweethearts'.

Grandniece Moira Whelligan-Fell said: 'From what we know, he was a typical 23-year-old, full of ambition and hoping to see the world and send some money home. We often think about him, full of dreams, boarding *Titanic* and waving goodbye … not knowing he was sailing to his death. It is so sad.'

THOMAS (FRANK) DONOGHUE (33) LOST

Steward.
60 Ludlow Road, Southampton.

Report of the American Red Cross (Titanic Disaster) 1913:
No. 121. (Irish). The husband was drowned. He was 33 years of age, a steward on the *Titanic*, earning $75 a month. He had made his home in this country [United States] for two years. He is survived by the widow, 33 years of age, and a son, 6 years of age.

Both husband and wife have relatives living in Liverpool, but none are able to assist this family. The widow is unwilling to return to England to live, because there are more opportunities in this country to earn a living for herself and her son. At present, she is employed as a domestic servant and cares for her son, who lives with her and attends school.

Immediately after the disaster, she went to England to recover for the death of her husband under the British Workmen's Compensation Act. She was awarded £300, of which one half was paid to her in cash. The remainder, placed in trust for the boy, is paid to her at the rate of £5 each quarter.

The appropriation by this Committee has been placed in trust for the widow with the Charity Organisation Society of the city in which she lives, and is paid as a pension to supplement her earnings until her son attains working age. From other American relief funds she received $81. ($2,700)

Donoghue's Irish origins are unknown. He was boarding at Ludlow Road with a fellow ship's steward named Thomas Phillips and his family.

LAURENCE DOYLE (27) LOST

Fireman.
From: County Wexford.
10 Orchard Place, Southampton.

Larry Doyle was formerly on the *Majestic*. He earned £6 a month as a stoker.

The only Laurence Doyle of the right age in Wexford in the 1901 census was a teenage servant on the Donohoe farm in Monamolin, with no prospects where he was.

WILLIAM LUKE DUFFY (36) LOST

Writer/Chief Engineer's Clerk.
From: Castlebar, County Mayo.
11 Garton Road, Itchen, Southampton.

Duffy: 15 April 1912, at his post on board the SS *Titanic*, William Luke, dearly loved husband of Ethel Duffy, 11 Garton Road, Itchen, Hants, late 103 Lr Baggot Street, Dublin, and grandson of the late Luke Ward, Castlebar. RIP.

(*Irish Weekly Mail & Warder*)

William's Baggot Street address was a boarding house run by his aunt, Mayo woman Marianne Ward. William's brother and sister, Mary and Joseph, meanwhile lived at No. 98, across the road. Mary appears to have inherited the most property after the death of their parents.

William had been a long time in Dublin. The 1901 census shows him as a 22-year-old commercial clerk in a bakery, living at 11 Stamer Street in the north inner city at the home of his aunt Mary. He was born on 8 October 1875 at Castlebar to civil engineer Joseph Duffy and his wife Ellen, formerly Ward. He was educated in St Jarlath's College, Tuam. He later spent two years as a clerk in Shackleton's Flour Milling Co., Dublin, before taking another job with James Walker & Co., Dublin. He married, and moved to England, settling in Southampton. The couple had a daughter, Mary.

Duffy opted to go to sea, re-crossing the Irish Sea and joining the *Titanic* at Belfast on 2 April 1912 as Chief Engineer's clerk. It was his first voyage.

From the Mansion House *Titanic* relief fund report, March 1913:

No. 88. Duffy, Ethel, widow; child: Mary. Marianne Ward, Aunt. All class D dependents.

Ethel was later granted a sum of £4 4s to buy a set of false teeth. Her daughter became sick, and she was granted further monies in 1914 for 'special nourishment'.

CECIL FITZPATRICK (21) SAVED

Steward.
From: William Street, Kilkenny.
93 Millbrook Road, Southampton.

William Cecil Norman Fitzpatrick was born at William Street, Kilkenny, on 26 April 1890, but was often referred to by his preferred name, Cecil. He was a mess steward, who found himself clinging to life on overturned lifeboat, collapsible B:

Amongst the survivors of the crew of the *Titanic* was a steward, Mr Cecil Fitzpatrick, son of Mr and Mrs Fitzpatrick, Bishop Street Tuam.

(*Limerick Chronicle*, 30 April 1912)

Fitzpatrick's parents, Robert and Mary (née Ryan), were married on 28 September 1885, in St Canice's Cathedral, Kilkenny. The groom was a policeman and on retirement he farmed horses at Foster Place, Tuam, County Galway.

Passenger Lillian Bentham (No. 12 lifeboat) told the *Rochester Times-Tribune* in April 1962:

'If it weren't for my fur coat, I believe I would not be alive today, nor would the young steward, Mr Fitzpatrick. I had on a hooded steamer coat over my nightclothes, and Bert [Denbury, a friend] grabbed my fur one from a chair as we left the stateroom. That "extra" I wrapped around Mr Fitzpatrick when we had rescued him from an overturned boat.'

In gratitude, the steward gave her the tiny Scout whistle from his belt. He had blown it all night in an effort to call some other boat to their aid. [Eventually] lifeboat No. 12, picked up about 20 men who had been for hours on the half-submerged hulk. One of them was dead.

'I have that whistle, some coins from the dead man's pocket, and a White Star Line button from the coat of an officer who later died in our boat,' Mrs Black [née Bentham] reveals.

On the night of the collision, Cecil helped passengers into the lifeboats. When the ship was low in the water where he stood, he jumped and swam for his life. He managed to scramble onto the overturned collapsible. Among the other shivering survivors there was *Titanic* Second Officer Charles Lightoller.

Mr Fitzpatrick, one of the stewards who were rescued from the *Titanic*, stated in an interview that on Sunday, 14 April as he was serving the lunch in the engineers' mess, the chief steward, who had been an old seafaring man, said that he knew ice was in the vicinity of the ship by the smell of the air.

'We retired to our cabin,' he continued, 'which was situated on the deck above the engine room and were settling down to sleep when we were aroused by a sudden lurch of the vessel. After a few minutes the engines were stopped. I enquired the reason for this sudden stoppage of the engines, and after being informed that the ship had struck an iceberg and that she was not seriously injured, I settled myself to sleep again.

'I was awakened by a foreman. I went on deck and the ship was listing to port. As one of the lifeboats was being filled with women and children, a foreigner tried to jump on the boat. The officer told him to go on deck. He refused, and the officer fired, and the man fell dead on deck. The crowd of foreigners who were hanging around the lifeboat cowed back when they found one of their countrymen dead.

'The lifeboat was lowered, and the officer kept on firing his revolver until he was level with the water. I saw a similar instance occur on the port side. A passenger tried to claim a seat in one of the boats. The officer told him to leave at once, and as he hesitated a revolver shot was fired, and he dropped dead in the water.'

(*Northern Constitution*, 4 May 1912)

The Liverpool *Journal of Commerce* of 30 April is similar, but adds in conclusion: 'As the liner was dipping I jumped over board in the icy water, and struck out with every effort I could in order to escape the suction. I was picked up by No. 12 lifeboat and afterwards taken on board the *Carpathia*.'

On 16 May 1912, Fitzpatrick wrote a letter to the *Southern Daily Echo* as follows:

Sir,
Referring to the various letters I have read in your columns under the heading 'Stewards as Life-savers', would you kindly allow me to enlighten some of your correspondents, who imagine that the stewards did not carry out their duties efficiently on the lost *Titanic* when she foundered, owing to lack of proper organisation.

Here is what I saw on the boat deck on that fatal Sunday night. Everywhere one could see the white jacket boys fastening passengers' lifebelts and assuring them that there really was no cause to fear.

Now I can see a group of them standing by the boat falls, ready to lower the boat load of women and children, and a few of their mates picked to man the boat, a very few, with steady, strong arms, and cool heads, for I assure anyone who has never been in a shipwreck that it requires gritty men to lower boats chock-full of living freight to the water 90 feet below, but thank God it was effectively carried out by the men who go on pleasure trips, in other words – stewards.

The firemen – brave fellows – were shoulder to shoulder with the stewards, and also performed their duties manfully.

The officers of the boat will be able to pass judgment on the stewards if they have not done their work efficiently. I was one of the few who had to swim for it, and I was under the command of Mr Lightoller. He is the only officer alive who had to swim.

Ask him if the stewards whom he was directing carried out his orders coolly and diligently, although the water where we worked was on the level with the boat-deck.

We were trying to get one of the two collapsible rafts launched when the vessel broke, and we had to go.

What do the feather-bed public want from stewards? I do hope that certain correspondents will kindly refrain from criticising the actions of men whom they do not know and who are ever ready to meet death bravely.

Yours faithfully,

C. W. Fitzpatrick
Engineers' Steward.
93 Millbrook Road.

Cecil W. Fitzpatrick married Elsie M. Moody in Hull on 2 August 1914. The certificate shows him as a 'cashier and building contractors' assistant', resident at 11 Commercial Road, Ipswich. Within days he was in uniform as the Great War broke out, and went on to serve on the Western Front in the Royal Garrison Artillery as a gunner, fortunately not on the front line. His photograph was taken on 8 December 1915, when he was 25.

Cecil and Elsie subsequently had four children – Patricia May, born 23 December 1920; Robert Cecil, born 2 October 1922; Anthony Evelyn, born 13 December 1923; and Anne Moody, born a decade later on 12 August 1933.

His son Robert wrote: 'Father was reluctant to talk about the *Titanic* and was I think rather ashamed to have lost his seaman's book one night in a pub. I have seen his discharge book, in which it notes that his employment with the White Star Line terminated at midnight on the day the *Titanic* sank.' The book's present whereabouts are unknown.

Daughter Anne said:

One day in 1933 my father took my two brothers swimming in the Hogsmill river in Surrey. My brother, Bob, noticed that my father was lying on his face in the water and not moving. He dragged him to the bank where he soon recovered.

Perhaps he had a similar experience to Officer Lightoller, who told in his memoirs how on one occasion he went to have a cold bath and his wife Sylvia found him lying on his face in the water unconscious. She believed the shock of the cold water brought back the memory of that terrible night and caused him to faint.

Cecil Fitzpatrick died on 11 July 1964 at Leeds.

JOHN 'JACK' FOLEY (46) SAVED

Storekeeper.
From: Youghal, County Cork.
Queens Road, Southampton.

Samuel Hemming (US evidence): Mr Lightoller called me and said, 'Come with me,' and he said, 'Get another good man.' I says, 'Foley is here somewhere.' He says, 'I have no time to stop for Foley.' So he called a man himself, and he said, 'Follow me.'

Jack Foley held the rank of quartermaster on the *Titanic*, but actually served as its storekeeper. He was originally from Youghal, County Cork.

He helped load women into boats in the last minutes, and was saved in lifeboat No. 4, the last standard lifeboat (as distinct from collapsibles) to be lowered from the ship. It went off at 1.55 a.m. Samuel Hemming and another seaman lowered No. 4. At the last moment, Hemming, Foley's pal, jumped down the fall ropes to escape the dying *Titanic* and swam 200 yards (without a lifejacket) to the nearest lifeboat – the same one he had last helped to lower. 'I pulled my head above the gunwale and I said, "Give us a hand in, Jack." Foley was in the boat. I saw him standing up in the boat. He said, "Is that you, Sam?" I said, "Yes," and him and the women and children pulled me in the boat.'

Foley returned to Britain and signed off the ship's articles, receiving the balance of his wages, £1 1s. He was given £9 7s 6d witness expenses at the British inquiry.

He had married Mary Murphy in 1895 and shortly thereafter moved from Youghal to Kinsale, where the 1901 census records the family in three rooms at No. 9 Cork Street. Foley is shown as a 35-year-old merchant sailor. His wife is 31, and they already have three children – Maurice, 5, Norah, 4, and Mary Ann, 2.

Within a decade the family had relocated to Southampton, where a 1911 population snapshot for No. 2 Queen's Road, Shirley, has Foley at 45, describing himself as a mariner. The number of children had expanded from three to seven. The initial trio had been joined by Nicholas, 9 (hospitalised with sleeping sickness for many years), Kathleen, 6, Margaret, 1, and newborn John.

Foley had seen service on the *Olympic*, the *Titanic*'s sister ship. A mishearing of Foley's birthplace is responsible for an error on *Titanic*'s crew manifest, whereby it was entered as

'York', instead of what he was saying – 'Youghal'. Foley was also aboard for the delivery sailing from Belfast to Southampton, and on these articles his Irish birthplace is named correctly.

He died of a blood clot on the brain in 1934, while still resident in Southampton. He was 69.

PATRICK GILL (41) LOST

Ship's cook.
From: County Kildare.
24 Waverley Road, Southampton.

Gill was born in Kildare and gave his age as 38 years old when he signed on the *Titanic* – two years younger than he had specified for his age in the previous year's census. He lived at 24 Waverley Road, Southampton, with his English wife, Mary, six years his senior. They had no children.

It seems Patrick Gill was from a locality named after his family, Gilltown, in County Kildare, east of Timahoe and north of Prosperous. He was an unmarried labourer in the 1901 census.

BERNARD HANDS (53) LOST

Fireman.
From: Killeshandra, County Cavan.
St Michael's House, Southampton.

Bernard was the only son of peddler Bernard Hands and his wife, Mary, née Maguire, of Clondrum, Killeshandra. He was born in 1858, and had five sisters. He is believed to have been unmarried.

JAMES HESLIN (45) LOST

Trimmer.
From: Cork.
Sailors' Home, Southampton.

James married Biddy Burns, an Armagh girl, and they lived in the Orchard County at Jonesborough. They had two children, Mary and Thomas, in 1912.

James' widow died in 1967, more than half a century after the disaster, at the age of 105. She had no way of knowing whether James' body was among the unidentified crew bodies recovered and buried either at sea or in Halifax, Nova Scotia.

VIOLET JESSOP (24) SAVED

Stewardess.
From: Shirley Road, Bedford Park, London.

William Jessop emigrated from Dublin in the mid-1880s to try his hand at sheep farming in Argentina. His fiancée, Katherine Kelly, followed him out there from Dublin, probably in 1886. They were married shortly after her arrival and their first child, Violet, was born in Buenos Aires on 2 October 1887.

The family left for Britain after William's death, but Violet still hankered to see the world and took a job as a stewardess with the White Star Line. Her unique claim to fame is that she was aboard all three sister ships of the White Star's *Olympic*-class liners when each of them came to grief. She was working on the *Olympic* when the vessel had a costly collision with HMS *Hawke* in September 1911, and half a year later endured the ghastly last hours of the RMS *Titanic*. She was also aboard the *Britannic* (third in the planned sequence of vessels, and originally to be called *Gigantic*, until the *Titanic's* fate deflated all claims to omnipotence) when that vessel, serving as a hospital ship, was torpedoed and sent to the bottom of the Aegean in 1916.

Violet said her thick auburn her had saved her from the *Britannic* sinking, because when she had jumped overboard she had been sucked under the keel, striking her head. Years later she was discovered to have suffered a skull fracture.

In the *Titanic* escape, Violet said she caught a baby thrown into her lifeboat from the deck. She carried it safely all night until they reached the *Carpathia* – whereupon a woman rushed up and snatched the baby back. She never found out who either of them were. Her own account gives no clue as to the lifeboat she escaped in. All but one of the eighteen stewardesses aboard were saved. Some escaped in No. 16, but she may have been in No. 13, which left from the starboard side, and into which a baby was tossed.

Lawrence Beesley was in this boat and wrote in his 1913 book *The Loss of the SS Titanic*: 'And so the coat was given to an Irish girl with pretty auburn hair standing near, leaning against the gunwale – with an outside berth – and so more exposed to the cold air.'

Violet indeed had auburn hair and was proud of the fact that she had never lost her Irish accent. First-Class passenger Lady Lucy Duff Gordon later recalled her 'merry Irish stewardess with her soft Irish brogue and tales of timid ladies she had attended during hundreds of Atlantic crossings'.

She returned to sea after the Great War and had a short-lived marriage to a ship's steward named John James Lewis. Violet reverted to her maiden name and eventually retired to a thatched Tudor cottage in Suffolk after more than four decades on the ocean wave.

Violet attended a reunion dinner of just four survivors in London in 1958, after they were brought together in the making of the movie *A Night to Remember*. Lawrence Beesley was one of them. It is fascinating to wonder whether he recognised her 'pretty auburn hair'.

The long-lived *Titanic* stewardess, escapee of two major sinkings, died in 1971, aged 83. Her unpublished memoirs, originally composed under the title 'Neptune's Greenroom' in 1934, were published posthumously in 1997 as *Titanic Survivor* and became a bestseller.

JAMES KELLY (44) LOST

Greaser.
From: County Meath.
12 Woodleigh Road, Southampton.

An engine-room greaser, Kelly was identified as being from Meath in a report in the *Irish World*, published in New York on 11 May 1912.

In the 1911 Southampton census, he listed himself as a marine fireman from that county, married eleven years to Mary, who was eight years his junior, from Monaghan. Three sons, James Jnr, 11, Frank, 9, and John, 3, had been born in Bootle while Kelly was working on the Liverpool-based liners.

WILLIAM KELLY (23) LOST

Assistant Electrician.
From: 1 Claude Road, Drumcondra, Dublin.

William had followed his older brother, Peter, into electrical engineering. His qualification brought joy to his proud parents, William and Annie, from County Tyrone, who had moved back to Ireland after years in Scotland.

Peter, William and Rose had all been born in Glasgow, with the arrival of William Jnr on 19 June 1888. Peter was already aged three, and Rose was born a year later. Two more children were born before the turn of the century when the family had moved to Dublin.

William Snr was a merchant tailor with a shop at 14–14a North Earl Street in Dublin city centre. Working also as a hatter and outfitter, he earned enough money to send his sons to the Christian Brothers. The family were devout Catholics – a faith perhaps forged stronger for the

THE IRISH ABOARD *TITANIC* 255

parents by Glasgow's sectarian divide – and William Jnr was encouraged to devote some of his time to the Church.

He was further educated at a commercial college before serving a three-year apprenticeship with the electrical engineering firm of T. E. Brunker Ltd in Dublin. In January 1912, he made the fateful decision to join Harland & Wolff, working on the final outfitting of keel number 401, the *Titanic*.

He went aboard as an assistant electrician. It was the first time he had ever been to sea.

One of the electricians employed on the *Titanic* is a son of Mr W. Kelly, tailor, Earl Street, who is almost prostrate with anxiety and grief.

(Irish Independent, 17 April 1912)

The Rev P. J. O'Hara, OP, preaching in St Saviour's church, Dublin, on Sunday morning, in asking the prayers of the congregation in connection with the disaster, made special mention of one of their choir members, Engineer Kelly, a native of Dublin, who was drowned.

(Irish Independent, 23 April 1912)

1911 census – Claude Road.
William, merchant tailor, and wife Annie. Both 50; married 26 years.
Children: Peter (25), elec. eng; **William P. (22)**, elec. eng; Rose (21), general clerk, Annie M. (14), Adrian J. (11).

ERNEST WALDRON KING (28) LOST

Assistant Purser.
From: Clones, County Monaghan.

Ernest had been delighted when a family effort helped to secure him work at last – even if it meant going away to sea. He had been unemployed for much of the past year, and at the age of 27 it was no joke to be without a job.

His parents had always been encouraging. His father, the Rev. Thomas Waldron King, was the incumbent Church of Ireland rector at Currin, Clones, County Monaghan. He was 53, four years younger than his wife, Caroline, who had borne him seven children in thirty-five years of marriage. Three of those children had died young, severely testing the faith of their parents. But Ernest, born in Galway, was one of the lights of their lives, even if his younger brother Charles, aged 21 in 1912, promised to be more successful in life, winning a coveted place in Trinity College Dublin, for undergraduate studies.

Ernest W. King had been aboard the *Olympic* in September 1911 when she collided in the Solent with the cruiser HMS *Hawke*, having to put back to Southampton with a large hole in her starboard quarter caused by the warship's ram. He gave his address as Currin Rectory, Clones, when signing aboard the *Titanic*.

His body was eventually found by the search vessel *Minia*, from Halifax, with Captain W. G. S. DeCarteret cabling the White Star Line on 1 May 1912:

> Today Tuesday, northerly gale, misty. Found body T.W. King, purser's assistant, Lat 41.30, Long 48.15, being forty-five miles east of that found yesterday, showing how widely scattered and difficult to find with no reports from passing steamers to help me. Icebergs numerous as far south as 40.30 in 48.30.

King's was the only body he had found that day. The day before, in another cable, DeCarteret had expressed his belief that late northerly gales had swept bodies into the Gulf Stream and had carried them many miles east. A little earlier, one of his crewmembers, Francis Dyke, had written to his mother during a stint on watch in the wireless room. 'There has been a lot of wind + bad weather since the accident so the bodies are much scattered, some we picked up over 130 miles from the wreck as they go very fast when in the Gulf Stream – very likely many will be washed up on the Irish coast, as they are all going East.'

The body was catalogued as number 321. Still floating more than two weeks after the sinking, only five more were recovered. King's age was estimated as 25, but no listing has been found for his clothing and effects. Returned to the morgue in Halifax, a permit for burial in Fairview Cemetery was issued on 9 May 1912, three and a half weeks after the wreck.

His impressive black granite headstone records 'in loving memory' that he 'died on duty, SS *Titanic*, 15 April 1912'. A verse at the base adds: 'Nothing in my hand I bring, simply to thy cross I cling.'

WILLIAM H. LYONS (25) LOST

Able Seaman.
From: Meat Market Lane, Cork.
27 Orchard Place, Southampton.

Young William Lyons almost managed to save himself. He was dragged alive into lifeboat No. 4 having jumped from the *Titanic* in its final throes and swimming through frigid seas that 'cut like a thousand knives', according to surviving Officer Lightoller. But the effort was too much. Exhausted, Lyons succumbed to the ravages of exposure and lapsed into a coma on board his means of salvation. He was later pronounced dead when taken onto the rescuing *Carpathia*.

Ironically, he could have survived – had Quartermaster Walter J. Perkis not peremptorily thrown away into the deep a bottle of brandy brought aboard No. 4 by another of those rescued, storeman Frank Prentice. Crewmen were forbidden alcohol. 'It might have been the means of saving life,' Prentice ruminated later, 'as we picked up two firemen who had been in the water a long time, and one afterwards died in the boat as the result of exposure.'

Fireman Thomas Patrick Dillon told how he recovered consciousness in lifeboat No. 4 after similarly swimming to safety 'and found Sailor Lyons and another lying on top of me dead.'

Stateroom steward Andrew Cunningham gave a flavour of death and comradeship in No. 4 when he told the US inquiry on its eighth day of evidence of his desperate leap overboard from the *Titanic* with fellow steward Sidney Conrad Siebert:

'I had a mate with me. We both left the ship together.'
Senator Smith: 'Did he have a life preserver on?'
Cunningham: 'Yes, sir … I waited on the ship until all the boats had gone and then I took to the water. I went into the water about two o'clock, I should say. About half an hour before the ship sank. I swam clear of the ship about three-quarters of a mile. We saw the ship go down then. Then we struck out to look for a boat.'
Senator Smith: 'Did you see one?'
Cunningham: 'No, I heard one and I called to it.'
Senator Smith: 'Did that lifeboat come toward you, or did you go toward it?'
Cunningham: 'I went toward it … It was No. 4 boat. They picked us up. There was my mate, who died just after he was pulled in…'

According to evidence given by *Carpathia*'s Captain Arthur Rostron, Lyons was alive but unconscious when taken aboard his ship at 8 a.m. on 15 April, dying some hours later. He is believed to have been finally pronounced dead at midnight. His remains were buried from that vessel in weighted canvas sacking with three others in a foggy 4 a.m. ceremony on Tuesday morning, 16 April. The other bodies are believed to have been those of Abraham Harmer (Third-Class passenger), William Hoyt (First-Class passenger), taken dead from No. 14, and Sidney Siebert (bedroom steward), whose body was removed from lifeboat No. 4.

A picture of William Henry Lyons appeared in *The Cork Examiner* of 23 April 1912:

W.H. Lyons, Market Lane, Cork, who was unfortunately amongst the victims. It seems that young Lyons was saved from the wreck but afterwards died through exposure in one of the lifeboats. The above photo was taken when he was only sixteen, during his apprenticeship.

The *Cork Constitution* recorded:

Cork Dramatic Society
At a special meeting of the Cork Dramatic Society held on Saturday, Mr D. Corkery in

the chair, Mr C. O'Leary proposed, and Mr D. P. Lucey, BA, seconded, the following resolution –

> That we, the members of the Cork Dramatic Society, desire to express our sincere sympathy with Mr J. F. Lyons, BA, on the loss of his brother in the *Titanic* disaster.
>
> (*Cork Constitution*, 22 April 1912)

The chairman was renowned English professor Daniel Corkery, who had founded the dramatic society with Terence MacSwiney, later lord mayor of Cork, who died on hunger strike. Corkery composed a poem on the tragedy, published in the *Irish Review* in May 1912. Entitled 'In Memoriam' and dedicated 'to my friend John F. Lyons, on the loss of his brother William H. Lyons of the crew of the *Titanic*', it contains these lines:

Because of one whose voice I never heard,
Whose face, whose eyes, to me were never known,
My heart, despite the clodding years, is stirred
And stabbed by every ruthless rumour blown
Across the breadths of sea.

1901 census – Lyons
Henry (44), publican. Catherine (45), wife.
Children: **William Henry (14)**, Denis James (12), John F. (11).
Ellen Lyons, servant (28), barmaid.

WILLIAM McCARTHY (47) SAVED

Able Seaman.
From: 9 Grattan Hill Road, Cork.

William's picture and address appeared in *The Cork Examiner* of 23 April 1912. He was said to be 'fortunately amongst the survivors'.

It is known that he survived in lifeboat No. 4, which he helped to crew. It left the port side of the *Titanic* at 1.55 a.m. and dragged in several men from the sea, including McCarthy's fellow crewmember from Cork, William H. Lyons, who died.

McCarthy returned to Britain on the *Lapland*, but was never called to give evidence at the official inquiry. He retired to Cork after a long seafaring career. He liked to make decorative anchors out of wood and shells, and is thought to have died in the 1930s.

1911 census – 9 Grattan Hill Road.
Widowed mother Catherine McCarthy, 80, born Cork. Daughter Kate, 35, born in England.

The 1901 census for the same address also showed Catherine, 69, as a widow, with Kate, 27, a dressmaker. Another daughter was present, May Ellen, 22.

HUGH WALTER McELROY (37) LOST

Chief Purser.
From: Tullacanna, County Wexford.
Polygon House, Southampton.

Chief Purser on the *Titanic* was a huge responsibility – and it was filled by an Irishman who was larger than life and the last word in gallantry.

Hugh McElroy occupied a critical shipboard position for the White Star Line. As Purser, he was the company's main interface with the bulk of passengers. They came to his office on C deck for everything – to lodge and retrieve valuables for safe keeping, to hand in wireless messages to pass on to the Marconi room, to report a leaky tap in a stateroom wash-hand basin, to organise a games of quoits on deck, right down to buying a ticket to the Turkish bath on F deck, and yes, renting the deckchairs ($1 per voyage).

McElroy was the perfect man for the job, because he clearly was an effortless arranger even during his short stays on shore. On 9 April, while still in Southampton, McElroy and his Wexford-born wife, Barbara, sent flowers in the Danish national colours of red and white to Miss Adeline Genée, a famous dancer. Perhaps she had been an important passenger in the past, but the gesture was particularly polished given the fact that Miss Genée was due to perform a special 'flying' matinee at the Southampton Hippodrome two days later – the afternoon after the *Titanic* sailed.

McElroy was still oozing charm and goodwill at Southampton when Francis Browne, the clerical novice soon to become famous for his photographs on board the *Titanic*, called to his office on C deck, 'where a letter of introduction served as a passport to the genial friendship of Mr McElroy'.

The soul of urbanity, McElroy was also a favourite of Captain E. J. Smith, and the two men were photographed together on deck, the Purser appearing with his hands joined behind his back, an image of strength at the master's right hand, and ever ready to do his bidding.

The Cork Examiner, which took the famous shot, noted in its issue of 15 April, while unaware of the unfolding tragedy:

> On the right of the picture is Commander E. J. Smith, R.D., R.N.R., to whose skill and watchfulness is committed the care of the great ship and her freight of close on four thousand souls. He is one of the heads of his profession, and he has a long and extensive connection with the White Star Line. The Captain may be the best, but unless the Purser knows everybody and everything, and combines the perfection of urbanity, tact, prompt appreciation of circumstances – in fact, is the best of fellows – his passenger list does not fill all the time, but on any ship on which Chief Purser McElroy has filled that position, the booking has always been complete well in advance of the sailings.

In fact the *Titanic* was by no means full. But that simply allowed McElroy to indulge

Purser McElroy with Captain E. J. Smith at Titanic's *last port of call, Thursday 11 April 1912.*

his special charm with the ladies. Mrs Henry B. Cassebeer recalled visiting the *Titanic's* Purser soon after boarding to ask for an upgrade from Second Class. It was done at once and Mrs Cassebeer ended up with one of the finest First-Class staterooms ever created for ocean-going luxury, the bulk of which were on this vessel. She remembered running into the Purser a little later and, pushing her luck, asked that it be arranged that she should dine at the Captain's table. McElroy's reply, quoted in Walter Lord's *The Night Lives On*, was: 'I'll do better than that. I'll have you seated at my table.'

On that fatal Sunday, just after midnight, when the *Titanic* engines had stopped after impact with the iceberg, bathroom steward Samuel Rule was investigating the oddity when he saw Purser McElroy on A deck 'in deep conversation' with Second Steward George Dodd. He expected to receive orders, but none were given.

At ten past midnight, stewardess Annie Robinson saw McElroy accompany Captain Smith in the direction of the mailroom, where water was within six steps of coming up onto E deck. 'About a quarter past twelve, or round about that time' Second Steward Joseph Wheat was going up to C deck when he met McElroy looking over the banisters. 'He saw me coming and told me to get the men up and get … lifebelts on the passengers and get them on deck.' The Purser had been talking urgently to two or three officers, including Chief Steward Andrew Latimer. At ten minutes or a quarter to one, Wheat was again given orders by McElroy, to get all the men to their stations at the boats.

McElroy's communication skills were at the fore when disaster struck and the Captain needed trusted men about him. There is evidence he played a major role in harnessing the passengers to their task of putting on lifebelts and preparing to abandon ship. Quietly, too, it seems he was passed a loaded revolver. Although not strictly one of Smith's officers, McElroy had assumed a position of veiled yet real power.

He was next seen outside his office on C deck, where a queue for valuables had begun and was being quickly processed by assistant pursers who emptied the safe. He later addressed the crowd, who were standing around in confusion, urging them to go up top. The Countess of Rothes moved close by and McElroy declared: 'Hurry, little lady, there is not much time. I'm glad you didn't ask me for your jewels as other ladies have.'

McElroy followed his clucking flock, then returned to his duties. He was later seen in the company of his fellow Irishman, Dr W. F. N. O'Loughlin, the senior ship's surgeon. Soon, however, he made his way to the boat deck, where chaos reigned and where every man of authority was desperately needed. McElroy answered the call.

Saloon steward William Ward witnessed Mr McElroy with First Officer Murdoch and J. Bruce Ismay, Managing Director of the White Star Line, at boat No. 9 on the starboard side. 'Either Purser McElroy or Officer Murdoch said: "Pass the women and children that are here into that boat",' said Ward. McElroy next ordered himself and bathroom steward James Widgery into the boat 'to assist the women'. They went.

Before anyone left on board could draw breath, it was nearly 2 a.m. Just two boats remained on the starboard side, with a collapsible hanging in the davits perilously close to the slowly submerging superstructure. A crowd had surged down to it, milling about the restraining officers and crew.

Elsewhere McElroy was bestriding a boat half-lowered to A deck, one hand clutching a fall rope, another wielding a gun. But his voice was his major weapon. At least that's the image conjured by the dramatic account of a First-Class passenger who was present at the last gasp. Seventeen-year-old Jack Thayer saw an armed McElroy attempting to quell panic at the last. His account was written privately for friends and family in 1940, more than a quarter of a century after the disaster. Then a mature 45, but with imperfect recall, Thayer wrote:

> There was some disturbance in loading the last two forward starboard boats. A large crowd of men was pressing to get into them. No women were around as far as I could see. I saw Ismay, who had been assisting in the loading of the last boat, push his way into it. It was really every man for himself …
>
> Purser H. W. McElroy, as brave and as fine a man as ever lived, was standing up in the next to last boat, loading it. Two men, I think they were dining room stewards, dropped into the boat from the deck above. As they jumped, he fired twice in the air. I do not believe they were hit, but they were quickly thrown out.

At some time there had been a lull in all this frenetic activity on the *Titanic*'s boat deck. McElroy found himself with Dr O'Loughlin and other senior colleagues near the First-Class entrance. They shook hands, and then McElroy turned for a final handshake with others – Assistant Purser Reginald Barker was certainly there, and probably Assistant Purser Ernest Waldron King, a third Irishman in the group. Junior Surgeon John Simpson, yet another Hibernian, shook hands with the senior medic and the rest. They were saying to one another, 'Goodbye, old man.'

Second Officer Charles Lightoller broke off his duties for a moment to also come over. He too, grasped hands with everyone and wished them all the best. They were, after all, all in the same boat. And it was sinking beneath them. Within minutes, the waves came.

McELROY – April 14th, on board R.M.S. *Titanic*, Hugh, beloved husband of Barbara McElroy, Springwood, Wexford.

(*Wicklow People*, 25 May 1912)

Hugh McElroy's family were originally from County Wexford and were staunchly Catholic. His parents had emigrated to Liverpool, where Hugh was born, like so many other Irish who went in search of work during the late nineteenth century when Merseyside was an engine of empire and the colonial trade. McElroy opted for a life at sea, and served three years on the troopship *Britannic* during the Boer War at the beginning of the new century. He had thirteen years with the White Star Line, serving on the *Majestic* and *Olympic* before transferring to the *Titanic*. In 1910 he married his long-time sweetheart, Barbara Mary Ennis, whom he had known growing up in Liverpool. She was the daughter of John J. Ennis, the passenger manager of the Allan Line of steamships in that city. The couple made their home in Tullacanna, Harperstown, County Wexford, when J. J. Ennis retired to his extensive family farm there. Barbara and Hugh were less than two years married when the *Titanic* sank, and had no children.

The Cork Examiner reported on 18 April 1912:

> Mr McElroy, the Chief Purser, was a Wexford man, and as fine a type as could be found. He was the Commodore Purser and only recently married the daughter of Captain Ennis of Wexford.
>
> Mr John J. Ennis JP … came to reside with his two daughters at his home place in Springwood (Ballymitty, County Wexford). Last year, one of his daughters, Miss Barbara Ennis, was married to Mr Hugh McElroy, who belongs to a very good Liverpool family, and is brother to Fr McElroy, who lives close to Bootle. He had been a purser in the White Star Line for a quarter of a century.

The remains of the Chief Purser were destined to be recovered from the ocean by the *MacKay-Bennett* search vessel. He was wearing a white dress uniform – leading to the initial mistaken conclusion that it could be the body of a steward. From a fragment, they came up with the name of D. Lily, but in fact there was no one of this name on board. The body was that of Hugh McElroy.

> No. 157. Male. Estimated age, 32. Dark Hair.
> Clothing – Ship's uniform; white jacket; ship keys; 10 pence; 50 cents; fountain pen.
> Steward. Name – D. Lily.

The body was buried at sea. A scrap of paper in the name of his wife was also taken from the remains and later provided corroboration of his identity.

Percy Mitchell, the White Star Line's manager in Montreal, later signed a declaration to obtain the above effects from the coroner's officer of Halifax, Nova Scotia. He certified the name of the deceased as H. McElroy, Purser, SS *Titanic*, his residence as Southampton, England, his religion as Roman Catholic, and his nationality as Irish. The official name of the claimant, issued in the space provided, was 'White Star Line'. It was perhaps appropriate. His white-clad corpse was the most senior member of crew to be recovered, and he had been one of their brightest lights for a long time, ever the embodiment of the White Star Line.

Dr J. C. H. Beaumont, for many years senior surgeon on the *Olympic*, claimed in his book *Ships and People*, published in 1927, that it was known that Purser McElroy had premonitions about the new liner prior to embarkation. He did not expand on the remark.

1911 census – 'Springwood', Tullacanna, County Wexford.
John Ennis (75), widower, retired steamship manager … **Hugh Walter McElroy (36)**, purser. Wife Barbara Mary (34). Married less than one year.
Six servants, including domestics, farmhands, a stableman and professional nurse.
First-class house with ten rooms and 15 outlying farm buildings.

GEORGE 'PADDY' McGOUGH (36) SAVED

Able Seaman.
From: Duncannon, County Wexford.
St George's Street, Southampton.

George McGough was a killer. He appears in the 1901 census as an inmate at HM Prison Winchester, fifteen miles from Southampton. He is the only George McGough born in Ireland in the entire census. The inmate is shown as a mariner.

George Francis McGough was born in Duncannon, County Wexford, Ireland, in 1875. His birthday, appropriately, was Bastille Day, 14 July – named for the storming of that prison. McGough is shown on the 1901 census, correctly, as aged 25. But eleven years later, aged 36, he is still claiming to be aged 25 when he signs on for the ill-fated RMS *Titanic*. Here AB George McGough is shown to be from Duncannon.

It's the same man – there was only one McGough family in Duncannon, and mariner George trimmed his age the better to sell himself at the hiring fair. Everyone did, but photographs from 1912 show McGough to be well-seasoned and no stripling. He has long since seen 25.

What caused George McGough, sometimes known affectionately to his shipmates as 'Paddy' because of his Irish origins, to be banged up in prison? On 10 March 1900, Able Seaman George Francis McGough engaged in a drink-fuelled brawl aboard the dreary collier *Rustington* while that vessel was anchored off Santos, Brazil. The fight was with another member of crew, Welshman John Dwyer, who was shoved over a hatchway and fell headlong into the hold, dashing his brains out on the tough timbers some 26 feet below.

Twelve years and one day before the *Titanic* struck her iceberg, the *Barry Dock News* of Friday 13 April 1900 reported to its Cardiff readers:

It appears, from a letter written from Santos by the Chief Engineer of the *Rustington* on the 13th March … that on the previous Friday, March 9th, the two men, Dwyer and McGough had some words on board and McGough, it is alleged, seized Dwyer, and whether deliberately or not it is not yet known, threw him down the forehold of the ship, Dwyer falling on his head, and death resulted shortly afterwards.

The terrible occurrence was witnessed by four members of the crew, and these men, together with McGough, who was at once placed under arrest, are now on their way home to England on board a Royal Mail steamer and are expected to arrive in Southampton in a day or two when McGough will be placed on his trial on a charge of 'wilful murder'. The deceased leaves a widow … and seven children.

George Francis McGough was committed for trial in Winchester. It emerged the prisoner and others had been ashore and got drunk. When McGough returned aboard, reeling and belligerent, 'he wanted to fight everybody'. He bodily picked up Dwyer and flung him down the forehold. The victim was found with bleeding from his mouth and both ears, dying within minutes. The *South Wales Echo* of Tuesday 3 July 1900 reported McGough's conviction of manslaughter on the high seas, and sentence of only fifteen months' hard labour. So McGough went off for his short stint in jail and was 'snap shotted' by the 1901 census. When released, he returned to the sea, sometimes using the alias George F. Bergin, instead of George F. McGough.

McGough's alternate name, for which he held a separate seaman's book, is shown on his marriage record as he wed a woman ten years his junior only months before the *Titanic* sailed. She was Beatrice Nellie Gannaway.

There is a certain irony in an interview with McGough (described as 'George M. McGough') carried in *The New York Times* on 20 April 1912 before his return to England, where the seaman 'complains that the crew of the *Titanic* were treated as prisoners by the White Star company'.

Irish Survivor's Story
Paddy McGough, an Irish seaman, according to the *Daily Mail*, said no-one was killed in the collision.

'When I left the *Titanic*,' he said, 'she was down to below the forecastle. I saw her back break, and I heard an explosion, either of her main steam-pipe, or of the boilers. I last saw Mr Murdoch, the first officer, when he was lowering No. 15 boat, and keeping back some Italians.

'From the boat deck I distinctly saw the lights of another ship. I saw Captain Smith, at some distance, swimming towards another boat. When they reached out to help him, he shouted at them – "Look after yourselves men. Don't mind me. God bless you." Then he threw up his hand and disappeared.'

(*Irish Independent*, 30 April 1912)

In an account reported by the *Irish News* on 20 May 1912, First-Class passenger May Futrelle declared:

One of the stewards, who relieved a sailor at the oar, couldn't row … I asked, not in anger, but in a sort of wonder, 'Why is that man in this boat?'

The Irish sailor, mistaking my meaning, I suppose, said: 'Madam, he wants to save his life as much as you do yours.'

Bertha Watt, writing in her Jefferson High School newspaper in 1917, said: 'The fellow at the tiller was an Irishman. Paddy had no authority, he was just a deckhand.'

Crewman George Kemish, in a letter of June 1955, wrote:

> I saw how desperate the situation was by now, all boats were away. We had been throwing deckchairs and anything movable overboard. I took a flying leap intending to grab the dangling boat falls and slither down them to the water, but I missed them. I swam until I got aboard that No. 9 or No. 11 boat, I don't know to this day what boat it was.
>
> A deck hand named Paddy McGough took charge of her. She was overloaded dangerously. Picking up one or two more persons from the water would probably have meant drowning about 80. That was the number in her …
>
> Well we drifted about until it started getting daylight. We could just see the berg. It had drifted on to the skyline with the help of the bump we gave it. There was a low icefield practically all round us. Paddy McGough suddenly gave a great shout – 'Let us all pray to God, for there is a ship on the horizon and 'tis making for us.' Some of our crowd had already passed out but those who were still able did pray and cry. The old SS *Carpathia* picked us up about 7 a.m.

A manifest for the *Lapland*, arriving at New York from Antwerp on 15 January 1920, names seaman George McGough, born at Duncannon, with an address at 15 St George Street, Southampton – the same street address he gave on the *Titanic*. This was the same vessel on which he returned from New York in 1912. Perhaps because of his manslaughter conviction, he was not called to give evidence at either the American or British *Titanic* inquiries.

Later, in 1920, George McGough arrived as a crewman on the *Gothland* from La Coruña, Spain, and in December set foot in Seattle, Washington, from the *Steel Ranger*. On 1 April 1921, he was aboard the Atlantic transport liner *Minnekahda*, plying between Boston and New York. A year later, he sailed into New York aboard the *Oropesa* from Southampton. This time the Irishman is noted as having a scar on his cheek. He was last seen on a crew list for the *Corbis*, arriving in New York from Tampico, Mexico, in 1924. McGough was aged 50, Irish by race, an able seaman. But the entry has a line through it, striking it out. A note reads: 'Deserted, Lisbon, October 19'.

ALFRED MIDDLETON (27) LOST

Assistant Electrician.
From: Ballisodare East, County Sligo.

Alfred spiritedly climbed access ladders inside the fourth, or aftermost, funnel in order to get a bird's eye view of the *Titanic* leaving Southampton on her maiden voyage, according to a letter home by his fellow assistant electrician Albert George Ervine. They were in no danger; the last funnel was for ventilation only. But it gave the *Titanic* symmetry and implied superiority over three-funnel steamers.

Someone was to repeat the funnel-climbing trick at Queenstown – poking a head above the parapet to watch the tenders bringing out steerage emigrants and their baggage. A few of those on the *Titanic's* decks noticed the figure, and it gave watching passengers quite a shock, for it must have appeared like a sweep popping out from the top of a chimney. Many fancied, perhaps psychologically influenced by the smokestack association, that the face was 'blackened'. They thought it was a daring stoker. Others commented that it was a bad omen. The face of a man wearing a flat cap does indeed appear at the top of the fourth funnel in a picture taken from the approaching tender *America* by a Mr Whyte of Queenstown.

Alfred Pirrie Middleton was the son of the local corn and flour-mill manager in Ballisodare, County Sligo. His father was Adam John Middleton, married to Annie, and Alfred grew up as one of three surviving sons from five births. His brother Bruce was two years older, while the youngest boy, born in 1900, gloried in the name of Wilbraham. The family were of the Plymouth Brethren sect – meaning Alfred was the same religion as his funnel-grappling friend, Albert Ervine. They may have known each other for some time.

Alfred went to intermediate school in Sligo and then went to Glasgow to train as an electrician. He later returned to Ireland as an electrical supervisor with the Scottish firm of Telford, Grier & Mackay. The 1911 census finds him a boarder in the Wilson household in 37 Lomond Avenue, Belfast, and also in digs at this address is Percy Scott, a fellow electrician, with whom he went to school. Middleton had by now joined Harland & Wolff, but the lure of adventure was too much to stay a landlubber and he signed aboard the White Star Line's *Demosthenes* for its maiden voyage to Brisbane, Australia, in August 1911.

Returning to duties alongside young Ervine in H&W, he itched for another opportunity to get away, and found it when the *Titanic* needed crew.

THOMAS MORGAN (26) LOST

Fireman.
From: Limerick.
16 Spa Road, Southampton.

Little is known about Morgan, apart from his Limerick allegiance. His body was recovered from the sea by the search vessel *MacKay-Bennett*, captained by F. H. Larnder.

No. 302. Male. Estimated age, 26. Hair Brown. Scar on Left Wrist.
Clothing – Blue coat; dark pants; no boots or socks.
Effects – Pocketbook with crucifix; Union book and discharge A book.
Fireman. Name – Thomas Morgan, Spar Tavern, Spar Road, Southampton.

Identified as a Catholic by his crucifix, Morgan was buried in Mount Olivet Catholic Cemetery in Halifax on 8 May 1912. He was actually a lodger at Mrs Steindel's Spa Tavern in Spa Road (not 'Spar'), Southampton.

From the Mansion House *Titanic* relief fund booklet, March 1913:

Case no. 191. Morgan, sister. Grant £25.

JOE MULHOLLAND (29) QUIT AT SOUTHAMPTON

Fireman.
From: Upton Street, Belfast.

Joe Mulholland wasn't on board the *Titanic* on the maiden voyage proper, but did escort the ship from Belfast to Southampton. His story, told on the fiftieth anniversary of the sinking, highlights long-rumoured stories of anti-Catholic sentiment among some members of crew and it points to the character of Thomas Andrews, shipbuilder.

His account of being aboard is true: his name appears in the ship's articles for the preliminary run to Southampton. He was the second-last man signed on, joining on 2 April 1912, the very day of the voyage. His stated last ship was the *Troutpool*. This was a much bigger fish.

Titanic: when his cat walked off, so did Joe
Old-time seamen are notoriously superstitious and 79-year-old Joseph Mulholland, of Upton St., Belfast, who sailed from Belfast in the *Titanic* on the first leg of her ill-fated maiden voyage, can still recall his feelings as he stoked down in the engine-room of the ship which Belfast boasted was 'unsinkable'.

Silver haired and vigorous despite his great age and a lifetime at sea, from square rigged grain ships on the Australian run to White Star liners on the Atlantic, 'Big Joe' Mulholland says:

'There was something about that ship I did not like and I was glad to lift my old bag and bid goodbye to my shipmates, like Hughie Fitzpatrick and "Pancake" Baker, when she arrived at Southampton. Hughie offered me a job as storekeeper on the trip across the Atlantic, but I did not accept. Hughie was lost when she hit the iceberg, but "Pancake" was picked up and I met him years later at La Plata.'

A Stray Cat
Big Joe is still fond of cats and perhaps he has reason. He recalls that on his way down to the *Titanic* before she set sail from Belfast with bands playing and crowds cheering, he

took pity on a stray cat which was about to have kittens. He brought the cat aboard and put her in a wooden box down in the stoke hold.

At Southampton, when he was ruminating whether to take on the job of storekeeper on the trip or sign off, another seaman called him over and said: 'Look Big Joe. There's your cat taking its kittens down the gang-plank.'

Joe said 'that settled it. I went and got my bag and that's the last I saw of the *Titanic*.'

Pride of Belfast

But there was plenty of drama on the journey down the Irish Sea as the great ship – the pride of the Belfast shipyard – headed for Southampton to take on board its complement of passengers, a cross-section of the social registers of England and America.

In Belfast in those days it was hard to get an experienced stokehold staff. Joe Mulholland said they scoured the Salvation Army hostel, the dockside and eventually got together a scratch team ranging from 'milk-men to dockers'.

'I had to mind six stokeholds, and the chief engineer told me to get the men to break up the big clinkers. I told them, but they must have lifted up the covers and kicked the clinkers down and affected the hydraulic pumps because the seas came back and we were soon standing up to our thighs in water. A young whippersnapper of an engineer came galloping up and he gave off something shocking. We got the water away, but I did not fancy that young fellow.'

Filthy slogans

Joe recalls a meeting in the engine room with Thomas Andrews, the designer of the ship, director of Harland and Wolff's, and a member of the noted Comber (County Down) family.

'I knew Mr Andrews because I often stoked ships on their trials after they were launched at Belfast. He came down to me and pointed to some of the insulting slogans about the Pope which had been chalked up on the smoke-box. Some of them were filthy and I had already heard about similar slogans which had been painted on the hull before the *Titanic* was launched.

'Mr Andrews said, "Do you know anything about these slogans?"

'I did not, so he said "They are disgusting" and went off and returned with some sailors and had them removed.

'Mr Andrews was a very decent man. He went down with the ship. Young Harland afterwards married his widow.'

Speed record

Joe has his own theory about the disaster. 'I was never in deep water in a White Star liner that we were not trying to win the blue ribbon for speed. That was the cause of the disaster. They were on a Northerly course to break the record for the Atlantic crossing.

'Any seaman can smell the ice from miles away, but instead of changing course South they kept on and hit that berg. The blue ribbon was the cause of the disaster and all those folk losing their lives.'

Old Joe was taken to see the premiere of the film *A Night to Remember* because he helped James McQuitty [*sic*] and his advisers with details for the production. He sat in the front row with the Belfast Lord Mayor.

What did he think of the film? 'Not much,' he said. 'It would make all the old sailors turn in their graves. The tiny crew they showed in the engine-room would remind you of a coal-boat.'

(*Sunday Independent*, 15 April 1962)

A 30-year-old fireman, John Baker, was on board for the Belfast–Southampton run, but the name does not appear on the crew list for the maiden voyage proper, indicating that he too signed off rather than remaining on board to be subsequently 'picked up'. Hughie Fitzpatrick, junior boiler-maker, was indeed lost. So too were all twelve men who served as junior storekeepers – Mulholland's offered job.

JOHN O'CONNOR (25) SAVED

Trimmer.
From: Wexford?
9 Tower Place, Bargate Street, Southampton.

One of twelve substitutes engaged on board the *Titanic*, O'Connor could have lost his life because of a split-second decision made by other men in allowing a train to go by before they crossed the road.

Jack Podesta, a fireman, much later told the *Southern Daily Echo* of Southampton that he had been among a large number of crew enjoying a last drink on shore in The Grapes public house before final muster and the ship's sailing. The crowd steadily thinned out – until an urgent effort to board the *Titanic* was called for:

Six of us left about ten minutes to twelve and got well into the docks and towards the vessel. With me and my mate were three brothers named Slade. We were at the top of the main board and a passenger train was approaching us from another part of the docks.

I heard the Slades say, 'Oh let the train go by', but Nutbean and myself crossed over and managed to board the liner. Being a rather long train, by the time it passed, the Slades were too late, the gangway was down – leaving them behind.

A party of substitutes were waiting aboard the *Titanic* for just such an opportunity. When Slade and others failed to board, twelve stand-by workers were taken on, including O'Connor. He must have savoured his good fortune.

Jack Podesta found himself working alongside new recruit O'Connor, whose work as a trimmer involved keeping the coals level in the boilers. And Podesta told the *Southampton Echo* on 27 May 1968 that O'Connor managed to escape from the *Titanic*. He stated that among survivors picked up from a raft, 'shivering terribly with cold', were two of his stokehold colleagues. 'My mate and I gave them blankets and rubbed their legs to start up their circulation. Their names were John Connor and Wally Hurst.'

John O'Connor was taken on board the *Carpathia*, where he recovered fully from the ravages of exposure. He returned to England on the SS *Lapland* and signed the crew discharge book on 30 April 1912. O'Connor's birthplace was entered as Southampton.

The *Enniscorthy Echo* reported on 20 April 1912:

> It is also stated that a sailor named Connors, from Coolcots (County Wexford) was on board the *Titanic*, but this report is not verified.

There was no 'Connors' on the *Titanic*. The only other similar name was Thomas O'Connor, a bedroom steward from Linacre Lane, Liverpool, who was lost.

WILLIAM F. N. O'LOUGHLIN (62) LOST

Senior Surgeon.
From: Nelson Street, Tralee, County Kerry.
Polygon House, Southampton.

Dr William Francis Norman O'Loughlin was very proud of his roots in Tralee, County Kerry, and retained his fondness for his birthplace through four decades at sea. In the ship's articles for the *Titanic* he inscribed his home town name in the space for place of origin, a piece of form-filling that didn't detain many others who were content to indicate 'Soton' or 'Hants', whether they came from Southampton or not.

The second son of William O'Loughlin Snr, he was a tender 16 years of age when he moved to Dublin to become a student at the Catholic University. He lived in a collegiate house on St Stephen's Green where his uncle was the reverend Dean.

> For three years he attended lectures regularly at the school, and in 1869 he had completed a distinguished course. But the Catholic university had neither public endowment nor even a charter enabling her to confer degrees. O'Loughlin then could obtain no degree from his own university. To Trinity College he would not go, and consequently, like many another distinguished Catholic student of those days, he obtained no university degree but only a licence.
>
> (*Irish News*, 21 May 1912)

O'Loughlin spent a short time thereafter working in a dispensary medical service in Clane, County Kildare, before leaving his native land. He joined the White Star Line when he was just 21.

He was described in the *New York Herald* as 'a most attractive character, a great lover of the sea, an affable man of most kindly and genial disposition', and as 'the strongest personal friend of every officer and seaman he ever left a port with. He would give his last dollar to charity.' He had friends in America, who established a pathological laboratory after his death as a tribute to his memory at St Vincent's Hospital, the same clinic that treated so many survivors of the wreck. He was said to have had 'many friends in Ireland, England and France', who were invited to support the project.

Edward C. Titus, Medical Director of the White Star Line, said simply that the doctor was 'the finest man that I have ever known'. Titus added, in the report carried by the *New York Herald* on 22 April 1912:

Once recently I said to him that as he was getting on in years, he ought to make a will and leave directions for his burial, as he had no kith or kin. He replied that the only way he wanted to be buried was to be placed in a sack and buried at sea.

In fact O'Loughlin had made a will, drawing it up during a brief trip home to Dublin a few years earlier. It was probated on 1 August 1912. The venerable surgeon, 'the doyen of the White Star service', according to *The Cork Examiner*, left a substantial £2,412 – about twice Captain Smith's annual salary, for instance – in spite of his reputation for giving away his last dollar. Many of the Irish Third-Class passengers left assets worth only £10, according to legal documents. By comparison, the ship's builder, Thomas Andrews, left more than £10,000. These values can certainly be scaled up 100-fold and more in order to attempt a present-day understanding of their value.

Money and value are indeed relative, particularly at 2 a.m. in the mid-Atlantic when the last boats are loading. Multi-millionaires stood by with paupers on the decks of the *Titanic* to submit to what God had ordained. John Jacob Astor's body was found with $2,440 in notes, £225 sterling, gold and diamond cufflinks and a diamond ring. It was worth nothing to him.

For Dr O'Loughlin it appears that the most valuable thing at this critical hour was a tot of whiskey. He was seen rummaging below decks close to the end by baker John Joughin who himself was after the hard stuff, and felt O'Loughlin was doing likewise.

O'Loughlin met stewardess Mary Sloan during the night. She later described him as 'a fine old man, and a great favourite with all on board'. Some survivors talk of O'Loughlin soothing the panicked and helping all he could, directing women to the boats. Irene Harris, the widow of theatre impresario Henry B. Harris, claimed she saw the doctor when she crossed with her husband from starboard to port, walking through the bridge area normally forbidden to passengers.

The Captain was standing with Major Archibald Butt and the little doctor. I saw the clock.

I can still see it with its hands pointing to 2.20. The captain looked amazed when he saw me: 'My God, woman, why aren't you in a lifeboat?' I kept repeating, 'I won't leave my husband. I won't leave my husband.' The little doctor said, 'Isn't she a brick?' to which the Captain replied: 'She's a little fool.'

(*Liberty Magazine*, 23 April 1932)

Finally O'Loughlin is seen with his medical colleague John Edward Simpson from Belfast, his fellow countryman Purser Hugh McElroy, and his assistant purser, standing on deck in an apparently relaxed and resigned mood. Some reports say O'Loughlin was casually swinging a lifejacket. 'I don't think I'll need to put this on,' he said. His desired burial at sea was only minutes away. The lifejacket, he had decided, had no value. Simpson then made a joke to Second Officer Charles Lightoller, who was feverishly working at filling the last boat and who had taken off his coat. He asked if he was too warm in the freezing conditions. It seems to have lightened the mood. Lightoller came over and the senior crewmembers all shook hands and said goodbye.

'As far as we can ascertain from the available accounts of the disaster,' a Fr Walsh told O'Loughlin's Requiem Mass at the University Church in St Stephen's Green in May 1912, 'his characteristic gentleness and philanthropy forsook him not in that last supreme crisis.'

He loved the sea. And the sea took him to her bosom.

Tralee man lost
Dr. Wm. F. N. O'Loughlin, the senior surgeon of the *Titanic*, and who went down with that great steamer on the morning of the 15th inst., was born in Tralee.

He was the second son of the late Mr William O'Loughlin, and some of the older inhabitants may (says the *Kerry Post*) remember his grandfather, the late Mr Benjamin Mathews, of Nelson Street, Tralee.

(*Limerick Chronicle*, 25 April 1912)

During a talk with me in the South Western Hotel he did tell me that he was tired at this time of life to be changing from one ship to another. When he mentioned this to Captain Smith the latter chided him for being lazy and told him to pack up and come with him. So fate decreed that Billy should go on the *Titanic* and I to the *Olympic*.

(Dr J. C. H. Beaumont, *Ships and People*, 1927)

Dr O'Loughlin was 62 years old and was born in Naase [*sic*], County Kerry. He was on the *Britannic* in 1887 when she rammed the steamship *Adriatic*.

(*Irish American*, 27 April 1912)

Dr O'Loughlin dined alone with the Chairman and Managing Director of the White Star Line, J. Bruce Ismay, on the night the *Titanic* sank. He mentioned to Ismay that the vessel had 'turned the corner', meaning it had changed course from a south-westerly track to steer west and slightly north towards New York. Ismay realised the course would put them directly headed towards field ice the *Titanic* had been warned about. The two men might even have discussed it. But Ismay presumably did not tell the White Star's surgeon of forty years that he had in his pocket an ice warning from another White Star ship, the *Baltic*, which had been wordlessly handed to him just before lunch by Captain Smith.

MICHAEL ROGERS (24) LOST

Steward.
From: Aughrim Street, Dublin.
13 Green Hill Avenue, Winchester.

The 1911 census shows Michael Rogers residing at the same address he gave in the *Titanic*, when signing on as 'M. Rogers'. Both the ship's manifest and the census confirm him to be from Dublin, the latter showing his occupation as 'steward at sea'.

Rogers had been staying with Dublin-born Ann Harris, her husband Tom (a night-watchman in a prison) and their five children. He was engaged to one of the Harris daughters. Son Edward Harris, 18, was a pantryman on the *Titanic* and also died. Michael had previously served on the *Olympic* and the *Adriatic*, and was reported as 'steward to the Marconi department of the *Titanic*'.

KATE WALSH (32) LOST

Stewardess.
From: Clonmel, County Tipperary.
57 Church Road, Woolston, Southampton.

Kate Walsh, formerly living in College Street, Clonmel, and afterwards married to a man named Roche, at one time storekeeper in Clonmel Asylum.
(*Clonmel Chronicle*, 19 April 1912)

I had just climbed into my berth when a stewardess came in. She was a sweet woman who had been very kind to me. I take this opportunity to thank her, for I shall never see her again. She went down with the *Titanic*.

'Do you know where we are?' she said pleasantly. 'We are in what is called the Devil's Hole.'

'What does that mean?' I asked.

'That is a dangerous part of the ocean,' she answered. 'Many accidents have happened near there. They say that icebergs drift down as far as this. It's getting to be very cold on deck, so perhaps there is ice around us now.' She left the cabin and I soon dropped off to sleep, her talk of icebergs had not frightened me, but it shows that the crew were awake to the danger.

(Charlotte Collyer, *Semi Monthly Magazine*, May 1912)

Kay Walsh was the only one out of eighteen stewardesses to die in the disaster. She appears to have been assigned to Second Class.

> Second-Class passenger Selina Rogers remembered: 'We had a very nice stewardess and steward whose names were Miss Walsh and Mr Petty. I was feeling very sick. The stewardess was very kind and brought me a glass of milk.'
> (*Titanic Voices*, 1997, Hyslop, Forsyth & Jemima)

JAMES B. WILLIAMSON (36) LOST

Postal Sorter, transatlantic post office.
From: Botanic Road, Dublin.

An extra-large postcard of the *Titanic* sent by James Williamson to his girlfriend just before the ship sailed fetched a hammer price of £11,500 in September 2002. The souvenir, known as a bookpost, was intended as a token of affection but instead became a symbol of wretched hopes. It proved especially valuable at auction because Williamson worked in the RMS *Titanic*'s transatlantic post office and the card carries the vessel's unique No. 7 postmark.

Williamson was from Botanic Road, Drumcondra, Dublin, and had just transferred to his post with five other sea post officers, all of whom were lost despite their heroic efforts to save the flooded mails. He met the young English beauty Gladys Copeland through her father, who operated the Queensland Hotel in Southampton. Gladys had promised him a kiss if he would provide her with a *Titanic* token before he sailed. Williamson wrote on the card: '*George wanted me to wait last night for you to fulfil your promise. This is a souvenir of* Titanic*'s maiden voyage.*' He never collected on the pledge, but the postal sorter had unwittingly just contributed to philatelic history himself.

The mailroom on the *Titanic* was on the starboard side of the Orlop deck, forward of boiler room six, and was one of the first places flooded. The water roared in and the shocked officials suddenly realised they had to get out. Heroically, they lugged large sacks stuffed with some of the ship's 500,000-plus pieces of mail up the ladder to the next level, F deck, where the post office proper was. Struggling through knee-level water, they tried to save registered mail first. But there was no going back for any more. From the deck above, they watched in alarm as water below began swallowing 3,418 mail bags.

Ten minutes after the collision, Fourth Officer Joseph Boxhall was at the post office, learning from John Jago Smith the grim severity of the problem. There were five officials of the sea post office on board the vessel, three American and two from the British side. Not one was saved.

Another Dublin man engaged on the *Titanic* is a postal official – Mr J. Williamson – who up to three years ago was employed as a sorter in the Dublin GPO. He was subsequently transferred to the Southampton GPO.

(*Irish Independent*, 17 April 1912)

The 1901 census confirms that Williamson was a sorter at the GPO in Dublin, which was to become the centrepiece of the Easter Rising just four years after the *Titanic* sank. He was then living at 2 Downham Villas on the northside of the city, the only son (among four daughters) of his Scots Presbyterian mother, a widow.

Postal clerks all drowned
Reuter's Cablegram Washington, Saturday
Of the five postal clerks employed on the *Titanic*, two were from the other side, namely respectively E. D. Williamson (Dublin) and Jago Smith. According to official advices received from the Postmaster-General here, all five completely disregarded their own safety when the vessel struck, and began to carry 200 sacks of registered mail to the upper deck, thinking they might be saved. As the situation became more desperate, they appealed to the stewards to assist them, and continued their work to the last. Every one of them was lost.

(*Irish Independent*, 22 April 1912)

Irish postal official
In reference to the postal official, Mr James B. Williamson, it should have been stated that he was unmarried, and that his widowed mother and sisters live at Botanic road, Glasnevin, Dublin.

(*The Irish Times*, 18 April 1912)

It appears that Fr Francis Browne, the renowned photographer of the *Titanic*, met Williamson. He wrote that as he passed down the gangplank in Cobh to leave the liner – with mailbags being taken on board – he encountered Purser McElroy 'and Mr Nicholson, head of the mail department'. The only Nicholson on board was a passenger, and the five postal officials were named March, Gwinn, Woody, Smith – and Williamson. Fr Browne, not yet a priest, wrote in the 1912 edition of the school annual *The Belvederian* that he said to the pair: 'Goodbye. I will give you copies of my photos when you come again. Pleasant voyage.'

He continued: 'And so they went. They never came back, one dying at his post far down in the heart of the ship as he strove to save the more precious portion of his charge, the other calmly facing death as he strove to reassure the terror-stricken, and to render up the jewels given to his keeping.'

The *Irish Independent*, printing a picture of Williamson on 8 May 1912, also referred to his being 'in charge of the mails on the *Titanic*', and to his mother receiving a handwritten letter of sympathy from the Lord Lieutenant, the Earl of Aberdeen:

Viceroy and Dublin victim
His Excellency the Lord Lieutenant has written an autograph letter to Mrs Williamson, Botanic road, Dublin, mother of Mr J. B. Williamson, who was one of those in charge of the mails on the *Titanic* and who perished in the disaster, expressing deep sympathy on behalf of Lady Aberdeen and himself.

'It is a matter of touching interest,' said his Excellency, 'to learn that as a mark of special confidence and approval, your son was selected for duty on the *Titanic* and that you have now received testimony that your son, after having, in conjunction with his brave colleagues, made every effort for the safety of the mails, devoted himself to the assistance of the women and children.

'And so his name is securely placed in the illustrious and imperishable roll of fame for those, who, under the supreme test of an appalling experience, manifested calmness, fortitude and unselfish care for others, thus bequeathing lasting solace for sorrowing friends, and an inspiring example to mankind.'

(*Irish Independent*, 6 May 1912)

All ranks of the Southampton postal staff attended a memorial service at St Peter's church yesterday in memory of their colleagues, Messrs Smith and Williamson, of the Sea Post Service, who went down with the *Titanic*.

(*Daily Sketch*, 6 May 1912)

WILLIAMSON – 15 April 1912, lost at sea in SS *Titanic*, James Bertram Williamson, postal official, Southampton, only surviving son of Eleanor G. Williamson, 11 Botanic Road, Dublin, and the late David Wallace Williamson; deeply mourned by his sorrowing mother and sisters.

(*Cork Constitution*, 25 April 1912)

The late Mr Williamson
A sympathetic reference to the late Mr J. B. Williamson, who was employed in the post office on the *Titanic*, appears in the *Irish Postal and Telegraph Guardian*.

Mr Williamson began his career in Dublin eighteen years ago. His ambition was to get on the sea post office staff, and with this end in view he obtained a transfer to Southampton and his wishes were granted.

He was in Dublin last March on a few weeks' leave, and spoke enthusiastically of his work and adventures. Poor Williamson died at his post. It will be remembered that one of the officers of the *Titanic* stated that when he visited the mailroom, whose floor was covered with water, he found the clerks removing the registered portion of the mail to drier surroundings.

(*Weekly Freeman*, 8 June 1912)

Questions in parliament
Loss of the Steamship *Titanic*
Mr J. P. Farrell: I beg to ask the Postmaster General whether his attention has been called to the case of James B. Williamson, a native of Dublin, who joined the sea-going post office at Southampton on 10th April 1911, and was lost in the *Titanic* wreck on 15th April 1912; whether he is aware that this young man was the sole support of his mother and

three young sisters; whether he is aware that for one year in this service he contributed £90 towards their support; and whether, under the circumstances, a bulk sum of £150 is all that is proposed to give his widowed mother in compensation for the loss of such a son who in one year nearly gave that amount of his earnings?

Mr Herbert Samuel: I am aware of the circumstances of this sad case and regard it with much sympathy. The sum specified by the honourable member is that due to the executors of the late Mr Williamson under the Superannuation Act of 1909, and is quite apart from any question of compensation for his loss. That question is complicated by unexpected legal difficulties, which have rendered it necessary to consult the Law Officers of the Crown. I regret, therefore, that at the present moment I am unable to give a more specific answer.

(*Longford Leader*, 20 July 1912)

Eleanor Grace Williamson, widow, of 11 Botanic Road, backed in surety by her daughter Eleanor, a spinster and railway clerk, later sought administration of the estate of James Bertram Williamson, 'Sorter in the Sea Post Office aboard the *Titanic*'. She declared that she was the lawful next-of-kin of her son, and agreed to pay his just due debts, certifying that his personal estate was worth £223. The family's solicitor was Gerald Byron of 7 Lr Ormond Quay, Dublin.

Eleanor herself did not long outlast the crushing heartbreak of losing her only son, an unfairness piled on top of the death of her husband. She died on 6 July 1913 at the Adelaide Hospital. Her estate amounted to £851 7s.

A memorial plaque was erected by lamenting colleagues to the Dublin sorter aboard the *Titanic*. It is found in the Abbey Presbyterian Church on Parnell Square, Dublin, also known as Findlater's Church:

To the Glory of God and in Memory of
James B. Williamson
Of the Transatlantic Post Office
Who died on duty in the foundering
of the SS 'Titanic' April 15th 1912

By this tablet the members of
the Postal and Telegraph Services
Record their Deep Sorrow at his death.

A RELATED INCIDENT

TRAGIC AFFAIR AT THE CURRAGH

Castlebar Man's Brother Lost on Titanic

Inquest into the death of Private John T. Young of the Connaught Rangers.

Sergeant Thomas Duffy told the inquest that the deceased was 33 and unmarried. He had been corporal, but had been reduced to private on the 28th March last.

As store man, the deceased slept in the store by himself, and on entering yesterday a witness found him lying on his right side about 18 feet from the bed.

He saw the carbine examined that morning and an empty cartridge extracted from the bore of the rifle. Deceased had been worried about a brother of his who was on the *Titanic* and who had, he believed, been drowned.

Sergeant John Clinton RIC said the deceased's body was very much stained with blood. Having pulled the trigger, the deceased must have fallen back and then got off the bed.

The jury found that the deceased died from gunshot wounds, self-inflicted, while of unsound mind. The deceased is a native of Castlebar.

(*Western People*, 18 May 1912)

Drowned fireman Francis Young of Russell Street, Southampton, was the only man with his surname on board. His picture (above) appeared in the *Daily Sketch*, of 22 April 1912. Recent research indicates, however, that he had been born in Southampton and had no connection at all with Mayo. Therefore the soldier from Castlebar had deceived himself about his brother being lost on the *Titanic*.

Private John Young's family lived at 11 Ellison Street, Castlebar, County Mayo. William Young and his wife, Emily, had had ten children, nine of whom lived. They had been married for 34 years. Son Francis appears to have been working as a seafarer from English ports, but was not on the maiden voyage.

In the 1911 census, as in previous population snapshots, Francis James Young of the *Titanic* disaster and of Russell Street, Southampton, is shown as having been born locally. His parents were Frank and Louisa, the former also a seafarer. Son Francis married Amy White at Southampton in 1901 and died in the North Atlantic at the age of 33.

Master's Name.	Registered Tonnage.	Aggregate Number of superficial feet in the several compartments set apart for Passengers, other than Cabin Passengers.	Total Number of Statute Adults, exclusive of Master, Crew, and Cabin Passengers which the Ship can legally carry.	Where Bound.
E J Smith	21831	26992	1735	New York

...rd this Ship are sufficient, according to the requirements of the Merchant Shipp...

...Statute Adults, for a voyage of _____17_____ days.

(Signature) _Edw J Smith_

(stamp: BOARD OF TRADE, SURVEYORS' OFFICE · No. 408 · 13 APR. 1912 · QUEENSTOWN.)

PASSENGERS EMBARKED AT THE PORT OF _Queenstown_

Detail of final clearance papers, with Captain Smith's last signature and the stamp of the Board of Trade Surveyors' Office at Queenstown, dated and filed two days after Titanic's *call.*

The offices of local agents James Scott & Company in a contemporary postcard. The White Star burgee, or swallowtail flag, is flown. St Colman's Cathedral had no spire in 1912. In the left foreground is 'Heartbreak Pier,' the jetty for embarkation of the tenders, some of whose rotting timbers can still be seen a century later.

NON-IRISH PASSENGERS EMBARKED AT QUEENSTOWN

FIRST-CLASS PASSENGERS EMBARKED AT QUEENSTOWN

WILLIAM EDWARD MINAHAN (44) LOST
LILLIAN MINAHAN (37) SAVED
DAISY (IDA) MINAHAN (33) SAVED

Only three First-Class passengers went aboard the *Titanic* at Queenstown. They were members of the first-generation Irish family called the Minahans. Dr William Edward Minahan was a 44-year-old physician with a practice at Fund Du Lac, Wisconsin. His wife, Lillian, was 37 years old and was formerly an artist's muse. William was her second husband. Also travelling with them was William's sister, Daisy Minahan, aged 33, from Green Bay, Wisconsin.

William and Daisy were both children of William Burke Minahan and Mary Shaughnessy, who had been childhood sweethearts from the village of Adare, County Limerick, before emigrating to a new life in America in the lean years after the Great Famine. The trio had been in Ireland on a sightseeing tour, and had stayed at the Imperial Hotel in Cork just prior to making the short journey to Queenstown and the luxury vessel that was supposed to convey them back to America. William lost his life in the ensuing tragedy. Lillian and Daisy were saved in lifeboat No. 14, launched from the port side.

They shared cabin C-78, dead amidships on the port side. Daisy told how she and her brother and his wife went to dinner at the Café Parisien on B deck at 7.15 p.m. on Sunday night, before the collision. When they entered a party of a dozen men and three women were already enjoying themselves at another table. The company included the Wideners, Major Archibald Butt (President Taft's personal aide-de-camp) and Captain Edward John Smith. Daisy said Captain Smith remained at the gathering, drinking coffee, for more than two hours, finally bidding goodnight between 9.25 and 9.45 p.m. William Minahan also suggested going to bed at this time, but was persuaded to remain on for one more piece of music from the ship's orchestra. The *Tales of Hoffman* was played and the Minahans retired.

Daisy told in an affidavit to the US inquiry what happened next:

I was awakened by the crying of a woman in the passageway. I roused my brother and his wife, and we began at once to dress. No one came to give us warning. We spent five minutes in dressing and went on deck to the port side. The frightful slant of the deck toward the bow of the boat gave us our first thought of danger.

An officer came and commanded all women to follow, and he led us to the boat deck on the starboard side. He told us there was no danger, but to get into a lifeboat as a precaution only. After making three attempts to get into boats, we succeeded in getting into lifeboat No. 14. The crowd surging around the boats was getting unruly.

Officers were yelling and cursing at men to stand back and let the women get into the boats. In going from one lifeboat to another we stumbled over huge piles of bread lying on the deck.

When the lifeboat was filled there were no seamen to man it. The officer in command on No. 14 called for volunteers in the crowd who could row. Six men offered to go. At times when we were being lowered we were at an angle of 45 degrees and expected to be thrown into the sea.

As we reached the level of each deck, men jumped into the boat until the officer threatened to shoot the next man who jumped. We landed in the sea and rowed to a safe distance from the sinking ship. The officer counted our number and found us to be 48. The officer commanded everyone to feel in the bottom of the boat for a light. We found none. Nor was there bread or water in the boat. The officer, whose name I learned afterwards to be Lowe, was continually making remarks such as, 'A good song to sing would be, *Throw Out the Lifeline*', and 'I think the best thing for you women to do is take a nap.'

The *Titanic* was fast sinking. After she went down the cries were horrible. This was at 2.20 a.m. by a man's watch who stood next to me.

Daisy Minahan

At this time three other boats and ours kept together by being tied to each other. The cries continued to come over the water. Some of the women implored Officer Lowe, of No. 14, to divide his passengers among the three other boats and go back to rescue. His first answer to those requests was, 'You ought to be damn glad you are here and have got your own life.'

After some time he was persuaded to do as he was asked. As I came up to him to be transferred to the other boat he said, 'Jump, God damn you, jump!' I had showed no hesitancy and was waiting only my turn. He had been so blasphemous during the two hours we were in his boat that the women at my end of the boat all thought he was under the influence of liquor.

Then he took all of the men who had rowed No. 14, together with the men from the other boats, and went back to the scene of the wreck. We were left with a steward and a stoker to row our boat, which was crowded. The steward did his best, but the stoker refused at first to row, but finally helped two women, who were the only ones pulling on that side. It was just 4 o'clock when we sighted the *Carpathia*, and we were three hours getting to her.

On the *Carpathia* we were treated with every kindness and given every comfort possible.

It is remarkable that Daisy makes mention nowhere in her account of what became of her brother William, who evidently accepted his fate. The sea yielded up his corpse nine days later:

No. 230. Male. Estimated Age: 60. Hair, Grey.
Clothing – Black suit and overcoat.
Effects – Pocketbook; papers; gold watch, 'Dr W.E. Minahan'; keys; knife; fountain pen; clinical thermometer; memo book; tie pin; diamond ring; gold cuff link; nickel watch; comb; check book; American Express; $380; 1 collar button; £16 10s. in gold; 14 shillings; nail clipper.
Name – Dr W.E. Minahan.

William's body was brought to the Morgue in Halifax by the rescue vessel *MacKay-Bennett* and later buried in his native Wisconsin.

Gypsy told doctor he would lose life in a sea disaster
Fond du Lac, Wis., 17 April – Dr William Minahan, the Fond du Lac surgeon who met his death in the *Titanic*, was told five years ago by a soothsayer that he would meet his end in a marine disaster.

Minahan with a number of friends visited a gypsy camp and all had their fortunes told. The fortune teller told Dr Minahan he would die while on a steamer on his second trip abroad.

The physician went to Europe shortly after, spending a year there in medical research. Last January he went again. Friends joked with him about the prediction of death made by the fortune teller, but he ridiculed the idea. However he arranged all his affairs before he went, taking his wife and sister with him.

He carried life insurance to the amount of $100,000 and $60,000 accident insurance. He was one of the foremost surgeons in Wisconsin.

(*Denver Post*, 17 April 1912)

Incredibly, shortly after the discovery of the *Titanic* wreck by Dr Robert Ballard in 1985, cultists broke into the Minahan mausoleum and stole his skull. The grotesque trophy was later recovered by police and reinterred in solemn ceremony.

After the *Titanic*, Daisy Minahan survived just another seven years. She died at the age of 40 on 30 April 1919 – and her officially certified cause of death was chronic TB.

Lillian Minahan, William's widow, lived for another half century, dying at the age of 86, after a total of four husbands, on 13 January 1962.

Dr William Minahan

SECOND-CLASS PASSENGERS EMBARKED
AT QUEENSTOWN

CHARLES KIRKLAND (71) LOST
Ticket number 219533.

Kirkland was a Free Will Baptist minister, originally from Glasgow, who had taken a sabbatical from his pastoral work in Canada to settle up a relative's estate in Scotland. He was journeying to the United States and Canada, where he intended to visit a married sister in Tuxford, Saskatchewan.

Records of lawsuits against the White Star Line show that Rev. Kirkland had family members living in Old Town, Maine. He had six children, named as sons Algie, Henry and Allen, and daughters Alma Jipson, Myrtle Treadwell and Maude Elden.

HILDA SLAYTER (30) SAVED
Ticket number 234818.

Miss Hilda Slayter, one of the First-Class [*sic*] passengers saved from the *Titanic*, was coming back to Canada on the big liner to marry Mr Reginald Lacon, of the big ranch owners of British Columbia, and son of the late Hon. Mr Lacon.

Miss Slayter, who is a Halifax girl, and a sister of the Captain of Queen Victoria's private yacht, has been in England and France visiting friends, and incidentally collecting a beautiful wedding trousseau, in view of her coming marriage to Mr Lacon. The trousseau will, of course, be lost, but one may well imagine that the coming bride will be none the less welcome for that.

(*Edmonton Daily Bulletin*, 25 April 1912)

Hilda had been in Ireland to visit her younger sister, Margaret, 26, who was married to an army officer and living in Anglesea Street, Clonmel, County Tipperary. She was travelling home to get married herself in Moon Island, British Columbia. Just turned 30, Hilda was the daughter of a wealthy doctor in Halifax, where the bodies of *Titanic* victims were later landed, and where she now lies buried herself. She had been living in Europe for many years and had trained as a professional singer in Italy.

The Cork Examiner reported: 'Miss Hilda Slater, sister of Mrs Haslam, wife of Captain [Gerald Willoughby] Haslam, Royal Irish Regiment, Clonmel, is among the rescued, and a cable announcing the glad tidings has been received by her relatives'. It appears certain that Hilda was saved in boat No. 13 – the same starboard boat entered by Dulwich College teacher Lawrence Beesley, who seems to be describing her in the course of relating a coincidence:

One conversation took place that is, I think, worth repeating. One more proof that the world, after all, is a small place. The ten-month-old baby which was handed down [into lifeboat No. 13] at the last moment was received by a lady next to me – the same who shared her wraps and coats.

The mother had found a place in the middle and was too tightly packed to come through to the child, and so it slept contentedly for about an hour in a stranger's arms; then it began to cry and the temporary nurse said: 'Will you feel down and see if the baby's feet are out of the blanket? I don't know much about babies but I think their feet must be warm.'

Wriggling down as well as I could, I found its toes exposed to the air and wrapped them well up, when it ceased crying at once. It was evidently a successful diagnosis. Having recognised the lady by her voice – it was much too dark to see faces – I said 'Surely you're Miss –?' 'Yes', she replied, 'And you must be Mr Beesley, how curious we should find ourselves in the same boat!'

Remembering that she had joined the boat in Queenstown, I said: 'Do you know Clonmel? A letter from a great friend of mine who is staying there at —— (giving the address) came aboard at Queenstown.'

'Yes, it is my home and I was dining at —— just before I came away.' It seemed that she knew my friend too, and we agreed that of all the places in the world to recognise mutual friends, a crowded lifeboat in mid-ocean at 2 a.m., twelve hundred miles from our destination, was one of the most unexpected.

(Lawrence Beesley, *The Loss of the SS Titanic*, 1912)

Hilda Slayter was duly married on 1 June 1912, and had a baby of her own the following year with the arrival of Reginald William Beecroft Lacon. She died in British Columbia on 12 April 1965, three days before the fifty-third anniversary of the sinking. She was 83.

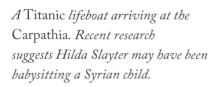

A Titanic *lifeboat arriving at the* Carpathia. *Recent research suggests Hilda Slayter may have been babysitting a Syrian child.*

The Titanic *casting off in Southampton at noon on Wednesday 10 April 1912.*

EPILOGUE

What follows is an extract from Lawrence Beesley's *The Loss of the SS Titanic*, 1912. This piece is an unrivalled evocation of land and sea, what it is like to be on a ship, and the optimism of a journey begun. But it also counterpoints the splendour of the *Titanic* with nature's own prowess, and in reference to the evolving sport of aviation, points to a threat to the golden age of the luxurious liners profoundly more potent than any iceberg or individual disaster.

The coast of Ireland looked very beautiful as we approached Queenstown Harbour, the brilliant morning sun showing up the green hillsides and picking out groups of dwellings dotted here and there above the rugged grey cliffs that fringed the coast. We took on board our pilot, ran slowly towards the harbour with the sounding-line dropped all the time, and came to a stop well out to sea, with out screws churning up the bottom and turning the sea all brown with sand from below. It had seemed to me that the ship stopped rather suddenly, and in my ignorance of the depth of the harbour entrance, that perhaps the sounding-line had revealed a smaller depth than was thought safe for the great size of the *Titanic*; this seemed to be confirmed by the sight of sand churned up from the bottom – but this is mere supposition.

Passengers and mails were put on board from two tenders, and nothing could have given us a better idea of the enormous length and bulk of the *Titanic* than to stand as far astern as possible and look over the side from the top deck, forwards and downwards to where the tenders rolled at her bows, the merest cockle-shells beside the majestic vessel that rose deck after deck above them. Truly she was a magnificent boat! There was something so graceful in her movement as she rode up and down on the slight swell in the harbour, a slow, stately dip and recover, only noticeable by watching her bows in comparison with some landmark on the coast in the near distance; the two little tenders tossing up and down like corks beside her illustrated vividly the advance made in comfort of motion from the time of the small steamer.

Presently the work of transfer was ended, the tenders cast off, and at 1.30 p.m., with the screws churning up the sea bottom again, the *Titanic* turned slowly through a quarter-circle until her nose pointed down along the Irish coast, and then steamed rapidly away from Queenstown, the little house on the left of the town gleaming white on the hillside for many miles astern. In our wake soared and screamed hundreds of gulls, which had quarrelled and fought over the remnants of lunch pouring out of the waste pipes as we lay-to in the harbour entrance; and now they followed us in the expectation of further spoil. I watched them for a long time and was astonished at the ease with which they soared and kept up with the ship with hardly a motion of their wings; picking out a particular gull, I would keep him under observation for minutes at a time and see no motion of his wings downwards or upwards to aid his flight. He would tilt all of a piece to one side or another as the gusts of wind caught him: rigidly unbendable, as an airplane tilts sideways in a puff of wind. And yet with graceful ease he kept pace with the *Titanic* forging through the water at twenty knots: as the wind met him he would rise upwards and obliquely forwards, and come down slantingly again, his wings curved in a beautiful arch and his tail feathers outspread as a fan.

It was plain he was possessed of a secret we are only just beginning to learn – that of utilising air-currents as escalators up and down which he can glide at will with the expenditure of the minimum amount of energy, or of using them as a ship does when it sails within one or two points of a head wind. Aviators, of course, are imitating the gull, and soon perhaps we may see an airplane or a glider dipping gracefully up and down in the face of an opposing wind and all the time forging ahead across the Atlantic Ocean.

The gulls were still behind us when night fell, and still they screamed and dipped down into the broad wake of foam which we left behind; but in the morning they were gone: perhaps they had seen in the night a steamer bound for their Queenstown home and had escorted her back.

All afternoon we steamed along the coast of Ireland, with grey cliffs guarding the shores, and hills rising behind gaunt and barren; as dusk fell, the coast rounded away from us to the northwest, and the last we saw of Europe was the Irish mountains, dim and faint in the dropping darkness.

THE DAILY MIRROR

A LAST GLIMPSE OF THE ILL-FATED TITANTIC.

The last time the Titanic was seen from the shores of the United Kingdom. The photograph shows the mighty vessel steaming away from Queenstown on Thursday last.